A DAY OF BATTLE

MARS-LA-TOUR
16 AUGUST 1870

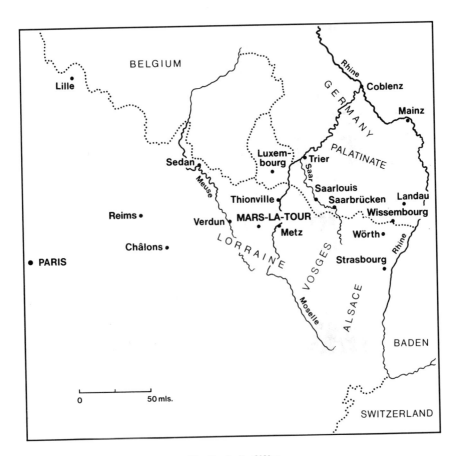

The Cockpit of War

A DAY OF BATTLE

MARS-LA-TOUR
16 AUGUST 1870

DAVID ASCOLI

HARRAP
LONDON

BY THE SAME AUTHOR

A VILLAGE IN CHELSEA

THE QUEEN'S PEACE

THE MONS STAR

**A COMPANION TO THE
BRITISH ARMY
1660-1983**

For
C.R.B.

First published in Great Britain 1987
by HARRAP Ltd,
19-23 Ludgate Hill, London EC4M 7PD

© David Ascoli 1987

ISBN 0 245-54250-7

Designed by The Design Team

Printed and bound in Great Britain
by R. J. Acford, Chichester

CONTENTS

ILLUSTRATIONS

Maps and diagrams

Plates

AUTHOR'S NOTE

1 The war of 1870−1 is commonly, but inaccurately, called the Franco-Prussian War. The defeat of Austria and her Saxon and South German allies at Sadowa (Königgrätz) on 3 July 1866 destroyed the German *Bund* which Metternich had created fifty years earlier under the presidency of Austria. As a result of the Treaty of Prague on 23 August, Prussia annexed Hanover, the Elbe Duchies and several smaller territories, and proceeded to form a Confederation of all the German states north of the river Main (this instrument specifically excluded Austria). Under a secret clause in the preliminary negotiations at Nikolsburg (26 July), the southern states — Bavaria, Württemberg, Hesse and Baden — agreed to remodel their armies on the Prussian pattern and to join with the Confederation in the event of a war. Thus on the outbreak of hostilities with France in July 1870, while the supreme command was exclusively Prussian, the army was that of a united *Germany*, as the Order of Battle on pp. 340-354 clearly demonstrates. The conflict should therefore properly be called the Franco-German War.[1] And the most significant result of the armistice signed on 28 January 1871 was the election of King William I of Prussia as the German Emperor.

2 The critical battles of August 1870 were fought in the provinces of Alsace (Elsass) and Lorraine (Lothringen) (see Map 1). This ancient region, since Roman times the gateway to invaders from both east and west, had been German in its ethnic origin until its annexation by successive French monarchs: the bishopric of Metz in 1559; Alsace in 1648; and Lorraine in 1766. As a result, place-names had — and still

---

1 A more cynical, but equally plausible, title would be the Second War of the Spanish Succession (see pp. 37-47).

have[2] — a hybrid pattern which, especially east of the Moselle (Mosel), reflects the historical ebb and flow. For example: Strasbourg (Strassburg); Thionville (Diedenhofen); Wissembourg (Weissenburg); Haguenau (Hagenau); Sarreguemines (Saargemünd). Since, however, at the period of this narrative the area was French territory, I have used French orthography except where (viz: the river Saar) a strict application would be pedantic. Only in minor and isolated instances will a reader of contemporary French and German sources encounter linguistic solecisms.

3   The battle on 16 August 1870 which forms the centrepiece of this narrative is known to British historians as Mars-la-Tour. This title is misleading, since the village of that name lies at the farthest extremity of the battlefield, and action was not joined there until the afternoon. German accounts refer to 'the day of battle' as *Vionville*, the village at the heart of the fighting, and whose occupation denied Bazaine the escape-route to Verdun. French sources — for reasons which will become only too apparent in the text — refer to the battle of *Rezonville*, which lies a little more than two miles to the east of Vionville on the main road. However, since it was at Mars-la-Tour that the French threw away the last — and most golden — chance of a stunning victory, I have chosen to use the conventional English title.

4   To distinguish between the formations of the two opposing sides, I have adopted the following formula:

a)   *German*
The three Armies are shown as First, Second and Third. Army Corps are shown in roman numerals, viz: III, IX, X, to distinguish them from their French equivalents. Cavalry and Infantry Divisions and Brigades are given in Arabic numbers, viz: 5th Cavalry Division, 19th Division. The Order of Battle on pp. 340-354 shows the territorial provenance of the whole German Army.

b)   *French*
At the outbreak of war the two groups of French Army Corps were combined to form the 'Army of the Rhine,' under the supreme command of the Emperor. After the two defeats at Spicheren and Wörth on 6 August 1870, the Field Army was briefly split into the 'Army of Metz' and the 'Army of

---

2   The process continued inexorably. After the peace treaty in 1871, the whole of Alsace and northern Lorraine became part of the new German Empire; the Treaty of Versailles returned both provinces to France in 1919; both were reoccupied by Germany in 1940; and both reverted to French sovereignty in 1945.

Strasbourg'.[3] When, on 12 August, with MacMahon in full retreat towards Châlons, Napoleon appointed Bazaine overall Commander-in-Chief, the five Army Corps grouped around Metz were redesignated — with a splendid disregard of both truth and geography — the 'Army of the Rhine'; and I have used this title throughout. Army Corps are shown in Arabic numerals, viz: 2, 3, 4, 6 etc. Cavalry and Infantry Divisions and Brigades are shown by the names of their commanders as at the evening of 15 August, viz: Vergé's, Bataille's, Forton's, du Barail's, Lapasset's etc.

c)   Individual German units are shown in italics; French in roman.

****

PREFACE

'The policy of your Government', said the French Minister, M. de Moustier, to Bismarck during the Crimean War, 'will bring you to Jena.' 'Why not', replied Bismarck, 'to Waterloo?'

In the event, it was Bismarck who got it right. Yet not even that shrewdest of diplomatic manipulators could then have foreseen that within fifteen years a self-styled 'parvenu' Emperor Napoleon would have met the same fate as his ambitious uncle; and that the unambitious King of Prussia would find himself the unopposed leader of the first united German Empire. Nor that the crucial decision would be reached between dawn and dusk of a single August day. What would then flow from the collapse of the Second Empire on 2 September 1870, and the rise of imperial Germany, Bismarck could not tell. We, with the benefit of hindsight, know better. We know that the German arrogance, ambition and duplicity brought that great nation, within fifty years, to a second apocalyptic Jena. In that sense, and that alone, M. de Moustier's observation was wiser than he knew. History is a catalogue of tragic ironies.

****

It is strange that, in modern times, so little attention has been paid to the Franco-German War; for poised as it is between Waterloo and Mons, it represents one of the great watersheds in the political and military history of Europe — and so, by extension, of the world. It is remembered, if at all, by Sedan, an immemorial town whose name would haunt both French and German military leaders half a century hence; by the Siege of Paris; and by the excesses of the radical Commune which, after the armistice, revived the sick spirit of revolution in French politics.

Yet these are only lightning flashes in a sombre sky. The thunder echoed far into the future. Out of the wreckage of one ill-founded Empire arose another, deeply rooted in history, instinct with nationalism, resolved to resurrect the grandeurs of the great Frederick. It is not the least of the charges against Louis Napoleon that, in his pursuit of his own 'dynasty', he created the German Empire. And who shall say what miseries for Europe flowed from that awesome abdication of responsibility?

Here lies the peculiar fascination of the Franco-German War; for it illustrates more strikingly than perhaps any other conflict the truth of Clausewitz's dictum that war is an extension of policy. Here is Moltke writing in 1888, shortly before his death:[1]

> As long as nations exist distinct from one another, there will be quarrels that can only be settled by force of arms.... Generally speaking it is no longer the ambition of monarchs which endangers peace, but the impulses of a nation, its dissatisfaction with its internal conditions, the strife of parties and the intrigues of their leaders.... A peace-loving sovereign is less rare than a parliament composed of wise men.... Today the question is not so much whether a nation is strong enough to make war, as whether its Government is powerful enough to prevent war.... It was, indeed, from such a condition of relations that the war of 1870-71 originated.

On his own carefully rehearsed role in bringing that war about, Moltke is silent.

There is ample evidence that, for different reasons, the Emperor of the French (the title has a subtle inflexion) and the King of Prussia wished for a peaceful solution: Louis Napoleon, because his fragile dynasty could not — and did not — survive the shock of a military defeat; William, because the victory over Austria at Sadowa in 1866 had already ensured the primacy of Prussia and the eventual unification of Germany. But neither man was a match for his politicians or for public opinion.

The French went to war because press, people, and politicians — Imperialists and Republicans alike — were gripped by that fatal mass-hysteria (and false pride) which is so signal a mark of Gallic temperament. The Germans went to war because Bismarck and Moltke wished it so, and because the newly aroused sense of German nationalism provided a formidable engine to drive the chariot wheels. If it is true that the road to hell is paved with good intentions, it is also illuminated by the fierce light of power politics and melancholy misjudgment.

****

The war of 1870-71 is unique in a particular — and peculiar — sense. Within four weeks of the opening action at Saarbrücken, the French field

---

1 Moltke, *The Franco-Prussian War of 1870-71*.

armies had been comprehensively defeated. By 19 August Bazaine's Army of the Rhine had withdrawn within the defensive perimeter of Metz where, on 28 October, after two half-hearted sorties, it capitulated. On 1 September MacMahon's hastily assembled Army of Châlons had surrendered at Sedan after a classic battle of encirclement. With it went into captivity the Emperor of the French.

Yet the collapse of the Second Empire signalled an extraordinary revival of French pride and passion. On 4 September the Third Republic was proclaimed in Paris under a Government of National Defence dedicated to the continuation of *guerre à outrance*. By a *levée en masse*, by Gallic improvisation (with considerable material assistance from Britain), but above all by the resurgence of national will, the seasoned armies of Germany were harassed and frustrated for five more months; and even after the signing of an armistice on 28 January 1871, resistance continued in many parts of the country. History has few parallels.

****

For France, the humiliation of Sedan long remained. It is conventional wisdom that it was there, in what Moltke called his 'mousetrap', that the French Army suffered its most crushing defeat since Waterloo. This is not so. Sedan was the natural and inevitable result of a lethal conjunction: a stricken man, an interfering wife, and a divided nation bent as much on private revenge as on public retribution, which sent MacMahon on a despairing crusade to relieve the beleaguered Bazaine in Metz.[2]

The truth is otherwise. The fate of France was sealed on another day and on another field. And it is with the extraordinary events of that day and of that field that this narrative is largely concerned.

When, on the morning of 16 August 1870, Napoleon took his leave of Bazaine at Gravelotte, he enjoined him: 'Put yourself on the route for Verdun as soon as possible. And no more reverses!' It was a simple and unequivocal instruction. Yet because Bazaine — the French Foreign Legion sergeant made Marshal — lacked both military expertise and moral authority, the warning implicit in that order was to be his undoing.

Already, on 14 August, Bazaine had allowed the process of disengagement of the Army of the Rhine to be halted for twelve crucial hours by the unnecessary battle of Borny on the right bank of the Moselle. Even then, the withdrawal up the Rozérieulles escarpment had become an administrative shambles, and by 15 August the advance-guard of Forton's cavalry division had reached no farther than Vionville, ten miles west of Metz. As

---

2 History was kind to MacMahon. Wounded during the action at Bazeilles on the day of the surrender, the ignominy of defeat attached to his deputy Wimpffen. MacMahon was rewarded with the presidency of the Third Republic. But he was not allowed to forget his complicity in defeat. The cynics of Paris saw to that when they celebrated his achievement under the soubriquet *'l'illustre vaincu'*.

we shall see — and Bazaine's orders are dreadfully explicit — there was no sense of urgency. And while one eye was fixed on Verdun, the other was fatally attached to the fortress behind him. Thus this sadly incompetent soldier was caught between an imperial devil and a deeply personal blue sea.

Not so Moltke. By 14 August he had pushed forward Prince Frederick Charles's Second Army to the Moselle crossings above Metz at Pont-à-Mousson and Dieulouard; and by that afternoon Rheinbaben's 5th Cavalry Division was ranging far to the north-west in search of the Army of the Rhine on the road to Verdun. Here, at dawn on 16 August, the two sides encountered each other; the French convinced that they were confronted by a whole German Army instead of a single cavalry brigade, the Germans thinking that the enemy had made good his escape and not realizing until the day was far advanced that what they had engaged was not a small rearguard but the entire Army of the Rhine.[3]

There followed during that long, hot summer's day an extraordinary battle, or series of battles, in which were compounded heroic endurance and moral cowardice, desperate bluff and dreadful incompetence, moments of splendour and acts of criminal folly, a bloody demonstration — as the casualty figures will presently show — of human fortitude and human frailty. Throughout the morning of Mars-la-Tour, French numerical superiority — albeit notional — was never less than four to one. Even by late afternoon it was still five to two. Four times during that day Bazaine was presented with the opportunity of an overwhelming victory. Four times, through lack of leadership and lack of resolution, he cast that opportunity away. The chance would come again two days later, but by then Bazaine had wasted the most vital asset of a military commander — the will to win.

I am entirely persuaded that the Franco-German War was won and lost at Mars-la-Tour. All that preceded this crucial battle was in the nature of a preface to an unwritten scenario. All that followed was an inevitable epilogue. That is my justification for this book, and for my belief that the history of our times would have been very different if one man had not so wantonly blotted the copybook.

****

The source material for the battle of Mars-la-Tour, for its preliminaries, and for its aftermath, raises problems. Shortage is not one of them.

The official German history, compiled by the Historical Section of the General Staff, runs to five weighty volumes, supplemented by thirty-six

---

3 Not for the only time during the events leading up to the battle of Mars-la-Tour, the reader may well speculate upon the dramatic difference that a single squadron of reconnaissance aircraft would have made to both sides.

detailed analyses and six special studies. It is meticulous, exhaustive and unreadable.

The French counterpart, similarly compiled by the Historical Section of the General Staff, is covered in twenty-two volumes. It is ill-organized, meretricious, and some way short of authoritative.

Both of these military monoliths are available only in specialist libraries, and accessible to those whose knowledge of languages is matched by profound patience.

But no previous war created a comparable literary industry. Within three decades more than eight thousand books had been published in French and German alone. *Souvenirs* and *Denkwürdigkeiten* proliferated from the presses; from almost every leader on both sides (the gaps are revealing) down to humbler participants, casual observers, academics, and soothsayers.

The personal accounts of the two main actors are both, for different reasons, unsatisfactory.

That of Moltke, the German Chief of Staff, is superficial (a mere 75 pages out of 477 are devoted to the first four decisive weeks of the war) and, despite the availability of the official History as a source of reference, extremely inaccurate.[4] This may be partly because Moltke died before the book was published, and the editing was left to his nephew, the same nephew who was to be the unstable and ineffective German Chief of Staff during the first month of the 1914-18 war.

Bazaine, Commander-in-Chief of the French Army of the Rhine, wrote three books which as cosmetic exercises are in the same class as the memoirs of Sir John French. They should be read — with some caution — in conjunction with the massive transcript of Bazaine's court-martial.[5]

Books in English are surprisingly few, and mostly date from before the Great War. Perhaps for that reason, they are perversely pro-German and uncompromisingly critical of French administration and command, if not of the French fighting soldier.

Fortunately, there is one comparatively recent study (1961) which is a model of its kind, Sir Michael Howard's *The Franco-Prussian War*, which covers the whole conflict from its political origins to the Treaty of Frankfurt in May 1871. Professor Howard's book is a rare — very rare — combination of scholarship, readability, Olympian detachment, and wit. For French politicians — with the possible exception of Jules Favre — he has little pity and less patience. Towards Bazaine he is more ambivalent, with a proper sense of criticism and compassion. But the special virtue of his book is its carefully documented demolition of the myth of German infallibility, from the insubordination of Steinmetz in the first encounter

4 A revised English translation by Archibald Forbes, correspondent of the *Daily News* at Royal Headquarters, was published in 1893.

5 *Procès Bazaine.*

battle[6] and the irresolution of Blumenthal in Alsace, to the assorted invitations to disaster between the morning of 16 August and the evening of 18 August. How frail can be the seemingly irresistible combination of a political dynamo and a military magneto may be seen in the clash of personalities between Bismarck and Moltke at the gates of Paris. But by then vendetta had been up-staged by victory.

So in choosing my bibliography I have been deliberately selective, and have held to the lower ground rather than climb inaccessible peaks. It is easy to be clever and parade an apparatus of scholarship. It is wiser to be modest and accept the limitations of language and libraries. I have therefore made a selection of books which will, I hope, provide a useful background to my own interpretation of events.

****

I would like to end on this note. The battlefield of Mars-la-Tour (and that of St Privat–Gravelotte two days later) is scarcely changed from its shape and substance of August 1870. The villages — Gravelotte, Rezonville, Vionville, Flavigny — are still there, small and sleepy, as if they had never heard the thunder of guns or the clash of cavalry. The woods are still there, too — Bois de Tronville, Bois de Vionville, Bois des Ognons. It is as if nothing had disturbed this peaceful plateau, were it not for the many memorials which mark that day of battle.

****

---

6   History was to repeat itself in the disobedience of the commander of another First Army, Kluck, to the orders of another Moltke in August 1914.

INTRODUCTION

THE WATCH ON THE RHINE

When, on the evening of 1 September 1870, the French General de Wimpffen presented himself at Donchery to discover what terms would be offered for the surrender of the Army of Châlons at Sedan, the Chancellor of the German Confederation, Bismarck, reminded him with pardonable exaggeration that during the previous two hundred years France had declared war on Germany thirty times. Exaggerated — for two reasons.

First, because throughout those two hundred years, French aggression had largely ignored the diplomatic convention of a formal declaration of war; secondly, because neither before nor since the dismemberment of the Holy Roman Empire after the battle of Jena had there ever existed any such national or political entity as 'Germany'. Prussia, certainly; and upward of fifty other states and petty principalities. But, as reference to any political map of Europe of the period will show, no German nation.[1] But it was due as much to Bismarck's sense of history as to Louis Napoleon's obsession with the political and military heritage of his uncle that the Franco-German War came about.

Yet Bismarck was not alone in his remembrance of things past. In the September weeks following the collapse of the Second Empire, the veteran Orléanist, Adolphe Thiers, volunteered for the role of emissary of the French provisional government in search of a mediator between Paris and Berlin. In Vienna he met the celebrated historian Ranke and asked him with whom Germany was really at war now that the Bonaparte dynasty had fallen. 'With Louis XIV,' replied Ranke drily.

****

1   This, notwithstanding the resounding title of the Austrian Emperor: *'Kaiser des Heiligen Römischen Reiches deutscher Nation'*.

19

It is not the province of this book to rehearse the long and complex power struggle between two inveterate enemies divided by temperament, religion, and culture, and by a geographical symbol of conflict, the river Rhine. Thomas Carlyle was expressing not only his own pro-German obsession but the received wisdom of a whole continent when he wrote in a letter to *The Times* in July 1870, two days after no words could any longer arrest the engines of war: 'No peoples ever possessed so bad a neighbour as the Germans had in France for the last four centuries; insolent, greedy, insatiable, irreconcilable, and incessantly aggressive.'[2]

Yet by the time Carlyle pronounced this verdict, the political and military scenario in central Europe had changed significantly, and for more than fifty years the old antagonists had gone their separate ways: France in pursuit of a new colonial dream; Prussia, proud and Protestant, in search of an historic role as heart and head of an united German empire. Between the two, the great river still flowed; and fifty years were not to prove enough for all its waters to wash away the ancient animosity.

In November 1813, with the armies of France in disarray and Prussia newly arisen from the ashes of Jena, the allied Powers offered Bonaparte peace terms, the chief of which, in an echo of Danton, set the Rhine as France's eastern frontier. It was a breathtakingly insensitive hostage to fortune which a wiser and less arrogant man than Bonaparte might eagerly have grasped; but wisdom is not the best counsellor of arrogance.[3] The terms were rejected; and on 1 December the allies invaded France. It was the first time in centuries of confrontation that a Prussian army found itself fighting on French soil. It was to be by no means the last.

When the Congress of Vienna was reconvened in 1815, Prussia had reason to expect a rich reward for her contribution to the defeat of Bonaparte. But there was no statesman in Berlin to match Metternich (or Talleyrand) and when the former Holy Roman Empire was recycled as the German Confederation, or *Bund*, its seat was at Frankfurt, and its presidency assigned to Austria. It was to prove a political blunder of the first order; and it was at once compounded by another.

Mindful of France's long record of aggression against her Eastern neighbours, the statesmen repaired to the map of Europe, there to devise a *cordon sanitaire* behind which they might contain French avarice and ambition.

The new frontier was a compromise, for while it largely restored the pre-Revolutionary *status quo*, it also left untouched several contentious bones. Thus the boundary between France and the Germanic states now

2   Danton, done to death in 1794, had set the 'natural' boundaries of France as 'the Ocean', the Rhine, the Alps, and the Pyrenees.' The geography was tidy; the ambition too modest for a hungry Bonaparte.

3   History has an uncomfortable way of repeating itself. When the victorious Allies imposed their treaty on Germany in 1919, they ignored the evidence of Jena, of Leipzig, and of Waterloo; and more critically of German imperialism.

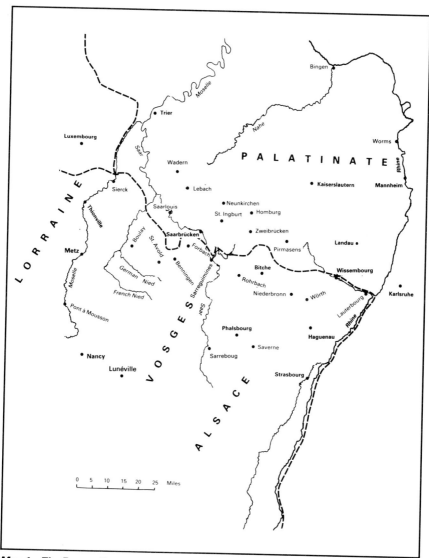

Map 1   The Franco-German frontier in 1870

followed the Rhine from Switzerland north as far as Lauterbourg opposite
Karlsruhe. There it turned west along an ill-defined line through the
Vosges mountains, crossing the Saar above Saarbrücken and the Moselle
below Thionville, whence it turned north to the Luxembourg frontier (see
Map 1). Both the disputed provinces of Alsace and Lorraine remained in
French hands, and Metternich could congratulate himself that a continuing
French presence on the upper Rhine would keep the South German states
in a suitable degree of apprehension.

Prussia, however, had little to show for her exertions.[4] The new peace treaty restored to her the territory she had lost at Tilsit in 1807. In addition to her former territory to the east of the old Mark Brandenburg, she acquired the Rhenish provinces as far south as the city of Mainz. The new kingdom, whose origin dated from the crowning of the Elector Frederick III in 1701, was a piece of political patchwork; but when, half a century later, the seams were subjected to strain, they were to prove formidably strong.

****

The same could not be said of France. During the 'interregnum' of 55 years between Waterloo and the final confrontation with the old enemy, the nation was a house divided against itself, fatally infected at home with the contagion of revolution, wistfully seeking new conquests abroad to restore the lost lustre of the old régime. Grandeur and misery went hand in hand.

The pale Bourbons came and went. In 1830, Parisians enthusiastically manned the barricades and, amid much bloodshed, installed as 'King of the French' the Orléanist Louis-Philippe who, during eighteen troubled years, survived four attempted assassinations, presided over an unprecedented economic decline, and launched the country upon a new era of colonial adventurism with the occupation of Algeria, a military seed-bed which was to nurture a generous crop of discredited Marshals and untutored Generals. By 1848, when all Europe was in political and social turmoil, France was ripe for another Bonaparte; and another such was at hand, in name if not in stature.

Louis Napoleon was a nephew of the great Emperor and, since the death of the young Duke of Reichstadt in 1832, the titular head of the Bonaparte family. Not for him the Orléanist usurper and 'Citizen King'. A mismanaged *coup* in Strasbourg in 1836 sent him into exile, first in Switzerland, then in America and England. Four years later he was back in Boulogne where a comic performance worthy of Offenbach left him behind bars in a prison at Ham. Plainly the road to power did not lie through private enterprise. The call to duty must come from public consensus; and in the summer of 1848, the people of Paris consented. In the savage 'July Days' Louis-Philippe was hustled away, and the Second Republic was proclaimed under the absurdly titled Prince-Presidency of Louis Napoleon. Another Bonaparte was come to judgment.

'Well-meaning republics', observed Philip Guedalla, 'are apt to be short-lived in Paris.' And so it now proved. As Prince-President, Napoleon, his head full of past glories and future aspirations, felt inadequate. His opportunities were limited so long as he seemed to be, in

---

4   The Prussian contribution to the Waterloo campaign amounted to nearly 117,000 men as against a total of 31,385 British troops.

his own words, 'the Prince Albert of the Republic' and so, by a *coup d'état* on 2 December 1851, he took supreme power. A year later on the anniversary eve of Austerlitz — monarchists, liberals, and radicals strongly dissenting — he became the first 'Emperor of the French' and the second and last Emperor of France.

His rule was autocratic and, like all autocrats, his authority rested on the support of the army.

The French Army had not greatly changed during the period since Waterloo. Certainly the long years of war and the rigorous conscription laws of the Revolutionary armies had created a wide gulf between professional soldier and contemptuous civilian, a gulf which was never to be bridged and which was to contribute in large measure to the disasters of 1870.

In 1818 a new conscription law had been introduced. It was a classic example of the French passion for *débrouillage* — the art of 'muddling through' — or, as the cynics called it, *Système D*. From this date, men from each age-group liable for service were chosen by ballot in sufficient numbers as the Legislative Body considered necessary to carry out defence at home and adventures abroad. Such men served for seven years with the colours on the curiously French idea that at the end of that period they would, as one optimistic Deputy observed, 'be so decontaminated of civilian attitudes that they would subsequently re-enlist as volunteers (*rengagés*)'.

But that was not the whole story. Side by side with the ballot there came into existence the principle of 'substitution', by which a man who had been unfortunate enough to draw a *mauvais numéro* could opt out of his obligations by the simple expedient of paying someone to take his place. This produced some interesting results. In 1836, for example, out of a ballot of 78,000, no fewer than 41,000 places were filled by substitutes; and by the following year it was even possible to take out an insurance policy against conscription. Thus while the upper and middle classes of society effectively insulated themselves against the risk of compulsory service, the military fate of the nation was largely entrusted to an army of unenthusiastic peasants. It was to cost the country dear.

Unfortunately for France, the new Emperor had illusions of Napoleonic grandeur, soon reflected in a revival of the old glories of the First Empire and a soldiery resplendent in its refurbished peacock feathers. In Africa a new generation of leaders — figures like Canrobert and MacMahon, Bourbaki and Bazaine (especially Bazaine), Ladmirault and Leboeuf, who would presently find themselves acting very different roles on a more sombre stage — were earning their spurs in the romantic kind of campaigning which made bubble reputations and concealed in clouds of desert dust the grim realities of modern war.

But Africa was a domestic affair. The Second Empire was in search of public battle honours, and these the Emperor now provided.

The Crimean War has been described as one of the bad jokes of history, not least because it brought together in improbable partnership the imperfect armies of France and Britain. It proved, if nothing else, a common valour in adversity and a mutual incompetence of leadership and administration. But in Paris it was hailed as a signal victory, and Sebastopol took its place beside the sonorous litany of Jena and Austerlitz, Eylau and Wagram, on the regimental standards of France.

Five years later, in a campaign of comparable rigour and equal incompetence, the Emperor rode to the rescue of Sardinia and defeated the army of Austria on the plains of Lombardy. And in July 1859, the honours of Magenta and Solferino were added to the standards. The French, so long 'les vaincus de l'Europe', warmed themselves before the glow of the new Imperial fire and counted themselves the military masters of the moment. In that they were gravely mistaken.

If pride comes before a fall, it may do so in the most unexpected way. In 1861, with no readily available jousting-ground in Europe, Napoleon lighted upon an extravagant folie de grandeur. Its origin, which need not detain us here, was a seedy financial scandal involving a Swiss banker and the President of Mexico. Out of this improbable scenario, the Emperor devised a comic improvisation which ended in predictable tragedy. If there was a shortage of Empire in the Old World, why not create a fresh one in the New? A single stone might kill several birds — Austria's injured dignity, Italy's demand for Venetia, France's imperial ambitions. In the event, Napoleon's wild adventure ended in the dust of distant Querétaro. There were two victims. One, the brave, forsaken Archduke Maximilian, brother of Franz Joseph, and briefly Emperor of Mexico, who paid the price of all those idealists who foolishly trust in princes; the other, the Emperor of the French, who would presently learn at bitter cost that it is wiser to preserve the old empires than to hazard new ones.

****

Meanwhile, another story was being played out beyond the Rhine.

When in 1815 the new German Confederation assembled in Frankfurt, it did so under the presidency of Austria, a decision which flew in the face of history and ensured that sooner or later the question of German hegemony would lead to armed conflict. Prussia, resentful of Austria's diktat, brooded over her past misfortunes and dreamed only of the day when a Hohenzollern King would master a Habsburg Emperor and achieve at last the unchallengeable leadership of an united Fatherland. It was to take fifty years for the dream to become reality. During this time, Prussia's sole political advance was the establishment in 1834 of a customs' union, or Zollverein, which, in liberalizing commerce did much to stimulate the pursuit of national unity. There remained as a chief priority the reform of the Army.

Since the death of the Great King in 1786, the powerful instrument which Frederick had bequeathed to the nation had become a poor shadow of its former self, deeply politicized and infected with the newly fashionable Liberalism. The Convention of Paris had limited the Standing Army to 42,000 men, but by an ingenious cadre system, this figure was exceeded and, thanks to the reforming zeal of Scharnhorst and Gneisenau, by 1813 Prussia could call to arms a force of nearly 250,000; and in that year a royal edict created a civilian reserve — the Landwehr and the Landsturm — which included all fit men between the ages of eighteen and forty-five.

The following year a Conscription Law was passed. Every man (with a few specialist exceptions) became liable for military service from the commencement of his twentieth year, serving three years with the colours and two with the reserve. He then passed to the 'first section' of the Landwehr for seven years, and at the age of thirty-three to the 'second section' for a further seven years. At the age of forty he could then, if necessary, be transferred to the Landsturm, a kind of Home Guard of last resort.

The former territorial provenance of the regular army was put on a permanent and extended footing so that it consisted of a corps of Guards, and eight corps districts (see Appendix A) which provided cadres to staff local Landwehr regiments. This reorganization was not completed until 1830, when the strength of the active army stood at 130,000, with a similar number available on the embodiment of the Landwehr. During the long years of peace until 1859 this organization remained little changed. Still based on the Conscription Law of 1814, it was too small to provide any serious threat to its European neighbours, and during its involvement in the social unrest of the 1840s the Landwehr had shown itself to be politically unreliable.

****

In 1858 Prince William of Prussia became Regent in place of his unbalanced brother Frederick William IV. The Regent was a veteran of the Wars of Liberation, and a professional soldier for whom military efficiency was, as it had been for his ancestor Frederick William I, an end in itself.

During that year General Albrecht von Roon, a dedicated supporter of absolute monarchy, drew up a detailed memorandum for the Regent in which he set out proposals for a radical reform of the whole Prussian military system which would provide the 'inexpensive but at the same time impressively strong army' that alone would make possible Prussia's claim to leadership of the German bloc.

Chief of these proposals concerned the suspect status of the Landwehr, and for this Roon's solution was to integrate this large reservoir of manpower into a restructured regular Army — 'the training school of the entire nation for war'. The separate civilian organization must be abolished and in its place area commands should be formed, staffed by regular officers who would train the Landwehr as an immediate reserve. Roon's plan was as follows. Universal military service would be retained. Conscripts would serve for three years with the colours, beginning at the age of twenty. They then passed into the regular reserve for four years, and thence into the Landwehr for five years (during their first years of Landwehr service they remained liable to be called out with the regular reserve in any national emergency). This, Roon estimated, would provide a trained army of nearly 500,000 men on mobilization.

The Regent warmly endorsed Roon's plan; but the proposals were strongly opposed on constitutional and financial grounds in the Assembly, and by the Liberal War Minister, von Bonin. When, however, a partial mobilization was ordered in 1859 on the outbreak of the Franco-Austrian War, the defects in the existing system were such that William dismissed Bonin and replaced him by Roon.

Three years later Parliamentary opposition to the reforms was such that William, who had succeeded as King, summoned the astute and ruthless Otto von Bismarck as Minister-President. Bismarck at once advanced the ingenious theory that, in the event of a constitutional deadlock, the Crown was entitled to take such action as it deemed necessary for the welfare of the state. In 1863 the Assembly was dissolved, and it was not until four years later — by when Prussian arms had ousted Austria from the leadership of a newly federated Germany — that a retrospective Bill of Indemnity was passed in Berlin.

****

While Roon pressed ahead with his military designs, Bismarck addressed himself to the political humiliation of Austria.

Since 1848, Prussia had been ineffectively meddling in the internal affairs of Denmark, ostensibly in support of the German-speaking Duchies of Schleswig and Holstein. In 1863 he decided to set a trap by inviting Austria to join in 'liberating' these provinces. Austria, happy to demonstrate her superior stewardship of the German *Bund*, readily agreed and in the following year went to war.

The Schleswig-Holstein campaign was short-lived and, until the octogenarian commander, General von Wrangel, was replaced by the Prussian Chief of Staff, Helmut von Moltke, incompetently conducted. Moltke had occupied his post since 1857 and had made a signal contribution to Roon's reforms by his intellectual grasp of the new complexities of warfare in an industrial age where such novelties as the railway and the electric telegraph had lent a whole new dimension to the deployment of great armies on the modern battlefield. His own particular innovation had been the creation of an uniquely trained and superbly efficient General Staff which served as the brain that guided and directed armies of a size undreamed of by past leaders. If Bismarck was the political dynamo of Prussia, Moltke was to prove the architect of military victory.

It was now the turn of Austria. During 1865, Bismarck applied his diplomatic skill to isolate her from potential allies; first Russia, then Italy, and finally, in his most celebrated poker-game, France. And in the summer of the following year, on the thinnest of pretexts over the rightful control of the Elbe Duchies, he seduced the Viennese government into declaring an unnecessary and wanton war.

The seven-week campaign, brilliantly master-minded by Moltke and dominated by the battlefield superiority of the newly minted Prussian needle-gun, ended in the defeat of Austria and her main allies, Hanover, Saxony, and Bavaria, at Sadowa in Bohemia on 3 July 1866. It was a victory at once comprehensive and unexpected. And from it Prussia emerged as the unchallenged leader of the Germanic states.

Bismarck moved quickly; and within two weeks the old German *Bund* in Frankfurt was dismantled and a new North German Confederation, consisting of all the states north of the river Main, was established in Berlin under the supreme control of the King of Prussia. On 26 July, under Napoleon's nose, a secret treaty was signed with the South German states at Nikolsburg, by which they agreed to accept Prussian leadership in the event of war.

Prussia's triumph was nearly complete. Now the all-powerful triumvirate of Bismarck, Moltke, and Roon were ready to seek a final confrontation with France. The old imperial dream was about to be fulfilled.

The news of Sadowa was greeted with profound consternation in Paris. How could it be that the Prussian army, so long derided and so unimpressive in the Schleswig-Holstein campaign, had achieved so swift and stunning a victory against an opponent who, for all his shortcomings, should have been more than a match for what had been slightingly described as 'a collection of lawyers and oculists'? There were various inadequate explanations advanced: Prussian perfidy; the superiority of the breech-loading needle-gun; Austria's long love-affair with military disaster. Wiser heads — and wisdom was at some discount in Imperial France — read the signals very differently: Bismarck's astute political judgment; the quality of the military machine which Roon had so patiently constructed; the strategic and administrative flair of Moltke and his uniquely professional General Staff; and, perhaps most tellingly, the newly arranged spirit of German nationalism.

It has been argued that Prussia's invasion of Bohemia provided France with a golden opportunity to occupy with impunity the Palatinate and the Rhine provinces on the left bank of the river, thus acquiring by default a prize which she could only achieve thereafter by force. (This danger had not escaped the watchful Bismarck, who had persuaded Moltke to support his main strategy by a diversionary attack on Hanover on his western flank.[5]) But no such logic commended itself to the imperial pundits in the Tuileries. First, the humiliating failure of the Mexican adventure had sent ripples of doubt and discontent across an already troubled political pond in Paris. The opposition parties, Orléanists and Republicans alike, were more suspicious of domestic danger than of Prussian sabre-rattling. Secondly — and more significantly — there was the comfortable perception, complacently compounded by arrogance, that Austria would win the war, and that France would be rewarded for her 'statesmanship' with rich territorial pickings at Prussian expense.

But in the event there was no such easy option. Sadowa saw to that; and France, so heedless of history and so falsely certain that past glories would guarantee a famous fortune, suddenly found herself confronted by a formidable threat, not only to her assumed superiority but to her security itself. So quickly does storm follow calm. So soon does pride precede fall.

****

The sudden and totally unforeseen emergence of the North German Confederation, the menace of a resurgent Prussia, the humbling of Austria — all these dramatic consequences of six short summer weeks swept away the semblance of stability which during the fifty years since Waterloo had flattered only to deceive the statesmen of central Europe. Throughout those years the balance of power had been held in silent equilibrium by the Rhine. Now the old river roused itself again to play the power-broker.

For France, the convention of Nikolsburg, with all its implications of pan-Germanism, aroused an extraordinary response, part anger, part envy, but above all fear. All the comfortable assumptions of a glittering Imperialism, of rakish prosperity, of an anodyne Liberalism to soften the asperity of the autocratic *coup d'état* of 1851, were overshadowed by a sense of diminished prestige, and by the brutal truth that her primacy among the European powers, as heir to Richelieu, to Louis XIV, and to the first Bonaparte, had been called in question by Prussia, so long despised and now so suddenly menacing. Thus, with a proper premonition of impending disaster, the Imperial government embarked upon a course of desperate diplomacy.

****

In the immediate aftermath of Sadowa, Napoleon officiously offered his services as an intermediary at the armistice negotiations, representing himself as an honest broker between the two chief Germanic States. It was a role for which he was almost comically unsuited, and Bismarck, with a

---

5 Curiously, the commander chosen for this show of strength was the inept Vogel von Falkenstein, who had demonstrated his incompetence in the Danish Campaign and now added insubordination to his military inadequacy.

comprehensive victory on his hands and a grandiose political strategy in prospect, carefully baited the trap for his arrogant and unwary mouse. He had no illusions about the inveterate enemy of Europe — dissolute and divided, with a dynasty precariously poised on the narrow edge of popular disapproval.

Napoleon had not gone to Nikolsburg to see fair play. He had gone to play Shylock, and his pound of flesh was 'compensation' for Prussia's territorial gains, and for France's 'statesmanslike' neutrality during the *Brüderkrieg*. There is an awful symmetry between the ailing, apprehensive Emperor and the shrewd, self-assured Pomeranian squire.

The French government lost no time in setting out its stall. During the first week in August, its ambassador in Berlin was instructed to 'claim' the left bank of the Rhine as far as, and including, the fortress of Mainz. It was a breathtaking impertinence, to which Bismarck replied with prophetic restraint: 'Should a war arise out of this complication, it might be a war attended by a revolutionary crisis. In such a case, the German dynasties are likely to prove more solid than that of the Emperor Napoleon.' Four years later, in a small weaver's cottage near Sedan, Bismarck was to remind Napoleon of those warning words.

But the warning was not heeded. On 16 August, the French government forwarded a fresh set of demands to Berlin. They were nothing if not ambitious: a return to the frontiers of 1814 (*viz. the left bank of the Rhine*); the annexation of Belgium; the annexation of Belgium and Luxembourg; or Belgium and Luxembourg, without Antwerp (this a sop to British commercial sensitivity).[6] 'The minimum we require (*sic*) is an ostensible treaty which gives us Luxembourg, and a secret treaty which, stipulating an offensive and defensive alliance, leaves us the chance of annexing Belgium at the right moment, Prussia engaging to assist us by force of arms, if necessary, in carrying out this purpose.' So ran the French demand. It received a reply from Berlin, at once Delphic and dusty: 'Why', suggested Bismarck, 'did you not annex these territories when they were there for the taking?' It was a fair question, to which Bismarck knew the answer, and the hesitant Emperor did not.

The year turned. In Berlin Bismarck was occupied with the complex problems of welding together the North German Confederation, and with the more delicate diplomacy which would bring the Southern states, Catholic and cautious, into his great pan-Germanic enterprise. In Paris, with the opposition parties in the Assembly still pressing with relentless rhetoric for some territorial compensation for '*l'agrandissement de la Prusse*', the Emperor embarked upon an alternative diplomatic ploy, at once ingenious and ingenuous.

Since the resettlement of Europe after Waterloo, Luxembourg had been

---

6   There is an irony in this demand, for France was a signatory to the 1839 Treaty of London which guaranteed the perpetual neutrality of Belgium — that same 'scrap of paper' which Germany was to tear up in 1914.

an integral Duchy of the Kingdom of Holland.[7] By ethnic origin its small population was French and its 'perpetual neutrality' later guaranteed by the Treaty of 1839. It had not been incorporated by Metternich in the *Bund*, but to complete the *cordon sanitaire* it had been garrisoned by Prussian troops since 1815 and absorbed into the German *Zollverein* in 1836.

Rebuffed in his absurd attempt to obtain the Rhenish provinces as a reward for his virtuous neutrality, Napoleon now sought to answer his political critics at home by acquiring at — as he believed — no great risk some French crumbs from Prussia's solidly Germanic crust. His logic, such as it was, reflected Bismarck's pan-German strategy. Let the Rhine rest, and the present frontier be preserved; and as a political counterpoise between the inveterate adversaries, let each absorb within its sphere of influence those territories on either bank of the river whose ethnic origins attached them to either East or West. It was a tidy equation, but fatally flawed, for it ignored the critical question of Alsace and Lorraine; and it was in these two long-disputed provinces that the future of Europe would presently, and most bloodily, be decided.

Now, in the early Spring of 1867, Napoleon made the first move towards his intended *Anschluss*. He began with Luxembourg; and in March he opened negotiations in The Hague for the purchase of the Duchy, his peaceful intentions to be ratified later in open court by a plebiscite. He proceeded with all the apparatus of 'secret' diplomacy — his every proposal monitored with amused contempt in Berlin.

The King of Holland, caught in a political cross-fire between two great power-blocks, played for safety; but he shared with the Emperor of the French a common incubus — a meddlesome and ambitious wife. His own consort, a Princess of the Catholic house Württemberg, and with a deep distaste for all things Prussian, pressed him to accept. A formal instrument of transfer was awaiting signature when the Dutch King paused on the brink and, with a wisdom born of apprehension, sought the opinion of the Prussian government. Bismarck's reaction was entirely in character. First the velvet glove. To the French ambassador in Berlin, thus: 'Luxembourg belongs to the King of Holland. It is his to keep or dispose of. If you want the Duchy, why do you not take it, and with it the consequences, which are for you to judge?' Then the iron hand. On 25 March, Bismarck caused to be printed on the front page of the *Official Gazette* details of the treaty which gave the King of Prussia full control of the Bavarian army in the event of war. The 'consequences' to which he had drawn Benedetti's attention could not be more explicit.

Moltke, however, still riding high on the crest of Sadowa, and eager to settle old scores with France, was more concerned with military advantage

---

7 By another historical irony, Napoleon III was the youngest son of a *parvenu* 'King of Holland', brother of the first Bonaparte.

than with diplomatic finesse, and pressed for the Luxembourg crisis to be the *casus belli* for a war which he believed to be inevitable and, in his own phrase, 'sooner rather than later'. Bismarck, while sharing the certainty of a future conflict, was in no such hurry. He had his reasons. First — and Moltke here let jealousy override judgment — the reorganization of the army of the North German Confederation was by no means complete;[8] each year would provide a significant intake of first-line conscripts. Secondly, much work had yet to be done to ensure in full the political and military co-operation of the South German states.[9] Thirdly, the astute Chancellor was busily engaged in seducing Italy from her tenuous relationship with the Ultramontane party in France. Fourthly, the world and his wife were in Paris for the opening of the glittering Exhibition on 1 April 1867, and Bismarck wisely had no wish to touch the tender consciences of the world and his wife. But lastly — and most importantly — the war, when it came, must be seen to be the result of French arrogance and not of Prussian provocation. Thus, in the summer of 1867, Chancellor and Chief of Staff returned to their drawing-boards. Neither could then have foreseen the tragic absurdity which brought about the final *dénouement*.

****

The collapse of the Luxembourg negotiations cast a cloud over the brilliant landscape of the Paris Exhibition.[10] If, at this hour, it was still no bigger than a man's hand, the man was Bismarck and the hand was Prussia's. The Emperor could claim one small success when a meeting of the central powers in London agreed that, with the dissolution of Metternich's *Bund*, the Prussian garrison should be withdrawn from the Duchy and the guarantee of its neutrality under the 1839 Treaty should be confirmed. So modest a concession to the cause of peace had small significance in Berlin, but in Paris it occasioned some anxious reflection. With Luxembourg — 'that rag of territory' as the French Foreign Minister now dismissively described it — eliminated from the political pawnshop, the more ambitious plan to annex Belgium was revived in Paris. Thus, during the summer of 1867, the French ambassador in Berlin submitted a memorandum[11] to Bismarck which set out in more specific terms the vague 'demands' which his government had made during the previous August: namely, that France

---

8   The new federal structure would create three new Army corps (IX – XI) and embody that of the Kingdom of Saxony (XII).

9   Bavaria, Baden, Württemberg, and Hesse-Darmstadt.

10   Another shadow fell across the sunlit scene, as news reached the capital of the execution of the hapless Maximilian by a firing-squad in distant Querétaro.

11   Bismarck made shrewd diplomatic use of Benedetti's handwritten note by arranging for it to be published in *The Times* a month after the outbreak of war in 1870.

and the North German Confederation should enter into an 'offensive alliance' by which the former would be left free to occupy Belgium and the latter, as a reward for 'acquiescence', be permitted to absorb the South German states into the Confederation.

As a political ploy this proposition had upon it the hallmark of desperation. As an exercise in diplomacy it invited Bismarck's derision. He left Benedetti in no doubt that the annexation of Belgium would have even more serious 'consequences' than the Luxembourg affair. And he was careful to conceal from him the progress of his own peaceful negotiations with the Southern states. 'It was', as he later wrote, 'as if the Rhine was flowing between us as we talked'.

This exchange marked the end of French attempts to negotiate any kind of territorial 'compensation' for Prussia's spoils of war; and the Belgian question degenerated into desultory discussions between Paris and Brussels, of which the chief ingredients were a Customs' Union and the acquisition by France of control over the Belgian railway system. Like so much else during these last fateful years, they fell on stony ground. Meanwhile, Napoleon, under growing pressure from the political opposition and from angry public opinion, played his last card. It had upon it the mark of an amateur gambler playing for stakes which he could not afford.

Baulked at each successive turn by Bismarck's courteous invitations to disaster, he turned to the last infirmity of ignoble diplomacy. If he could not parcel out what has been neatly called 'the ribs of the Rhine' with Prussia, he might perhaps find a like-minded ally with whom to threaten the heart of the new and menacing Confederation. Thus in September he set out, accompanied by a large and ostentatious suite, to meet the Austrian Emperor in Salzburg. The purpose of this loudly publicized visit was to exchange condolences over the sad demise of the late Archduke Maximilian in Mexico, but no one was deceived by Napoleon's calculated discourtesy in failing to pay his respects to the Bavarian King in Munich; and every interested party — and there were few disinterested parties east of the Rhine — read the writing correctly. There was mischief afoot in Salzburg:

> The days spent in Salzburg were given up to mirth and feasting — not to sorrow and gloom. The irrepressible spirit of politics intruded upon the brilliant company gathered round an open grave. Both Emperors felt aggrieved: one by the loss of his high estate in Germany, the other because his demand for the Rhenish territory had been rejected, and he had not been allowed to take Belgium or buy Luxembourg. The common enemy was Prussia, who had worsted Austria in battle, and France in diplomacy.[12]

12 Hooper: *The Campaign of Sedan.*

The Emperors went their several ways, and with their several thoughts: Napoleon, convinced that he had trumped Bismarck's every ace; Franz Joseph, convinced that lame ducks make poor allies. In Paris, there was enthusiasm. In Vienna, there was cautious optimism.

****

Yet there were few grounds for enthusiasm in Paris; for behind all the display of diplomatic activity there lay a most uncomfortable truth. Sadowa had demonstrated conclusively that the newly minted Prussian army was a formidable instrument of war, now buttressed even more solidly by the addition of the Federal provinces and by the treaty commitment of the South German states. In the autumn of 1866, the military authorities in Paris estimated — only too accurately, as it was to prove — that in the event of war, the available field army of France would be outnumbered four to one by the mobilized strength of the North German Confederation.

In December, the Emperor called a conference at Compiègne to discuss the crisis of manpower. His own inclination was to follow von Roon's path and introduce universal, short-term conscription, on the simple mathematical equation that only by a sharply reduced term of service could the perilous gap in numerical strength be narrowed. But France, dedicated to the doctrine *of débrouillage*, lacked the national will which had fuelled the Prussian military machine.

Soldiers and civilians alike resisted, for equal and opposite reasons, so radical a break with the *status quo*. The politicians, reflecting public opinion, were firmly opposed to any constitutional change which might revive the autocratic power of the Emperor and of the military junta which had helped to engineer the *coup d'état*. What had been good enough for Africa, the Crimea, and Italy (Mexico was conveniently ignored) was adequate for Europe; and a people, long divided between the pursuit of pleasure and the threat of military repression, resisted bitterly any demands on the public purse in the name of national security.[13] For nearly ten years, Roon had faced the same sterile opposition in Berlin, but he had behind him the unique combination of a soldier-king and the political purpose of Bismarck.

Nor, at Compiègne, did Napoleon's belated wisdom receive much military encouragement. His Minister of War, the arch-conservative Marshal Randon, was adamant. An army, he insisted, was only as good as its professional soldiers. If the matter was a distinction between quality and quantity, and if an increase in the head-count could not be achieved by an addition to the annual intake, then the numbers must be maintained by extending the length of regular service.

---

13 Much the same argument had long bedevilled the patient endeavours of military reformers in Britain.

In this sterile argument, an alternative proposal was made by one of the conference members, Marshal Niel.[14] Niel was an able, articulate soldier who clearly understood both the cause and the effect of French military weakness. Almost alone he shared with Napoleon a true perception that time was fast running out.

His suggestion was the revival of the Garde Nationale, as a kind of makeshift equivalent to Roon's carefully integrated Landwehr (a closer parallel would be the British cheerful addiction to amateurism on their Militia and Volunteers). The Garde Nationale was an unloved child of the French Revolution, fostered by the first Napoleon, suckled briefly by Louis XVIII and Louis-Philippe and, after the 'July days' and the *coup d'état* of 1851, swiftly sent packing by the new Emperor. It had never been intended as anything more than a police force to maintain internal order. Niel's proposal that it should now be revived as a trained and equipped reserve for the field army sent shudders of anxiety throughout the political and national spectrum.

Randon stood his ground; and accordingly, in January 1867, the Emperor dismissed him and appointed Niel Minister of War, with the brief to set up a Commission to examine and report on the manifest shortcomings in the organization and administration of the army as a whole. And with almost indecent haste the Commission submitted its findings in a confidential document at the end of February.[15] The subsequent events may be briefly summarized.

The Bill which Niel presented to the Legislative Body found few friends. The governing party viewed with apprehension the effect on public opinion of what was a thinly veiled, if clumsy, attempt to introduce a form of universal military service; the radicals and liberals, reflecting the opposition which Roon had encountered in the Assembly in Berlin, bitterly disputed the financial burden which, despite the unparalleled prosperity of the country, would be imposed upon all classes of society. The greatest stumbling-block was the proposal to revive the Garde Nationale, with all its imagined implications of a return to the worst excesses of past history 'Do you want to turn France into a barracks?' cried Jules Favre in a heated debate in the Assembly. 'Take care,' replied Marshal Niel, 'that you do not turn it into a cemetery!' This celebrated exchange tells us much. By the summer of 1867, while the elected representatives of France indulged in noisy rhetoric, the Germanic states beyond the Rhine had become the very barracks which so exercised Jules Favre; and within three years, France had become the very cemetery which Niel had so sadly foreshadowed. By

14 A name celebrated to-day by a suitably delicate climbing rose. Niel was already a dying man, afflicted by the same ailment — the stone — from which the Emperor was suffering. Napoleon would be reduced to a physical wreck on the crucial battlefields which lay ahead.

15 These findings were leaked by a member of the Commission, General Trochu, in an anonymous book, *L'Armée Française en 1867*, which reprinted fifteen times in six weeks.

then, Niel was dead; and with striking irony, Favre was left to pick up the empty pieces of his own oratory.

Niel's Bill became law in January 1868. Its main thrust represented a dangerous compromise.

Conscripts would serve for five years with the colours and four years with the reserve (absurdly the principle of 'substitution' was retained so that, at the very moment when the army needed a steady source of leadership, the leader-class was seduced into the pursuit of private pleasure rather than the imperative of public duty).

Nor was that all. The annual intake was still divided into two parts, of which the second would be required to serve for no more than five months — 'enough', as one cynical Deputy observed, 'to count the cockroaches in the barrack-room.'

It fared even worse with the Garde Nationale,[16] that reservoir on which Niel's whole expansion plan depended, and which had aroused such universal animosity. The new Act required that all men who, for whatever reason, had escaped the annual contingent should have a legal obligation to 'serve' for five years. If Niel believed that this cosmetic exercise would match in either quality or quantity the German Landwehr, he was swiftly disabused. In the event, the law required that all such men (and there remained every manner of subtle exemption) would serve no more than fourteen days in each year; no more than a single day at a time; and none would be subjected to the contagion of a night in a barrack-room.

In such a climate of military folly and political prejudice, France stumbled slowly into the arms of a confident and expectant enemy.

****

'*Arma virumque cano*.' Though the new army of France was short on men, management, and morale, it was more wealthy in weaponry.

The infantry was equipped with the 'chassepot' rifle (so named after its designer and developer). It was a breech-loaded weapon of such exceptional quality that even the penny-pinching politicians (though not for want of trying) could not obstruct its adoption, and when war broke out, more than one million were in production. Sighted up to 1600 yards, it far outranged (by nearly 1000 yards) the legendary German needle-gun, and its small calibre enabled the infantryman to carry up to 100 rounds of ammunition. In other hands and in other circumstances it could well have dominated the battlefield.

The chassepot was accompanied by another novelty, the mitrailleuse. This embryonic 'machine-gun', Napoleon's own brain-child, was a light, horse-drawn weapon consisting of 25 concentric barrels which, operated by a crank-handle, could produce a fire-rate of 150 rounds a minute with a

16   The force was notionally divided into two sections: Garde Mobile and Garde Sédentaire.

maximum range of 2000 yards. Its development had been financed by the Emperor from his private funds and was conducted in such secrecy that there were barely sufficient trained men to operate the 156 pieces available on the outbreak of war. Its obvious tactical employment should have been that of a close-support infantry weapon, but in the event it was deployed as part of the divisional artillery, sited in batteries, and fired indiscriminately at extreme range. On the battlefield it achieved little more than consume an inordinate quantity of ammunition.

There remained the artillery; and here the Germans had a decisive superiority. French batteries were still equipped with the bronze muzzle-loaders which had done service in the Italian campaign — 4-pdrs and 8-pdrs, with a few antique, smooth-bore 12-pdrs, firing exclusively air-burst ammunition with only two settings. They were no match for the German steel breech-loaders whose range, weight of percussive shell, and brilliant handling were to dominate each successive battlefield and finally pound the French into submission at Sedan.

Yet in the last analysis the Germans possessed the most formidable weapon of all, more miraculous than the mitrailleuse, more effective than batteries and battalions. It was a small, exclusive arsenal of brain and expertise; and it was called the Great General Staff.

****

In August 1869, Niel died, as much a victim of his political opponents as of his physical frailty. He was replaced at the War Ministry by Leboeuf. It was a curious appointment.

Leboeuf, an artilleryman, was the junior Marshal of France. His record of service, from Africa to Italy, had been exemplary if undistinguished. Now he inherited a bed of nails, but lacking Niel's intellectual rigour and political skill, he floated with the tide and the tide was ebbing fast. He has been harshly judged for his complacency; but on that account he was in good company. Given the five years which Napoleon had sought to rebuild the ramparts of France, he could well have succeeded; but within fifteen months, he had joined his more illustrious contemporaries in Wilhelms-höhe as a prisoner of the Prussian King.

****

By January 1870, complacency had become the received wisdom of the day in Paris, and Emile Ollivier was presiding over a new Liberal ministry. It was a situation which Candide, cultivating his little garden, would have enjoyed. In May, a national plebiscite strongly endorsed the new face of imperialism. All, it seemed, was for the best in the best of all possible worlds.

****

THE WAY TO WAR

There were many similarities between the months of June 1870 and June 1914. The weather had been perfect. There was prosperity in the air. And Ollivier's optimistic view to the Chamber on the 30th that 'at no period has the maintenance of peace seemed better assured' was echoed in London by Lord Granville, who could detect 'no cloud in the sky'. In Paris the newly liberalized constitution had cooled the political temperature. In Berlin, Bismarck, Roon and Moltke had left to spend the summer on their estates, while the King prepared to take the waters at Bad Ems. All seemed to be sweetness and light when suddenly, three days later, the blow fell in a quarter as improbable and unexpected as Sarajevo would one day be.

In September 1868 a military coup had disposed of the 'fat, oversexed and grossly incompetent'[1] Queen Isabella II of Spain, who had occupied the throne since her accession (with French assistance) as a child in 1833. It was, given the long decline of Spanish influence in European affairs, an unremarkable event; but it created a vacuum, and politics abhors a vacuum no less than nature.

The Cortes, or Spanish Parliament, had a problem. Despite the steady growth of republican sentiment in Europe, the monarchical system had not only prevailed but prospered, for in the recent past five countries had become independent sovereign states, even if under a curious assortment of foreign Kings. Thus the Prime Minister, Marshal Prim, was authorized to hawk the crown around Europe, on two conditions: the prospective candidate must not be a member of the Spanish Bourbon line; and he must be a Catholic. So Prim went trawling.

Among the royal or princely houses of Europe the offer was received with less than enthusiasm, not least in Vienna where the memory of the ill-fated Maximilian was still all too fresh. Indeed, it is a matter for

1 Aronson: *The Fall of the Third Napoleon*.

speculation that if, in his absurd pursuit of an empire in the New World, Napoleon had not embarked upon his Mexican adventure, he could well have held in his hand seven years later an Austrian Archduke, a Habsburg ace to trump Bismarck's Hohenzollern prince.

The canvassing process continued upon its casual way until, during the summer of 1869, Prim made a fateful decision. In September he approached Prince Charles Anton of Hohenzollern-Sigmaringen, King William's cousin and head of the Catholic, South German branch of the Prussian royal house, and inquired whether his eldest son, Leopold, would accept the Spanish crown. Given French apprehensions of the growing menace of German nationalism since Sadowa, it was at best a tactless, at worst a dangerous proposal; and it was to have consequences which Prim neither intended nor foresaw.

Charles Anton, a great deal more attracted by the offer than the unambitious Leopold, proposed instead his second son Charles, King of Romania. But Charles had all the crowns he needed, and duly declined the honour.[2] And there the matter might have rested; for when news reached Paris of the offer to Leopold the French ambassador to Prussia, Benedetti, was instructed to convey his government's absolute opposition to the candidature. He received polite assurances from Bismarck that this was entirely a domestic matter for Sigmaringen and of no concern to Prussia. Knowing Bismarck's acute diplomatic flair and his careful manipulation of public and political sentiment in France since the 'insult' of Sadowa, it is difficult to believe that his bland *démenti* could possibly have deceived Benedetti, let alone Napoleon. But in the autumn of 1869 Bismarck was having problems with the Catholic states of South Germany, and it undoubtedly suited him to play the innocent bystander and await events. A velvet glove matched with a silver tongue are formidable weapons of diplomacy. He did not have to wait long.

When early in 1870 it was obvious that Prince Leopold was unmoved by Spanish flattery or paternal calls to duty, Prim played his last card. In February he sent a private delegation to Berlin to seek the intervention of the King, as head of the family, in bringing royal pressure to bear on the reluctant Prince. William, whose conduct throughout this dangerous poker game was, and to the end remained, impeccable — if naive — refused to be party to this new approach, and indeed made clear his formal opposition in Sigmaringen. But Prim's decision to involve Protestant Prussia in the domestic affairs of the Catholic Hohenzollerns provided the quick-witted Bismarck with a rare opportunity to hatch a double-yolked diplomatic egg: the simultaneous encouragement of the South German states and the provocation of France. How better to achieve this neat objective than by placing a Catholic Hohenzollern on the throne of Spain?

2 Charles Anton was a persistent man, for early next year he tried unsuccessfully to persuade his third son, Frederick, to accept 'this great historic opportunity'.

To this end Bismarck now applied his devious skills. Aware of the King's opposition, he shrewdly represented Prussia as a disinterested third party, and concentrated his persuasive talents on the ambitious Charles Anton and the persevering Prim. He also proceeded behind a smoke-screen of secrecy. Thus there came about a development the full significance of which has been curiously ignored by historians and misrepresented by the participants.

On 15 March a private meeting was called by the King in Berlin and attended by the Crown Prince of Prussia, Prince Charles Anton and Prince Leopold. Left to themselves, they would certainly have put an end to speculation and finally rejected the candidature. But they were not left to themselves. Also called into consultation were Bismarck, three cabinet ministers — and Roon and Moltke. As Chancellor of the North German Confederation and self-appointed king-maker, Bismarck could hardly be excluded from the discussions. But the presence of Roon and Moltke gave to a council of state the character of a council of war, and indeed such was Bismarck's not oversubtle intention. No detail of the discussions at that fateful gathering has been recorded (Bismarck some years after his dismissal from office in 1890 even denied it had taken place[3]), but in the light of subsequent events it is not difficult to rewrite the scenario.

At the centre of the argument lay Bismarck's dream of a united Germany under Prussian leadership, and excluding an already humiliated Austria. This at once called into question the attitude of France if confronted with the *fait accompli* of a Hohenzollern king of Spain. Not one of those present could have doubted that, given the instability of the Bonaparte dynasty and the volatile state of political opinion in France, the certain outcome would be war. Moltke's opinion needed no rehearsing. Ever since Sadowa — even as early as the Luxembourg crisis — he had advocated a final reckoning with Prussia's historic enemy, and 'sooner rather than later', while German military superiority so far outmatched the ill-organized armies of an effete and divided French nation. If France were provoked into striking the first blow, so much the better for Germany at the bar of history and world opinion.

If that was the advice offered by the politicians and soldiers, it certainly did not reflect the view of kings and princes. William was dedicated to the cause of German nationalism, but he had seen enough of war. He was elderly, peace-loving and had no wish to become master in any house other than his own. It must also have come as a severe shock to the unfortunate pawn, Leopold, that the price of the Spanish crown might be a European conflict; and the following day, 16 March, to William's recorded relief, he again declined the offer.

Undeterred, Bismarck continued to fish for trouble through his agents in Madrid and through personal ('private' was his own word) persuasion in

3 Bismarck: *Gedanken und Erinnerungen* (1898).

Sigmaringen. 'I impressed upon the Prince and his father that the assumption of the crown was a sacred duty to the cause of German unity', he wrote later, while studiously avoiding any suggestion of his more sinister and more cynical purpose; and in the end his persistence was rewarded. For on 19 June, Leopold informed William that *at his father's request* he had decided to accept the offer subject to the unanimous vote of the Cortes, and asked for formal approval from the head of the family. Had the King been wiser — or less ignorant of his Chancellor's intrigue — the course of history might well have been changed. But with a due sense of family propriety, he gave his consent, though 'with a very heavy heart'.

That the news was at once conveyed to Madrid by Bismarck rather than Charles Anton tells its own story. But now capricious fate, so often the joker in the pack, decided to intervene. By an error in decoding, Bismarck's telegram to Prim was taken to mean that Leopold's acceptance could not be presented to the Cortes for a further three weeks. Prim duly adjourned the Cortes *sine die*, and suddenly the truth was out. Thus on 3 July, only three days after Ollivier's comfortable assurance to the Legislative Assembly, the doves of peace were rudely disturbed by the dogs of war. And Paris was in ferment.

Even then cool heads and common sense might have defused the political time-bomb. But fate had already played another wild card. On 15 May, after a national plebiscite had endorsed the new liberal constitution,[4] the moderate, pacifist Foreign Minister of France, Lavalette, had been replaced by the Duc de Gramont.

Gramont was an intemperate warmonger, *plus impérialiste que l'Empereur*, an ardent anti-Prussian, latterly the ambassador in Vienna, and now deeply involved in stitching together some kind of offensive-defensive alliance with Austria and Italy. Ollivier could not handle him. Napoleon did not try. Only Bismarck could count himself lucky that instead of a poker-player, he found himself matched against a card-sharper.

On 6 July the Assembly met in Paris. Gramont, after dismissing the right of the Spanish Cortes to choose its own king, had this to say:

> We do not believe that respect for the rights of a neighbouring people obliges us to endure that a foreign State, by placing one of its princes on the throne of Charles V, should be able to derange, to our injury, the balance of power in Europe, and to imperil the interests and honour of France. We have a confident hope that such an occurrence will not take place.... Should this, however, turn out contrary to our expectation, we shall know how to do our duty without hesitation or weakness.

The threat was explicit; and the message was plain. France had been

---

4 Napoleon should have been warned, for a large part of the Army had voted 'Non!'

insulted once too often. And France — like some romantic Dumas duellist — sought satisfaction from a provocative Prussia. Despite a few muted voices, the deputies greeted Gramont's dreadful rhetoric with wild applause.

Despite the outburst of public anger, there was still time for wiser counsels to prevail. Thiers, the monarchist, and Gambetta and Favre, the republicans — all three of whom would, within two months, find themselves confronted with the curious dilemma of responsibility without power — held back. Ollivier was not even sure that Prussia was directly involved.[5] Napoleon was not unkindly disposed to Leopold, for ironically enough he was related to the house of Hohenzollern-Sigmaringen through the Beauharnais family, and did not identify this hesitant prince as another potential Spanish ulcer. But the war-party in Paris — and historically the voice of French extremism has always been the voice of Paris[6] — was now in full control, and Gramont, determined to exact from Prussia an inexplicable retribution for years of invented insults, embarked upon a collision course. What followed is a very curious passage in the historical process of diplomacy.

Gramont's technique had all the subtlety of a bull in a china-shop (Bismarck was to use the same analogy in a famous aside a week later). Without consulting his colleagues, he decided to by-pass the normal channels and involve the King of Prussia personally in a way which only a political innocent or a dangerous firebrand could have imagined to be either profitable or acceptable. Unfortunately for France — and for the future of Europe — Gramont combined in himself both these perilous qualities.

Early in July, William had gone to Bad Ems to take the waters. By all accepted standards of diplomacy he was incommunicado, an elderly head of state in relaxation and retreat. Gramont accepted only the standards of an arrogant aristocrat for whom the privacy of a king was no obstacle to the making of mischief. Now, on 8 July, he dispatched Benedetti to Ems with an impertinent brief: to demand that the King should formally and personally *order* Prince Leopold to renounce his acceptance of the Spanish crown. It was, in other words, a crude attempt to pre-empt Bismarck and to involve the King directly in a situation already aggravated by Gramont's intemperate speech of 6 July.

William received Benedetti with his customary courtesy, and in answer repeated that the matter did not in any way concern him as King of Prussia but only as head of the Hohenzollern family, and that the decision was purely one between Sigmaringen and Madrid. It was, in effect, the same

---

5 Ollivier: *The Liberal Empire.*

6 When, on 15 July, the question was put to departmental Prefects, sixteen voted for war, thirty-four for peace, and the remainder 'abstained'. So much for *vox populi.*

reply that Bismarck had given in his communications with the French government, but with this significant difference: the King, at least, meant precisely what he said. Benedetti duly reported his conversation to Paris.

But by now Gramont was beyond reason, intent only on extorting from the King a public confession of complicity in a conspiracy against the honour and security of France. He bombarded the embarrassed Benedetti with telegrams — '*Brusquez le Roi!*' is a fair sample of his intemperate approach. 'If the King will not advise the Prince to renounce his design, well, it is war at once, and in a few days we shall be on the Rhine.' It was not the language of brinkmanship, but of Gadarene hysteria. There have been ambassadors who would have resigned rather than be the accessory to implicit disaster. But Benedetti was his master's servant, and did his bidding. In the last remaining days of peace, he is one of the very few actors — he was later to describe himself with some accuracy as playing the Messenger in a Greek tragedy — for whom it is possible to have much sympathy. Now, in carefully moderated form, he conveyed his government's urgent instructions to the King. It was 11 July, and time was running out. Of this the King was well aware, and while repeating his earlier refusal to shift his position, he promised to consult with Sigmaringen.[7]

Then suddenly, on the following day, the Spanish ambassador in Paris informed Gramont that Prince Charles Anton, on behalf of his son, had decided finally to withdraw his candidature.[8] There are many versions of the reason for this change of heart, even that Napoleon on his own initiative pulled the rug from under the feet of his Foreign Minister. More certainly, the pressure was brought to bear by a group of related royals who had watched the mounting crisis with deep apprehension. Both Napoleon and William expressed their relief. 'A great weight has been lifted from my heart,' confessed the King. '*C'est la paix!*' observed the Emperor. Both spoke too soon; and both were wrong. The politicians saw to that.

Bismarck was despondent, for the withdrawal of the candidature removed the main plank in his carefully constructed edifice of provocation. He could not have imagined, therefore, that within twenty-four hours the situation would have been transformed again, not through any stroke of diplomatic ingenuity on his part but by the criminal folly of his opponent.

The news from Madrid was received without enthusiasm in Paris. Ever since 8 July, when Benedetti had been dispatched to Ems, Gramont's sole purpose had been the public humiliation of the King of Prussia. Now he found himself with a hollow victory and an innocent 'victim'. In Paris there

7   While the fate of Europe hung in the balance at Ems, Prince Leopold was happily enjoying a walking tour in the Alps.

8   The crown was eventually accepted by Amadeus, Duke of Aosta, a member of the Italian House of Savoy.

was a sense of anti-climax. The original issue of the Spanish Succession was swept away in a tempest of synthetic anger. Prussia had insulted France. Prussia must prostrate herself before the altar of French 'honour'. And so Benedetti was directed to exact his pound of flesh, blood and all. That sadly tried man failed to extract the one, and in so doing let flow in dreadful measure the other.

Early on the 13th, without requesting a formal audience, he buttonholed the King during his morning walk, and there issued what amounted to an ultimatum. His government, he said, required that the King should at once send the Emperor a written apology for the insult to France, and that he should further give a personal undertaking that never again — *à tout jamais* — would he endorse a candidature for any foreign crown. To this insolent demand the King replied with understandable coolness that, while Benedetti had his authority to say officially that Leopold's decision to step down had his royal approval, in no circumstances would he undertake to write a blank cheque against every future eventuality.

If Benedetti thought that honour was thus satisfied, he little knew Gramont, who fired off a succession of importunate telegrams demanding that the King should be brought to heel.

Three times during that fateful day the ambassador sought a further interview. Three times he was politely informed by an aide that the King had nothing further to say; but courteous to the last, William was present at the railway station when Benedetti took leave of him on the following morning.

While Paris seethed with indignation and war-fever gripped the capital, a different but parallel drama was being played out in Berlin. Bismarck had arrived there during the afternoon, to be greeted with the news of Prince Leopold's defection. He at once recognized that the French had scored a palpable hit, although he did not yet know that Gramont had that same morning trumped his own ace. His immediate concern was the effect that this diplomatic rebuff might have on his patient efforts to woo the South German states into his Confederation. It was therefore with thoughts of resignation that he invited Roon and Moltke to dinner. It was not a very convivial occasion. 'My two guests', he wrote later, 'were so downcast that they would neither eat nor drink'.[9]

Into this melancholy symposium there now entered an unscripted visitor in the shape of a long, factual telegram from Ems describing in detail the events of that day, Benedetti's peremptory demand, and the King's refusal to discuss any further a matter which he considered to be closed. The telegram ended with these words: 'His Majesty leaves it to the discretion of Your Excellency whether this new demand of Benedetti and its refusal should be forthwith communicated to our ambassadors and published in the press.'

9 Bismarck: *op. cit.*

43

This seemingly routine bulletin did nothing for the appetites of Roon and Moltke; but it worked like a charm on the astute Bismarck. 'Examining the document again, I saw the significance of the authority given me by the King to publish the refusal of Benedetti's new demand.' Without altering a word, but by careful editing and emphasis, he changed a simple situation report into what he rightly described as 'a red rag to the Gallic bull'. This is the Bismarck version:

Telegram from Ems, July 13th, 1870

After the Royal Government of Spain had informed the Imperial Government of France that the Hereditary Prince of Hohenzollern had withdrawn his candidature, the French ambassador in Ems made a further demand upon the King, asking him for authority to wire to Paris that His Majesty had bound himself that in future he would never again give his consent in case the Hohenzollerns should resume their candidature. His Majesty thereupon declined to receive the French ambassador again, and sent word to him by one of his Aides-de-Camp that he had no further communication to him.

'That', said Moltke, 'has a different ring. The first sounded like a parley. This is a bold reply to a challenge.' By midnight, Bismarck had forgotten about resignation. Assured by Roon and Moltke, he had embarked on war.

By a curious irony, the news broke in Paris on 14 July. It was Bastille Day, a public holiday, and an occasion for heady parades and demonstrations. It was therefore only a short step from the celebration of one historic decision to the hysterical prosecution of another. Suddenly the symbolic military parades assumed a fearful and immediate symmetry, for as the marching soldiers dispersed, Marshal Leboeuf, the War Minister, issued instructions to call out the reserves.

No one, senator and deputy alike, paused at the cliff's edge. Bismarck's press-handout was wildly assumed to be a formal 'diplomatic note' (not for nothing had he also circulated copies to every Prussian embassy).[10] For France, the passage of events in Ems was the final insult. The Emperor's representative — and so, by curious French logic, the soul of France — had been subjected to intolerable humiliation. No one, senator and deputy alike, paused to think that traps are set for the unwary, and that only clever foxes escape their fate. No one, senator or deputy alike, consulted Benedetti. And Benedetti, who alone knew the truth, would have told them that throughout that last day he had been treated with perfect

---

10 Not until six months later was King William's telegram in its original form made available in Paris. By then one Empire had been swept away and another, more formidable and more durable, had risen beyond the Rhine.

courtesy by the King of Prussia, and that the only insult had been the provocative policy of his own government, which, handed peace on a plate, preferred to shatter the plate.

At a Cabinet Council at St Cloud at noon on the 14th, it was decided to go to war. Napoleon, ill and frightened, asked for 'guarantees'. Guarantees of what?

Of victory; for the option was a simple one. To retreat in the face of Bismarck's challenge would mean the death of the dynasty, swept away in the rising tide of public anger. 'That child', said the Empress, pointing to the fourteen-year-old Prince Imperial, 'will never rule until we have won satisfaction for Sadowa.' To advance beyond the Rhine and teach an insolent Prussia and her allies that France was still the France of Bonaparte and of Jena, that would secure the dynasty and much, much more. The national will was echoed in the streets of Paris by the singing of the *Marseillaise*, banned since the *coup d'état* of 1851.

But if the armies of France, with their wonder-working weapons of chassepot and mitrailleuse, were to go down to defeat, what hope then for the dynasty? 'On the evening of the 14th', recorded Filon, the tutor of the Prince Imperial, 'the emperor appeared very ill at ease.' Small wonder. There are no guarantees in war. For every Jena there is a Waterloo.

By the following day, there was no option left. By a massive majority — 267 votes to 10 — the Legislative Body voted the necessary war credits. Much nonsense was talked by men who should have known better. '*L'armée*', announced Leboeuf, '*est prête au dernier bouton des guêtres*', without adding that the buttons and the gaiters were not always in the same places. Gramont hinted darkly at successful negotiations for an alliance with Austria and Italy. And Ollivier delivered himself of one of history's great *obiter dicta* when he foolishly confessed that he went to war '*à coeur léger*.' It is a dreadful man indeed who goes to war with a light heart.

On the other side of the hill, Bismarck watched with interest as his red rag enraged his prize bull. The King left Ems on the afternoon of the 15th and was met at Brandenburg by the Crown Prince and by the triumvirate. He was briefed by Bismarck on the political developments, and by Roon and Moltke on the military state of readiness. And shortly before midnight, the order went forth: 'Call out the army of the North German Confederation. The 16th of July is the first day of mobilization.'

At 11.20 a.m. on 19 July, the French chargé d'affaires in Berlin, M. le Sourd, presented his government's formal declaration of war. It was the first and only written communication between the two governments since the start of the crisis. *Jacta erat alea.*

****

Where, then, lies the true responsibility for a war which was as unnecessary as it was inevitable? Certainly it was France which, in language highly charged with emotive words like 'injured dignity', 'national pride', and 'honour', made the formal declaration. Undoubtedly the politicians, led by the arrogant and unstable de Gramont and urged on by an inflammatory press, pursued their vendetta against Prussia despite having achieved a more than adequate diplomatic victory. Complacency, political naivety and a wanton disregard of the military facts of life drove a volatile nation to its certain destruction. Napoleon, sick and insecure, wished only for peace. Almost alone, except for the patriotic Thiers and the discredited Trochu, he understood the scale of France's unpreparedness and the price of reckless adventurism, but in July 1870 he was an Emperor without authority, pathetically aware of his own inadequacy to command, but unable to resist an Empress for whom the dynasty was everything, and a war-party hell-bent on exacting vengeance for imagined injuries.

William too wished only for peace. True, he was a soldier-king, but he sought no territorial advantage in his pursuit of a historic dream, the creation of a united Germany. To him, the distasteful *Brüderkrieg* with Austria had been represented as a political necessity. But unlike Napoleon he was secure in his crown, a father-figure to his pious and industrious people. 'War', he once wrote to the Crown Prince, 'can only be an end, never a beginning.' Having, therefore, all the authority that Napoleon lacked, his dynasty assured, his country prosperous, he cannot be absolved from his failure to perceive, if not from his refusal to halt, the political thrust of Bismarck and the military purpose of Moltke. History shows him to have been a stern, courteous and excessively naive man; and he has much to answer for.

The architects of the war, if not the ultimate aggressors, were Bismarck, Roon and Moltke. It is significant that all three were present at the meeting on 15 March; that they were dining together when the Ems telegram reached Berlin on 13 July; and that, as if to ensure no royal backsliding, they all accompanied the King's headquarters throughout the entire war, even if at the end Bismarck and Moltke were barely on speaking-terms. There is no comparable example in history of Clausewitz's dictum that war is an extension of policy.[11]

In this triumvirate, each man played a carefully co-ordinated part. It had started with Roon and his detailed proposals for the reorganization of the Prussian army; it had continued with Moltke, who provided the brain behind the sinews and the purpose behind the planning; and from the power base of the North German Confederation, the fate of France had been orchestrated by Bismarck with flair and finesse.

After Sadowa, it was Bismarck who conducted the band, while his accomplices rehearsed the players until they were note-perfect. There would be no performance until all three were confident that the platform had been well chosen and that the invited audience had taken their places.

11 *See also* Moltke's comments on p. 14.

The true tragedy of the Franco-German War is that it reflects, in a tiny time-capsule, the moral predicament of man: greed matched by temptation, revenge visited with retribution, pride preceding a fall. In all the German literature on the origins and outcome of the war there is neither humility nor sense of guilt, barely even an awareness of those elementary errors which, as we shall presently see, would have provided a more resolute adversary first with the chance of success and then with the assurance of victory.

On the French side the whole sombre story dissolved in a welter of mutual recrimination and personal animosity, and culminated in the ritual slaughter of a man who was innocent of warmongering and whose only crime was moral cowardice when confronted with a responsibility beyond his sadly limited competence. In hammering home the nails, the prosecution at Bazaine's court-martial chose thus to describe his inertia on the afternoon of 18 August: 'His conduct may be likened to that of a common soldier who deserts his post in the face of the enemy'. On the criminal arrogance and ineptitude of the politicians who placed this former private of the line in his predicament, the prosecution remained silent. When, on 13 July, the luckless Benedetti was driven to an absurd extremity by his intemperate masters in Paris, not even Bismarck could have guessed his good fortune. Bazaine had no illusions. Three days later, as he was leaving the Gare de l'Est to take up his command in Metz, he turned to a friend and said: '*Nous marchons à un désastre.*' He had always been a man of few words.

Bismarck has passed into history as the Iron Chancellor. That does him more than justice. More simply, he was an evil man. When all is weighed in the balance — the pursuit of German unity, the professions of injured innocence, the blatant hypocrisy, the clever provocations of an all too easily tempted adversary — he remains the undoubted instrument of German imperialism, the malign genius of his time, and the prophet of a later doom. He got the war he wanted, in his own time, and on his own terms. If it is possible to attribute the responsibility to any one man, then it is Bismarck. Only one historian, and that of our time, has properly placed the blame, when commenting on the manipulation of the Ems telegram:

A simple falsification had enabled German statesmanship, which had already initiated the wars of 1864 and 1866, to enrich its country's history with the war of 1870.[12]

He might well have added 1914 and 1939.

12 Guedalla: *The Two Marshals.*

MOBILIZATION[1] AND THE FRONTIER BATTLES

It might be supposed that a great military power which arbitrarily declared war on a formidable opponent would do so after meticulous preparation and with a clearly perceived plan of action. But French arrogance and the deadly sin of *débrouillage* conspired to lose a war even before it had been entered upon. When, in the heady July days, Leboeuf had described the French army as *archiprête* he may well have believed that a little lie might conceal a massive miscalculation. He may even have succeeded in squaring his political conscience with his military judgment. If so, he was in a lonely minority. There was not one other Marshal or General who shared his rhetorical view. Three years earlier, Trochu had offered a Churchillian warning.[2] And when the blow fell Trochu, who might well have been a match-winner where Bazaine and MacMahon failed, was sent to cool his heels on the Pyrenees. His time was yet to come.

Towards the end of 1871, when wise words had long been overtaken by events, there appeared an anonymous pamphlet, whose authorship has on good grounds been attributed to the deposed Emperor.[3] It was not widely read, and was soon forgotten in the contemporary welter of charge and counter-charge. This is a pity, for it dwelt not on personalities but on some uncomfortable home truths. For example: 'An army is always a true reflection of the social condition of the population out of which it is formed.' And later, with benefit of hindsight: 'There was lacking in the nation that unity of purpose which alone can lead to military success.' It was by no means all that was lacking on the French side.

1 See *Orders of Battle* at Appendix A.

2 Trochu, *op. cit.*

3 *Des causes qui ont amené la capitulation de Sedan*, par un officier attaché à l'état major général.

First, a clearly defined plan. Back in 1868, when Marshal Niel was fighting a losing battle with the Corps Législatif, and well before de Gramont's headlong rush to war, a 'strategic deployment' had been agreed, and filed away. The plan, such as it was, envisaged a purely defensive stance in *'positions magnifiques'*, facing the frontier with the Palatinate on either side of Saarbrücken. The author was General Frossard,[4] an able and industrious engineer officer and military tutor to the Prince Imperial, who would later command 2 Corps in the very positions he had chosen, but in circumstances he had certainly not envisaged.

By the first weeks in July 1870, however, and with the streets of Paris echoing to cries of *'À Berlin!'*, no one dusted down the Frossard file. It is barely conceivable, but none the less true, that the French field army was within a matter of days bundled into battle (no other word will serve) without a plan. Instead, there were two vague 'options', both owing more to political expedients than to military capability.

The first of these options was an immediate strike across the common Rhine frontier at Maxau with the object of overrunning the South German states, linking hands with an enthusiastic Austria, and then turning together to crush the insolent Prussian-led North German Confederation beyond the Main.

It was by any standard an absurd improvisation. It presupposed the virtual acquiescence of South Germany, and tacitly ignored the agreement four years earlier at Nikolsburg, when those states had aligned themselves with Prussia in the event of French aggression. More importantly, it assumed that Austria would be ready, willing and able to enter the lists by the end of July. But the Austrians were none of these things. They had been taught a bloody lesson by Prussia at Sadowa; they had an explosive problem on their hands in Hungary; they were rightly wary of Russian intentions; and above all, they were under no illusions about the military capability of France. So, while Vienna made suitably Delphic responses to Paris, Paris continued to confuse confidence with incertitude. As late as 12 August, by which time the French armies were in full retreat and the Emperor had abdicated his military — and with it his political — authority, the only straw of comfort that he could offer to his new and reluctant master of ceremonies, Bazaine, was the dead spark of Austrian intervention.[5]

The second option was pure extravaganza — a rapid thrust with all forces combined into the Palatinate, and with the fortress of Mainz as the primary objective, before the German armies could complete their own mobilization. The naive assumption of this grandly Napoleonic stroke was twofold: first, that it would fatally disrupt German counter-measures

4 The same idea, on an altogether grander scale, was foisted on a credulous French government sixty years later by André Maginot.

5 But *see also* p. 32.

beyond the Main; and secondly, that such a display of French military superiority would bring the South German states, Austria, and even Italy hastening to share the fruits of victory.

That both these options depended on speed of execution and a degree of organizational fine-tuning far beyond anything that the French had ever attempted, let alone demonstrated, was conveniently ignored. Traditional *élan*, the chassepot, and the mysterious mitrailleuse would do the trick. In his one and only Order of the Day, the Emperor summoned up the old glories of the Grande Armée and evoked the spirit of Austerlitz and Jena; but the fires of the First Empire no longer burned in the Second, and the pale and pain-wracked Louis Napoleon was a Bonaparte in name alone.

****

In the summer of 1870, despite the warnings of Trochu and the military attaché in Berlin, Colonel Stoffel, and for all Leboeuf's comfortable reassurances to the Assembly, no war establishment existed in France. The country was divided into six military districts (with a seventh in Algeria), and regiments were moved around at frequent intervals within this framework — for no better reason than to provide a kind of political safety-valve.[6]

When war broke out, and when, as we shall see, Leboeuf decided to concentrate the line regiments in Alsace and Lorraine without the formality of an orderly mobilization, this policy resulted in an almost comical confusion. The order to call in the reservists went out on 14 July, and the men were instructed to report to their regimental depots where they were to be embodied, kitted out and forwarded to their respective units. But a few examples will illustrate the inevitable degree of chaos.

The 98th Regiment (destined for 4 Corps at Thionville) was stationed at Dunkirk, with its depot at Lyon; the 86th was at Lyon, with its depot at Ajaccio in Corsica; the depot at St Malo; the 32nd at Châlons, with its depots of all 'home' regiments serving in Algeria were in France; and reservists of Zouave regiments were required to report to Oran. The staffs at the various depots were insufficient, and incompetent to deal with the work-load; and thus during the critical early weeks men wandered around France in search of their units, *enfants perdus* indeed. So it was that by 6 August, the day that battle was joined in earnest, only half of the reservists had reached their regiments, and many of these lacked the most basic items of uniform and equipment.

More seriously — and this is reflected in the lack of any mobilization plan — the scattered units were not, with three exceptions, organized into tactical formations, while the different arms of the service had received no

6   In early July, of the hundred Infantry Regiments of the Line, only thirty-six were stationed in their 'home' depots.

practical training in mutual co-operation and support. In the event of war (and even when war was inevitable) it was envisaged that the first and second lines of the field army would notionally be formed into seven army corps, and the Imperial Guard, of which three would comprise the Army of Alsace based on Strasbourg, four be concentrated on Metz as the Army of Lorraine, and the eighth held back at Châlons as a general reserve.

It was on this vaguely strategic basis that preparations were being set in train early in July when there occurred the first of the many *ordres, contre-ordres, et désordres* which were to cause such fatal confusion in the French conduct of the campaign. On the 11th, Napoleon suddenly decided to assume sole command of a united army of all eight corps, a prospect which would have daunted even a Moltke. The decision was purely political rather than military, and almost certainly stemmed from the Empress and her kitchen cabinet, the future Regency Council, who threw Napoleon to the wolves of public opinion on the shallow premise that the dynasty depended on him, and that Bonapartes did not lead from behind. It could not possibly have been an imperial *grand geste*. He had no great pretensions as a soldier and he was a desperately sick man; and there is something infinitely pathetic in the final decline and fall of this unwarlike warrior as, within a month, he accepted defeat, handed over his command to Bazaine, and trailed disconsolately to his eventual humiliation at Sedan.

****

As with the cavalier attitude to field formations, so too with the higher command. With the one exception of Bazaine, the superior ranks in the French army were all products of the so-called 'special schools' — St Cyr and the Polytechnic — and there is a certain irony in the fact that when the Emperor abdicated the supreme command at Metz on 12 August, public (and especially republican) sentiment demanded that the succession should pass to an ex-Légionnaire whose chronic inferiority complex was to affect his every judgment when the margin between defeat and victory hung upon strong and resolute leadership; so that his conduct on the critical day of battle could later be described (by his most savage critic) as that of '*un simple colonel*', rather than that of a Marshal of France.

There were other ingredients in the process of advancement. Social position and especially Court favour was one (all eight corps commanders on the outbreak of war were aides-de-camp to the Emperor); a dashing career in Africa was highly regarded; and a successful reputation in the Crimea and Italy was a necessary passport to a Marshal's baton, and even, in MacMahon's case, to a dukedom, no less.

But professionalism, the *métier*, was a secondary consideration in an army which dwelt on past glories and, counting its virtues, turned a blind eye to its blatant vices. The entire system was socially divisive, and discipline (never a strong suit) was left to the most junior officers, themselves for the most part elderly *rengagés* whose humble origins and lack of authority were not the best equipment for handling a volatile and, in large measure, politically suspect rank and file.

Battle-training, skill at arms, physical fitness[7] — all singular features of the German army — were given scant attention on the French side. The single field-service manual had not been updated for more than twenty years, and dwelt almost lovingly on the well-worn theme of chasing *goums* around the African desert. Students of a future war like the young Ardant du Picq, killed by a stray shell at the Emperor's headquarters on the eve of Mars-la-Tour, were dismissed as dangerously *avant-garde*. And the annual 'manœuvres' at Châlons, the Aldershot of France, bore no more relationship to military realities than a colourful and spectacular demonstration of Trooping the Colour on a grand and theatrical scale. Now, after the wasted years, and without even benefit of dress rehearsal, the French rang up the curtain, while a confused cast hurried from the wings.

****

The leading actors, armed with an unedited script which left them to mull over their lines until the stage-directors, Napoleon and Leboeuf, decided which play should be performed, were allotted the following roles.[8]

> *Stage right*: the Army of Alsace
> *Stage left*: the Army of Metz
> *Backstage*: the Army of Châlons

The improvised nature of this *force de frappe* threw up a number of absurdities which may be briefly summarized thus:

1   The commander in Alsace was Marshal MacMahon, Duke of Magenta, a glittering star of the Crimean and Italian campaigns, who would survive the later humiliation at Sedan, crush the Commune uprising in Paris, and effortlessly emerge as the improbable President of the Third Republic. Early in July he was Governor-General in Algeria, and did not reach Strasbourg until ten days after the declaration of war. There, until battle was joined, he combined his Army command with that of 1 Corps, until a week later he delegated the latter authority to General Ducrot. The rest of MacMahon's command consisted of 5 Corps and 7 Corps, neither of which existed on the peacetime establishment, and which were now being hastily

7   As the reader will presently see, the march-discipline and stamina of the German infantry during the encounter battles of August had a decisive influence on the whole campaign.

8   The broad delegation of responsibility remained unchanged even after the Emperor assumed supreme command on 11 July; and again during the critical period between 6 August and 12 August.

improvised at Châlons and Belfort under, respectively, Generals de Failly and Félix Douay.

Two examples will illustrate the tragi-comic preliminaries. On 21 July the cavalry general Michel addressed a plaintive telegram to Paris: 'Have arrived at Belfort. Can't find my brigade. Can't find the General of Division. What shall I do? Don't know where my regiments are.' Then on 27 July Leboeuf, newly appointed Chief of Staff to the Emperor, inquired of Félix Douay: 'How far have you progressed with your formations? Where are your divisions?' — seemingly unaware that the commander of 7 Corps was still in Paris, occupied with the ritual duties of an Imperial aide-de-camp. Douay arrived in Belfort the following day. With pardonable irritation he replied to Leboeuf (equally unaware that Imperial Headquarters was by then established in Metz):

> For the most part troops have neither tents, cooking-pots nor flannel belts; no medical or veterinary canteens, medicines, nor forges, or pickets for horses. Am without hospital staff, *ouvriers*, and train. The magazines of Belfort are empty.

It was on such a tide of incompetence that the French went forth to war.

2 To the west of Alsace, and dangerously divided by the Vosges massif which ran from Belfort northward into the Palatinate, the Army of Metz (Imperial Guard, 2, 3 and 4 Corps) was being assembled. Here the problems were less acute, for the area was served by two railway lines from the interior through Nancy and Thionville.[9] Furthermore, of this Army, three corps — 2 Corps in the camp at Châlons, the Imperial Guard and 3 Corps in and around Paris — were to a greater or lesser degree organized into tactical formations.

2 Corps was commanded by Frossard, slightingly nicknamed 'the Professor'; and, in a sense, it was to be his misfortune that his advanced state of readiness would ensure that when the curtain rose he would be first to the footlights.

The Imperial Guard, so precious a jewel in the crown that in the bitter battles of August it was scarcely committed and never hazarded, was commanded by General Bourbaki, young by French standards of advancement (he was fifty-four), rich, well placed at Court, and sufficiently unstable to indulge in two attempts at suicide before the war was over. The Guard, with its long and glamorous tradition, was élitist, the one true heir to the *grognards* of the Grande Armée; and a tiny footnote will illustrate how soon it slipped from grace. It reached Metz on 25/26 July in its heavy gold-frogged uniforms which had graced the parade-ground at

---

9 The third line from Verdun to Metz, one that could well have been of critical importance, was still under construction.

St Cloud, but which were scarcely a suitable *tenue de campagne* in the summer heat of Lorraine. Thus when two days later the Emperor arrived from Paris, the first of his many mindless compromises was to replace the proud bearskin caps of his Grenadiers with the unsoldierly *bonnets de police*, a perky little headdress which in more ways than one (as a cynical critic put it), 'cut the Praetorian Guard down to size'.

The commander of 3 Corps was Marshal Bazaine, thirty-nine years a soldier of France from Africa to Mexico,[10] famous for his courage if not for any military brilliance, risen uniquely from the ranks (although born at Versailles, his ancestral home was the tiny village of Scy within a cannon-shot of Metz) and thus the darling of the Left to which he owed no allegiance and from which he certainly sought no favour. Yet it is a melancholy irony that it would be this brave, loyal, unambitious soldier who would all too soon find himself saddled with a desperate situation not of his making, with a responsibility far beyond his limited competence, and with — at the end — a public humiliation which did more credit to him than to his persecutors.

There remained in the Army of Metz 4 Corps, commanded by General de Ladmirault, the then military Governor of the Lille district and a veteran of the Crimean and Italian campaigns.

3   The general reserve consisted of 6 Corps, an entirely new and improvised formation.[11] Curiously, it was commanded by Canrobert, the senior serving Marshal of France, whose outstanding record and long experience of active service might have presupposed a much more prominent role, such as Chief of Staff to the Emperor or even as commander-in-chief of what would be presently, if grandiloquently, called the Army of the Rhine. But Canrobert was, and remains, an ambivalent character who, as we shall see, declined the honour and responsibility of supreme command at a critical moment when his duty lay with his Emperor and his country, and left the fate of France to a man of whose incompetence he was already cynically aware.

****

Despite his assurances to the Assembly that the French Army was in a state of perfect readiness, Leboeuf was uncomfortably aware of the physical — to say nothing of the moral — superiority of the German military machine. The previous year Colonel Stoffel, the attaché in Berlin, had estimated

---

10   See *Appendix D*.

11   When, after the French defeat at Spicheren on 6 August, the major part of 6 Corps was hurried forward from Châlons to Metz, another improvised formation, 12 Corps under General Lebrun, was hastily cobbled together just in time to march away with MacMahon to its melancholy fate on 1 September at Sedan.

that the Germans could mobilize 1,000,000 men within 25 days of a declaration of war. The figure was accurate so far as it went, but he ignored — or was unaware of — the contribution from the South German states, bound by treaty to the Confederation if it should come to a war with France.[12] Indeed, it is arguable that the two Bavarian corps, and the infantry divisions from Württemberg and Baden, significantly tilted the balance, first during the early encounter battles on the German left wing, and finally at Bazeilles a month later at the gates of Sedan.

The effective strength which the French could hope to put *into the field* by the end of July was, at the most optimistic guess, 567,000, but it was a purely notional figure, based on a number of absurd miscalculations. It included a large number of 'ineffectives' — the garrison required for Algeria, the brigade group stationed at Civita Vecchia to protect the Papal States, a division held back to watch the Spanish frontier, and, in a climate of political uncertainty, a substantial number of second-line troops for internal security duties. Twenty thousand highly trained Marines stood idly by while Ministers debated a diversionary (and in the event aborted) combined operation on the German Baltic coast. Leboeuf more realistically put the figure at 300,000, but even this proved to be an overestimate, for reasons which will presently become apparent. In the administrative shambles which followed the declaration of war no one troubled to count heads. Various sources later gave very various figures. The official French history gives the effective strength on the morning of 16 August as 288,000; and by a singular irony it was on that day, the day of Mars-la-Tour, that the Army of the Rhine enjoyed for the first and only time a crushing local superiority over its enemy.

****

For Leboeuf, therefore, time was of the essence; and accordingly he took a hazardous decision for which in the circumstances he has been unjustly criticized — even if as Minister of War he bears a heavy responsibility for the wasted years, and the almost total disregard of even the most elementary preparations for war. Now every day counted; and so instead of waiting until his field formations had completed the process of mobilization, and of absorbing and equipping reservists together with the assembly of administrative services, he decided to press forward immediately with the concentration of his eight army corps on or near the German frontier, irrespective of their state of battle-readiness. He was later to justify his action not as a pre-emptive strike but as a defensive deployment in accordance with Frossard's dusty and forgotten file.

This is not true. A government and a bloodthirsty nation bent on

12   In the event, the combined German armies embodied 1,183,000 men within 21 days of mobilization.

teaching an ancient adversary a salutary lesson does not declare a defensive war. Leboeuf knew this. He was aware of the two alternative 'options', as his deployment of the newly minted 'Army of the Rhine'[13] demonstrates; he knew that the Empress and the war-party, if not a hesitant and apprehensive Emperor, wanted quick and inspiring victories. But an army cannot conduct itself in the field without those sinews of war which lend it vigour and flexibility. 'Thus a plan already faulty in principle was further marred by faults in execution; and as the army assembled around Metz and Strasbourg it found itself lacking not only men but the most elementary supplies.'[14]

These supplies certainly existed; but thanks to the dead hand of bureaucracy, a grossly inefficient and understaffed *intendance* and an overburdened and disorganized railway system, the vital marriage of men and material did not happen until it was too late.

The villain of the piece was the French passion for centralization. From the outbreak of the war the Ministry in Paris was inundated with demands ranging from ammunition and administrative personnel down to cooking-pots and shelter-tents. In the forward area there was a shortage of food, even a shortage of money to pay an already sullen soldiery. The only maps available were, by a perverse irony, those of Germany, except for a strictly limited edition of an outline sketch of the frontier area marked simply 'Routes leading to Rhine'. The wonder is that this undernourished, unpaid, ill-equipped, and improvised army was in any state to resist the hammer blows of its superbly organized and confident opponent when the collision came in the early days of August; and that, much more remarkably, its fighting spirit twice brought it within measurable distance of a wholly improbable victory.

****

When Leboeuf decided to dispense with the time-consuming preliminaries of mobilization, the Army of the Rhine moved forward into the following concentration areas:[15]

Imperial Guard (Bourbaki)
    To Nancy. Thence on 25 July to Metz.

13   The title, both grandiose and significant, which had been coined on 11 July, was dropped discreetly on 28 July, and rather pathetically revived on 12 August as the armies of France retreated in disarray.

14   Howard, *The Franco-Prussian War*.

15   *See* Map 2.

1 Corps (Ducrot/MacMahon)

To Strasbourg, with a division (that of Abel Douay, brother of the commander of 7 Corps) pushed forward to Wissembourg on the frontier between Alsace and the Palatinate.

2 Corps (Frossard)

To St Avold midway between Metz and Saarbrücken.

3 Corps (Bazaine)

To Metz from Paris. Bazaine, commanding this corps, was also responsible for the whole Lorraine sector until the arrival of the Emperor on 28 July, on which date he moved his own headquarters to Boulay on the right bank of the Moselle.

4 Corps (Ladmirault)

To Thionville, with a division forward at Sierck on the frontier.

5 Corps (Failly)

Holding a dangerously exposed position on the frontier between Bitche and Sarreguemines, and notionally acting as a link between the two main armies in Alsace and Lorraine.

6 Corps (Canrobert)

From Châlons to Nancy. Then on 26 July back to Châlons, and finally, in part, from Châlons to Metz on 9 August.

7 Corps (Félix Douay)

Forming in Belfort. This corps was so bedevilled by shortages of both men and material that only one division (Conseil-Dumesnil) reached MacMahon, and then only in time to join in the general retreat after the battle of Wörth on 6 August.

Reserve Cavalry

Three divisions assembled at Lunéville, whence one (Bonnemain) was directed to Strasbourg, and two (de Forton and du Barail) to Metz.

Thus the Army of the Rhine was strung out over a front of 100 miles from Wissembourg to the Luxembourg frontier, its two wings separated by the Vosges mountains and loosely connected by 5 Corps. There it awaited the signal to advance.

The signal never came. When Leboeuf reached Metz on 24 July his mind was set on the second of his two options — the thrust north-eastward into the Palatinate with his whole force combined. His reasoning, such as it was, ran thus: with Austria and Italy both still ambivalent, an attack across the Rhine frontier would have neither military nor political significance beyond encouraging press headlines and some cheerful demonstrations in the capital. But that road led to a cul-de-sac, and this Leboeuf and his two

A gallery of French leaders

Louis Napoleon Bonaparte, Emperor of the French (62)

Marshal Bazaine, 3 Corps, then C-in-C, Army of the Rhine (59)

Marshal MacMahon, 1 Corps, then Army of Alsace (62)

Marshal Leboeuf, Chief of Staff, then 3 Corps (64)

Marshal Canrobert, 6 Corps (61)

General Bourbaki, Imperial Guard (54)

General Frossard, 2 Corps (63)

General Ladmirault, 4 Corps (62)

assistant chiefs of staff, Lebrun and Jarras, recognized.[16] On the other hand, a quick advance in strength beyond the Saar might catch the Germans off balance and disrupt their own concentration in the area of Mainz. Thus the first orders to Bazaine, the nominal commander in Lorraine, were to push Frossard's 2 Corps forward to the wooded heights above Saarbrücken astride the main road from Metz to Forbach, while 3 Corps followed along the same axis to St Avold, and 4 Corps and a division of 5 Corps closed in on either flank. It looked splendid on paper — a solid wedge of eleven infantry divisions poised to knock a great hole into the heart of Germany. But like every other French improvisation, it was fatally flawed.

First it took no account of the terrain — difficult enough for a small, mobile force, let alone a cumbersome, ill-organized army, with poor lateral communications. Secondly, MacMahon's three scattered corps could only with extreme difficulty be concentrated by rail to the west of the Vosges, and their movement would uncover Alsace; and thirdly, and most importantly, the gap between the Army of the Rhine and a formidable enemy which outnumbered it by two to one was closing rapidly.

Four days later, on 28 July, the Emperor arrived at Metz to assume command. In the few weeks that remained before he was led away into captivity, he was to take only three decisions. All were, in the circumstances, right and proper in purely military terms; each was to prove a successive nail in his political coffin.

His first decision was to countermand Leboeuf's intended offensive. For all his fine words,[17] Napoleon was uncomfortably aware that the Army of the Rhine was in no state to embark upon even limited heroics. Failly had reported from his exposed concentration area around Bitche that his first reservists had only reached him on the 26th. Bazaine's 3 Corps, as it moved forward on the same day to St Avold, was entirely lacking in ambulances and medical staff. In Metz itself there were only 36 bakers to provide bread for upward of 130,000 men. There was a grave shortage of artillery ammunition. And already there was an inescapable atmosphere of insubordination. It was in such circumstances, charged with doubt and hedged with hesitancy, that Imperial headquarters in the Préfecture 'discovered' the electric telegraph, a potent new weapon in the right hands and, in the wrong ones, an invention of the damned. So, armed with this formidable instrument for good or ill, the Emperor and his staff moved their pieces round the chequerboard — those *marches et contre-marches*

16   MacMahon had not yet arrived from Algiers and his stand-in, Ducrot, in Strasbourg was loud in his objections.

17   'I place myself at your head to defend the honour of our country's territory... Wherever our steps may lead beyond the frontier, we shall everywhere find the glorious traces of our fathers...' So ran the rhetoric of his short-lived Order of the Day.

which so distracted Frossard — as they contemplated the next move. Meanwhile in another part of the forest...

****

When on the evening of 13 July Bismarck decided that the Ems telegram provided him with a perfect opportunity to provoke the war party in Paris into precipitate action he did not need to ask Roon and Moltke if their military preparations were complete. Moltke had indeed pressed for a pre-emptive strike as far back as 1867 at the time of the Luxembourg crisis, but had been restrained for sound political reasons. Since then war plans had been polished and perfected year by year. Four new railway lines had been constructed, running from the interior to the Rhine; three more annual classes of conscripts had been absorbed and trained; the armies of the Southern states had been re-equipped largely in conformation with those of the Confederation; the lessons of Sadowa had been minutely studied and applied by a General Staff moulded in the image of its demanding taskmaster; the intricate machinery of mobilization had been so refined that a single order on the evening of 15 July set a million men in orderly motion. Germany, unlike France, was truly *archiprête*.

Moltke, unlike Leboeuf, had a plan, ambitious in scale but precise in purpose. He was later to explain his intellectual grasp of the art of war in these words:[18]

> The plan of campaign was fixed, from the first, upon the capture of the enemy's capital, the possession of which is of more importance in France than in other countries.... Beyond everything [the plan] was based on the resolve to attack the enemy at once, wherever found, and keep the German forces always so compact that this could be done with the advantage of superior numbers. The specific dispositions for the accomplishment of these objects were left to be adopted on the spot; the advance to the frontier was alone pre-arranged in every detail.

Then:

> It is a delusion to imagine that a plan of campaign can be laid down far ahead and fulfilled with exactitude. The first collision with the enemy creates a new situation in accordance with its result. Some things intended will have become impracticable; others, which originally seemed impossible, become feasible. All that the leader of an army can do is to form a correct estimate of the circumstances, to

18 Moltke, *op.cit.*

decide for the best for the moment, and carry out his purpose unflinchingly.

There remained the greatest of all imponderables: the human factor. And it was this which came close to disrupting Moltke's master-plan almost before battle was joined.

****

The detailed project for an offensive war against France was drawn up by Moltke and the General Staff during the winter of 1868/69.[19] Thereafter it was constantly updated and refined, the process of mobilization checked and rechecked, rail timetables perfected, maps of Alsace and Lorraine revised to the point where, by July 1870, not only were the smallest roads shown (including the unfinished railway line from Verdun to Metz) but also the number of inhabitants of each individual town and village. Nothing, so far as ingenuity and application could ensure, was left to chance. In this project military science was elevated to a new art-form; and such was the artistry that the original project became in the event, and with only modest amendments, the master-plan which set in train the great *Aufmarsch* when the final issue was joined.

Moltke's *modus operandi* (his own phrase) proceeded from the classical starting-point of all military operations: courses open to both sides. He accurately estimated the relative strengths available within seven, fourteen, and twenty-one days of mobilization, and correctly judged the effect of *débrouillage* on French military readiness.

From the outset he perceived that the first enemy concentration on the frontier would be dictated by the deficiencies of the French railway system, and thus he arrived at precisely the same options as Leboeuf — a deployment on the line Strasbourg–Metz and a pre-emptive strike across the Rhine into southern Germany, with the Main as the first objective and the Elbe as the second. That such a deployment on an east-west axis would mean that the French armies were split in two by the Vosges massif did not escape him, although it seems not to have occurred to Leboeuf until 6 August, and by then the heady optimism of July had turned to defeat and desperate disengagement.

Moltke summed up thus:

> The military forces, such as must be brought into the field against France, can evidently only operate by being combined into several armies. The strength of each army must depend upon the special object it has in view, and the different Corps to comprise it must be so

19 See *Official German History*, Vol I, Pt I.

allotted that no delay takes place in concentrating for battle.

****

The resources available to Moltke on mobilization were formidable: the Guard Corps and eleven army corps of the Confederation; the Royal Saxon Corps, numbered XII; two army corps from Bavaria and an infantry division each from Württemberg and Baden; six cavalry divisions in addition to those of the Guard and Saxony; a combined artillery of 1194 guns; and accompanying each formation a full complement of pioneers, bridging companies, supply and medical services. With the forward troops moved field post-offices; and also, at the ready invitation of the astute Bismarck, a large corps of press correspondents from neutral countries.[20] Less welcome to Moltke and his professional staff was a startling assembly of princes and potentates with their swollen suites who attached themselves to Royal Headquarters when it reached Mainz at the end of July, as if for all the world war was a glorified shooting-party.

No comparable military machine, whether in numbers or quality, had ever before been arrayed for battle.

****

The German advance on the frontier moved south-west on a wide arc between the Moselle and the Rhine, and was so poised as to counter and contain either or both of Leboeuf's offensive options if the French should strike first. The entire force was organized into three Armies disposed thus.

On the right, concentrated around Wadern to the south of Trier and with its objectives Saarlouis and the Moselle below Metz, First Army, consisting initially of VII and VIII Corps.

In the centre, Second Army, an unwieldy group of six corps (III, X, Guard, IV, IX[21] and XII) moving through Kaiserslautern and Neunkirchen with Saarbrücken as its first objective, and then the line Metz—Nancy on the upper Moselle. In Moltke's original project IX and XII Corps had been formed into a separate Reserve Army, but on the outbreak of war were placed under command of Second Army, despite the not unreasonable objections of its C-in-C. In the event, Moltke's second thoughts were to be fully vindicated in the critical fighting on 18 August.

On the left, Third Army (V and XI Corps, the two Bavarian corps, and the Württemberg and Baden divisions) assembled around Landau, Rastadt

20 William Russell of *The Times* accompanied the headquarters of Third Army, and Archibald Forbes of the *Daily News* was attached to Second Army.

21 This corps consisted of 18th Division and a division from the Grand Duchy of Hesse numbered 25th. Its 17th Division was left initially to watch the Baltic coast and did not come forward until the latter part of August.

and Karlsruhe, with as its objectives the capture of Strasbourg and the occupation of Alsace.

The six independent cavalry divisions were allocated thus: 1st and 3rd to First Army; 5th and 6th to Second Army; 2nd and 4th to Third Army.

There remained unallocated three army corps: I, II, and VI. On mobilization these were held back, partly as an insurance policy against any aggressive action by Austria, and partly because, for all the carefully planned strategic network of railways,[22] they could not be fitted into the intricate timetables. But on 7 August, the day after the two successful engagements at Spicheren and Wörth, Moltke released his reserve.[23] Thus on the twenty-first day after mobilization, and precisely according to plan, 468,000 German troops had been deployed along the French frontier.

The supreme commander of this great array was the soldier-King of Prussia, William. In his seventy-fourth year, he had fought against the first Bonaparte in the Wars of Liberation as far back as 1813, and as his unqualified support for Roon's army reforms demonstrated, he shared the devotion of his ancestor, the great Frederick, to the strengthening and perfecting of the old military traditions of Prussia. He had not wished — indeed, at the last hour, had tried to avert — the present war. But in his peaceful pursuit of German nationalism, he found himself the prisoner of both his political and his military mandarins, and that formidable combination in the end proved too strong. So, as the assembled states of Germany embarked upon their settlement of old scores, this sad but stubborn man took his place at their head, revered and respected, a true father-figure with behind him a united people and, pressing forward to battle, a devoted and dedicated soldiery.

When on 28 July Royal Headquarters moved forward from Berlin to Mainz, it was accompanied by Bismarck and Roon, and by representatives of all essential departments of state, thus ensuring a smooth and integrated political transition from peace to war. It is difficult to imagine a greater contrast than the situation on that same day beyond the Rhine. There, newly arrived in Metz, sick in body and hesitant in mind, the Emperor of the French, saddled with the supreme command, anxiously surveyed a bleak horizon. Certainly he had brought with him his Minister of War, but Leboeuf was required to combine that office with the overriding responsibilities of Chief of Staff, and an untutored staff at that. It was a grotesque burden which a Berthier might have borne; but Leboeuf was no Berthier, and the burden broke Leboeuf.

When Napoleon left Paris the political conduct of the war was delegated

---

22   It is instructive to note that in Moltke's master-plan for the *Aufmarsch* each formation detrained *on the Rhine*, first to protect the line of advance against a surprise incursion by the enemy, and secondly — and more importantly — to toughen up his infantry reservists by some hard foot-slogging. As we shall see, this wise precaution was to pay a rich dividend.

23   This reserve was allocated thus: I Corps to First Army; II Corps to Second Army; VI Corps to Third Army.

to his Empress and a Regency Council. The chief result of this intemperate improvisation was to alienate the anarchist and republican factions in the capital and undermine an already sensitive public opinion. Thus while those behind cried 'Forward!', those in front faltered on the brink.

****

While the King of Prussia exercised supreme authority in all matters, he wisely left the executive command of his armies to his incomparable Chief of Staff. Certainly all orders in the field were issued in the King's name, but the voice was that of Moltke, the plans were those of Moltke and, until unforeseen human error entered the balance, the execution was that of Moltke.

Helmut von Moltke was seventy, a remote and dedicated professional, whose intellectual mastery of the art of war had been tested in the Schleswig-Holstein campaign of 1864, and triumphantly vindicated in the Austrian war of 1866. Roon's army reforms had provided him, as it were, with the body. He himself furnished the brain — the Great General Staff which served as a nerve-centre through which were transmitted, sometimes intuitively, Moltke's detailed strategic intentions. This élite body, not greatly loved for its exclusivity and *hauteur*, was a formidable innovation without which the whole machine (as, indeed, was demonstrated by the total absence of any comparable organization on the French side) would have been reduced to a lumbering, uncoordinated military mass. Yet it is a measure of Moltke's guiding philosophy of war that every outstanding officer earmarked for service on the staff was periodically returned to regimental duty to ensure that brain and body should work constantly together in the process of teaching and learning.

A striking example of this system of cross-fertilization is shown in the military career of Konstantin von Alvensleben, who commanded III Corps on the crucial day of battle on 16 August and whose conduct of that battle reflected in a dramatic way Moltke's precepts. Alvensleben, born in 1809, entered the army as an officer from the military academy in 1827. In 1853 he was seconded to the General Staff, first as a Major and then as a Lieutenant Colonel. In 1861 he was given a regimental command. Three years later he was back on the staff in the rank of Major General, and served in that capacity during the Danish campaign. In the war of 1866 he was a divisional commander and, as a Lieutenant General, took III Corps to war in 1870. Curiously, he was the only German corps commander not to hold the rank of full General, and for that he may perhaps have had to thank his elder brother, whose command, IV Corps, was a virtual bystander in the August campaign.

When Royal Headquarters assembled in the latter days of July, Moltke's chain of command ran thus. His chief of operations, styled Quartermaster General, was Lieutenant General Podbielski. At the next level were three

heads of sections, responsible for movement, supply and intelligence.[24]
These men apart, the staff consisted of eleven officers and seventy-six
other ranks, which reflects Moltke's studied view that the effective control
of even the most bulky body depends on the quality, and not the size, of
the brain.

****

Moltke's choice of Army Commanders is of particular interest in the light
of his considered opinion that a plan is only as good as the chief executives
charged with carrying it out.

First Army was commanded by General von Steinmetz, aged seventy-
four and, like the King, a veteran of the Wars of Liberation. He was widely
thought — rightly, as it proved — to be too old and certainly too
impetuous, but he owed his position to his brilliant handling of V Corps at
the battle of Nachod in the Austrian war which alone made possible the
victory at Sadowa six days later. He resented the fact that his Army,
initially consisting of only two corps, was cast in the supporting role of
flank protection to the main German thrust, and his contempt for Moltke
had long been well advertised. In the event his obstinacy and insubordination not only hazarded the entire master-plan but came close to causing an
irreversible disaster within two weeks of the first collision.

The commander of Second Army was the King's nephew, Prince
Frederick Charles, aged forty-two, whose lack of years belied a professional expertise and a reputation — not universally accepted — as the
architect of victory as an Army Commander at Sadowa. For all his
glamorous image as the 'Red Prince' in his Hussar uniform, he was a
curious combination of caution and audacity, and his handling of his Army
during the early encounter battles owed much of its success to the
incompetence of his chief adversary. Reading between the lines of
Moltke's narrative of events, it is not difficult to detect a strong sense of
irritation at the unpredictable conduct of his royal subordinate. By the end
the antipathy was mutual.

Third Army was commanded by the Crown Prince of Prussia, who
although now only thirty-nine, had served with distinction on the staff
during the Danish campaign and had commanded Second Army at
Sadowa. His present appointment was as much political as military, since
his Army included the contingents from the Southern states, and it is likely
that his choice was dictated by Bismarck as much as by Moltke. In the
event it may properly be argued that his defeat of MacMahon in the early
engagement battle at Wörth opened the road to Paris, threw Bazaine into
confusion at Metz, and within three weeks sealed the fate of France at the
gates of Sedan.

24 Respectively Colonels Bronsart, Brandenstein and Verdy du Vernois. For an instructive
and entertaining account of their activities, see the latter's *With the Royal Headquarters.*

****

All but two[25] of Moltke's fifteen corps commanders were in their sixties. All had held senior posts — on one side or the other — in the war of 1866; all those of the former Prussian Army had been meticulously schooled by Moltke in his own image, so that repeatedly — and most notably on the night of 16/17 August — these subordinate commanders instinctively anticipated the intentions of their mentor. In sharp contrast with French practice, decision-making was delegated right down through the chain of command, and while this freedom of action caused its quota of crises, it undoubtedly tipped the balance when, as on 16 August and again two days later, all initiative was lost and companies found themselves commanded by corporals.

It has nowhere been remarked that, for all their years, Moltke's senior subordinates demonstrated an extraordinary resilience and physical stamina. The two corps commanders who were to fight the crucial battle on the 16th provide a striking illustration.

Alvensleben (III Corps) and Voigts-Rhetz (X Corps) were both aged sixty-one, and both had been subjected to the harsh rigours of campaigning ever since the great advance of Second Army had been set in train on 1 August. This entailed long hours in the saddle on dusty roads and throughout days of summer heat and drenching rain. Unlike their French counterparts — sybarites to a man — they lived rough without regard to rank, and if they referred to their men as *Kinder*, it was with pride and not condescension.

Frederick Charles's orders for the pursuit of the Army of the Rhine were issued at 11 p.m. on the 15th.[26] At 4 a.m. the following morning, after barely two hours' sleep, the two leaders of the hunting pack were on the road, Alvensleben making for the village of Gorze and the Gravelotte plateau and Voigts-Rhetz heading farther west towards Thiaucourt. From dawn to dusk, under a burning sun and with little food or sustenance, these two men fought a series of desperate engagements throughout that day. Certainly some of the heat and burden was borne by their untiring staff officers, but despite the long hours of physical strain, both men displayed a clarity of mind and a quality of leadership which, against all the odds, decided the issue and fashioned an improbable victory out of impending disaster. Nor as night fell on the bloodstained battlefield did either of them relax in mind or body, for both were aware that their exhausted men faced the likelihood of another dangerous dawn. Alvensleben permitted himself a glass of wine and 'a soldier's ration' towards midnight, but he did not sleep. And at 4 a.m. on the 17th both he and Voigts-Rhetz were ready and

25 Prince Augustus of Württemberg (Guard Corps), fifty-seven, and the Crown Prince of Saxony (XII Corps), forty-two.

26 See p. 108.

A gallery of German leaders

King William I of Prussia (73)

Count Otto v. Bismarck, Chancellor (55)

General v. Moltke, Chief of Staff (70)

Crown Prince of Prussia, C-in-C, Third Army (39)

Prince Frederick Charles, C-in-C, Second Army (42)

Prince Augustus of Württemberg, Guard Corps (57)

Lt. General K. v. Alvensleben, III Corps (61)

General v. Voigts-Rhetz, X Corps (61)

alert when Frederick Charles came forward from Pont-à-Mousson to the plateau at Flavigny to face a still uncertain break of day.

This resolution and stamina was to have a profound result, for in the end it broke Bazaine. The Marshal chose to fight a complex battle virtually single-handed, for most of the morning playing truant from his staff and uselessly involving himself in the eye of the storm. But by nightfall he was physically and — which was more important — morally drained. When towards 11 p.m. on the 16th Jarras, the chief of staff, came to receive his orders for the following day he found Bazaine surrounded by maps and guttering candles, and muttered to a staff-captain that he thought that the Marshal was asleep. He may well have been right. It had been a long, lonely day.

****

By 30 July, two weeks after German mobilization, Moltke was ready. His First Army was already deployed to the south of Trier; Second Army, still farthest from the frontier, was advancing through the difficult wooded country beyond Kaiserslautern; Third Army was assembled on the left bank of the Rhine between Speyer and Landau. Already Moltke had a clear picture of the disarray in the French camp, but he continued to reckon on the possibility of an offensive thrust on either or both flanks. He was in no hurry. In his original project his first objective was the line of the Saar, and he had calculated that his main instrument, Second Army, would not be ready tuned and prepared to strike from that position until 9 August. Meanwhile it was essential that his own left flank was fully protected and that the French army in Alsace should be prevented from acting in concert with the main body concentrated to the west of the Vosges in Lorraine. Thus on the evening of 30 July an order was sent to the Crown Prince to launch an immediate attack across the frontier along the line of the Lauter. And at once Moltke's master-plan began to go awry.

The order from Royal Headquarters was not well received at Third Army. The Crown Prince's chief of staff, General von Blumenthal, protested that the Army was not ready; that it lacked trains and much of its artillery; and that it still awaited the arrival of VI Corps. Curiously, Moltke did not choose to impose his will, and accepted that Third Army would not be capable of striking a major blow until 3 August at the earliest. It is probable that he was overruled by reasons more diplomatic than military, for, as we have seen, a large part of Third Army — six divisions in all — was drawn from the South German states. He himself dismissed this serious setback to his strategic timetable in a single laconic sentence: 'Whereupon, regardless of this delay, Second Army was put in march towards the Saar, where the French were beginning to be active'.[27]

27 Moltke: *op cit.*

****

The activity to which Moltke referred was as modest as it was confused. Since the Emperor's arrival in Metz on 28 July, precious time had been wasted in semantic argument and aimless manœuvring between the Moselle and the Saar. French intelligence about enemy strength and dispositions was negligible, indecision feeding on rumour and rumour stifling decision. In Paris, as July turned to August, there were already the rumblings of public disquiet. Two weeks had passed, and angry questions were being asked. When would the expected offensive begin? Where were the promised victories? And it was in this climate of impatience that the Empress and the Regency Council demanded action.

Napoleon's response was to launch a reconnaissance in force along the axis St Avold—Saarbrücken. The 'force' was impressive; the execution less so. On the left 3 Corps marched up the Forbach road towards Völklingen; on the right, 5 Corps made a cautious movement across the river at Sarreguemines; and in the centre 2 Corps, accompanied by the Emperor, so pain-wracked that he could scarcely sit his horse, and by the eager little Prince Imperial whose baptism of fire it was to be, advanced along the Spicheren heights which commanded the valley of the Saar. The sun shone. Flags flew and bands played. It was a splendid spectacle, and in the French ranks spirits rose as the men recognized a Bonaparte in their midst.

In Saarbrücken the Germans had, with exemplary foresight, assembled a strong outpost consisting of twelve companies of the *40th* and *69th Regiments*, four squadrons of cavalry, and a battery of horse artillery, under the command of Colonel Pestel. Pestel's orders were to avoid a pitched battle and, if heavily engaged, to retire a few miles north to the village of Lebach.

There was in the event no heavy engagement. Frossard's men halted on the great bluff above the Saarbrücken parade-ground and engaged in a desultory exchange of fire. A spent bullet landed near the Prince Imperial, and he was to carry it proudly on his person until his melancholy death nine years later in Zululand. Meanwhile there was much sound, if little fury, and during the afternoon Pestel withdrew his small force across the river to the suburb of St Johann. In the two hours of skirmishing the French had lost eighty-six officers and men; the Germans eighty-three. The savage blood-letting was yet to come.

Towards evening a brigade of Laveaucoupet's division made its cautious way across the valley into Saarbrücken. It found the small town unoccupied by the enemy, but satisfied with the day's work, and rightly fearing that the German main body was close at hand, Frossard recalled his men to their earlier positions on the high ground overlooking the river.

The news of this modest encounter spread like wildfire, gathering a rich embroidery of exaggeration as it went. An entire German army corps had been destroyed. Saarbrücken had been reduced to rubble. 'Our army', said a Press announcement the following morning, 'has taken the offensive, and crossed the frontier and invaded Prussian territory. In spite of the strength of the enemy positions, a few of our battalions were enough to capture the heights which dominate Saarbrücken.' In the capital cheering crowds thronged the streets and church bells rang. It was the first demonstration of public euphoria; and it was to be the last.

****

Moltke watched the events of 2 August impassively. He had assumed — indeed, invited — an offensive strike by the enemy; and he was not surprised when the extravagant French gesture petered out in a tame withdrawal. His timetable, largely governed by the physical problems of moving six army corps and their attendant trains through the difficult country to the east of the frontier, had counted on a full deployment along the line of the Saar by 9 August whence, pivoting on Saarlouis, he would deliver a crushing blow against the French centre and right. It was conceived, as the victory at Sadowa had been conceived, as another Cannae on a heroic scale. That this plan had been in part compromised by Blumenthal's excessive caution on the Lauter we have already seen. That it would be effectively wrecked by Steinmetz's insubordination on the right flank we shall presently discover. Now, however, the order went forth to the Crown Prince to prosecute the invasion of Alsace without further delay.

****

Here, on the evening of 3 August, MacMahon's Army was disposed thus. The main body of 1 Corps (Ducrot) was assembled on the high ground to the north of Haguenau. In the triangle of villages overlooking the Sauer stream — Wörth−Froeschwiller−Morsbronn[28] — were three divisions and three cavalry brigades, with the fourth division (Abel Douay) pushed twelve miles forward to the small but exposed stronghold of Wissembourg on the frontier. The main position above Wörth was in fact one of those which Frossard had noted in his defensive plan two years before, but it was now fatally flawed by the detachment of Douay's division to the line of the Lauter where it could not hope to withstand the full weight of an attack by the German Third Army. Indeed, it has been argued by both French and German sources that, in sacrificing this division, MacMahon sacrificed Alsace.

To the west of 1 Corps stood Failly's 5 Corps along the Metz−Strasbourg railway line from Bitche to Sarreguemines, notionally part of MacMahon's

28 The battle which took place here on the 6th is known variously as 'Wörth' and 'Froeschwiller'.

command, but constantly subjected to conflicting orders from Metz. A resolute intervention by this corps on 6 August would have caused serious embarrassment to the Bavarians on the German right flank; but, in the event, Failly was to cover himself with less than glory, as he turned a deaf ear to MacMahon's calls for help and beat a hasty retreat through Saverne and to a safer shore beyond the Vosges.

There remained 7 Corps. On 3 August, this could in no sense be called a fighting formation. One incomplete division with a cavalry brigade was being railed up from Colmar to Strasbourg; a second was still forming at Belfort; and a third, at little more than half-strength, was far to the south at Lyon. Twelve days were to pass before these scattered elements were to find some sort of safety in numbers at Châlons; but by then the entire stage setting had changed dramatically.

****

During the evening of the 3rd, Abel Douay sent out cavalry patrols from Wissenbourg across the frontier; and it is a measure of the perfunctory attitude to reconnaissance which marked the conduct of the French cavalry throughout the campaign that these patrols returned at dusk and reported that the enemy was nowhere to be found. In fact at that very hour the advance guard of no fewer that six German divisions had reached their bivouac positions less than three miles from the Lauter. A single scout of even modest ambition could scarcely have failed to discover that Douay's division was in the presence of a formidable and numerous opponent. What Douay's true reaction to this intelligence may have been we do not know, for he did not survive to tell the tale. But, from the disposition of his slender force, it is clear that he decided to defend the indefensible. Had his patrols provided him with a true picture of the massive threat to his position, remote and unsupported as it was, he must surely have decided to slip away during the night and rejoin MacMahon on the main defensive bastion of 1 Corps covering Wörth and the Sauer stream. But he chose to stand his ground. And his ground was occupied thus.

Wissembourg was a small, fortified place which had earned a certain reputation during the Revolutionary Wars of the 1790s. It stood astride the narrow Lauter stream, and here Douay posted two infantry battalions and a single battery of artillery. Whether by oversight or complacency, no orders had been given to destroy the two bridges which gave access to the fortress from the east.

A mile to the south-west a spur runs out from the main Vosges massif. Here on the Geisberg, a prominent feature crowned by a citadel-like château, Douay had deployed his nine remaining battalions, three artillery batteries, and a battery of mitrailleuses whose gun-crews, it was later said, were entirely unversed in the handling and firing of their novel weapons.

Thus the French strength totalled fewer than 8000 men when, shortly after 8 a.m. and in circumstances very similar to those which would herald the day of battle on the 16th, a battery of II Bavarian Corps opened fire on the unsuspecting garrison in Wissembourg.

The Germans, unsure of the strength of the opposition, attacked cautiously and on a wide front with the Bavarians on their right, V Corps in the centre, and XI Corps working its way round through the wooded country to the east of the town and directed on the main French position on the Geisberg. And at once a pattern was established which would be sharply underlined in the battles ahead: the dominance of the French chassepot over the German needle-gun, and — decisively as it would prove — the crushing superiority of the German breech-loader artillery over the elderly and out-classed French muzzle-loaders; and in tactical and technical terms, the versatility of the modern percussion fuse against the old-fashioned air-burst. Somewhere within this equation the mitrailleuse might well have bridged the gap. The German infantry came to fear 'the infernal rattle' of this embryo machine-gun, spewing in one minute the discharge of a hundred chassepots. But like so much of French military planning, it was a case of too little and too late; and what might have been a potentially virtuoso weapon became, in inexpert hands, an anonymous quasi-artillery piece rather than a formidable access to the fire-power of the infantry arm.

The Bavarians, on the German right, outranged by the French chassepots in the town, could make no progress and indeed showed little enthusiasm to come to grips with the enemy. Thus more than two hours passed while the artillery of V Corps, some eighty guns deployed on the rising ground to the east, smote the beleaguered garrison. Abandoned to its fate by MacMahon, Douay's division, out-gunned if not out-fought, bravely stood its ground. Discretion, not always the better part of valour, suggests that the growing threat of encirclement should have prompted Douay to order a retreat from the Geisberg, but shortly before noon when the German XI Corps had begun to work its way round the French right flank, a shell struck the ammunition wagon of the mitrailleuse battery near the Geisberg château and Douay was mortally wounded. The command passed to his senior brigadier, General Pellé.

An hour later the leading infantry brigades of V Corps, followed at a respectful distance by the Bavarians, stormed the battered defences of Wissembourg and after a brief but bitter hand-to-hand fight, the garrison — two battalions of the 74th Regiment and their supporting battery — surrendered.

At almost the same hour 41st Brigade of XI Corps, having worked its way across the Lauter and through the thick woodlands to the east, attacked up the steep slope of the Geisberg towards the château and the nearby farmstead of Schafbusch. There the Germans, moving forward in close column, learned the first of many bloody lessons, losing more than 800 officers and men within a few minutes. With the utmost gallantry the

French repeatedly counter-attacked with the bayonet and it was not until four batteries of artillery were brought into action at the foot of the slope that the chassepots were silenced. At 2 p.m., without hope of rescue and with dwindling ammunition, General Pellé accepted defeat and ordered his weary men to retreat westward to Wörth, covered to the last by two stubborn companies of the 1st Algerian Tirailleurs.[29] The Germans, much chastened, paused to lick their wounds and made no effort to pursue a beaten enemy.

So ended the first serious clash of arms. If it may be said that the Germans had drawn first blood, it had been at bloody cost. Their casualties, partly the result of mindless infantry tactics and partly a tribute to the power of the chassepot, numbered 91 officers and 1463 other ranks. There is no record of comparable French casualties, but 1092 officers and men were left as prisoners in German hands.

****

If the excessive caution of the Crown Prince and his chief of staff had given early cause for concern on the German left, it was the headstrong and insubordinate Steinmetz on the right who came close to wrecking not only the careful timing of Moltke's plan but also his entire strategic concept (see Map 2).

As we have seen, the main instrument in this plan was Frederick Charles's Second Army, directed on the Saar between Saarbrücken and Sarreguemines and with its main objective the line of the Moselle between Metz and Nancy. If the French delivered a pre-emptive strike towards the Palatinate, then Second Army would hold fast in the centre while the Crown Prince wheeled up from Alsace and First Army took the enemy in flank from the north.

The short-lived demonstration by the French against Saarbrücken on the 2nd did nothing to deflect Moltke from his original plan, and on the following morning he ordered Steinmetz to concentrate VII and VIII Corps in the area of Wadern and Tholey, there to await further instructions.

> But Steinmetz had different ideas. It was only with the greatest difficulty that he was brought to accept Moltke's authority at all: to understand Moltke's strategy was beyond him and he had no intention of implementing it. By 3 August his army was ready and he intended to attack.... He informed Moltke that he proposed next day to move south on Saarlouis and St Avold, and instead of holding back round Tholey he firmly pushed the units of his left wing forward to

---

29 This was one of the native regiments known as 'Turcos', and as celebrated for their indiscipline as for their savage fighting spirit.

the St Wendel-Ottweiler road [*that is, towards Saarbrücken*] — straight across the Second Army's line of march.[30]

There followed an acrimonious exchange of letters, ending with a magisterial face-down from Moltke:

His Majesty has expressly reserved the giving of orders for the execution of this operation, since the manner of undertaking it, and the direction it is given, will depend upon the turn which events will have taken with the Third Army.[30]

But the damage had been done; and it is to Third Army that we will return.

****

The Crown Prince made no effort to exploit his initial success at Wissembourg, partly because his leading cavalry division (4th) was still a day's march to the rear, and partly because of the continuing caution of his chief of staff; and it was not until the morning of the 5th that the advance was resumed in the direction of Haguenau to the south-west.

At Third Army H.Q. there was an air of uncertainty. Little was known of MacMahon's dispositions, and less of his intentions. Blumenthal noted in his diary that the most likely option was that he would march to the north-west behind a strong rearguard and, collecting Failly's corps around Bitche, join the Army of Lorraine at Metz — a shrewd appreciation which seems not to have occurred to the French Emperor and his advisers until two defeats and four days later. There were other alternatives: that MacMahon would concentrate every available division and give battle on the eastern approaches to the Vosges; that he would conduct a fighting withdrawal on Strasbourg; that he would retire immediately behind the line of the Saar; or that he would strike first at his pursuers. Thus, during the 5th, Third Army moved warily forward.

No such wide-ranging options were in fact available to MacMahon. On the morning of the 5th he had at his immediate disposal three divisions of 1 Corps, the remnants of Douay's division which had escaped from Wissembourg, and Dumesnil's division of 7 Corps, lately arrived from Strasbourg. The two remaining divisions of this corps were still detained far to the south at Belfort and Lyon and could not possibly be counted upon as reinforcements.

Certainly on the morning of the 5th 5 Corps had been put under MacMahon's command, and he had sent an urgent order to Failly to march his three divisions the 15 miles or so which would have brought them within the perimeter of the strong defensive line on either side of Froeschwiller.

30 Howard: *The Franco-Prussian War.*

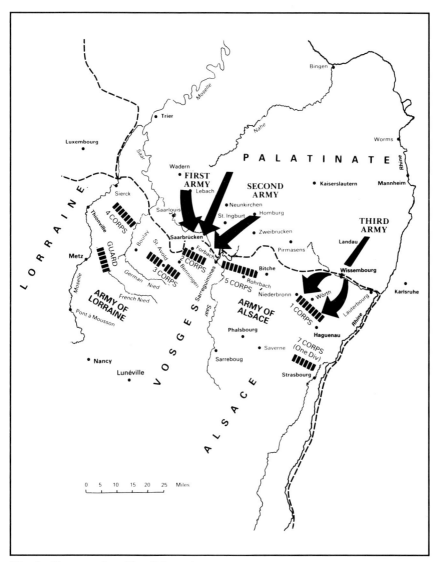

Map 2   The opposing sides, 6 August

But while MacMahon proposed, Metz disposed; and Failly was ordered to stand fast, even when, on the following morning (when a crucial battle was inevitable) MacMahon summoned him again.[31]

There remained the option of retreat. But here — and throughout the

31   Failly's conduct on this and the following days was to call down upon him — and rightly — a storm of criticism only marginally less than that visited on Bazaine. It is a measure of French *débrouillage* that the Imperial decree relieving him of his command on 22 August did not reach him until the curtain fell on 31 August.

77

rest of August — political imperatives outweighed military wisdom; for this time, while Metz proposed, Paris disposed. To retire without even striking a blow against the invader would mean the tame surrender of Alsace; the humiliation of France; even the death of the dynasty. In the event MacMahon, '*L'illustre vaincu*', survived by a mixture of gallantry and good fortune to achieve an unwarranted public esteem; and Bazaine, on whose shoulders MacMahon's final defection fell, went, by a mixture of gallantry and incompetence, to a court-martial and to public degradation. Such is the pity of war.

****

MacMahon deployed his five divisions in a strong defensive position on a steep and wooded ridge running north and south and facing east across the valley of the small river Sauer and overlooking the village of Wörth which, mindful of Douay's fate at Wissembourg, he sensibly did not occupy. On his left, a refused flank to which he had fruitlessly summoned Failly's corps from Bitche, stood Ducrot's division at Nehwiller and Niederbronn. In the centre, closely entrenched around the key village of Froeschwiller and with the bulk of the artillery, stood Raoult's division, and on the right, dangerously — and in the event fatally — exposed to an enveloping attack, were Lartigue's division and Dumesnil's late arrival from 7 Corps, covering Morsbronn and the Niederwald forest. The reserve on the right consisted of the weary survivors of Wissembourg, and the Cuirassier Brigade of Michel, that angry cavalryman whose righteous indignation at Belfort has been earlier recorded, and who was presently to preside over a great and glorious disaster. Behind the centre, also destined for destruction at the final crisis of the battle when MacMahon, as the story goes, called for '*vingt minutes*' of breathing-space to cover his retreat, stood Bonnemain's cavalry division.

Thus at dawn on the 6th MacMahon could marshal an immediately available force of no more than 45,000 and fewer than 100 guns. Advancing on his defensive line were two Prussian and two Bavarian corps and the Württemberg and Baden divisions, with nearly 300 guns, and numbering in all nearly 85,000 men.

For different reasons, neither the Crown Prince nor MacMahon expected or indeed sought a collision until the following day; the former because he still had no certain knowledge of where and in what strength the French lay, and thought it prudent to wait until his cavalry division and his third corps (VI) had closed up from the rear; the latter because he was still waiting — and would wait in vain — for Failly to march to his assistance from Bitche. 'But when, as in this case, the adversaries are in such close proximity, the conflict may break out at any moment, even against the wishes of the higher commanders.'[32] And so it came about.

---

32   Moltke: *op. cit.*

Moltke should not have been surprised, for the essence of his whole concept of battle was that, as his great offensive developed, the enemy should be attacked *wherever found*, the basic principle of Clausewitz writ large, and tested and proved four years before at Sadowa. To this doctrine he had added something of his own distinctive philosophy which Clausewitz, in the now remote past before science had changed the whole geometry of warfare, would not have understood: that as the battleground grew even larger, so the authority to take decisions was delegated further and further down the chain of command. That no such freedom of action was ever contemplated in the French military canon surely led from one disaster to another. That Moltke's military ethic might well have invited comparable crises, the reader may presently judge for himself.

****

The battle of Wörth–Froeschwiller may be briefly summarized. By the evening of the 5th the leading columns of Third Army had closed up on the Sauer and were disposed thus: on the right, II Bavarian Corps near Langensulzbach and towards the main road from Bitche to Haguenau; in the centre, V Corps opposite Wörth; on the left near Gunstett, XI Corps. I Bavarian Corps was in reserve behind the centre, and the combined Württemberg and Baden divisions under General von Werder behind the left.

Early on the 6th, the commander of the leading infantry brigade (20th) of V Corps, observing considerable activity on the heights beyond the Sauer and assuming that this indicated the preparations for a French withdrawal, decided on his own initiative to investigate the position more closely and pushed forward a strong reconnaissance force with an artillery battery. His skirmishing line, finding the bridges on either side of Wörth broken and the village itself unoccupied, waded across the stream. But on the further bank the movement was halted in its tracks by heavy chassepot and mitrailleuse fire from the direction of Froeschwiller, and the skirmishers fell back across the stream under the protection of their own artillery on the left bank.

The sound of battle alerted the Bavarians farther to the north, and the corps commander, General Hartmann, assuming that it signalled the start of a general engagement, launched an ill-considered attack against the French left flank where Ducrot, strongly entrenched on the wooded slopes to the south, easily repulsed an unenthusiastic enemy. There was a lull.

It was 8 a.m. At Froeschwiller, MacMahon rightly judged that, with Ducrot, his left flank was in safe hands. In the centre, Raoult[33] could be relied upon to hold the fort against a frontal attack. The danger lay on the

---

33 Raoult was killed in action shortly after noon, as also was MacMahon's chief of staff, Colson.

right. Here the whole French position could be decisively turned — as, indeed, events were to prove — and here MacMahon pushed Lartigue's division forward to the river crossing beyond the Niederwald opposite Gunstett. It was too little, and too late.

It was 8 a.m., and the Crown Prince was disenchanted. He had not planned a battle for this day, and now he had a battle on his hands. Moltke's comment on p. 61 is *à propos*. This same pattern, for much the same reasons, was to be repeated on this day at Spicheren; on the 14th at Borny; on the 16th at Vionville; and on the 18th at Amanvillers. Not until the assembled armies of Germany closed in upon Sedan three weeks hence could it be said that a grand strategy was signed and sealed by a single battle.

Accordingly, towards 10 a.m. the Crown Prince issued an urgent order that the fighting should be broken off until the deployment of Third Army had been completed. Hartmann's Bavarians on the right complied with some alacrity, but General von Kirchbach, commanding V Corps in the centre, replied that he was already too deeply involved and that any attempt to disengage would invite summary punishment from the strong enemy force assembled on the high ground overlooking the Sauer. He therefore, noted Moltke, 'determined to continue the contest on his own responsibility'. It was a costly but, in the event, vital decision.

During the forenoon V Corps sustained the battle in the centre against repeated attacks by Raoult's division. Here the pattern of Wissembourg, and of all the bloody battles which followed, was sharply illustrated; on the one side the superior range and accuracy of chassepot against needle-gun; on the other the irresistible power of the German artillery, swiftly and solidly deployed, both covering and creating the killing-ground. By 11 a.m. Kirchbach had assembled his entire orchestra of 84 guns.

Within half an hour his ring of steel had been strengthened by 24 guns from the artillery of XI Corps on his left. It was this massive arsenal which was to win the day.

The morning wore on. There is no doubt that had Failly responded to MacMahon's order of the previous evening to join him at Froeschwiller, the German centre — Kirchbach's artillery notwithstanding — would have collapsed.[34] Even then V Corps could do no more than maintain a fragile bridgehead on the west bank of the Sauer, while XI Corps and the Württemberg division hastened forward on the left, and it was here that numbers told and the critical issue was joined.

Shortly after noon the Crown Prince, realizing that the situation demanded sterner measures, ordered a general attack on the main French positions in the villages of Elsasshausen and Froeschwiller. On his right the

34 One division of Failly's corps — that of Guyot de Lespart — did in fact set out from Bitche early on the morning of the 6th, but it took nearly *twelve* hours to cover the few miles to Nehwiller, and arrived only in time to cover MacMahon's headlong retreat that evening (*see* below).

Bavarians resumed their encounter with Ducrot's division; in the centre, V Corps, despite heavy losses and repeated counter-attacks, succeeded in bringing a large part of its artillery across to the right bank of the Sauer; and thus, while the right and centre pinned MacMahon down, XI Corps and the Württemberg division developed a strong flank attack against Lartigue and Dumesnil from the south.

Here a bitter battle was joined for possession of the Niederwald, a thickly wooded area which covered the approaches to the commanding ridge beyond. The French infantry fought with exemplary resolution, repeatedly forcing the Germans to retire under cover of their greatly superior artillery; but by 1 p.m. XI Corps succeeded in driving a wedge between Lartigue and Dumesnil and captured the village of Morsbronn to the south of the Niederwald, and with it control of MacMahon's lateral communications. The French flank was turned.

There followed a famous, if fearful, passage of arms. Lartigue, his last infantry reserve committed, called on the cavalry to cover his retreat. Nearest to hand were Michel's Cuirassier brigade and the 6th Lancers of Duhesme's division, and this body of horsemen, 1000 strong, launched itself against Morsbronn, across, in the words of the official acount, '*un terrain détestable*' of tree-stumps, ditches, and tangled vines. Within moments all cohesion was lost, and the disordered squadrons were met at a range of 300 paces by the concentrated fire of the *32nd* and *80th Regiments*. Thereupon '*un quart de la brigade tomba en route. Le reste s'engouffra dans les rues barricadées du village où l'infanterie prussienne installée dans les maisons le décima en tirant des fenêtres.*' Only a handful of survivors managed to escape, pursued by an eager regiment of German Hussars. Thus in a matter of minutes the breech-loader rifle had called in question the whole future of the cavalry arm. It was a question presently to be repeated.

It was now 2.30 p.m. XI Corps had stormed the burning village of Elsasshausen, where it joined hands with the left wing of V Corps. Thus MacMahon's position was fatally compromised. Certainly on his left Ducrot, by his resolute defence against the Bavarians, kept open the vital avenue of escape; but the right flank was in disarray and Froeschwiller, the final bastion, was caught in the crossfire of five German divisions and their assembled artillery.

Even then the French defenders offered bitter resistance, and a spirited counter-attack by two Algerian regiments (1st and 3rd Tirailleurs) drove the Germans out of the eastern part of Elsasshausen and back into the Niederwald. It was a brief, brave and bloody gesture, but a forlorn hope; and beset by overwhelming numbers, the Turcos, their ammunition if not their spirit exhausted, fell back fighting. In half an hour they had sustained more than 1000 casualties.

At 4 p.m. MacMahon ordered a general retreat. He has been criticized for not disengaging earlier, but it is an unjust charge. He had fought a clever battle against a greatly superior opponent; he had reasonably supposed that Failly would obey his order to march 5 Corps to support him at Froeschwiller; he could not then have known of the climate of confusion in Metz, or of the day's development far to the west near Saarbrücken.

Now, as Lartigue had earlier done, he turned to the cavalry as a line of last resort to provide, however briefly, the breathing-space he needed. To the rear of Froeschwiller stood Bonnemain's reserve cavalry division, four regiments of Cuirassiers numbering some 2000 sabres. Without hesitation, Bonnemain launched his men in close formation against the infantry masses as they pressed forward from Elsasshausen.[35] The result was a disaster even more comprehensive than that suffered by Michel at Morsbronn. Here, as there, the ground was broken by ditches, vineyards, and hop gardens. Here, as there, a charge of massed cavalry was an invitation to destruction; and so it proved. The leading brigade, met at point-blank range by rifle-fire and artillery case-shot, was overwhelmed within ten minutes, losing both its regimental commanders and more than three-quarters of its effectives. The same fate met the second brigade as it sought to avoid the debris of fallen men and horses in its path. It is said that not one cuirassier succeeded in charging home. It was, as has been recorded in another context, magnificent; but it was not war.

Yet Bonnemain's sacrifice was not in vain. By 5 p.m. MacMahon had succeeded in breaking off the battle and was in full retreat. His right wing — the divisions of Dumesnil and Pellé — separated from the main body since early afternoon, made good its escape on the southerly road through Haguenau, whence some 4000 men hurried on to take refuge in Strasbourg.[36] The centre and left wing retired on the roads through Reichshoffen and Niederbronn, covered first by Ducrot and then, as evening drew on and with some sort of tragic irony, by Guyot de Lespart's division from 5 Corps which reached the battlefield after a wasted day, and just in time to fire a few Parthian shots at the Bavarians before it too hastened away to the west and to the saving grace of the Vosges and of the mountain passes through Saverne, La Petite Pierre, and Phalsbourg. And Failly? Caught in the cross-fire between Metz and MacMahon, conscious only of messengers of doom on either flank throughout that day, he abandoned Lapasset's brigade at Sarreguemines, and marched away from Bitche through the summer night along roads already crowded with the survivors of 1 Corps as they hurried to safety beyond the welcoming hills.

The Crown Prince made no effort to pursue a demoralized enemy. His hunting pack — 4th Cavalry Division — was still a day's march to the rear. He had fought, at savage cost, an entirely improvised battle. German

---

35 Most accounts wrongly describe this action as 'the charge of Reichshoffen', a village which lay two miles behind the French lines.

36 On 7 August the Baden division was detached from Third Army to invest the fortress. Strasbourg eventually surrendered on 28 September.

losses had been extravagant — no fewer than 489 officers and 10,153 rank and file killed and wounded. Third Army was in no condition to seek another confrontation.

MacMahon had also suffered grievously. His casualties in killed and wounded were 5884. But he had also 9212 officers and men as prisoners of war, together with 28 guns, five mitrailleuses, one eagle, four standards, and his personal baggage train. Thus he had lost one-third of his effective strength. More critically, he had abandoned Alsace, and uncovered the road to Paris.

****

If 6 August had resulted in an unexpected victory on the German left wing (unexpected, because the Crown Prince had not intended a battle on that day), it produced, for precisely opposite reasons, an unforeseen drama on the right; for where the Crown Prince's indecision had been redeemed by the initiative of one subordinate, Steinmetz's indiscretion, faithfully reflected in the arrogance of one of his divisional commanders, came close to sustaining a disastrous defeat.

It will be remembered that on 3 August, Steinmetz had informed Moltke that, with or without authority, he proposed to assume the offensive, with his objectives St Avold and Saarbrücken; VIII Corps marching on the right by Völklingen and VII Corps on the left taking the main road from St Wendel. Since he omitted both the courtesy and precaution of informing Frederick Charles of his decision, VII Corps thus struck in across the main axis of advance of Second Army. So much for that human factor with which all Moltke's precious planning and meticulous march-tables had failed to reckon. Steinmetz, old enough to be Frederick Charles's father and contemptuous of Moltke's royal patronage, decided to be first to the footlights when the curtain rose. And so at dawn on the 4th, First Army blundered forward.

****

After the demonstration at Saarbrücken on the 2nd, Frossard had occupied the bluff overlooking the parade-ground and the river. From there he had good observation across the valley and the approach roads from beyond the frontier, but, as he later wrote, '*ma position était aventurée*'. So, with two German armies closing in on him, it was; and accordingly on the evening of the 5th, after informing Bazaine and under the watchful eyes of German cavalry patrols in St Johann, he withdrew 2 Corps one mile south covering the Spicheren heights, and occupied, with a nice sense of irony, one of the very '*positions magnifiques*' which he had so carefully reconnoitred before the war, and before the politicians had made mincemeat of military wisdom.

It was indeed a magnificent position. The centre was dominated by a towering ironstone cliff called, from its colour, the Rotherberg, or Red Hill. To the left, the ground fell sharply to a narrow valley through which ran the main road from Saarbrücken to Forbach, and thence by Forbach to St Avold. This way any main attack must come, and here stood a strong defensive 'fortress' in the great ironworks of Stiring-Wendel. To the right the ground sloped downward through a large wooded area, the Gifertwald, towards the river — difficult country for infantry and virtually inaccessible to the other arms.

Frossard occupied this position thus: the centre and right were held by Laveaucoupet's division, well entrenched, since Frossard, unlike some of his more celebrated contemporaries, was an engineer who understood that in modern warfare the spade was partner to the rifle. On the left stood Vergé's division, straddled across the Forbach valley and strongly established at Stiring. In reserve was Bataille, on the high ground about Spicheren village.

Behind Frossard the remainder of the Army of Metz was assembled in a curious pattern which owed more to inevitable retreat than to the expectation of an advance. On the left 4 Corps was bivouacked around Bouzonville, anxiously watching the Saarlouis road. Not until too late on the 6th did Ladmirault obey an order to close inward on Boulay. The four divisions of 3 Corps, under Bazaine, were strung out along country roads from St Avold to Sarreguemines on a front of nearly 16 miles and some 6 miles behind the Spicheren position. The Imperial Guard, not for the last time, was carefully relegated to the sidelines, and stood now 15 miles to the west of St Avold where, if it could come to no harm, it could equally provide little support.

These dispositions, however haphazard, provided enough offensive options if the enemy overplayed his hand. That he did so, and was not made to pay heavily for his intemperate actions, was due to that fatal lack of resolution which was to mark the whole French conduct of the August campaign.

****

On the morning of the 6th, thanks to Steinmetz's blatant disobedience, the planned movements of First and Second Armies had been entirely dislocated. Moltke's comment is a masterpiece of restraint:

> The protrusion to the south-westward[37] of First Army towards the Saar, which had not been intended by the supreme Command, had brought its left wing in upon the line of march laid down for the Second, and detachments of the two armies had to cross each other at

37   Moltke: *op.cit.* His reference to 'south-westward' should have read 'south-*eastward*'.

Saarbrücken on the 6th. Thus there was indeed no lack of strength at that point; but as a battle that day was neither expected nor probable, the synchronous arrival of troops had not been pre-arranged, and so detachments could only come up by quite unprescribed routes and arrive one after the other at different hours.

The inference is clear. Had Frossard held his original ground overlooking the parade-ground and the Saar crossings, with 2 Corps firmly entrenched and 3 Corps in close support on the Spicheren position, Bazaine could have picked off his opponents one by one as they arrived piecemeal at Saarbrücken, while keeping in reserve the luxury of at least two divisions to protect his railhead at Forbach against the very flank attack which finally drove Frossard to surrender his *'position magnifique'* that evening. But by the morning of the 6th Frossard had drifted back; and Bazaine was at St Avold trying to reconcile his tactical problem with the flood of conflicting orders which clogged the telegraph from Imperial headquarters. Thus a curious combination of French indecision and German indiscipline brought on a totally unexpected battle. It came about in this fashion.

The cavalry patrols which observed the French withdrawal on the evening of the 5th belonged to General Rheinbaben's 5th Cavalry Division, which in accordance with Moltke's plan was covering the advance on the Saar valley between Saarbrücken and Sarreguemines of III Corps, the right wing of Second Army. Moltke's march-table had allotted to this corps the main road and rail communications running from St Wendel south to Neunkirchen, and thence to the river crossings at Saarbrücken. No battle was planned until 7 August at the earliest.

Steinmetz, however, had effectively scotched this tidy staff-work when, on the morning of the 4th, he had decided to run the war his own way and had taken the ground of III Corps by pushing his own left wing (VII Corps) on to the St Wendel–Neunkirchen road, the 'protrusion' to which Moltke so drily referred.[38] The leading formation of Zastrow's VII Corps was the 14th Division (von Kameke) which, cutting across the main road from St Wendel, brought III Corps to a standstill as it marched southward on the Saar. The confusion was complete.

It was nearly noon when Kameke started pushing his division across the river at Saarbrücken. Rheinbaben's cavalry patrols on the parade-ground had reported Frossard's withdrawal towards the Spicheren heights, and now Kameke, matching the impetuosity of Kirchbach earlier that morning at Wörth, decided that the enemy was in full retreat towards Forbach and asked permission of his corps commander, Zastrow, to attack. It was an act

---

38 Steinmetz's axis of advance, as laid down in the march-tables, directed First Army from its concentration area around Tholey and Wadern upon Metz by Saarlouis. It has nowhere been remarked that by pulling his right-hand division inward on Forbach, the commander of VII Corps presented an open flank to Ladmirault's 4 Corps at Boulay, an invitation which neither Bazaine nor Ladmirault accepted.

of stunning folly, for it exposed VII Corps to an improvised assault upon a position of exceptional strength, on a battlefield where natural obstacles and poor communications demanded the most careful co-ordination.

Zastrow, elderly and cautious, found himself caught between two fires — Steinmetz going for glory and Kameke going for broke. He chose the line of least resistance and told Kameke 'to act as you think best'. Later Steinmetz explained that his object was to facilitate the advance of Second Army by drawing the French on himself and attacking them vigorously. Moltke merely annotated the despatch: 'Would have exposed the First Army to defeat.'[39] And so indeed it should have done.

****

Kameke did not even wait for his division to complete the crossing of the Saar. Shortly after 1 p.m. he ordered General von François's 27th Brigade, accompanied by three artillery batteries, to attack not the rearguard of a retreating enemy as he rashly assumed, but an entire army corps strongly entrenched on a line running from the Stiring valley on the left, across the great Rotherberg spur and the Spicheren heights, to the thick Gifert woods which covered the eastern slopes on the right.

François was soon in deep trouble. As his leading infantry emerged from the valley on to the foothills beyond, they were met by heavy artillery and chassepot fire. Facing him was the daunting spectacle of the Rotherberg, and accordingly he pushed the Fusilier battalion of the *74th Regiment* forward to the foot of the bluff where the sheer cliff face provided a fair measure of protection. Simultaneously he sought out the enemy flanks with his remaining five battalions, supported by his eighteen guns which came into action on the Galgenberg and Folster Höhe, two features lying to the east of the Forbach road.

On the right the remaining battalions of the *74th* attempted to work their way towards Stiring, but faced by a large part of Vergé's division and four well-sited batteries, they were driven back with heavy losses. On the left, the *39th Fusilier Regiment* pressed forward through the Gifert forest but on emerging on to the open plateau beyond was smitten by a violent cannonade from Laveaucoupet's massed ranks on the Spicheren heights and fell back in disorder to the safety of the woods.

Here then was the well-scripted scenario for a German defeat of the first magnitude: a single isolated infantry brigade with modest artillery support confronted by a whole army corps established on dominant ground, with at least three more divisions and ample cavalry at close call. Why then did Frossard not seek to exploit his overwhelming advantage? From his command post at Spicheren he could see the whole Saar valley and its northern approaches spread out before him and identify the strength and

39 Quoted by Howard: *op.cit.*

thrust of his opponent. A glance at his map would have shown him that any major German attack would have to be channelled through the bottleneck of Saarbrücken, and that any attempt to outflank his position could only be made by a hazardous approach march from the direction of Völklingen.

His own explanation was that, without any order from Bazaine to the contrary (it would soon become fashionable to blame Bazaine for every error of commission and omission), he considered his prime function to be the defence of Forbach and the supplies accumulated there.[40] This was a craven argument. On the morning of the 6th — that is to say, before events at Wörth and here at Spicheren had infected Imperial headquarters with the contagion of defeat — Forbach still remained a springboard and not a safety-net. Reflecting upon the situation as François's battered brigade awaited the tidal wave which could sweep it away, a recent French critic had this comment to make:

What greater opportunity can be imagined? Frossard had only to throw himself on the Prussian formations and destroy them as they arrived one by one in the valley. But that did not happen. Frossard, an excellent engineer officer but a second-rate tactician, sat tight, and so succeeded in losing a battle which he should with minimum effort have won, while Bazaine, with 40,000 men close at hand, watched impassively the defeat of an army corps for no better reason than that its commander enjoyed a greater esteem than he in Imperial circles.

Steinmetz would have applauded both the sentiment and the cynicism.

****

It is a measure of Kameke's reckless initiative, and of Frossard's failure to profit by it, that two hours passed before the second brigade of 14th Division (Woyna's 28th) came into action on the German right. By then the issue should have been beyond doubt, and Moltke left with the debris of a disaster on his hands. But instead French lack of resolve left the door ajar, and through it the Germans passed six more batteries to join those already deployed on the Galgenberg and the Folster Höhe. They should have served no other purpose than to cover Kameke's retreat. In fact — and the reader will be left in no doubt of the decisive part played by the German artillery during the August battles — these guns, and the six further batteries which were brought into action before evening, succeeded in sustaining the fire-fight against the most improbable odds; indeed as the afternoon wore on, Frossard abandoned any offensive intentions he may have had. First he committed his reserve division (Bataille) to bolster an already adequate concentration in and around Stiring where the great

---

40 Frossard: *Rapport sur les Opérations du deuxième corps de l'armée du Rhin.*

ironworks provided a solid bulwark; and with the penchant of many French commanders to start crying before they were hurt, he sent the first of many calls to Bazaine for help.

****

Bazaine's reaction may be briefly dismissed. Since dawn he had been at St Avold where he had received a vague indication from Leboeuf in Metz that a German attack might presently be expected from the direction of Saarbrücken. He was now responsible for the operational control of three army corps — 2, 3, and 4 — which was by far the largest force that he had ever commanded in the field. His task was made no easier for him by Leboeuf's oversight in not providing him with a staff; and from this he deduced with peasant logic that Metz would continue to make the decisions that mattered. In this he was sadly wrong.

Like MacMahon at Wörth, he had been left in the absurd position of having to double as an army and a corps commander. And it was his own corps — 3 — which he had aimlessly deployed in a straggling 15-mile line between St Avold and Sarreguemines as a kind of *cordon sanitaire* behind the Spicheren position. He should not be too harshly judged for this apparently supine stance, for as hour succeeded hour, his authority was overridden by conflicting orders and counter-orders from Imperial headquarters. Thus the telegraph tied him to St Avold when the battlefield beckoned.

When, during the afternoon, Frossard's repeated cries for help reached him, Bazaine had three divisions on hand: Montaudon's at Sarreguemines; Castagny's at Puttelange; Metman's on the Forbach road near Benningen. All three were ordered forward. All three advanced with circumspection. All three were swiftly halted and ordered back as the meddlesome men in Metz continued to harass Bazaine at St Avold. A wiser man would have distanced himself from the telegraph. A more competent commander would have hurried forward to Spicheren to judge for himself Frossard's true situation and the glittering prospect which it offered. In the event, three strong divisions, which could and should have ensured a famous victory, spent a wasted day wandering weakly to and fro within an hour's march of the battlefield. Towards evening Bazaine ordered Montaudon to close inward from Sarreguemines on St Avold; and there as night fell he learned that Frossard had been driven from the commanding heights, and that MacMahon's Army of Alsace was in full flight away to the south-west. So easily can the pendulum of war swing in a single day.

****

No such doubts and indecisions clouded activities on the German side. Certainly, Kameke's precipitate attack had invited summary retribution;

but even when he recognized the scale of the disaster to which he had exposed not only his own division but also the entire First Army, his reaction was to die in the last ditch rather than surrender the initiative to Frossard, confident that behind him eager formations would be hastening forward to the sound of the guns. There can be no more striking example of the mental and moral gulf which separated the senior commanders on either side.

Now, at 3.30 p.m., with every battalion committed and no immediate help at hand, Kameke played his last card — a frontal attack on the formidable cliffs of the Rotherberg, linchpin of Frossard's position.

The assault was made by the Fusilier battalion of the *74th* and three companies of the *39th*, led in person by General François. Facing them on the crest in a long entrenchment and supported by a battery of mitrailleuses were the 10th Chasseurs firing down an almost vertical slope. There followed a most singular and sanguinary encounter, as the German infantry, despite savage losses, worked their way up from crag to crag and from ledge to ledge. At their head, François fell, pierced by five bullets. Yet with extraordinary spirit the Fusiliers clung to their precarious foothold, sustained by the potent guns in the valley below; sustained even by the cavalry.

As the Fusiliers held their ground, Kameke sent forward a squadron of Hussars to override the French trench-line. It was a gesture at once grandiose and grotesque:

> The Hussars were not long in discovering that their riding-school lessons did not include practice in crag-climbing, and they went back wiser than before... They saw before them a track which looked practicable, and they dashed on and up, strewing the path with dead and living debris as they advanced. How near the summit one at least of them may have got I never knew till the next day, when I saw a dead hussar and a dead horse tumbled over into a ravine thee-fourths of the way up. I saw them ride up. I never saw any of them ride back.[41]

An hour passed while the fate of Kameke's Fusiliers hung on the balance. Frossard, fearful for his left wing and for the safety of his base at Forbach, strongly reinforced an already strongly held position at Stiring. None of his reserve (Bataille's division) was used to settle the issue on the Rotherberg; and it was here that the battle of Spicheren was won and lost. For shortly after 4.30 p.m. help began to reach Kameke in great and growing numbers.

First on the scene was the *40th Regiment*[42] which, pressing forward

41 Forbes, *My Experiences of the War between France and Germany.*

42 It is a measure of the confusion caused by Steinmetz's wanton disobedience of orders that this was the *only* unit of the entire VIII Corps to reach the battlefield before darkness fell.

between Rotherberg and the Gifert wood, drove the French Chasseurs from the small plateau which crowned the crest and there joined hands with Kameke's men. There now followed a famous passage of arms as first four, then eight, guns were bravely manhandled up a narrow track on the eastern face of the Rotherberg and, despite severe losses among their crews, were brought into action against the village of Spicheren lying 1000 yards to the south across a neck of open ground. Against this stoutly held position three French counter-attacks foundered; and here towards evening the fighting ceased.

It will be remembered that Kameke's impetuous advance during the forenoon had taken the ground of Second Army as it moved south-west from Neunkirchen. The leading formation of this Army was III Corps, commanded by Lt. Gen von Alvensleben. Here, cast in a supporting role, this corps would ten days later find itself in the eye of the storm, and by its heroic exertions change the course not only of a battle but arguably of the entire war.

Now, towards 5 p.m., its artillery hastening ahead, the foremost column[43] crossed the Saar and at once struck in upon Laveaucoupet's division in the Gifert wood. For two hours a bitter battle raged among the trees. The French fought with exemplary ferocity 'at bayonet point and with clubbed rifles'. Twice the Germans won the western fringes of the forest; twice they were driven back in disorder. Small wonder that Frossard repeatedly called on Bazaine for support. Small wonder that Bazaine's silence sealed Frossard's fate, and thus cast away a victory that was there for the taking. Small wonder, too, that the simple soldiery of France began to feel that bravery was not enough, and that they were being betrayed by lack-lustre leaders.

****

It was on the French left that the day's climax came. Here Vergé, reinforced by Bataille, had stubbornly resisted every German attempt to capture Stiring and so open the road to Forbach, to St Avold, and so to Metz, even when towards 6 p.m. Schwerin's brigade of 5th Division entered the battle. There remained a joker in the pack.

When Kameke directed his advanced guard on Saarbrücken his movement carried him away from the other division of VII Corps[44] which was moving according to Moltke's plan on Völklingen, five miles to the west and separated from the Saar by a broad spur of wooded hills. A long march would bring this division directly in on Forbach. Of this Frossard was well aware, and mindful of the threat to his flank and to the critical

43 9th Brigade of 5th Division.

44 13th Division (Lt. Gen von Glümer).

arteries of road and rail, he sent an early warning to St Avold. Bazaine's response was to issue a quaint order to Metman of 3 Corps 'to move your division to a defensive stance on the highway'. Metman duly obliged by advancing some three miles to Benningen, where he could be of no service either to Frossard or indeed to Bazaine. Frossard was later to claim with every justification that had Metman hastened to Forbach and pushed out a strong force on the narrow approaches from Völklingen, night would have fallen before the Germans could have played their joker.

It was 7 p.m. Frossard had fought a brave and lonely battle. He has been roughly criticized for his lack of commitment when, early on, he had Kameke at his mercy. That is unfair. Certainly he had made a serious error of judgment when, on 5 August, he had surrendered the ground overlooking Saarbrücken. But he had done so in order to narrow the gap between 2 Corps and 3 Corps. And he had occupied with some skill the *position magnifique* which he had so carefully reconnoitred all those years before. He had every right to expect that Bazaine would grasp the opportunity and sally forth to his support. In that he was to find himself sadly mistaken.

****

As darkness fell, Frossard decided to break off the battle. His right had bravely held firm against the mounting assault by Alvensleben's corps. His centre was caught in a vice. His left was threatened by the advance of Glümer's division. He thus mounted a great battery of 58 guns around Spicheren, and behind this screen he slipped discreetly and cleverly away — not, as Bazaine would have supposed, along the main road to St Avold, but south and south-east by Oettingen to Sarreguemines, only to find there the remnants of Failly's fugitive corps.

It had been a bitter battle. German casualties amounted to 4871. French losses were 4078, which significantly included nearly 2000 unwounded prisoners. The Germans, greatly shaken and disorganized, wisely made no attempt to pursue their enemy through the dark night. But as the news of MacMahon's defeat at Wörth and Bazaine's 'surrender' at Spicheren reached Moltke, the master-plan was subtly and swiftly altered.

****

The absurd euphoria generated in Paris by the minor episode at Saarbrücken was swiftly dissipated by the news from Wörth and Spicheren; for the descent from Olympus to the Styx was ever precipitous. Certainly Moltke had won the first round, if at great cost and serious dislocation to his master-plan; certainly the French had been driven from the commanding ground on both flanks. But the two defeats were in no sense decisive. At Wörth MacMahon's men had fought with a savage bravery which had called into question the tactics and even the resolution of the vaunted German infantry; and at Spicheren a rash German attack on a position of exceptional strength had been allowed to go unpunished by Bazaine's failure to march to the support of Frossard, when a combined counter-attack would have put Moltke's whole right wing at serious risk. In Alsace, MacMahon's cleverly conducted retreat had prevented a defeat from becoming a rout. In Lorraine, Frossard's equally skilful withdrawal had preserved the Army of Metz virtually intact. Only Failly in the centre had little to be proud of.

On the 7th, Paris was placarded with a despatch from the Emperor which, by its very understatement, foreshadowed the fall of an Empire: 'Marshal MacMahon has lost a battle on the Sauer. General Frossard has been obliged to retire. The retreat is being conducted in good order.' And then: *'Tout peut se rétablir'*. The final sentence, the false optimism of which cannot be precisely caught in translation, was not lost on its disenchanted readers. France was in mortal danger, and the time for private vendettas was past. The nation, so wantonly launched upon an aggressive war, began belatedly to close its ranks.

The crisis which now faced the Government was as much political as military. The dilemma may be stated thus. For the Empress and the Regency Council the survival of the dynasty hung upon the slender thread of a military success; and if that were so, then the Emperor, in the Bonaparte tradition, should be seen to be the chief instrument of victory. The contrary view of the radical opposition, carefully ignoring its complicity in the mindless march to war, was a cynical belief that a military disaster might succeed in bringing down a dynasty whose stability had survived twenty years of political in-fighting. It was scarcely the best scenario for conducting a major war; but both pride and prejudice combined to bring the rival factions to some sort of national unity.

On the 9th the Assembly met in an atmosphere of tense excitement, for there is nothing more dear to the hearts of the elected representatives of France than the thunderstorm of a political crisis. The gravamen of the opposition's attack, led by Favre and Gambetta, was that the régime stood accused not of making war, but of making it complacently and with culpable incompetence. There were few who could dispute either change, and fewer still who did not identify the Emperor as both political and military scapegoat.

Ollivier, who only a month earlier had so 'light-heartedly' embarked upon a collision course, bowed before the storm and resigned. The previous day leaders of all parties had invited Trochu to form a new Ministry, but when Trochu (as Canrobert would very shortly do in the face of a parallel challenge at Metz) declined to put his reputation on the line to salvage a lost cause, the Assembly turned to a distinguished and uncontroversial old soldier, General Cousin de Montauban, whose exploits in the Chinese expedition of 1860 had earned him the exotic title of Comte de Palikao. When, to his duties of chief executive, Palikao added the poisoned chalice of Minister of War, it almost seemed as if the Regency Council had forgotten that the present incumbent of that office, Leboeuf, was alive and well and much preoccupied with the realities of war as the Emperor's chief of staff in Metz. Thus, invigorated by a transfusion of new blood, the Assembly addressed itself to the task of mobilizing the nation for a war which, if not already lost, had upon it the stigmata of defeat.

* * * * * * * *

While political passions ruled in Paris, military problems occupied Imperial headquarters in Metz, where confusion was the order of the day. On the 7th, MacMahon was hastening his scattered army westward to a rendez-vous beyond the Meuse at Châlons, deaf to Leboeuf's repeated summons to close inward on Metz while the remaining railway-line from Nancy was still in French hands and when, on the following day, a heedless order had been sent to Canrobert to occupy the same lifeline in bringing 6 Corps back again from Châlons to the battlefield in Lorraine. On the 7th, Imperial headquarters had no precise knowledge of the whereabouts of Frossard's corps as it retreated unexpectedly to the south on Sarreguemines and Puttelange. On the morning of the 7th, the Emperor took train for St Avold, there to co-ordinate a bold riposte to the German advance from Saarbrücken, only to learn at the railway-station in Metz that the enemy was already in occupation of Forbach with its accumulated stocks of military material. He returned to the Préfecture, there to contemplate a desperate dilemma, to which nature now added a measure of artifice.

The cynical gods of war had the last laugh; for on the morning of the 7th, after days of burning heat, the heavens opened and a succession of torrential thunderstorms flooded the Moselle valley, sweeping away the improvised river crossings on either side of Metz and bringing on an unforeseen drama.

* * * * * * * *

On this same day, Moltke also had his problems. The battle of Spicheren, thanks to Steinmetz's impetuosity and disobedience, had left First Army and the right wing of Second Army inextricably confused around the narrow exits from Saarbrücken. None the less, Moltke, while making several tactical adjustments as a result of the two engagements of the 6th, kept his strategic intention steadfastly in mind. He was not greatly assisted by some of his senior subordinates.

First, he had to clear First Army out of the path of Frederick Charles, whose great mass of six army corps was moving south-west on the Saar from Neunkirchen and Zweibrücken. Thus he ordered Steinmetz, now reinforced by I Corps — which by a miracle of organization had been brought forward to the battlefield in four days from distant Königsberg in East Prussia — to secure the railhead at Forbach; to revert to his original axis of advance on the road from Saarlouis to Metz; and to maintain close contact with the French left wing.

Steinmetz would have none of it. He was sulking; he did not accept Moltke's authority; and when it was made clear to him that the role of First Army was to protect the right flank of the great advance, he, as it were, broke off diplomatic relations with Royal headquarters, and — to make his point — insolently withdrew his hunting-pack of two cavalry divisions, deploying one to no purpose watching the Luxembourg frontier, and the other to even less, cluttering the roads behind his infantry. So it was that Ladmirault's 4 Corps on the French left slipped away under dark and drenching skies towards the protective guns of Metz.

In the centre, Moltke's problem was one of logistics. His staff had worked wonders in devising march-tables which accommodated so great a mass of men and vehicles on for the most part narrow country roads; but when the rains came their difficulties became almost insuperable. In any other army, less disciplined and less resilient, the advance to the Saar would have been halted in its tracks.

In these circumstances it was imperative that close contact should be maintained with the retreating enemy; and for this purpose Moltke had six cavalry divisions available. As we have seen, Steinmetz on the right ignored every order to co-operate and allowed the French to disengage unobserved. On the left the Crown Prince moved forward so cautiously through the Vosges passes that all contact with MacMahon had been lost by the morning of the 8th. But more seriously, the two cavalry divisions in the centre (5th and 6th) under the command of General von Rheinbaben were handled with such lack of urgency that Frossard, after collecting an abandoned brigade[45] of 5 Corps from Sarreguemines, was allowed to make good his escape towards Metz on the Puttelange–Faulquemont road. Fortunately for Moltke, however, Rheinbaben's lack of enthusiasm was largely redeemed by the enterprise and initiative of his most junior commanders.

Operating far ahead of the main body of Second Army, these intrepid young patrol-leaders not only kept a close watch on the enemy's movements as he retreated to the west but also scouted as far south as the main crossings of the Moselle above Metz. As early as the 11th, indeed, one particularly daring group of Hussars was surprised by a troop of French Chasseurs as it was busily engaged in dismantling the railway line below Pont-à-Mousson.

The incident, minor as it may have been, is doubly revealing. First, the

---

45 This was Lapasset's brigade group, including a regiment of Lancers and a battery of artillery which was presently to give an outstanding performance on the 16th and again on the 18th.

counter to an inquisitive cavalry advance guard is a resolute cavalry rear guard.[46] Yet at no stage, neither now nor throughout the August battles, were the French divisional or reserve cavalry divisions used to screen or succour their infantry. And never during those battles — except at four moments of crisis when they were summoned to save their infantry — were the German cavalry used except as watch and ward. Secondly, the brisk affair at Pont-à-Mousson should have alerted Imperial headquarters to the growing threat to their open flank. It did not. And as the Army of Lorraine drew back within the perimeter of its fortress's guns, the bridges over the Moselle upstream from Metz remained unbroken, and the crossings unprotected.

It was the reports from these vigilant cavalry outposts which confirmed the view at Royal headquarters that the two wings of the French army were irrevocably retreating away from each other, and that the main force on the left was closing back on Metz. For Moltke, the moment had come to realign the German advance.

To bring the three armies abreast of each other, a wheel to the right was necessary. The movement of First and Second Armies had, however, to be delayed until the Third Army on the left had come into line [*to Moltke's ill-concealed irritation, it took the Crown Prince five days to cover the thirty miles from Froeschwiller to the upper Saar*]. The whole manoeuvre was so arranged that Third Army was to close in on its right, using the roads from Saarunion and Saarburg, thence by Dieuze towards the upper Moselle; Second Army on the roads by St Avold and Pont-à-Mousson, and further south; First Army, by Saarlouis and Boulay in the direction of Metz.[47]

The order for this grandiose manœuvre was issued on the evening of the 10th. It occupied no more than four short paragraphs. There was to be no impetuous pursuit of MacMahon. MacMahon could be dealt with in due time. Moltke's eyes were firmly fixed on Bazaine and on Metz. And while to the south MacMahon slipped out of sight and — for ten decisive days — out of mind, Royal headquarters moved boldly forward from Saarbrücken to St Avold.

****

As the Army of Lorraine fell back on the fortress under sullen skies which matched the mood of the dispirited troops — most of whom had yet to fire

---

46   It is a melancholy commentary upon this fact that when MacMahon decided to quit the field at Froeschwiller, the cavalry which should have covered his retreat had been destroyed in two brief, bloody and bootless charges.

47   Moltke: *op cit.*

a shot in anger, but whose anger was instead directed against a leadership which provided the barest sustenance and nightly bivouacs in waterlogged fields — another battle was being fought in Metz. This was to be a conflict of hearts and minds, and if its casualties were few, they were to be profoundly significant.

The news that the Germans had occupied Forbach and Sarreguemines, and with them the accumulated material to support an invasion of the Palatinate, swiftly disabused the Emperor and his advisers of any further offensive intentions. In the week that remained before the argument was to be bloodily resolved, a bleak drama was played out.

On the 8th, with Paris in ferment and Ollivier's ministry on the brink, the Emperor delegated the command of 2, 3, and 4 Corps to Bazaine, while retaining under his own command the Imperial Guard and that part of Canrobert's 6 Corps which was hastening forward from Châlons. It was the first act of abdication of his supreme authority and a revealing commentary on his growing defeatism. For on that same day the confidential secretary of the Cabinet, Pietri, put to him in gentle terms a question which now exercised both public and private opinion in the capital: 'Do you consider yourself to be physically quite competent to go through the fatigues and hardships of an active campaign, all day long on horseback, and at night in the bivouac?' Tactfully Pietri did not add the necessary corollary: 'Are you competent to *command* the armies of France?'

Napoleon grasped eagerly at this straw, and in a pathetic reply confessed himself too sick a man to carry the burden of his military responsibilities. Already his mind was occupied with the spectre of retreat, with the surrender of Alsace and Lorraine, and with the reorganization of his scattered armies at Châlons, there to turn upon the invader and save the soul of France. This achieved, he might then return to Paris and, relieved of the physical strain of campaigning, resume the reins of his imperial office. But he had reckoned without his Empress.

Eugénie has much to answer for. She knew, far better than Pietri, that Napoleon was physically incapable of providing the military inspiration of a Bonaparte, but in her ruthless obsession with the survival of the dynasty she imposed her personal and political will on her hesitant husband. Ignoring the military imperatives which daily demanded purely military decisions in Metz, she coldly reminded him where his imperial duty lay. That he should even contemplate returning alone and disgraced to Paris was politically unacceptable, for public opinion (let alone her private conviction) would precipitate the end of the Empire. Although she did not spell that conviction out, the impression still remains that she was not averse to sacrificing Napoleon as a hostage to fortune, and that a soldier's death might prove the salvation of the dynasty, and the secure succession of the Prince Imperial. In the event, her meddlesome intervention led inevitably to both political and military disaster.

****

By the morning of the 10th, after wasted hours of doubt and indecision, the Army of Lorraine had struggled back to a hastily improvised defensive stance behind the French Nied, a small river running east by north into the Saar below Saarlouis (see Map 2). On this day the Army of Lorraine was disposed thus: the main position was occupied by 3 Corps, now commanded by General Decaen[48] when Bazaine assumed a notional authority for the retreating army; on the left, covering the advance of Steinmetz's First Army, was Ladmirault's 4 Corps; 2 Corps, withdrawing after the battle of Spicheren, crossed the Nied and deployed behind Faulquemont; in reserve, though not assigned to Bazaine's command, stood the Imperial Guard and, as it made its hazardous way forward from Châlons, the available elements of Canrobert's 6 Corps. On the evening of the 10th, by whatever means and with whatever prospect, the Army of Lorraine stood uneasily to arms.

It was at once apparent that the Nied position could not be sustained in the face of Moltke's concentric advance on either side of Metz. From Paris came conflicting reports of the strength and thrust of the German armies which, even if they owed more to fantasy than to fact, were sufficiently accurate to fuel the fires of indecision at Imperial headquarters. The various options were becoming daily, even hourly, fewer and more hazardous. By now, when the fall of Forbach had put paid to the Emperor's brief excursion into the realm of heroics, only two alternatives remained: to stand and fight on the Moselle, or to retire and regroup beyond the Meuse.

Bazaine advanced the idea — supported, if without much enthusiasm, by Leboeuf — that the Armies of Alsace and Lorraine should be concentrated in the triangle Toul—Nancy—Langres where, protected by the Vosges, a strong counter-attack could be delivered against either flank of the German left and centre. It was a most curious improvision, for it would have meant the abandonment of Metz by a man for whom, within a week, Metz would become an obsessive symbol of security.[49]

This proposal, fleetingly considered, was as swiftly dismissed; and with good reason. For by the morning of the 11th rail and telegraph communications between Metz and Nancy had been cut, and unknown to Imperial headquarters MacMahon, hastening ever farther to the south-west, was already entraining his leading columns at Lunéville and

48   Decaen was killed in action four days later during the battle of Borny, and the command of 3 Corps passed, for want of a better alternative, to the then discredited and deposed Chief of Staff, Marshal Leboeuf.

49   On 10 August the Commandant of Metz, General Coffinières de Nordeck, reported that the fortress could not survive on its own for more than fourteen days. In the event the siege of Metz, its resources strained by the presence of nearly 200,000 troops and refugees, was to last for ten weeks.

Neufchâteau, and thus by devious ways bringing his scattered command to the great camp at Châlons. Suddenly the whole house of cards, always fragile, began to collapse.

Thus during the 11th the Army of Lorraine fell back on its last defensive option under the guns of Forts St Julien and Queleu on the right bank of the Moselle. The new shortened frontage covered less than five miles. No effort was made to maintain any connection with the small garrison at Thionville fifteen miles to the north. Much more seriously, the vital river crossings upstream from the fortress — Ars, Corny, Novéant, Pont-à-Mousson — remained unwatched, unguarded, and unbroken. At least, by that evening, the incessant rain of the past four days stopped, and that, for the sorely tried soldiers of both sides, was a small but welcome mercy.

****

The following day, the 12th, was to be an occasion of profound importance on the French side since, whether for good or ill, it was to be a long-overdue day of decisions; one in Paris and one in Metz.

In Paris, where the full implications of MacMahon's defeat were now only too clear, all eyes were concentrated on Metz. None could any longer doubt the Emperor's inadequacy as a commander capable of inspiring his army with the necessary resolution of a Bonaparte. The tide of public opinion was irresistible, and even the Empress was compelled to swim with the current, although, obsessive to the last with her rock-like faith in the dynasty, she demanded that not only Napoleon but also the hapless little Prince Imperial should remain among their soldiers.

To whom then the succession? Palikao's options were severely limited. There were in the field four serving Marshals of France: MacMahon, Leboeuf, Canrobert and Bazaine. MacMahon was, not to put too fine a point on it, otherwise employed. Leboeuf, no longer War Minister, was as discredited as his Emperor. Canrobert, the most senior and experienced, had all the obvious military qualifications, but a questionable track record. Fifteen years earlier, and in a very different crisis, he had resigned his command at Sebastopol in a fit of pique and had then tamely agreed to serve under his junior, Pélissier. His part in underpinning the *coup d'état* in 1851 had not endeared him to the Radical left; and Palikao knew that he must now carry the opposition with him.

So there remained Bazaine. His record of service spoke for itself, despite strong criticism of his conduct in Mexico. But his humble origins commended themselves to the Republicans. Even the monarchist Thiers described him in an excess of admiration as '*notre glorieux Bazaine*'. He was trusted by the rank and file, a rare military virtue in the army of the Empire. And he was loyal to a fault. Yet this seeming paragon was doubly, and in the event fatally, flawed. He had never commanded a formation greater than an army corps in the field; and he suffered from an inferiority complex so acute that he could not bring himself to assert his authority over colleagues and subordinates whom he felt even to the end to be his social superiors.

Palikao's decision was made easier when Canrobert, true to character, declined to assume the honour — and responsibility — of supreme command. And thus on the morning of the 12th an Imperial decree, no less, was issued appointing François Achille Bazaine, ex-Fusilier and now Marshal of France, as Commander-in-Chief of all the French forces in the field under their original, if now hollow, title of the 'Army of the Rhine'.

At his trial three years later, Bazaine was to give his own version of events which now took place.

> I received word of my appointment during the afternoon. I at once went to see the Emperor [*in Metz*] and told him that there were Marshals both more senior and more capable than I of taking over command in the difficult situation in which we found ourselves. I had been given no other details; no statement of further intentions, no word about the retreat of 1, 5, and 7 Corps, no intelligence regarding the enemy. The Chief of Staff [*Leboeuf*] who was present at this meeting had nothing to add. There had been no mention, none whatever, at this meeting of the concentration of troops at the camp at Châlons. The Chief of Staff should have informed me of the orders which had been given to Marshal MacMahon. He did not do so...[50]

There are no possible grounds for thinking that Bazaine's account was not true. Not only Leboeuf, but also Canrobert, was present at the meeting. Both were called as witnesses for the prosecution. Neither disagreed with Bazaine's evidence. It is difficult to avoid the conclusion that by the afternoon of the 12th the contagion of defeat had so infected the French high command that the chief players needed no prompting to make for the wings and leave the darkening stage to the lonely figure of '*notre glorieux Bazaine*'. If that is so, it leaves one critical question unanswered.

Two decisions were taken on the 12th. One, as we have seen, was Palikao's act of political courage in clipping the Emperor's military wings.[51] But even as the wires from Paris were humming, Napoleon had pre-empted Paris. Early that morning he had decided, after consultation with Leboeuf, and with Leboeuf's two assistants, Lebrun and Jarras[52] (though *not* with Bazaine), to surrender the Moselle, surrender Lorraine,

---

50 *Procès Bazaine.*

51 Palikao: *Un Ministère de la Guerre de vingt-quatre jours.*

52 Leboeuf, a casualty of Palikao's policy of new blood, assumed command of 3 Corps when General Decaen was killed in action on the 14th. Lebrun hurried away to Châlons to take command of the newly formed 12 Corps. Jarras was left, despite Bazaine's objections, as Chief of Staff of the Army of the Rhine.

and fall back on Verdun, there to join hands with MacMahon at Châlons. It was a decision which should have been taken as early as 7 August when the French front began to crumble. Precious days had been lost. Futile hours had gone while Paris played politics, and Metz aimlessly manœuvred. Now, too late, Napoleon gave the order for a general withdrawal behind the Meuse, forty miles to the west.

How then, it may properly be asked, was this decision not the first and foremost direction given to Bazaine when, on that August afternoon, he came back to Metz to assume his new appointment 'in the difficult situation in which we found ourselves'?

There is no rational answer. As we shall presently see, Bazaine was deeply and dangerously committed to Metz. But for the moment he was equally — and equally dangerously — committed to the Emperor's person, if no longer to his military authority. It was a dilemma to which he was not equal. Caution and instinct suggested that he should stand and fight on the Moselle; but it was not until late on the 12th that he was informed of the Emperor's earlier directive for a general retreat on Verdun.

Thus Bazaine found that he had inherited not only a difficult situation but a hazardous solution. It was therefore the ex-Fusilier Bazaine, accustomed to obeying orders, who overruled the Marshal of France, Bazaine, to whom had been entrusted the sole authority for issuing them. There is no question that Napoleon's last executive decision — however belated and, for whatever reason, tardily communicated to the new commander of the Army of the Rhine — was the right and proper one. Only by disengaging now, while time and space for manœuvre ebbed away, could something solid be salvaged. When at dawn on the 16th the Emperor took his leave of Bazaine at the Gravelotte cross-roads his final injunction — for he could no longer issue orders — was: *'Mettez-vous en route pour Verdun dès que vous le pourrez.'* And then, sadly, as he drove away: *'Je vous confie la dernière armée de la France. Songez au Prince Impérial.'* It was a melancholy exit line.

****

When Bazaine assumed command he was required to do in haste what his predecessor might have done at leisure. Even then he proceeded with no great sense of urgency.

His first decision was to distance himself from the Emperor, whose continued presence in Metz would have proved an embarrassment even to a man of greater self-assurance than Bazaine. The situation may be likened to that of an understudy required at short notice to take the stage while the company's leading light, stricken and paralysed, watched his performance from the wings. Thus Bazaine, pointedly leaving his new chief of staff, Jarras, in Metz, set up his headquarters at Borny two miles to the east of the river, with a small group of confidantes, and with two of his young nephews to run errands for him. Even as a corps commander, he had never learned the art of delegating decisions. Now, at the head of more than 170,000 men, and with an inherited problem which would have taxed the ingenuity of a Bonaparte or a Wellington, he addressed himself single-handed to disengaging the Army of the Rhine. He began in almost leisurely fashion as if unaware — as indeed he appears to have been — of the true measure of the peril in which that Army stood.

****

On the same day that a critical decision was being taken in the Préfecture in Metz, another, long since planned, was being set in train a few miles away in St Avold.

By the morning of the 12th the German armies had completed their great wheel to the right, and occupied a front of some sixty miles from the German Nied to the upper Saar facing west. On the right Steinmetz, now under tight control, was moving on the axis Saarlouis−Metz, with the heads of his columns on either side of Boulay. In the centre, with his rear corps closing up on the Saar, Frederick Charles was advancing slowly towards the Moselle crossings above Metz, with reports from his cavalry patrols hourly confirming that the French appeared to have evacuated their earlier positions on the French Nied and that the roads leading to Pont-à-Mousson were clear. On the left the Crown Prince had lost all contact with MacMahon and was scouting cautiously towards Lunéville and Nancy.

Moltke has been accused of making haste too slowly, but his critics ignore the iron will which kept one single purpose in view. Clausewitz had taught him that the essence of war is battle; but Clausewitz had also preached the gospel of concentration of force. He had only to remember that a failure to practise what Clausewitz preached had almost lost him the battle of Sadowa. He had only to see the vengeance visited on the French for ignoring the principle of safety in numbers. And when presently he relaxed his grip, first on the 16th and again on the 18th, he twice came close to hazarding the whole campaign.

Thus he moved now not leisurely but deliberately. Not for two days could he be certain of Bazaine's intention. He had before him a numerous enemy, sustained by a potentially strong fortress base. He reasoned thus. If Bazaine turned upon Steinmetz on the Nied, then Second Army would be poised to strike in from the other flank. If Bazaine chose to defend the Moselle and attack Frederick Charles in the act of crossing the river, then Second Army could retire on the Third at Nancy, while Steinmetz fell upon the fortress from the rear.

And if Bazaine decided that discretion was the better part of valour and abandoned Metz and the Moselle? For such an eventuality Moltke sharpened his sword, as he pressed the leading cavalry of Second Army forward to the river crossings. It was now Saturday the 13th.

****

Bazaine spent that day issuing orders for the retreat, which was to begin the following morning. He was later to claim that this vital day was lost because the floodwaters after the days of rain had swept away the twelve pontoon bridges which General Coffinières had thrown across the river at Metz. This is partly true, but there still remained three permanent bridges and a railway crossing which with proper staff organization could have accommodated the Army of the Rhine. There were other more serious problems.

Metz lies at the foot of a steep escarpment which rises sharply to the west. There were then two main exit roads, one climbing through a long defile to the plateau at Gravelotte and thence by way of Rezonville−Vionville−Mars-la-Tour to Verdun, forty miles away. At Gravelotte this road branched to the right and followed across the plateau through Doncourt and Etain. The second road, skirting the forts of Plappeville and St Quentin, passed farther north by Woippy and St Privat, and thence also made its way to Verdun. (There was a third, still more northerly road by Briey, but this did not come into play during the imminent battles.) These roads apart, there was a secondary route, little more than a country lane, which branched right from the main *chaussée* to Gravelotte and, following the narrow Châtel valley, made its way by Amanvillers to St Privat. Thus the line of retreat was forced to pass through a bottleneck eight miles long before the leading column reached the open country beyond. This alone should have convinced Bazaine that every hour was precious.

The congestion in the narrow streets of Metz itself was further compounded by a massive congregation of nearly 5000 vehicles, to say nothing of the apparatus of a numerous artillery; and indeed Bazaine spent much of that day sorting out a confusion which was properly not his concern but that of his improvised and incompetent staff. Nothing illustrates more clearly his inability to delegate responsibility; nor the poverty of the disenchanted team which he had inherited.

The Army of the Rhine marched away on the Sunday morning in the following order, using only the southerly road up the escarpment to Gravelotte (the route by Woippy was expressly forbidden in the march-table, and was only taken by Ladmirault two days later when no alternative remained).

The cavalry divisions of Barail and Forton were followed by Canrobert's 6 Corps, Frossard's 2 Corps, and the Imperial Guard, the first two going into bivouac by the morning of the 15th on either side of Rezonville, while the Guard took station a little to the rear at Gravelotte. Around noon Ladmirault's 4 Corps began to cross the Moselle by the permanent bridge below Metz. The withdrawal was covered by Decaen's 3 Corps on the line of the narrow brook between the villages of Colombey and Nouilly on the right bank of the river and a mile to the east of Bazaine's ill-chosen headquarters at Borny. The hours ticked away.

****

By the evening of the 13th, while Bazaine was wrestling with his problems in Metz, Frederick Charles was pressing steadily forward to the river crossings above the fortress, with III Corps on the right and X Corps on the left, closely followed by IX Corps. Ahead of the infantry, 5th Cavalry Division (Rheinbaben) advanced without opposition to Pont-à-Mousson and the Guard Cavalry occupied Dieulouard farther upstream. Still farther south, IV Corps reached Marbache, where early the next morning it joined hands with the right wing of Third Army. Thus the last link was forged, and at the very hour which Moltke's meticulous timetable had laid down. It is difficult not to feel a proper pity for the lonely man at Borny, whose military virtues did not match the moment, and whose timetable, such as it was, demanded a competence and an authority of which he was not capable.

Sunday the 14th was to be a day of unexpected fortunes. Early that morning, Frederick Charles pushed the three brigades of Rheinbaben's 5th Cavalry Division across the Moselle at Pont-à-Mousson. Since dawn great dust-clouds had been observed to the west of Metz, although whether these signalled a partial or a full-scale retreat was still uncertain. Rheinbaben's orders were to scout to the north-west towards Mars-la-Tour and Etain and there seek out and observe the Army of the Rhine if it should that day be marching on the roads to Verdun. It was a bold and hazardous operation, for it would carry 5th Cavalry Division, accompanied only by two horse-artillery batteries, some twenty-five miles beyond the Moselle and a full day's march from the nearest river crossing ahead of any infantry support.

Rheinbaben had already shown something less than a spirit of adventure after passing the Saar. Then his lack of enterprise had been redeemed by his junior patrol-leaders. Now he was to prove fortunate in the quality and initiative of his three brigade commanders.[53]

There was a thick fog that morning, and progress was slow on the steep road up the escarpment to Thiaucourt. Redern, with the leading brigade, reached the village shortly after noon, and, reporting no sign of the enemy, rode on five miles to Xonville, where he bivouacked for the night, while an apprehensive Rheinbaben waited for the rest of his division to close up from the rear.

53   11th Brigade (von Barby); 12th Brigade (von Bredow); 13th Brigade (von Redern). The divisional strength on the morning of the 14th was 5145, together with twelve 4-pdr guns.

Meanwhile, of danger all unconscious, the Army of the Rhine was winding its weary way towards the plateau, the long caravan encumbered by a disorderly mass of vehicles, its soldiers sullen, and disheartened by the stigma of a retreat which they did not understand. Leading this desolate array were the cavalry divisions of Forton and Barail. At Gravelotte the former rode on to Rezonville, where it halted for the night, while the latter turned aside on the upper route to Doncourt. The infantry slogged forward.

On the following morning Redern detached the Hussar squadrons, accompanied by two guns, with orders to reconnoitre as far as the Verdun road; and shortly after 11 a.m. his scouts, breasting a slope north of Puxieux, saw before them a long column moving on Mars-la-Tour along the main *chaussée*. This was the leading brigade of Forton's cavalry division, commanded, by an irony of history, by General Prince Murat, whose appetite for action now proved to be sharply less enthusiastic than that of his legendary forebear. There followed a desultory exchange of artillery fire, and an hour later Redern recalled his men to Puxieux, where the rest of his brigade was assembled. Thence he reported his brief encounter to Rheinbaben, and stood to arms. He need have taken no such precaution.

Murat made no attempt to follow the German withdrawal or to investigate the true situation to the south of the Verdun road. Had he done so, and had Forton remotely understood the proper function of cavalry in covering the retreat of an army, Rheinbaben's apprehension of being launched into open country without visible means of support might well have been justified. Instead, frightened by his own shadow, Forton summoned his own leading squadrons back from Mars-la-Tour, and by evening his division was comfortably installed in a tidy tented camp around Vionville. He duly reported the day's entertainment to Bazaine, adding for good measure that the enemy cavalry was 'strongly supported by infantry at Puxieux'. So much for vivid imagination. So much for faint hearts. And so much for the wild surmise in Bazaine's order issued from Ban St Martin that evening.[54]

****

But while Rheinbaben was feeling for the enemy on the plateau during the 15th, events had taken an unexpected course in the valley below during the previous day.

As we have seen, Saturday the 13th had been a wasted day on the French side, when the situation demanded that the withdrawal of the Army of the Rhine be set in train without a moment's delay. And we have seen how a conjunction of natural misfortune and primitive staff-work had created a

54 *See* p. 109

state of chaos in the narrow approaches to and exits from Metz. None the less, by the forenoon of the 14th all the cavalry and three of the army corps (2, 6, and Imperial Guard) had been transferred to the left bank of the Moselle; 4 Corps was in the process of crossing the river by the permanent bridge below the fortress; and the whole operation was covered by 3 Corps along the Colombey brook. By then, if Bazaine had acted with less maddening deliberation, the greater part of his army should have been firmly established on the plateau, and Rheinbaben's worst fears would have been confirmed. But it did not happen. Effectively, another day had been lost.

On the far side of the river, Steinmetz had meanwhile been playing devil's advocate. Having been informed that First Army was to act as pivot to the right wheel, and to serve as flank protection to the princely commander of Second Army, he assumed an attitude of calculated indifference. He had now been joined by the whole of I Corps which was moving slowly on the main roads from Saarlouis and Saarbrücken, with VIII Corps echeloned to the rear on its right, and VII Corps on its left; but he was in no mood to invite any further royal reprimands. Thus he dragged his feet and watched developments with an insolent detachment.

He had not, however, reckoned with the bold initiative of his subordinates. As at Wörth, as at Spicheren, so now under the guns of Metz. Shortly before 4 p.m., General von der Goltz, commanding 26th Infantry Brigade,[55] came forward to the rising ground which overlooks the Moselle valley from the east. There he saw the outposts of Decaen's 3 Corps lying before him, and beyond, the clear indications of retreating columns towards the river. 'I knew,' Goltz wrote later, 'that the sound of gunfire would bring strong support to the scene of battle', and without waiting for authority from his divisional commander, Glümer — who had saved the day at Spicheren by his timely intervention when Zastrow's corps was in disarray along the Forbach road — Goltz launched his brigade against the centre of Decaen's line, four divisions strong. He received a bloody welcome.

The engagement which followed — known variously as the battle of Borny, and the battle of Colombey–Nouilly — lasted for little more than three hours. It sucked in the best part of five divisions on each side.[56] It has been dismissed by several historians as a pointless rearguard action, but that is not so. The casualties alone — 3915 French and 4620 German — tell a different tale.

But battles are not always to be judged by blood-counts. This unforeseen engagement sent ripples out on either side.

55   13th Division of VII Corps.

56   3 Corps and Grenier's division of 4 Corps (French). Elements of VII Corps, I Corps and — at the end — IX Corps (German).

Even though Goltz's precipitate action had succeeded in disrupting the French retreat, Moltke had serious misgivings that the habit of bringing on improvised battles might prove a source of considerable danger; though curiously the order which he was presently to give to Frederick Charles invited — and indeed resulted in — precisely the kind of collision he sought to avoid. He was well aware that an able and enterprising French commander would have made the German advance-guards pay heavily for their excessive zeal, first at Spicheren and now again at Borny. This time he could not blame Steinmetz, but as a matter of reinsurance, he sent him the most specific instructions during the night of the 14th/15th that First Army was in no circumstances to become involved in any further offensive action.

If Moltke was anxious, Bazaine was exceedingly angry. When during the afternoon the guns began to sound across the valley he had ridden out from Borny and insisted that the action be broken off and the withdrawal to the left bank of the river resumed without delay. But a battle lightly begun is not so lightly stopped, and Bazaine was at his best on a battlefield rather than in a bureau. When the corps commander, Decaen, was mortally wounded, he was soon busy moving battalions about. A shell-fragment struck his shoulder, but he remained under fire until, as darkness fell, the Germans withdrew to their previous bivouacs, and the five French divisions remaining on the right bank resumed their retreat.

****

Later that night Bazaine moved his headquarters to Ban St Martin on the western outskirts of Metz and then made his way along the Verdun road to Longeville to report the day's proceedings to the Emperor. Even now, after a battle which had come as close to victory as Bazaine would ever get, this strange man could not bring himself to accept the fact that Napoleon was no longer his military master, and that the responsibility for the Army of the Rhine was his alone. Perhaps it would be charitable to describe his visit to the Imperial villa as a courtesy call. It did little for Bazaine's peace of mind.

When he arrived, Napoleon was in bed. Bazaine has described the brief exchange which followed.

> The Emperor greeted me with his usual kindness, and when I explained my fears lest the Germans should cut in on my line of retreat, and referring to my wound asked to be relieved of my command, the Emperor, touching my bruised shoulder and the broken epaulette, gracefully said: 'It will be nothing, a matter of a few days, and you have just broken the spell [*Vous venez de briser le charme*]. I await an answer at any moment from the Emperor of Austria and the King of Italy. Compromise nothing by too much

precipitation and, above[57] all things, no more reverses. I rely on you.'

And on that note, full of foreboding, monarch and Marshal took leave of each other.

During the morning of the 15th the Imperial entourage made its way up the escarpment to the inn at Gravelotte, its passage marked by a disrespectful counterpoint of comment from the marching columns. At Ban St Martin, Bazaine slept until noon. Then, after a reassuring examination by his doctor, he gave Jarras some inconsequential orders, and rode up the hill. It was, by a melancholy irony, the Emperor's name-day, and Bazaine took with him some flowers from the garden of his suburban villa. It was a touching gesture which tells us much about this simple, kindly soldier to whom history has been less than kind.

At the crossroads there was a short discussion as the long columns filed past, and Bazaine interrupted the conversation to indicate their proper destination to various tired units. He had always had an exceptional memory for faces and places, and for seemingly unimportant military detail. That had served him well in the African desert, in the Crimea, in Italy, and in Mexico. The wider vision which his new command now required was beyond his intellectual grasp, and Canrobert — who should surely have stood in the dock beside him three years later — might have spared him the cheap jibe that he was incompetent to command 'an army of 140,000 men'.

The Emperor asked if he should leave at once for Verdun, but Bazaine counselled caution until the situation was clearer; and wisely, too. For at that very moment, unknown to all at Gravelotte, Redern's outposts had intercepted Forton's division six miles away on the outskirts of Mars-la-Tour. Time had run out.

****

It was early in the afternoon of the 15th that Moltke at last decided that the moment had come to release Second Army. The battle of Borny had been as unexpected a diversion for him as it had been a fatal check to Bazaine. Now Moltke saw — or thought he saw — the way ahead. That he made a serious misjudgment we shall presently see; but that his error was redeemed by the incompetence of his opponent he could not then have guessed. This conjunction of error and irresolution was to result in the battle of Mars-la-Tour.

At 5 p.m. Moltke issued his orders. Steinmetz's First Army was to leave a corps (I) at Courcelles-sur-Nied and place the other two (VII and VIII) on the right bank of the Moselle.

---

57   Bazaine: *Episodes de la guerre de 1870.*

It is only by a vigorous offensive movement of the Second Army [so ran his order] upon the roads from Metz to Verdun by way of Fresnes and Etain that we can reap the fruits of the victory obtained yesterday [14th]. The commander of the Second Army is entrusted with this operation which he will conduct according to his own judgement and with the means at his disposal, that is to say all the corps of his Army.

It was a tidy order, very precise and very Prussian. It presupposed every kind of presupposition. It assumed several false assumptions. And it came very close to bringing about a disaster.

Frederick Charles took Moltke at his word. His orders, issued at 11 p.m., read thus:

X Corps will march tomorrow [16th] in a straight line westward from Pont-à-Mousson towards Verdun on the supposition [sic] that the enemy's advanced troops on his retreat may be already approaching that town. The troops will complete more than half the distance during the day [25 miles], and their advanced guards will push on as far as St Hilaire. Not before reaching that place is it thought possible that they can come up with the enemy. III Corps will move on Gorze and is likely to make contact with some [sic] of the enemy tomorrow evening.

With 'all the corps of his Army.' At midnight on the 15th, these were disposed as follows. On the right III Corps, which had already started to cross the river by the intact bridge and by pontoons at Corny/Novéant; five miles upstream at Pont-à-Mousson, X Corps with part of one division already on the westerly road to Thiaucourt; five miles farther to the south and closing up to the Moselle at Dieulouard, the Guard Corps; and on the far left, in touch with the Crown Prince's Third Army, IV Corps in the direction of Toul. Behind these leading formations, IX Corps was marching on Corny/Novéant, XII (Royal Saxon) Corps was a day's march from Pont-à-Mousson, while much farther to the east, and the last to cross the frontier, was II Corps. By midnight on the 18th, all these corps (except IV) would be involved in a series of desperate actions which, within 72 hours and at a cost of nearly 40,000 casualties, settled the fate of France.

****

As one army gathered itself to press forward, another, only fifteen miles away, was stumbling back towards Verdun. Neither had any clear picture of the other. Neither was sure if — or where — a collision might occur. The Germans at least had made a bold investigation beyond the river. The French marched away without heed to their security or to the rising risk to their open flank. We have seen that during the 15th, Forton's cavalry

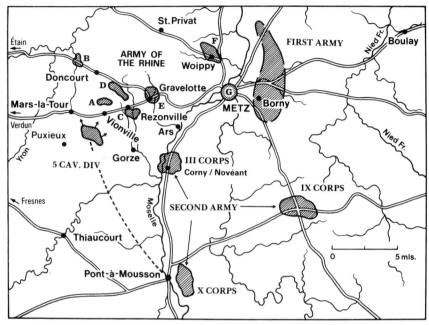

KEY

A   Cav. Div Forton
B   Cav. Div du Barail
C   2 Corps
D   6 Corps
E   Imperial Guard
F   3 Corps
G   4 Corps

Map 3   The situation at midnight, 15/16 August

division had clashed with Rheinbaben's patrols near Mars-la-Tour, and had tamely fallen back to Vionville while Frossard's 2 Corps and Canrobert's 6 Corps had emerged onto the plateau and bivouacked on either side of Rezonville. And at almost the same hour that Frederick Charles issued his orders for the 16th, Bazaine, still tied in fancy, if not in fact, to the authority of the Emperor (now anxiously installed in the inn at Gravelotte) issued his:

> *La soupe sera mangée demain matin à quatre heures. On se tiendra prêt à se mettre en route à quatre heures et demie, en ayant les chevaux sellés et les tentes abattues. Les 2ᵉ et 6ᵉ corps doivent avoir 30,000 hommes devant eux; ils s'attendent à être attaqués demain. Les reconnaissances doivent se faire comme d'habitude.*[58]

58 'Troops will have their breakfast tomorrow morning at 4 a.m. They will hold themselves ready to move at 4.30 a.m. with horses saddled and tents struck. 2 and 6 Corps are likely to have 30,000 men facing them; they must expect to be attacked tomorrow. Reconnaissance will be carried out as usual.'

This order invites the closest attention, for it was — rightly — to be subjected to much scrutiny at Bazaine's trial three years later.

First, it was based like that of his opponent on pure guesswork, even if the estimate of the likely enemy strength available *some time* during the following morning was surprisingly accurate. But then at once Bazaine reveals in a single word the fatal flaw in his character and in his subsequent conduct. 'They [*2 and 6 Corps*] must expect to be *attacked* tomorrow.' Already, regardless of the massive superiority — which he had and would still have on the following morning — the implication was that of a defensive stance. No word of resolute action to brush the enemy aside. No suggestion of aggressive action such as Moltke had demanded of Frederick Charles. No reference to the Army of Alsace or the retreating MacMahon. No mention of Verdun or of the day's objective for the Army of the Rhine.

Bazaine's final sentence, flat and plucked as it were from some anonymous training-manual, says all that is left to say: 'Reconnaissance will be carried out as usual.' No reconnaissance was carried out, or had been since the retreat began on the 14th. Not one squadron of Forton's division was sent to watch the Moselle crossings. Not even a small patrol ventured the few miles to Gorze, where it would have learned much to Bazaine's advantage, if not adding to his anxiety. But curiously this elementary lack of flank protection deceived the Germans into believing that the Army of the Rhine had made good its escape, and so encouraged Frederick Charles to commit a series of comparable blunders.

And yet... If Bazaine had left well alone and had marched at first light on the roads to Verdun as his order of the 15th, however vaguely, proposed, he would have had a headstart of at least five hours before Alvensleben's III Corps could reach the plateau to intercept what would then in reality have been the French rearguard. He might thus have brought the Army of the Rhine to safety beyond the Meuse. He might then have joined hands with MacMahon at Châlons. And it is just possible that the war would have taken a less disastrous course for France.

But it did not happen; for early on the morning of the 16th, for reasons good or bad, for purposes creditable or craven, and with results of the most profound historical significance, Bazaine countermanded his order. His decision was to bring on the battle of Mars-la-Tour; and to this most singular day we shall now address ourselves.

THE
DAY OF BATTLE
16 AUGUST

THE BATTLEFIELD

The plateau of Gravelotte is virtually unchanged since the day of battle over a hundred years ago. The villages and farms destroyed in the fighting still bear their former names, and have been rebuilt in the solid style typical of the Lorraine countryside. The area was largely untouched by the two world wars. All the woods which played so critical a part in the battle still stand, and remarkably continue to yield up the rusty wreckage of war. Even the old Roman road remains. Indeed, it would be difficult to believe that during 72 hours more than 64,000 men were killed and wounded on this now peaceful landscape, were it not for the multitude of memorials which mark those desperate encounters. Around Rezonville alone there are sixteen.

But while the fields are the same, the roads have changed. The poplars which lined them have gone. The so-called Gran' Route *from Metz to Verdun, the artery which crosses the battlefield and is today a four-lane highway, was then a* chaussée *25 feet wide, but narrowing to 15 feet along the causeway which crosses the deep Mance ravine. More strikingly, the two roads which climb through the dense woods from Gorze to Rezonville and Vionville were then little more than dusty tracks 12 feet wide and bordered by vineyard walls.[1] Yet up such roads the Germans were allowed to pass half an army corps with all its guns and attendant transport. Two regiments and a couple of batteries properly and prudently deployed during the ample hours available could have bolted and barred these vital gates. For want of a nail ...*

---

1   The French defined those roads which were passable to wheeled transport as *carrossable*. Their own antiquated maps showed only five such roads between Metz and Verdun. The German maps, updated to May 1870, showed eleven; and they were right.

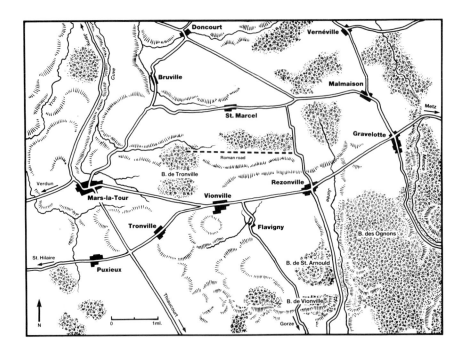

Map 4   The battlefield, 16 August

The Gravelotte plateau is approached from the east and south-east up a steep, wooded escarpment. To the west of Gravelotte the southerly of the two main roads to Verdun runs straight for seven miles to Mars-la-Tour, passing through the villages of Rezonville and Vionville which lie in shallow depressions that serve to gather the limited drainage from the sparsely watered plateau. Near Rezonville a small brook, the Jurée, follows a modest ravine through Gorze to the Moselle valley at Novéant; at Vionville there is a pond sheltered by a clump of trees. This pond was to play an important part in the fighting around the village, for 16 August was a day of burning heat.

The road runs like a red thread across the plateau; for the battle of Mars-la-Tour — or, more exactly, the two related battles of the 16th — was centred on and around it; from 9.15 a.m. when the first German shells surprised Forton's bivouac at Vionville, until nightfall when Frederick Charles ordered a suicidal attack on Rezonville. The road also gives a striking symmetry to the battlefield, for it divides almost exactly a rectangle measuring eight miles by six miles. This geometrical pattern can best be described as 'the morning and the evening of the 16th day'; or, seen through German eyes, survival in the south (III Corps) and salvation in the north (X Corps). Seen through Bazaine's eyes, the picture is very different;

for while he occupied the same rectangle, and for him salvation lay to the west, he cast away a succession of opportunities by nervously looking over his shoulder for survival to the east, where no threat lay. In this sense the battle of Mars-la-Tour, unplanned and unforeseen by either side, is a very unusual passage of arms.

The Gravelotte plateau is an upland of fields and woods, then given to cattle-grazing, now thick with arable crops. It has much in common with Salisbury Plain and with the landscape around Gettysburg. It has the lowest water-table in France, and one of the smallest farming communities in Lorraine. It is also, ironically, famous for its rough-shooting.

But it is, in the strictest sense, a plain. In every account of the battle of 16 August, writers — even eye-witnesses — repeatedly refer to topo-graphical features such as 'the heights' or even 'the hills' on either side of the main road. Such descriptions are both inaccurate and misleading. The landscape,[2] in fact, is gently undulating, much broken by woods and copses to the south and north of the main road, and there are no features which entirely dominate the battlefield — no Chemin des Dames, no Vimy ridge. For example, the 'heights' to the south-west of Vionville where Körber's horse-artillery batteries came into action on the morning of the 16th are no more than a gentle swell of ground rising only 30 feet above the level of the road, and giving only a partial view of the village. Similarly, the open fields across which Wedell's brigade advanced to its destruction slope very gradually down to the wooded ravine beyond which the divisions of Grenier and Cissey awaited it.

Yet the ground, with its quiet contours, its re-entrants, and its woods, provides a surprising degree of concealment, and this explains how Bredow was able to move his six squadrons north of Vionville without detection before wheeling into line for his celebrated charge. It also partly explains why so many hours passed before the German commander realized that he had before him not simply a rearguard but the whole Army of the Rhine; and why throughout the long day Bazaine so signally failed to grasp the extreme vulnerability of his adversary. Throughout the battle of Mars-la-Tour, except for the great cavalry clashes, fewer than 2000 yards separated the two sides.[3] In that sense, it was to prove an artillery duel between two ill-matched opponents.

South of the main road from Gravelotte to Mars-la-Tour, where the 'morning battle' was concentrated, bare fields slope down to a series of thick woods — Bois des Ognons, Bois de St Arnould, Bois de Vionville — through which lead the approach roads up the escarpment from the Moselle valley. Here Stuelpnagel's 5th Division clung to a precarious foothold against greatly superior odds. But farther to the west Budden-

2 See illustrations *passim.*

3 Significantly, a total of sixteen General Officers were killed or seriously wounded on both sides.

brock's 6th Division captured the villages of Vionville and Flavigny by noon, and this enabled Alvensleben to deploy his entire divisional and corps artillery on a low ridge which forms a natural amphitheatre overlooking Rezonville. It was these guns which were to be the key to the battle.

North of the road the ground slopes gently up to a line of woods bordering an old Roman road and flanked to the west by a number of thick copses. Here, during the morning, the German left flank lay open to attack by four French divisions. The attack never came. As the map shows, the Tronville copses were the pivot of the whole battlefield — the *point d'appui* between the morning and the afternoon — for they provided a natural buttress to the Germans' perilously exposed left flank until the arrival of X Corps at 4 p.m., and an obstacle to the faltering French attempts to envelop this flank. They were won, lost, and won again. The measure of their importance is that although Mars-la-Tour was there for the taking until late in the afternoon, not one French soldier set foot in that village throughout the day of battle.

Beyond the copses and to the north of the main road lies the scene of the 'afternoon battle'. Here the ground stretches away towards Bruville, and is cut through like a knife by the Fond de la Cuve, a deep, dry gully thickly covered by bushes and scrub, which was to be the scene of the disastrous attack by the *16th* and *57th* Westphalians, the heroic counter-charge by the Guard Dragoons, and the failure — even the refusal — of the French corps commander, Ladmirault, to drive a disordered enemy from the field.

Even then the day of battle reserved a final and suitably Wagnerian climax when, as evening drew on, the massed cavalry of both sides met in a stupendous encounter on the farthest flank in the rolling fields above the little Yron river. 'A victory, an undoubted victory!' said Ladmirault as he rode back to Bruville across a forsaken field. In Mars-la-Tour, the Germans rested wearily on their laurels. Against absurdly improbable odds, they had cut Bazaine's lifeline. He had bled them nearly dry. Now they would bleed him to death.

Such is this strikingly beautiful and strikingly moving battlefield. 'It was a murderous day,' recorded a German sergeant. 'We are all too old for a war like this,' lamented General Bourbaki, commander of the Imperial Guard. He was just fifty-four. The battlefield had the last word. So baked was the ground that it took many days to bury the dead — in unmarked graves. And by then another and even bloodier battle had been fought — not to the easeful west, but to the unlikely east.[4]

---

4   The terrain for the set-piece battle on 18 August is very different; as, for example, Plates 21 and 22 dramatically illustrate.

THE BATTLE

Tuesday, 16 August dawned cloudless and clear. Since the previous morning the ceaseless rain which had earlier interfered with the withdrawal of the Army of the Rhine across the Moselle had given way to hot sunshine. It was to be, in every sense, a dusty day.

At first light, Bazaine rode up from his headquarters at Ban St Martin to the inn at Gravelotte. Napoleon was already sitting in his carriage with his cousin and the Prince Imperial, '*son visage fatigué portant l'empreinte du chagrin et de l'inquiétude*'.[1] 'I have decided to leave for Châlons,' he said to Bazaine. 'Put yourself on the road to Verdun as soon as you can.' And with that he set off — fortunately, as events were to prove — on the northern road by way of Doncourt and Étain, accompanied by two regiments of Imperial Guard cavalry. Emperor and Marshal were not to see each other again for ten weeks, and then as distinguished prisoners of the King of Prussia in Wilhelmshöhe.

For the first time since the overall command had been placed squarely on his unwilling shoulders, Bazaine was on his own. If we are to believe Colonel d'Andlau's highly suspect account[2] 'he [Bazaine] loudly expressed his pleasure at being rid of this embarrassing encumbrance'. Whether this was so or not, his immediate action was to prove a grave commentary upon his subsequent conduct, and a flagrant defiance of the Emperor's last instruction. It was also to result in a battle which should never have happened.

On returning to his headquarters, Bazaine at once countermanded his warning order of the previous evening; and since this decision has been the subject of much controversy, it is proper to quote Bazaine's exact words:

1 D'Andlau: *Metz: Campagnes et négociations.*

2 D'Andlau: *Ibid.*

Plate 1 The inn at Gravelotte where Napoleon spent the night of 15/16 August

Plate 2 The crossroads at Gravelotte looking east. To the left the central road to Verdun by way of Doncourt and Étain

Dès que les reconnaissances seront rentrées et que tout indiquera que l'ennemi n'est pas en force en proximité, on pourra dresser de nouveau les tentes. Nous partirons probablement dans l'après-midi, dès que je saurai que les 3ᵉ et 4ᵉ corps sont arrivés à notre hauteur en totalité. Des ordres, du reste, seront données ultérieurement.[3]

In all the official — and unofficial — accounts of Mars-la-Tour, many errors of commission and omission have been attributed to Bazaine; and to some of these we will return. But this order is so critical — and so revealing — that it deserves a careful analysis.

First, the complacent assumption about enemy activity, completely at odds with Bazaine's order of the previous evening. In fact, he was simply guessing, and it was a remarkably uneducated guess. He knew that Frederick Charles's Second Army had crossed to the left bank of the Moselle upstream from Metz at Novéant and Pont-à-Mousson, and that his own cavalry had been in action as far west as Mars-la-Tour the previous day. Yet he made no effort to reconnoitre the southern defiles leading from the river to the plateau, nor did he give Forton, in the vanguard of the withdrawal, instructions to send out strong patrols to the south and west where Rheinbaben's cavalry, totally without infantry support, was at large. His previous laconic direction — *'les reconnaissances doivent se faire comme d'habitude'* — was followed precisely. There was no reconnaissance.

'Permission is given to pitch tents again.'[4] This was in direct disobedience of the Emperor's parting instruction to make all haste on the road to Verdun. It was a complete negation of the paramount need for urgency — and this decision is underlined by the next sentence in his order: 'We shall probably [*sic*] resume our march during the afternoon.' What sort of resolute command is it that, in such a situation, could only contemplate 'probabilities'? As we shall presently see, Frederick Charles had already issued to his nearest corps commanders — Alvensleben and Voigts-Rhetz — clear, simple, even reckless orders; and that he had done so with no more precise knowledge of the movements of the Army of the Rhine than had Bazaine of the German Second Army. Even on a clear August day, the fog of war already obscured the battlefield.

Then, at last, Bazaine's order provides a clear insight into his confused mind. There was to be no resumption until Leboeuf's 3 Corps and

---

3 'Since our own returning patrols have reported that the enemy is not in any strength in our vicinity, permission is given to pitch tents again. We shall probably resume our march during the afternoon as soon as I know that 3 and 4 Corps have completed their arrival on the plateau. Further orders will be issued in due course.'

4 Unlike the enemy, the French persisted in treating war as if it was simply an extension of peacetime manœuvres. Even on 18 August, when Bazaine had retired to his *position inexpugnable* on the Amanvillers Line, the Germans were astonished to see the little white, two-man tents neatly pitched.

Ladmirault's 4 Corps had struggled out of the Moselle valley and arrived on the Gravelotte plateau — '*à notre hauteur en totalité*'. This was absurd. By daybreak only part of 3 Corps had managed to reach Vernéville. 4 Corps, driven by paralysing congestion on the *routes carrossables* to take the Woippy road to the north-west of Metz, had not even left the Moselle valley. If Bazaine's order was to be taken seriously (and he did not even communicate with Ladmirault throughout that day), then it meant that the Army of the Rhine was being instructed to mark time for a vague and indeterminate period in order to close up on its centre without the slightest regard to the activities of an eager, thrusting — *and highly vulnerable* — enemy. Already, Bazaine had lost control.

At his trial, he explained that he had taken this decision at the request of Leboeuf, who was worried about the confused situation north of Gravelotte. This may be so. It may be that he felt that the Army of the Rhine should be fully concentrated on the plateau before the westward march was continued. Had not the Emperor told him: 'On no account compromise the army'? But had the Emperor's last words to him not been: 'Put yourself on the road to Verdun as soon as possible'? It was a classic example of the split definitive. Hence the weasel word '*probablement*'.

But while a commander-in-chief should rightly consult his subordinates, he alone must take the final decisions.[5] The responsibility was not Leboeuf's. But — and it is important to understand this — while Leboeuf was the junior Marshal of France, Bazaine, the ex-ranker, could never bring himself to impose his will on his social superiors. How different on the other side of the hill, where — for all their errors — princes proliferated.

Yet the reason for Bazaine's ready, even eager, acceptance of Leboeuf's call for caution is this (and it was to influence his every action in the hours that lay ahead). It may be simply stated in a single word: Metz.

Metz held Bazaine like a magnet. It was for him, during the day of battle and its aftermath, an image — or more accurately a mirage — of security from which, with his eighteenth-century, fortress-minded concept of war, he could not bring himself to be separated. No matter that, by whatsoever means, he had assembled a greatly superior force on the plateau. No matter that he had been enjoined to make all haste and bring his Army of the Rhine to a safer haven beyond the Meuse a day's march to the west. Extraordinary that on the 17th he decided to take his whole army back to replenish supplies rather than bring those supplies forward the mere ten miles to his army. No such negative notion occurred to an opponent whose hazardous communications stretched far back beyond the Moselle, and were for more than two days at the mercy of a resolute counter-stroke. This obsession with Metz was to cost France first a battle, and then a war.

---

5   This was to be the argument advanced for good — and often not so good — reasons by the prosecution at Bazaine's trial.

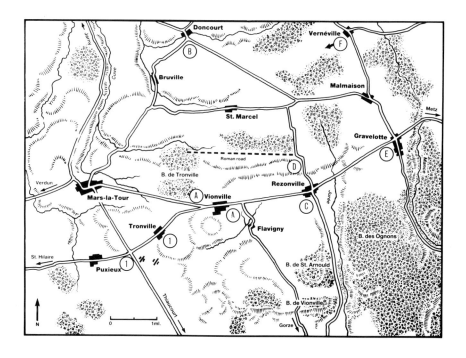

KEY

FRENCH	GERMAN
A. Cav. Div Forton	1. 5 Cav. Div and Horse Artillery Batteries
B. Cav. Div Barail	
C. 2 Corps	
D. 6 Corps	
E. Imperial Guard and Bazaine's HQ	
F. 3 Corps	

Map 5   Situation at dawn, 16 August

It was also to cost Bazaine his reputation, and nearly his life.

There remains the last, flat sentence: 'Further orders will be issued in due course.' No such orders were issued; for within hours a single German cavalry brigade and four horse artillery batteries had stopped the Army of the Rhine in its tracks.

****

This was the situation at first light on 16 August.

After its encounter with Rheinbaben's cavalry near Mars-la-Tour on the previous day, Forton's division had fallen back cautiously to Vionville, not so much to protect Bazaine's infantry as to be protected by it. Here it went into bivouac with all the leisurely composure of peacetime manœuvres. Tents were pitched; men took their horses to water at the village pond; and officers sat down to a pleasant *petit déjeuner sur l'herbe* at tables set with clean linen and polished cutlery. Not even the most elementary precautions were taken. In the words of the official History: 'The outposts of Forton's division were established to the *north* of the road and to the *east* of the Tronville copses less than 500 metres from the bivouac and in a position from where they could see nothing.' Not a single patrol scouted to the south where the real and obvious danger lay. At daybreak, some horsemen were seen on the skyline near Tronville. Various silly suggestions were made; that they belonged to Barail's cavalry division, then four miles to the north near Doncourt; even more absurdly, that they were part of Ladmirault's 4 Corps, which at that early hour was still trying to extricate itself from the Moselle valley ten miles away to the east. No one was sent to investigate. More significantly, no officer had ventured to Vionville from Bazaine's headquarters — in sharp contrast to the activities of the German staff, as we shall presently see. No matter. It was a pleasant day. Breakfast was served.

To the east of Vionville, on a road crowded with civilian transport and further encumbered by Valabrègue's cavalry division of 2 Corps, the Army of the Rhine was disposed as follows.

To the south of the main road in a narrow arc around Rezonville was Frossard's 2 Corps: on the right, Bataille's division, on the left Vergé's, and straddling the road to Gorze, Lapasset's brigade group which had joined the Army of the Rhine on 7 August after McMahon's precipitate retreat from Wörth.[6] This corps, which faced towards the main access roads from the Moselle valley, was disposed in a tight circle no more than 1000 yards from Rezonville. Despite Frossard's later protestations to the contrary, no outposts were thrown forward to the southerly woods whence a likely threat would come. No single spy, let alone a battalion, was sent to reconnoitre the village of Gorze three miles away. Forton, the engineer who had preached the doctrine of defence in his famous *positions magnifiques*, sat tight while the enemy closed in.

To the north of the main road, and echeloned slightly behind Frossard, was Canrobert's 6 Corps — or more precisely those elements of the army reserve which had been sent forward to Nancy from Châlons, shuttled back again on 2 August, and then brought up to Metz on 9 August. It lacked its cavalry division, all but one regiment (the 9th) of Bisson's infantry division, a major part of its artillery, and its entire engineer park.[7] Canrobert's corps lay thus, facing rather nonchalantly to the west, cooking its breakfasts and innocent of any information about the enemy: on the right Tixier's division a little to the north of the Roman road; on its left the

6   The third division of Frossard's corps, Laveaucoupet's, which had borne the brunt at Spicheren, had been left behind to garrison Metz.

7   The lack of the engineer and pioneer units was to have serious consequences at the battle of St Privat two days later.

Plate 3 Rezonville, looking north along the road from Gorze. This was the position held by Lapasset's brigade. In 1870 this road was only 12 feet wide

Plate 4 The road from Gorze, looking east to the Bois des Ognons

Plate 5   A general view of the position held by Frossard's 2 Corps

Plate 6   The Bois de St Arnould and the Bois de Vionville, looking south

9th Regiment from Bisson's division at the point where the memorial to the Ziethen Hussars now stands; and linking loosely with Frossard's corps around Rezonville, Lafont's division. In reserve, behind the Rezonville ridge, lay Levassor-Sorval's division. 'I did not know what was required of me,' said Canrobert at Bazaine's trial. Canrobert had only himself to blame. A Marshal of France who refuses the honour of commanding an Army deserves small sympathy.

Farther to the north, on Canrobert's right, Leboeuf's 3 Corps had struggled out of the Moselle valley by midnight on the 15th. It lay at dawn on the plateau, with Clérambault's cavalry division towards Doncourt and the infantry divisions of Montaudon, Aymard and Nayral bivouacked between Vernéville and St Marcel. The fourth infantry division, Metman's, was still far behind, and indeed did not reach the battlefield until evening. To the east 4 Corps — one cavalry division and three infantry divisions — which, according to Jarras's half-baked march-plan, should have been leading the withdrawal on the northerly road to Verdun (its commander, Ladmirault, had been refused permission to use the *route carrossable* by Woippy and St Privat[8]) was still in the general area of Metz.

There remained the Imperial Guard, France's pride and Bazaine's problem, in the sense that it embodied in his rank-ridden mind the epitome of Empire, not lightly to be committed nor compromised nor cast away. In the days that followed this corps was barely committed, never compromised, only its cavalry in part cast away. Its commander, Bourbaki, was a petulant *beau sabreur* who may be forgiven for wondering whether his elegantly uniformed regiments were heirs to one Bonaparte tradition or the colourful curtain to another. The Imperial Guard had been the last corps to leave Metz on the southerly route. Now, at dawn, it stood around Gravelotte, where Bazaine had set up his headquarters with the Army artillery park. A mile to the north, near Malmaison, was the Voltigeur division and two brigades of cavalry. To the south, with a battalion of Chasseurs thrown forward into the Bois des Ognons, was the Grenadier division.

So, when the Emperor took his leave at first light, the Army of the Rhine had assembled the equivalent of eleven divisions of infantry, four of cavalry, and some 340 guns and mitrailleuses on the plateau in an arc stretching from Vernéville, west through Vionville, to the fields south of Rezonville and Gravelotte. It numbered, at this hour, some 125,000 men. That was more than enough to ensure its westerly march. It was not enough to win a bitter battle. And this is why.

****

8 Despite this refusal, which can only be explained by Bazaine's bleak obsession with keeping his army 'concentrated', Ladmirault, with no other option, disobeyed orders. It was a memorable day of disobedience.

Plate 7 Looking west from Canrobert's gun-line (6 Corps). On the right the trees lining the Roman road. On the skyline the Bois de Tronville. The scene of Bredow's cavalry charge

Plate 8 The position of 6 Corps (a.m.) looking south to Rezonville

Since late on the 14th the German 5th Cavalry Division, under command of X Corps, had been reconnoitring the plateau to the north-west of Pont-à-Mousson as far as Mars-la-Tour, with patrols pushed even farther towards Doncourt. It consisted of three strong brigades and two batteries of horse artillery (12 guns), but no supporting infantry.[9] Its commander, Rheinbaben, had already shown a marked lack of resolution and initiative in the first frontier engagements. Now he had good reason to be apprehensive. His clash with Forton's leading brigade on the 15th had confirmed what he already believed — that the French withdrawal was in progress. But was Forton's cavalry the advance-guard, the rear-guard — or even a flank-guard to the main body on the more northerly route to Verdun? Rheinbaben was in no doubt. Had the enemy made good his escape, his patrols would have seen the evidence to the west of Mars-la-Tour. It is not possible to pass whole army corps and their attendant transport along a single dusty road without detection. Rightly, Rheinbaben decided that he had before him the entire Army of the Rhine, and that discretion was the better part of valour (the same idea, in reverse, had also occurred to Forton). Thus, while the latter fell back and bivouacked at Vionville, Rheinbaben kept him under observation and retired discreetly to the comparative security of the villages of Puxieux and Xonville farther south; and from there he made his report to his corps commander.

During the 15th, Voigts-Rhetz (X Corps), charged with the task of intercepting the French withdrawal to the west of Mars-la-Tour, had come forward to Thiaucourt with the leading brigade of 19th Division (Schwarzkoppen). There he received the intelligence of enemy activity to the north. His reaction was to bring on the day of battle.

Voigts-Rhetz was a Moltke-moulded general who had learned his trade with modest distinction at Sadowa. Now he found himself leading the Second Army pack across the Moselle. Behind him, to his right, Alvensleben's III Corps was pressing across the river at Novéant. Away to his left, the Guard Corps were crossing at Dieulouard on their way to the Meuse. For the moment, he was on his own.

His orders were clear: 'to push on as far as St Hilaire'. This wide sweep would carry him well to the west of Mars-la-Tour. But St Hilaire was twenty-five miles from Pont-à-Mousson. Could he arrive there in time? And what reception might he expect, with his slender resources and with no support within a day's march? Moltke's strategy was plain; and Frederick Charles had interpreted his freedom of action in the simple terms of a race to the Meuse. Of the enemy nothing was known except that he lay in considerable strength somewhere to the north.

Voigts-Rhetz had his doubts about Rheinbaben, and when on the 15th

9   At dawn on the 16th the nearest German infantry was still six miles from the Metz-Verdun road.

he received the report of the cavalry encounter near Mars-la-Tour he was unconvinced. To his tidily trained mind, it was inconceivable that the Army of the Rhine, despite the hours lost at Borny on the 14th, would not by now be at or close to Verdun — as indeed, by German march-standards, it should have been. Thus he reasoned that Forton's camp at Vionville was in fact Bazaine's rear guard. There was a simple, if reckless, way of finding out.

His chief of staff, Colonel Caprivi,[10] was not so sure. He had his own views on the competence of Bazaine and his staff, and suspected that Rheinbaben might well have caught the enemy by the nose rather than the tail. None the less, it was an unambiguous order that Caprivi took to Rheinbaben at Puxieux during the night of the 15th: to attack the French camp at Vionville at dawn the following morning.

We may remark here the striking difference between the opposing commanders. While Bazaine's order of the 15th had spoken of an 'expected enemy attack' on 2 and 6 Corps the next day — in other words, a purely defensive stance — and while his countermanding order of the 16th stood his earlier appreciation of the situation on its head, Moltke's directive of the 15th had been short and sharp: a vigorous *offensive* by Second Army against both of the escape routes to Verdun from Metz. It was, given the modest force available on the left bank of the Moselle, an ambitious decision and a potentially foolish one. But it was a *decision*. While Bazaine dealt in probabilities, Moltke was concerned only in possibilities. His sense of urgency was communicated right down to junior commanders. Bazaine scarcely troubled to communicate at all, even with his senior officers.

This delegation of responsibility lay at the heart of Moltke's concept of war. Once armies were committed, the commander-in-chief's plan stood or fell on the initiative and resolution of subordinates. We have seen how, on 6 August, the whole strategy nearly foundered at the first hurdle because of the insubordination of one Army commander and the excessive caution of another. Now Frederick Charles was given total discretion in bringing Bazaine to battle, and his order to his corps commanders reflected Moltke's sense of urgency. It also contained the seeds of disaster, for it was based on a false assumption about the enemy, and he projected his leading corps in pursuit with a flagrant disregard of any mutual support. Not until the afternoon was he aware of the crisis around Vionville on the 16th; and he did not reach the battlefield until 4 p.m., by when he should have been in time only to witness the debris of a comprehensive defeat. Instead he found the debris of a remarkable survival compounded of brilliant bluff, exceptional fortitude, and an irresolute adversary. He should have left well alone, but in an access of princely arrogance he added his own contribution by demanding of his weary men a final, futile attack at dusk on Rezonville

10 Caprivi was to succeed Bismarck as Chancellor of the new German Empire in 1890.

which was to draw from Moltke an angry verdict only marginally less caustic than that which he reserved for the conduct of Steinmetz two days later at Gravelotte.[11]

So to summarize the situation on the German side early on the 16th:

X Corps was on the march to St Hilaire with 38th Brigade of 19th Division at Thiaucourt and (a brilliant stroke, as it was to prove) the Guard Dragoon Brigade attached from Dieulouard to the south; 20th Division on the same westerly road from Pont-à-Mousson and on the march at 3.30 a.m.

III Corps lay at Novéant on the left bank of the Moselle with, under command, Colonel Lyncker's detachment from 37th Brigade of X Corps which had covered the crossing of the Moselle;[12] 6th Cavalry Division, sweeping a path to the north-west, was on the road at 4 a.m.; 6th Infantry Division (Buddenbrock) accompanied by the corps commander, Alvensleben[13] *en route* for Mars-la-Tour by way of Arnaville and Onville; 5th Infantry Division (Stuelpnagel) on the right making for Gorze up the escarpment at 7.00 a.m. III Corps had reason to believe that at best it might strike a blow at Bazaine's rearguard. It was about to receive a rude shock.

****

When Caprivi hurried to Puxieux on the night of the 15th he picked up two additional horse-artillery batteries. It was a prime example of Moltke's staff-training; and it is just possible that this modest extra muscle was enough to tilt the scale during the early hours of the 16th. At Puxieux Caprivi found a very nervous Rheinbaben who insisted that his function was only that of a reconnaissance in strength, and that a dawn attack by three regiments of Hussars, 24 guns and not even a single battalion of supporting infantry against the vanguard of an entire Army was not the received wisdom of any cavalry manual. From the swell of ground he could look down on the French camp at Vionville less than a mile away, but beyond that to the east his view was masked by the undulating plain. He could not see Rezonville, around which more than 50,000 enemy troops were bivouacked, and to the north of the main road the ground was screened by the Tronville copses. The question of a surprise attack would in fact have been an academic one if Bazaine had not countermanded his march-order of the 15th, for by dawn the Army of the Rhine should have passed Mars-la-Tour on the southerly road, and not even the thrusting Caprivi would have risked a flank-attack with the kind of small force

11 Moltke: *op. cit.*

12 Two battalions of the *78th Regiment*, two squadrons of cavalry, and a battery of artillery.

13 His elder brother commanded IV Corps far to the south between Marbache and Toul.

Plate 9   Vionville. The view from the rising ground near Tronville

Plate 10   Tronville, looking west from Forton's camp at Vionville

130

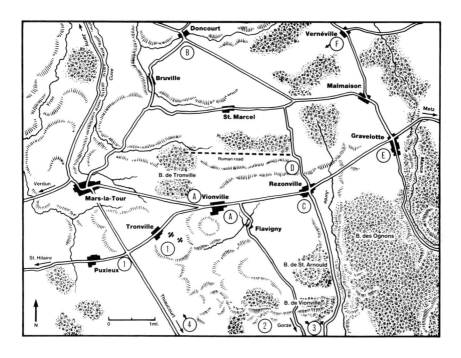

KEY

FRENCH

A. Cav. Div Forton
B. Cav. Div Barail
C. 2 Corps
D. 6 Corps
E. Imperial Guard and Bazaine's HQ
F. 3 Corps

Note
4 Corps still in the Moselle valley

GERMAN

1. 5 Cav. Div and Horse Artillery Batteries
2. 6 Cav. Div
3. 5 Inf. Div, III Corps
4. 6 Inf. Div, III Corps

Note
X Corps advancing on Thiaucourt to the south

Map 6   Situation at 9 a.m., 16 August

assembled to the south of Tronville. It was to be the first of many twists of fortune.

Rheinbaben, literally, stuck to his guns; and it was not until word reached him that Alvensleben's III Corps was on the march from Gorze and that he could expect support in some strength on his right that he agreed to move.[14] Even then he took his time, and it was not until 9.15 a.m. that his batteries opened up on the unsuspecting French camp at a range of 1200 yards and brought on the battle of Mars-la-Tour.

---

14   Rheinbaben was to be soundly — and most unfairly — criticized in the official History for not pressing the attack he had been ordered to make, and for his subsequent inaction.

****

The surprise was complete. As the first shells burst among the French tents and horse-lines, Murat's dragoons and de Grammont's cuirassiers — names resonant of former glories — broke and fled, sweeping away in their confusion the civilian baggage train which cluttered the main road behind them. It was not until the panic-stricken mob reached a safer haven beyond Rezonville that a measure of order was restored.

Emboldened by this rout, the German guns closed the range by moving down the forward slope towards Vionville. Now if ever was the classic moment for cavalry action — the pursuit of a demoralized enemy — but Rheinbaben shirked the opportunity for launching Redern's three Hussar regiments after the fugitive French, and indeed withdrew them to the west of the Tronville ridge. Thus Major Körber's batteries were left without support, and exposed to the full weight of any impending counter-attack. There in fact they stayed throughout the long day until their guns became too hot to handle and ammunition ran out, a vital buttress linking the two wings of Alvensleben's dangerously extended infantry divisions. As for Caprivi, he wisely decided to stay near Tronville and play Mephistopheles to Rheinbaben's irresolute Faust.

****

At the first sound of gunfire, Frossard stood 2 Corps to arms. The wasted hours of the 15th were now to cost him dear, not least his failure to have posted a strong force to deny enemy access through the woods and defiles to his immediate south. His subsequent excuses were particularly lame: that his third division, Laveaucoupet's, had been left behind at Metz and that his orders had been to keep his corps closely concentrated on Rezonville. Yet he had in addition under his command Lapasset's brigade group, which was to acquit itself with much distinction during the next 72 hours; and he had received no orders at all from Bazaine. In fact, he was thoroughly infected with the deadening contagion of defence which permeated the entire Army. As we shall see, throughout the battle every show of aggression by the French corps commanders was purely *defensive* in intention. The contagion stemmed from the top. At no time, despite his overwhelming superiority in numbers — infantry, cavalry and artillery — did Bazaine think in terms of victory, even though it was there for the taking until far into the afternoon. It has been said in his defence that he was burdened with the Emperor's words: 'On no account compromise the Army.' Yet that is precisely what his lack of resolution succeeded in doing. The truth is that Bazaine, swamped by responsibility, was no match for a determined, even reckless, adversary who though faced not once but four times with disaster would not accept defeat. He was a forlorn figure compounded of physical bravery and moral cowardice. And moral cowards do not win battles.

****

Frossard deployed 2 Corps thus. On his right he pushed Bataille's division forward and, despite the debris left by Forton's flight, occupied Vionville and Flavigny in the teeth of accurate artillery fire. This part of the line, already defensive in its stance, was held by Pouget's brigade, with the 12th Chasseurs in Vionville and the 23rd in Flavigny, linked by the 8th, and supported by five 4-pounder batteries. To Pouget's left was Bastoul's brigade facing south-west on open ground and with no cover or artillery support. Here the line was prolonged across the front of the Bois de Vionville and the Bois de St Arnould by Vergé's division: covered by the whole remaining divisional artillery in line of batteries, Valazé's brigade on the right, Jolivet's in the centre, and the 84th of Lapasset's brigade group astride the road from Gorze with its left resting on the Jurée ravine. The position it occupied consisted of a series of *mamelons*, or mounds, which overlooked, at a distance of nearly 1000 yards, the northern fringes of the woods and was accurately described in the official History as *un crochet défensif*. No attempt was made to block the difficult approaches. The siting of the infantry seems to have been dictated by the superior range of the chassepot rather than with any thought of giving rein to the famous *furia francese*.

The cannonade had also alerted Canrobert, although from his position north of the main road he had no view of Vionville two miles to his south-west (see Plate 7). His first awareness that serious trouble was afoot was the sight of Forton's and Valabrègue's cavalrymen galloping to the rear. His reaction was predictable. Instead of sending out reconnaissance parties to establish the situation at Vionville, he drew up his 6 Corps in a curious formation well to the rear of Frossard and facing due west along the axis of the lane running north from Rezonville (see Plate 8). On the left was Lafont's division, in the centre at the junction with the Roman road the 9th Regiment, and on the right Tixier's division towards St Marcel where, expecting to link up with Ladmirault, he was surprised to find Leboeuf. (It had not occurred to Bazaine or Jarras to inform him of the state of play in the northern exits from Metz.) The artillery was drawn up, also facing west, in the intervals between his formations.[15] The exception to this tidy phalanx was the third division of his corps, which was drawn up in the rear, but at right angles to the general line of battle and parallel to the main road. Already Bazaine's obsessive fears for his left flank were only too plain.

---

15 Most of the guns which had been left behind at Châlons were made good from Bazaine's Army reserve, including three batteries of mitrailleuses.

Such was the disposition of 6 Corps shortly before 10 a.m. It was little changed by dusk. Long before then it could and should have destroyed the entire German left wing and reopened the road to Verdun. That it did not was due to Canrobert's totally unwarranted caution, and a single and memorable gambler's throw by Alvensleben.

****

'III Corps will move on Gorze and is likely to make contact with some of the enemy tomorrow morning.' Frederick Charles's order of the 15th had been short and explicit. It had also been based on a series of false — if understandable — assumptions. During the day, cavalry patrols had scouted up the escarpment and had reported no sign of the enemy in the small, narrowly confined village of Gorze.[16] Thus Frederick Charles reasonably assumed that the absence of any cork in this vital bottleneck meant that the main body of the Army of the Rhine was well on its way to Verdun. Hence his simultaneous order to X Corps to make all haste on the more southerly road to Thiaucourt, and thence to St Hilaire.

By midnight reports coming in from Rheinbaben in the area of Mars-la-Tour were vague and inconclusive. These told of the encounter with Forton's cavalry that afternoon, but not of Voigts-Rhetz's order which Caprivi was even then carrying to Puxieux. Thus it was the general opinion at Second Army headquarters at Pont-à-Mousson that Bazaine had made good his escape, and that the best that III Corps could expect on the 16th was to intercept the tail end of the column or the rearguard of the Army of the Rhine somewhere between Rezonville and Vionville.

Alvensleben shared this view; indeed, it was not until nearly noon on the 16th that he finally realized that he was fighting the entire Army of the Rhine single-handed when, turning to his Chief of Staff, he said: 'I feel like Wellington at Waterloo. Would to God that night or X Corps would come!' So it was that at 7.00 a.m. he set III Corps in motion, not dreaming what lay in store for him.

It is appropriate to describe here the circumstances of III Corps' advance to battle. From Novéant there are two roads leading north-west to the Gravelotte plateau. As has already been remarked, both were then little more than country lanes enclosed by vineyards and thick woods. The right-hand road climbs up the escarpment for three miles to Gorze, where it divides, turning north on either side of the Bois de St Arnould and the Bois de Vionville, emerging on to the plateau some two miles south of Rezonville and Flavigny. The left-hand road runs due west from Novéant, climbing even more steeply. At Onville it turns north-west, crossing the plateau in a straight line to Mars-la-Tour. Thus it will be seen that these

---

16   At Bazaine's trial the Mayor of Gorze insisted that he had sent word to Frossard on the 15th of the presence of strong German patrols in the village.

roads closely bracket the 'morning' battlefield.

III Corps[17] — two infantry divisions with Lyncker's detachment, one cavalry division (6th), 90 guns, supply train, and ambulances, a total of some 30,000 men (and women) — moved as follows.

On the right-hand road to Gorze, 6th Cavalry Division; Stuelpnagel's 5th Infantry Division (9th and 10th Brigades); and Lyncker's detachment. Here, after a bare half-hour's halt, 9th Brigade and Lyncker took the Rezonville road, while, with cavalry and artillery leading, 10th Brigade headed for Flavigny.

On the left-hand road to Onville, with divisional and corps artillery in the van, Buddenbrock's 6th Infantry Division (11th and 12th Brigades). Moving on the outer arc of the advance, this column had a longer and even more exhausting march to make. Its objective was Mars-la-Tour. It never got there; for by 11 a.m. both artillery and infantry were fighting for their lives.

****

The approach-march of III Corps in the early hours of the 16th was an extraordinary achievement, part good planning, part improvisation, even if it was made possible by Frossard's failure to take the most elementary precautions. Alvensleben was not to know this. It has to be remembered that in August 1870 communications on a line of advance were only as fast as a galloping horse and as accurate as the information carried by the rider.[18] Here at least the initiative and training of junior cavalry officers on the German side serves only to emphasize the shortcomings of the French. '*Les reconnaissances doivent se faire comme d'habitude.*' In projecting his corps up a series of blind alleys, Alvensleben was taking a fearful risk, for which he was to pay a fearful price. But because his opponent was Bazaine, he was in luck. Napoleon Bonaparte once said that he liked lucky generals. He would greatly have approved of Konstantin von Alvensleben.

There is no evidence that Alvensleben knew of the timing — or indeed the intention — of Rheinbaben's cannonade at 9.15 a.m. In any event III Corps had already been set in motion two hours earlier and seven miles away. Mars-la-Tour is a classic example of an 'encounter' battle, largely unforeseen, entirely instinctive. There was no tidy co-ordination, no carefully prepared battle-plan. Within hours, if not minutes, it had degenerated into a bloody slogging-match, sustained on one side by a fatal lack of resolution and on the other by outrageous bluff. Yet lest it be thought that Moltke and his generals had a monopoly of wisdom, it must

17 This corps was raised and garrisoned in the province of Brandenburg.

18 Frederick Charles at his headquarters ten miles away at Pont-à-Mousson was not even aware of the desperate battle at Vionville until 12.30 p.m. Royal Headquarters twelve miles farther back at Herny did not receive the news until evening.

be remembered that two days later when, for the first time in the whole campaign, two German Armies were launched upon a deliberate 'set-piece' attack, they came close to disaster because of impatience, insubordination, and a flagrant disregard of the military unities of time and space.

****

Shortly after 9.45 a.m. 6th Cavalry Division, sweeping a path ahead of III Corps, emerged on to the lower slopes of the plateau near the Bois de Vionville. If Alvensleben had supposed that he was chasing Bazaine's shadow he quickly discovered that he had struck an obstacle of some substance; for as his horsemen broke cover they were received with a violent storm of shot and shell from Vergé's division deployed along the ridge south of Rezonville (see Plate 5). In some disarray they withdrew hastily to the cover of the Gaumont copse to the west of the Flavigny road.[19]

It was 10 a.m. Three miles away at Tronville, Rheinbaben's 24 guns were pinning down Pouget's brigade at Vionville and Flavigny. Less than 1000 yards separated the two sides. The reader may well wonder why 2000 riflemen with artillery support were unable to overwhelm four enemy batteries without cover or infantry assistance — the more so when, four hours later, in a dramatic *coup de main* 800 German horsemen overrode the gun-line and infantry of an entire French army corps. To answer this question is to explain the whole course of the day's action. On the French side the occupation of Vionville and Flavigny by Pouget's brigade was a purely defensive reflex, as when in a dark alley a man raises his arm to ward off a blow from some unseen assailant. Frossard had received Bazaine's countermanding order of the 16th; but he was also aware of the previous order of the 15th which had spoken of the likely presence of '30,000 men' facing him. Having secured the two villages and the fields south of Rezonville, he stood fast. His not to reason why.

On the German side it was the artillery which began, sustained, and ended the day. By evening 210 guns were in action stretching from Mars-la-Tour to the Bois de St Arnould, and during ten hours fired nearly 22,000 rounds of ammunition. Certainly during the morning, when III Corps stood in greatest peril with all its infantry committed and no reinforcements at hand, Alvensleben's batteries pressed forward into the line itself and drove back the divisions of Bataille and Vergé. They drew from Canrobert the apt and admiring description of *'tirailleurs d'artillerie'* — 'skirmisher guns'. Bitter though the infantry fight was, and dramatic the

19   6th Cavalry Division consisted of only 18 squadrons, compared with the 36 of 5th Cavalry Division. It took little subsequent part in the battle, and then to small purpose and at great cost.

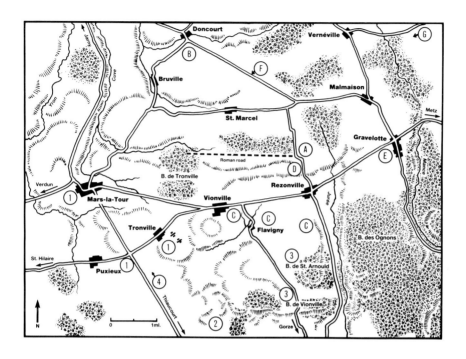

KEY

FRENCH		GERMAN	
A.	Cav. Div Forton	1.	5 Cav. Div and Horse Artillery Batteries
B.	Cav. Div Barail	2.	6 Cav. Div
C.	2 Corps	3.	5 Inf. Div
D.	6 Corps	4.	6 Inf. Div
E.	Imperial Guard and Bazaine's HQ		
F.	3 Corps		
G.	4 Corps, approaching Vernéville		

Map 7   Situation at 10 a.m., 16 August

cavalry clashes, Mars-la-Tour is memorable above all for the brilliant handling and deadly efficiency of the German artillery.

****

So it was that when 6th Cavalry Division hastily withdrew to the nearest cover shortly after 10 a.m., Stuelpnagel pushed forward his whole divisional artillery of 24 guns into the north-west angle of the Bois de Vionville, while Doering's 9th Brigade and Schwerin's 10th worked their way, company by company, through the thick undergrowth, only to be met by heavy chassepot fire far beyond the range of their own needle-guns as they struggled to get a foothold on the bare slope beyond the woods. The

48th managed to reach the Flavigny road but was driven back in disorder by a French counter-attack, the second battalion alone losing all its officers and more than 600 men in the space of fifteen minutes. Here too the brigade commander, Doering, was killed. At this moment a concerted effort by Frossard would have thrown Stuelpnagel's division back into the Gorze defiles. But Frossard received neither orders nor support from Bazaine, and he was not, as he had already shown at Spicheren, a man for bold decisions. As Stuelpnagel's infantry came piecemeal into action, it was met not by a single co-ordinated blow from the commanding position on the Rezonville ridge[20] but by a series of violent sorties and limited counter-punches. And despite savage casualties the German infantry not only held on, but even managed to gain ground towards the ridge running south-east from Flavigny.[21] It was to prove a vital success, and it was made possible (for neither the first nor the last time) by the German artillery.

Against the tightly grouped guns of 5th Infantry Division, Vergé had deployed six batteries of 4-pounders and 8-pounders and two of mitrailleuses on the bare slopes above the woods, but, constantly driven to shift their positions, they were no match for the German breech-loaders. 'Alone', says one French account, 'these batteries maintained the German position during the first two hours by their technical, if not their numerical, superiority.' In particular, they demonstrated the greater destructive effect of the percussion-fuse against the random and inaccurate air-bursts of the French.[22]

The pattern of ebb and flow continued throughout the first hour on the right flank. Most German — and English — accounts of the fighting suggest that 5th Infantry Division succeeded in gaining the high ground overlooking the Bois de Vionville and the Bois de St Arnould. For example: 'Stuelpnagel's division was now solidly established upon the most commanding uplands in that part of the field';[23] and: 'A brisk engagement ensued ending with the retreat of the French to Rezonville.'[24] This is not so. Until nearly 11 a.m. the German infantry was repeatedly driven back to the comparative safety of the woods, and as we have seen, was only sustained by the steadfastness of its artillery. The sombre evidence is there today in the cluster of German memorials which stand near the *western* edge of the Bois de Vionville. The monument closest to Rezonville, 1000 yards south of the village, is that of the *11th Grenadiers*, the *Leib-Grenadier Regiment*, of IX Corps which did not enter the battle until 5 p.m Indeed, at that point Lapasset's brigade held its original ground on the

20 At its highest point this ridge is no more than fifty feet above the village.

21 During the fighting on the 16th, III Corps alone lost 310 officers and 6744 men.

22 The artillery of the BEF in 1914 was to be at the same disadvantage.

23 Hooper: *The Campaign of Sedan.*

24 Borbstädt and Dwyer: *The Franco-German War to the catastrophe of Sedan.*

extreme left of the French position until dark. The withdrawal of Vergé's division and its replacement by the Grenadier division of the Imperial Guard about noon was the result of the collapse of Frossard's right wing at Vionville. And it is there that the centre of the action now moves.

****

It will be remembered that 6th Infantry Division, accompanied by Alvensleben and led by the corps artillery, had left Novéant at dawn on the southerly road up the escarpment by Arnaville and Onville. On a morning of burning heat, it was to be the first of many remarkable feats of endurance by German infantrymen during this long day.

The objective of this column was Mars-la-Tour, even, if necessary, Jarny on the northerly road from Gravelotte to Verdun; and by 9.30 a.m. the head had emerged from the defile near the village of Buxières. There it halted briefly. Two miles to the north-east 5th Infantry Division was just coming into action.

Alvensleben's orders were clear: to make all haste to intercept the retreat of the enemy on the Verdun road, and his order of march had been carefully planned to that end. When the noise of battle was heard from the Rezonville plateau he resisted a commander's instinct to march to the sound of the guns. Instead, he at once deployed the whole of his corps artillery and that of Buddenbrock's division along the shallow ridge running south and south-east of Flavigny (see Plate 11), so that by 11 a.m. Frossard's positions were ringed by a great arc of 105 guns stretching from the Tronville copses to the Bois de Vionville. It was a brilliant stroke, for without this circle of steel it is as certain as any military hypothesis can be that III Corps would have been swept away, long before X Corps could reach the battlefield during the afternoon.

Leaving Buddenbrock to march his division up the long, straight, sunburnt road to Mars-la-Tour, Alvensleben rode on ahead towards Tronville, where he met Rheinbaben and the watchful Caprivi. It was beginning to dawn on him that this was not the expected rearguard action, although he was not yet prepared to accept the full implications of Rheinbaben's certainty that before them lay the entire Army of the Rhine.[25]

If that were so, the only way of avoiding disaster was to give the French the impression that they were at grips with the entire German army; and that could only be done by an attack which would make up in boldness what it lacked in material strength. Few decisions on the

25 Caprivi, who had watched the deployment of Bataille's division in Vionville and Flavigny, had already guessed the truth, and had sent an urgent warning to Voigts-Rhetz at Thiaucourt.

Plate 11 The 'amphitheatre' on which Alvensleben deployed the guns of III Corps

battlefield can have been harder to take, more rapidly taken, and so completely justified.[26]

It was the first of a series of gigantic bluffs, not one of which was called by Bazaine throughout the day of battle. And accordingly Buddenbrock's march on Mars-la-Tour was halted at Tronville, and 6th Division was ordered to wheel to the east and launch a frontal attack on Vionville and Flavigny. The time was 11 a.m.

****

Meanwhile at Gravelotte ... When, five miles away, the German guns began to fire Bazaine was at breakfast — scrambled eggs and coffee. From the conflicting evidence of his two orders of the 15th and 16th, and from the three entirely different versions which he was to give in his published accounts and at his trial, it is impossible to know what his real intention was at that moment. Ever since he took command on the 12th he had been given a single option, but by the 16th he had decided on another. One was called Verdun; the other, Metz. In the immediate aftermath of defeat he was savagely arraigned by his numerous enemies for choosing 'the traitor's course'. But writing in 1904, General Bonnal, a highly professional critic — assessing Bazaine's conduct in purely military terms rather than with

26 Howard: *The Franco-Prussian War.*

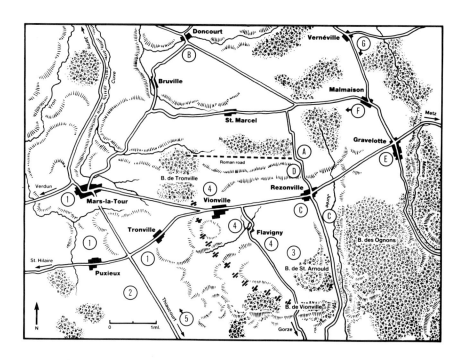

KEY

FRENCH	GERMAN

FRENCH

A. Cav. Div Forton
B. Cav. Div Barail
C. 2 Corps, driven out of Vionville and Flavigny
D. 6 Corps
E. Imperial Guard and Bazaine's HQ
F. 3 Corps
G. 4 Corps

GERMAN

1. 5 Cav. Div
2. 6 Cav. Div
3. 5 Inf. Div
4. 6 Inf. Div
5. 37 Inf. Bde, 20 Div, X Corps

Note
III Corps Artillery deployed between Bois de Vionville
and Bois de Tronville

Map 8   Situation at 11 a.m., 16 August

political animosity — said: 'Marshal Bazaine's solution was the only wise one, given the inadequacy of the high command and the waste of time between 7 August and 12.'[27] And that, given the situation which he inherited, disaster was *sooner or later* inevitable. The tragedy is that, obsessed with avoiding defeat, he was blind to a beckoning victory.

Breakfast finished, Bazaine addressed himself without undue haste to the matter in hand. The situation in which he found himself was not originally of his own making. The irreparable damage had been done long before the declaration of war, and for that the politicians — and in particular Leboeuf — had been to blame. It had been compounded by the Emperor's lack of authority, by administrative incompetence, by precious

27   Bonnal: *L'esprit de la guerre moderne: La Manoeuvre de Saint Privat.*

time critically wasted, and by MacMahon's defection and flight after Wörth. Now, however, it was too late for *arrière-pensées*, and much too early for inquests. Napoleon and MacMahon were a hundred miles away at Châlons. The eyes of France were on *'notre glorieux Bazaine'*. He was about to cover himself with something less than glory.

Bazaine's first reaction was to bind himself to his fortress base of Metz with a stout lifeline, apply a padlock, and throw away the key. During the rest of the day his chief contribution to a battle which should never have happened was to add padlock after padlock to an already secure back door, while refusing to march decisively forward across a thinly obstructed threshold.

A battle which should not have happened? If in accordance with his order of the 15th Bazaine had set the Army of the Rhine in motion at 4.30 a.m., using Forton's cavalry division and Frossard's corps as a strong flank-guard and moving, as the Germans later did, by every available road or even across country, he would have had a four-hour start over Frederick Charles, his sole obstruction Rheinbaben's dispersed cavalry, the nearest enemy infantry eight miles away; and even allowing for indifferent march discipline and administrative incompetence he must have been half-way to Verdun by 10 a.m. That, as we know, was certainly the view at Second Army headquarters.

But it did not happen. Now Bazaine's first action was revealing. It was an order to Bourbaki to stand the Imperial Guard to arms at Gravelotte, facing south to watch the defiles leading from the Moselle valley nearest to Metz. It was his first padlock. Then at 10 a.m. he rode forward to Rezonville.

There he met Frossard and Canrobert, and witnessed the distasteful sight of fugitives streaming back from Vionville. The three men had one thing in common. None of them had any clear idea of the strength of the enemy, or of the thrust of his developing attack, although it could not have required much imagination to assume that, after the inconclusive engagement on the 14th, Moltke's strategic plan would be to use his Third Army to drive the retreating MacMahon across the Meuse and away from Metz, and to launch his Second Army across the Moselle to intercept Bazaine on the road to Verdun. But Bazaine's limited grasp of the situation did not extend to such simple logic. Curiously, in his order of the 15th he had come quite close to guessing the force that Alvensleben could bring to bear the following morning on the Verdun road, although it is clear that he had no knowledge of the movements of X Corps farther south, or — and this was to prove crucial — of the dangerous dispersal of the rest of Frederick Charles's Army. Had he paused to measure his own strength against that of his adversary, and had he been gifted with the *coup d'œil* that is the mark of every great commander, he might well have rejoiced in the prospect of destroying his adversary in detail. But as we have seen — and as we shall see again and again — he was a prisoner of his own conviction. By the early hours of the 16th he was concerned with the security of his base; and his every subsequent action (or, more often, inaction) only reinforced — in every sense — his obsession with Metz.

Now he had to take some decisions. Frossard had already manned — however belatedly — the defensive positions to the south and west of Rezonville. Bazaine was content to leave the protection of that flank to so celebrated an apostle of the doctrine of defence, even if after Bazaine's failure to support him at Spicheren Frossard's confidence in his chief was some way short of mutual. Besides, as he loudly complained now and later, his third division, Laveaucoupet's, had been left behind to garrison the fortress. At Bazaine's trial he was to advance this as the main reason for the partial collapse of 2 Corps during the forenoon.

North of the road Canrobert had deployed 6 Corps facing west, although Bazaine told him not to move his reserve division, Sorval's, already drawn up parallel to the highway watching the left flank — the first, in fact, of Bazaine's extra padlocks designed to protect his communications with Metz.[28] As a *quid pro quo*, however, he called forward seven batteries of the Army reserve at Gravelotte, including three of 12-pounders, to make good the missing corps artillery which Canrobert had been obliged to leave behind at Châlons, and these were presently deployed to extend the gun-line of 6 Corps along the Roman road (see Plate 7). Beyond that, Bazaine gave Canrobert no orders. 'He was ten years my senior,' he said at his trial. On such laughable lip-service to protocol the Army of the Rhine was arrayed for battle. And Canrobert — the brave and beloved veteran Marshal who only four days earlier had declined to risk his reputation — assumed a posture of masterly inactivity while little more than a mile away a thin line of German guns, alone and unsupported, laid waste to Vionville. How different the reckless resolution of the junior colonel, Caprivi, in imposing *his* commander's will on the irresolute Rheinbaben at Tronville.

From Rezonville, Bazaine rode on towards St Marcel where 3 Corps was by now largely assembled (the fourth division, Metman's, did not reach the battlefield until after dark, in time to cover the eastward withdrawal of the Army on the 17th). Here he met Leboeuf, whose earlier intervention, according to Bazaine, had led to the postponement of the westward march until the afternoon. Now, with the same deadly deference to rank and status, he 'suggested' ('invited' was the word Leboeuf used at the trial) that 3 Corps should pivot on its left and, by extending Canrobert's right wing along the Roman road, help 'to clear the Prussians from your front'. At that hour there were no Prussians to the north of the main road; and by the time there were Bazaine had sent a laconic message to Leboeuf telling him

---

28 Sorval's division, although perfectly positioned to give offensive support to both Frossard and Canrobert, took no part in the fighting until late in the evening.

that there was no hurry because Ladmirault's 4 Corps[29] was not yet in position to complete the encircling movement from the direction of Bruville. Leboeuf should therefore not have been surprised when, towards 1 p.m., Bazaine suddenly decided to remove one of his divisions, Montaudon's, from the Roman road, and place it in the depression which runs between Gravelotte and Rezonville. It was the second additional padlock to seal the southern flank, and its movement across an area already thick with disorganized units and scattered transport only confounded an already serious confusion. 'It added to our population as well as our problems,' was the wry comment of an Engineer officer.

Bazaine did not return to Rezonville until after 11 a.m., by when battle had been joined in earnest.[30] Now he was in his element, brave as a lion, encouraging his men — '*Allons, mes enfants, suivez votre maréchal!*' — ordering the drums to beat, oblivious of his scattered and bewildered staff, for all the world as if he were back in the African desert rather than on the sunburnt uplands of his native Lorraine, where the fate of France was in his faltering hands. It might almost be true to say that, for the first and only time in the campaign, he was enjoying himself (the wound of which he had complained to the Emperor the previous day was now forgotten); and there is more than a hint of pity in the comment of his most dedicated critic:

> He involved himself in every detail, siting individual batteries here and there, showing battalions the positions which each should occupy. He was everywhere, not sparing himself for a moment, but entirely confusing his responsibility as a commander-in-chief with the more modest duties of a general or even an ordinary [*simple*] colonel.[31]

The fault in Bazaine was not in his stars, but in himself; that, called to be an overlord, he could not escape being an underling.

****

We left Buddenbrock's 6th Infantry Division marching on Mars-la-Tour. Alvensleben had ridden on ahead, and on reaching Tronville he could have been left in no doubt that the French 'rearguard', if such it was, posed at least as great a threat to Frederick Charles's reconnaissance in strength as did the widely dispersed Second Army to an enemy determined on

29 No orders were sent to Ladmirault, then on the march from the Moselle valley. 'I trusted', said Bazaine, 'to his experience to bring his corps into line *au son des canons*'.

30 'His prolonged absence was the reason why 6 Corps hesitated to attack in strength, awaiting orders which never came.' See Canrobert's craven evidence, *Procès Bazaine*.

31 D'Andlau: *Metz: op. cit.*

reaching Verdun. That the enemy had no such resolute intention he could neither know nor even suppose. The situation, as he later reflected, was this.

His orders had been simple — and hazardous: to march III Corps to the north-west and to intercept and arrest as large a part of the Army of the Rhine as he could bring to battle. He had no protection on his right, where Steinmetz's First Army was still on the far bank of the Moselle. On his left flank was X Corps, moving on a westerly track, four hours of marching-time distant. Of his two infantry divisions, one was fully committed, and held fast on the approaches to Rezonville. His corps artillery (with brilliant foresight) had been deployed on the long ridge south of Flavigny.[32] His two available cavalry divisions were covering the flank of 6th Infantry Division's approach-march, with one brigade (Barby's) detached to the west of Mars-la-Tour. Thus by 11 a.m. III Corps was strung out along a front of four miles while somewhere — certainly to the east, and probably to the north — lay the enemy he was seeking to intercept. There was no going back.

From the rising ground where Körber's batteries were maintaining the fire-fight with Bataille's division in Vionville and Flavigny, Alvensleben could see nothing beyond the immediate smoke and flame of battle which, with the rolling plateau, concealed not only Rezonville but also Canrobert's corps to the north of the main road. But he could see enough to convince him that Mars-la-Tour was no longer a valid option, should the enemy commit what now seemed likely to be most of, if not all, his strength to a determined attack. If the escape route were to be cut, then it must be cut here and now, at Vionville.[33] And so he took a desperate decision.

'I had', wrote Alvensleben later, 'to take the battle area for better or for worse as I found it and make "the most of it" [*he used the English phrase*]. This meant that I had to match the physical inferiority of my numbers by the moral superiority of my offensive action.'[34] As the head of Buddenbrock's division reached Vionville it was given the order to halt and, forming front to the east, to attack and capture the two enemy-occupied villages and thus secure the main road. If the decision was daring, its execution was a formidable tribute to German battle-training. The men of 6th Division had been on the march for six hours under a burning sun. There was no pause for rest, refreshment, or reconnaissance. 'I had no time to waste,' explained Alvensleben, 'since time was my only advantage.' So 6th Division, as it came up the long, dusty road supported by the great arc of guns, wheeled inward and into battle.

32 See also footnote on p. 113.

33 Thus, and rightly, the Germans call this day of battle 'Vionville'.

34 Moltke (*op. cit*) was to add a tribute of his own: '(Until the early afternoon) General von Alvensleben deceived the enemy with regard to the slenderness of his force by acting incessantly on the offensive.'

It was deployed thus, right to left: 11th Brigade (*20th* and *35th*) attacked from the south-west; 12th Brigade (*24th* and *64th*) with two batteries crossed the road north of Tronville and launched three battalions in a turning movement on Vionville. For the first and only time that day, the Germans — if only on the narrowest of frontages — had a notional superiority of numbers. They made remarkable use of it during the brief hour that it lasted.

Except in the context of Bazaine's obsession with his own left flank and his doubtful intention of prosecuting his westward march, it is not easy to understand why Alvensleben was able to bring off so spectacular a bluff. For one answer at least, we must turn to Canrobert.

Since the evening of the 15th, 6 Corps had bivouacked to the north of Rezonville awaiting the resumption of the withdrawal at first light and seemingly unconcerned at the prospect of serious business the next day, as Bazaine's warning order had suggested. South of the main road — and therefore in the immediate path of any enemy thrust from the Moselle valley — lay 2 Corps. Neither commander consulted with the other. They might, a road apart, as well have been on different planets.[35]

When Rheinbaben's guns opened up at 9.15 a.m. Frossard, as we have seen, was quick to occupy Vionville and Flavigny and the ground overlooking the approaches from Gorze. Canrobert's reaction was slow, and cautious to the point of absurdity. The precipitate flight of Forton's and Valabrègue's cavalry divisions was enough to convince him that Bazaine had been right and that the Germans already lay in considerable strength to the west. He made no attempt to find out. Had he pushed even one of his divisions forward on Frossard's right, Körber's batteries and their sole support, Redern's cavalry brigade, could not have stood their ground. A further advance to Tronville, and Alvensleben's precarious flank would have been turned.

Instead, Canrobert, with little urgency and less justification, deployed his corps facing west along the saddleback running north from Rezonville to the Roman road and thence towards Leboeuf at St Marcel, with his left thrown back along the road to Gravelotte, consoling himself that Frossard had no monopoly in the choice of *positions magnifiques*. How wrong he was we shall presently see, for he had reckoned without Alvensleben's resolution — and gambler's luck. Thus when Bataille's division occupied Vionville and Flavigny, 6 Corps lay more than a mile to its rear, without any mutual support or visual contact, waiting incuriously for Leboeuf — with even greater deliberation — to bring 3 Corps into line on its right. Not for almost four hours did Canrobert seriously attempt to fill the vacuum on the German left, apart from the ill-concerted use of artillery and

35 The original march-plan for the 15th — such as it was — assumed the following positions at midnight: Forton's cavalry division at Mars-la-Tour; Frossard's corps at Vionville; Canrobert's at Rezonville.

long-range chassepot fire. During that time Alvensleben, with four divisions facing him, could only count on his devoted gunners; and on two brigades of infantry masquerading as a mass of manœuvre. There can be few more singular examples in war of a nut being used so improbably to crack a sledgehammer, or of the primacy of nerve over numbers. Two days later Canrobert was to win renown for his brave, if doomed, defence of St Privat. On the 16th he had nothing to be proud of.

****

Buddenbrock's attack was directed first against Vionville, weakly held by a single battalion of Pouget's brigade (12th Chasseurs)[36], and by three 4-pounder batteries which were soon forced to shift their ground under heavy German artillery fire. South of the road one battalion of the *35th* struck in from Tronville, while on its right a second battalion advanced towards the village graveyard and the tree-girt pond where only two hours earlier Forton's troopers had unwarily taken their horses to water. North of the road and covered by a single battery, the *64th*, in close column, was sent forward in a turning movement. The battle to slam the door in Bazaine's face had been joined.

****

III Corps was now committed beyond the point of no return. That Vionville, the key to the door, was held by only one of Bataille's seven battalions is sufficient commentary on the confusion caused by Bazaine's abrupt *volte-face* after Napoleon's dawn departure. But this Alvensleben could not know. His ring of guns might or might not create the impression that it masked a great and growing assembly of arms. In the dead ground to the west of the Flavigny ridge four cavalry brigades provided his only mobile reserve (they were not long kept idle). Yet here, on his open left flank, his sole infantry resources were the twelve battalions of Buddenbrock's division. Somehow, since he could expect little succour from the south for several hours, this force had to be both hammered home and husbanded; deception without courting disaster. Thus, while Alvensleben pressed forward on Vionville, he held back two battalions of the *20th* in reserve at Tronville and then, as a brilliant improvisation, pushed the *24th* of 12th Brigade into the unoccupied copses north of the road, inviting the attention of Canrobert's artillery (then slowly coming into action along the line of the Roman road). Canrobert, believing that this hazardous extension of the German front signalled the arrival of new masses, took the bait and held his ample infantry back. When, two hours later, he

36 Frossard later claimed that Vionville was Canrobert's responsibility, but see footnote on p. 146.

Plate 12   Flavigny, looking south from the main road

summoned up the courage of his faint convictions, he was taught a short, sharp lesson in the virtues of bravery matched by bravado.

The fight for Vionville and Flavigny was brief and exceedingly bloody. As has been remarked, it was here for the only time throughout the long day that the Germans achieved — when they most needed it — a physical superiority which they were not to enjoy again. There can be no argument that if Alvensleben had not succeeded in winning — and holding — the two villages, III Corps must, even in spite of Bazaine, have been swept away by the tidal flood that was already threatening its left flank long before help could reach it from the south.

The battle was dictated as much by quality as by quantity. Against Pouget's chassepots and mitrailleuses, the needle-guns of 6th Division, outranged by more than 500 yards, could not come to grips; not unless the German artillery could, in the words of the official History, 'beat a path for the infantry'. And this the artillery now did, the men dragging their guns down the forward slope under a hail of bullets which cut great swathes in their ranks (in ten minutes the second battalion of the *35th* lost all its officers and over four hundred men). Pouget's Chasseurs fought with great courage, but overwhelmed by the crushing weight of shells from more than fifty guns, the survivors were slowly driven back on Rezonville. By 11.30 Vionville was in German hands. The road was cut.

To the south a still more bitter battle raged around Flavigny, for here the French lay in greater strength and the German infantry, attacking across a thousand yards of open fields, suffered appalling casualties. Yet once again

148

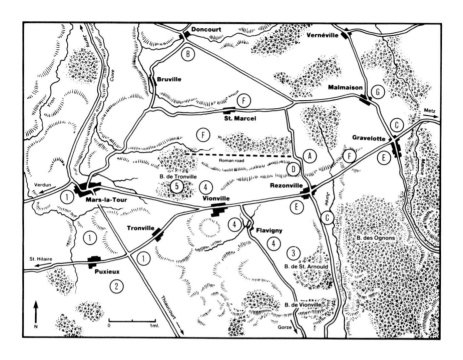

KEY

FRENCH

A. Cav. Div Forton
B. Cav. Div Barail
C. 2 Corps, withdrawn but with Lapasset's brigade still south of Rezonville
D. 6 Corps
E. Imperial Guard, with Picard's division now covering Rezonville
F. 3 Corps
G. 4 Corps

GERMAN

1. 5 Cav. Div
2. 6 Cav. Div
3. 5 Inf. Div
4. 6 Inf. Div
5. 37 Inf. Bde

Note
III Corps Artillery as in Map 8

Note
Montaudon's division of 3 Corps now deployed between Rezonville and Gravelotte

Map 9   Situation at noon, 16 August

it was Alvensleben's incomparable artillery which battered down the door while the Brandenburgers, using every fold in the ground, worked their way forward, first to within rifle range and then, as the *52nd* of Stuelpnagel's division struck in on their right, to the bayonet point. 'It was', wrote an eye-witness, 'a dreadful sight. Within minutes the village had been reduced to a blazing rubble, the flames reflected in the billowing smoke through which stampeded herds of terrified cattle.'[37] When that evening quiet descended on the battlefield the dead and wounded of both sides lay 'stacked in ramparts' in the ruins of Flavigny.

37   Many villagers had earlier sought refuge in Metz. The fate of those who remained is not recorded.

149

******

It was nearly noon. At long last Canrobert had deployed the reserve artillery along the line of the Roman road and was pounding the German left on either side of Vionville; and dust clouds to the north marked the leisurely arrival of Leboeuf with the infantry divisions of Nayral and Aymard, covered by Clérambault's cavalry towards Bruville, and supported by fifteen batteries. Alvensleben, bluffing it out, had sent his only reserve, the two battalions of the *20th*, into the Tronville copses. And it is a measure of his resolute approach that he answered Canrobert's defensive cannonade with a show of strength. To sit tight in Vionville and Flavigny was to invite destruction. To sit tight in Vionville and Flavigny was to invite a flood-tide which would sweep away the whole of III Corps. 'The only way that we could hold what we had won', he wrote, 'was to press forward'.[38] He pressed forward — and as he did so, a gleam of light appeared on the horizon.

We left X Corps marching by way of Thiaucourt to intercept the French on the Verdun road. During the 15th, the 19th Division had crossed the Moselle at Pont-à-Mousson and was heading west to the Meuse. Leading the division was Colonel Lehmann's 37th Brigade (*78th* and *91st*) less two battalions under Colonel Lyncker which had joined Stuelpnagel the previous evening at Novéant and were now hotly engaged on the forest fringes above Gorze.

Lehmann's action was in striking contrast to the doubt and indecision on the other side of the hill. Alerted by the sound of battle to the north and by an urgent message from Caprivi, he at once turned aside and, accompanied by two squadrons of hussars and one heavy battery, marched his four remaining battalions to the crossroads east of Puxieux where he reported himself to Alvensleben.

Alvensleben had three options: to use this small but precious access of numbers as a reserve to replace the fully committed *20th*; to thicken the ravaged ranks of Buddenbrock's infantry beyond Vionville and Flavigny; or to counter the growing threat to his left flank by securing the Tronville copses before Leboeuf's 3 Corps had completed its infinitely delayed change of front.[39] Alvensleben made a quick decision. With the whole of III Corps stretched in one line from the Bois de St Arnould to beyond the Verdun road, he could not afford the luxury of a reserve; beyond the two

---

38   Alvensleben was later to write that at this first crisis in the battle, he intended to fight his way back along the Verdun road. 'Bazaine might beat me, but he would not be rid of me for a long time.'

39   The reader should recall that Bazaine had advised Leboeuf that this change of front could be conducted 'at leisure' until Ladmirault's 4 Corps, now arriving on the plateau, was ready to extend the line still farther to the west. While this stately minuet was being conducted, Bazaine had no fewer than *seven* infantry divisions within two miles north of Vionville, not one of which was committed during the 'morning battle' when all that stood between them and victory was half an army corps.

villages, Buddenbrock's men were holding their ground while Bataille's division began to disintegrate under the ceaseless pounding of the guns; the fate not only of III Corps but, increasingly, of the entire Second Army lay on his left, and so, pinning his faith to offensive action, he bluffed once more and fed Lehmann's battalions into the Tronville copses. It was a desperate — but not, as we shall see, a final — gamble.

****

It was nearly noon. Bazaine had not long been in Rezonville but already it was clear that despite his massive superiority, his least intention was to match Alvensleben's resolute aggression.

> He never for a moment thought of *defeating* the Germans. He made no attempt even to clear the Verdun road, which Alvensleben's capture of Vionville had closed. Instead, he was obsessed with the danger to his left flank — with a possible thrust which would cut him off from Metz ... So on the 16th Bazaine devoted his entire energies to safeguarding his communications [with the fortress]; ignoring his right flank where victory might have been cheaply won.[40]

Instead, against every probability, it was the French centre which now found itself under threat. Bataille was dead, and the entire right wing of 2 Corps was at breaking-point. This, if ever, was the moment for 6 Corps to strike in on the German flank. Canrobert waited passively for the order to commit his infantry. The order never came; and France's senior and most respected Marshal stood idly by.

Without infantry support, Frossard turned to the line of last resort, the cavalry. All he had at hand[41] was the Lancer regiment (3rd) of Lapasset's brigade group. A half-hearted attempt to mount an attack on the German line foundered immediately, and Frossard was on the point of ordering a general retreat when Bazaine decided to intervene. From his exposed position in the forefront at Rezonville, he could see the repulse of the Lancers and the ebbing tide of Frossard's infantry. It did not occur to him to counter the threat by summoning Canrobert. In his despatch of 22 August (from Metz) he was to write: 'Keeping his positions a little in rear of the crests [*sic*] Marshal Canrobert had arrested the offensive movement of the enemy [*sic*].' A commander who could believe that could believe anything, for what then was causing the collapse of 2 Corps?

Instead — like MacMahon at Morsbronn — Bazaine resorted to a

---

40 Howard: *op. cit.*

41 Frossard's own cavalry division, Valabrègue's, had fled in disorder at the first cannonade, and now was assembled two miles away to the north of Rezonville.

Plate 13 Memorial to the 52nd Brandenburg Infantry Regiment near Vionville. 'On 16 August 1870 the Regiment lost 52 officers and 1002 men killed and wounded'

desperate remedy. 'It is absolutely necessary to stop them. We must sacrifice a regiment.' Whether true or not, the words have the authentic ring of Bazaine's voice, and of a mind obsessed by the spectre of defeat and of a phantom enemy pressing upon him in overwhelming numbers.

Bazaine's sacrificial lamb was the Cuirassier regiment of the Imperial Guard. It was not the most obvious instrument to launch against resolute infantry armed with the needle-gun,[42] but the brigade commander, de Preuil, in the heroic tradition of another Napoleonic army, formed his squadrons into three lines dressed with parade-ground precision, and with drawn sabres and cries of 'Vive l'Empereur!' charged down across a thousand yards of ground covered with the debris of battle against the remnants of a battalion of the *52nd* drawn up to the east of Flavigny.[43] The German infantry, with perfect discipline, held their fire until the leading rank was within a hundred yards. A single volley stopped the Cuirassiers in their tracks, and the mass of fallen men and horses threw the following squadrons into total disorder, while the German infantry continued to fire into the milling crowd of horsemen. Not one man succeeded in charging home. 'All that remained for the survivors was to extricate themselves from the wreckage and to rally as best they could behind their own infantry

42 But *see* p. 35.

43 This regiment, from Stuelpnagel's 5th Division, had earlier joined hands with Buddenbrock's 11th Brigade in storming the village.

in front of Rezonville.'[44] The regiment had ridden into action 47 officers and 651 men strong. It left on the field 22 officers and 243 men and horses. The only wonder is that the casualties were not even greater. It had been a futile sacrifice.

But the rout of the Cuirassiers provided Alvensleben with yet another chance to demonstrate his offensive spirit, for here was a classic cavalry situation — the pursuit of a disordered enemy. As the French squadrons struggled back to the safety of their own lines, he released the 11th and 17th Hussars of Redern's brigade, and this eager hunting pack went close to cornering a very unexpected fox; for, galloping up the slope, they came upon Bazaine calmly siting a horse-artillery battery of the Guard in front of Rezonville. That he was thus exposed tells us much about his personal bravery. That he was there at all tells us even more about his inadequacy as a commander-in-chief. Now, in a swirl of men and horses he was, in his own words, 'obliged to draw my sword' and indeed was almost captured by a Hussar sergeant before his cavalry escort and a battalion of Chasseurs intervened and drove the enemy back through the ranks of their own infantry in some disorder. The chief result of this furious mêlée was that Bazaine's staff was scattered in the general confusion and it was not until mid-afternoon that it managed to regain some semblance of order and cohesion.

Several French commentators have speculated on what might have been the consequences if Bazaine had in fact been killed or taken prisoner. The argument goes that, by virtue of seniority, the command would have devolved upon Canrobert, and that in his hands the subsequent conduct of the battle would have been very different. 'Perhaps', runs one optimistic view, 'we would that same day have thrown the army of Prince Frederick Charles into the Moselle and punished the Germans for their rashness which flew in the face of every principle and experience of war. Perhaps, at no distant date, we would have joined hands with the Army of Châlons and presented the invader with an impenetrable obstacle to his advance.' Perhaps. But the facts do not support any such bland hypothesis; and this is why.

First, this unnecessary battle only took place because of Bazaine's fatal change of plan after the Emperor's departure. And Canrobert — '*un soldat sans peur et sans raproche, dont le nom était déjà synonyme de loyauté et d'honneur*'[45] — had not demurred at the decision to postpone the retreat. Furthermore, this paragon of military virtue had already, on 12 August, declined the honour of commanding the Army of the Rhine. Throughout the morning, when the resolute intervention of 6 Corps would indeed have thrown the Germans back into the Moselle, he had confined his activity to

---

44 De Place: *History of the 12th Cuirassiers (formerly Cuirassiers of the Guard)*.

45 *Loyauté? Honneur?* Canrobert had readily led the military support for the parvenu, Napoleon, at the time of the *coup d'état* in 1851.

strictly *defensive* artillery fire. And when early in the afternoon, as we shall see, a single desperate cavalry charge disrupted his first deliberate attack on Vionville he retreated into his shell and took no further part in the battle. To understand Canrobert, it is only necessary to study his evidence at Bazaine's trial. This covers seven pages in the transcript, but it can fairly be summarized in a single phrase: 'There but for the grace of God ...'

Meanwhile the phlegmatic Bazaine, unruffled by his experience of hand-to-hand combat and separated from his staff, took advantage of a brief lull in the fighting to alter his strictly defensive dispositions covering his centre and left flank — that flank where all day long he continued to pile up massive reserves against an imagined threat to his communications with Metz, when a resolute blow two miles to the west would have severed his opponent's fragile link with his own base. In his despatch of 22 August he wrote: 'It was evident [*sic*] that the enemy was going to make a great effort on our left from the woods which sheltered his men, and to cut us off from any line of retreat on Metz.'[46] No word here of any effort, great or small, to break through the slender cordon which barred the road to Verdun. No hint of aggression, only of passive defence. Evidence only of a mind obsessed with security when it should have had visions of victory.

South of the main road Bazaine withdrew the battered right and centre of Frossard's corps to Gravelotte (Bataille's division and Valazé's brigade[47]) and brought forward Picard's Grenadier division of the Imperial Guard to protect Rezonville. That should have served his supine purpose adequately; but it did not. To make room for the infantry of 2 Corps, he moved the Voltigeur division of the Guard to his south, covering the approaches through the Bois des Ognons and then, as if Sorval's division of 6 Corps were not already sufficient cover to the east of Rezonville, he applied yet another of his padlocks by switching Montaudon's division from Leboeuf's 3 Corps to the area of Malmaison, where it served no purpose other than to weaken his own line where disaster most surely faced his opponent.

Thus, as the morning battle ran its course, Bazaine had assembled half his Army[48] around Gravelotte and Rezonville, his eyes fixed on Metz and on the southern defiles 'whence hourly I expected the appearance of large masses of the enemy'. In so deceiving himself, he also contrived to deceive his enemy. For Alvensleben, bent as ever on offensive action and seeking precious time to relieve his weary infantry and hard-pressed gunners, turned to his cavalry; and for the only time that day his luck failed him. Seeing the flight of Frossard's corps, he called forward three regiments of

46 See Appendix C.

47 Valazé had also been killed in action during the morning of the 16th.

48 The equivalent of six infantry divisions, three cavalry divisions, and the larger part of his available artillery, facing, until mid-afternoon, two and a half infantry divisions, two cavalry divisions, and fewer than half the number of guns.

6th Cavalry Division in pursuit through the gap between Stuelpnagel's and Buddenbrock's men. The move was ill judged and ill contrived, and before the squadrons were able to deploy they were met by a murderous chassepot and mitrailleuse fire from Picard's newly arrived Grenadiers and were driven to take refuge behind Flavigny after suffering heavy losses. The official German history reports laconically: 'This demonstration, apparently without any result, was still useful since it provided the artillery with an opportunity, so greatly desired, to press up closer to the front.' Bazaine congratulated himself on his foresight, and resumed his posture of masterly inactivity.

****

It was nearly 1 p.m., and Alvensleben was in deep trouble. Four hours had passed since Rheinbaben's cannonade had alerted Frossard, and three since Stuelpnagel's 5th Division had first struggled ineffectively to occupy the open ground above the Gorze defiles. Since then Buddenbrock's 6th Division, supported by every available gun in III Corps, had fought its way into Vionville and Flavigny, while beyond the main road the infantry of 12th Brigade and Lehmann's battalions had reached the northern fringe of the Tronville copses, inexplicably unoccupied by either Canrobert or Leboeuf. By now Alvensleben was fully and irrevocably committed, with not a single battalion in reserve. By now the first great crisis of the battle had been reached; and it is a proper moment to reflect upon the 'morning battle', and upon the conduct of the two adversaries.

****

It is necessary to remember that when III Corps was set in motion on the morning of the 16th, the view of Second Army HQ at Pont-à-Mousson was that it would at best strike in upon the rearguard of the Army of the Rhine, while X Corps hurried west to intercept the main body. Despite Rheinbaben's gloomy conviction that the Army of the Rhine still lay in strength to the east of Mars-la-Tour, Alvensleben had pressed forward in accordance with his instruction to cut not only the southern road from Gravelotte to Verdun but also the more northerly route by Doncourt and Étain.[49] He was therefore marching steadily away from the rest of Second Army, [50] persuaded by Frederick Charles's comfortable assumption that 'serious fighting with the French was no more to be anticipated on the Moselle'. It was neither the first nor last error of judgment by the German

49   This would still leave Bazaine a third, if difficult, line of retreat through the hilly country around Briey.

50   X Corps, XII Corps, Guard Corps, IV Corps and — still on the far side of the Moselle — IX Corps and II Corps.

General Staff; and it provided precisely the same recipe for disaster which the first Napoleon had turned to such stunning account at Austerlitz.

That disaster now faced Alvensleben; for by 1 p.m. he was fighting not just for time, but for his very existence. His reconnaissance in strength had turned from an encounter battle into a full-scale engagement for which he was neither prepared nor equipped. III Corps had crossed the Moselle at Novéant on the 15th as no more than a flank-guard to Second Army's main thrust to the Meuse, and the supply and service echelons had been almost entirely routed through Pont-à-Mousson seven miles upstream.[51] The village of Gorze through which 6th Cavalry Division and 5th Infantry Division had to make their way was (and is) tightly enclosed by the rocky cliffs of the ravine through which the Jurée stream makes its way to the Moselle. A single battery of mitrailleuses would have been enough to seal it off. Small wonder if Alvensleben assumed that the coast was clear as he pushed his right wing up the defiles. Small wonder that, as the day wore on, the village became an administrative nightmare as the plateau shed its mounting load of wounded on to the narrow streets encumbered with the ammunition carts which alone could sustain the battle ahead. And, as the day wore on, Bazaine sat waiting for the appearance of 'fresh enemy masses' from a small village which could only with difficulty pass a battalion along its packed thoroughfares.

But now, at 1 p.m., with the temperature in the 80's, III Corps — which had marched and fought without respite — was, had Bazaine made the slightest effort to discover it, a spent force, barely able to hold its own, quite incapable of the sustained effort necessary to capture the key prize of Rezonville. It had suffered the most severe casualties, not least in officers of every rank. It had no single uncommitted reserve. It clung to the cliff's edge by precisely those qualities which the French lacked: the will to win; battle training; individual initiative; mutual support; or, in a word, 'professionalism'. But above all it was animated by the indomitable spirit of Alvensleben, who, launched on a reckless road, turned a likely tragedy into an unlikely triumph.

'I had to match the physical inferiority of my numbers by the moral superiority of my offensive action.' But lack of numbers was not the most significant of Alvensleben's problems. Given the unforeseen development of a reconnaissance in force into a combat à outrance, the most pressing of these was the supply of ammunition. This was not Alvensleben's fault. It arose from a massive error of judgment by Frederick Charles, and — more significantly — by Moltke.

It is not surprising that Rheinbaben had been less than enthusiastic when Caprivi had ordered him to attack what he himself — rightly, in the event

---

51 It had also been necessary to use this crossing to pass the entire corps artillery of III Corps over the river during the 15th; and a glance at the map on p. 109 will underline the remarkable achievement in deploying these guns on the Gravelotte plateau between 10 a.m. and 11 a.m. on the 16th.

— believed to be not a modest cavalry rearguard but the entire Army of the Rhine. When action was joined early on the morning of the 16th the four horse-artillery batteries available to him had fewer than eighty rounds a gun; that, given 5th Cavalry Division's original role of a flying picket scouting far ahead of Second Army (and on a divergent track), would have been enough to maintain harassing fire against a rearguard, but certainly not for the pitched battle which, for the first hour at least, it had to fight single-handed.

Throughout the day of battle, first III Corps and then X Corps had to improvise, in regard both to men and to materials. Both were — indeed, had to be — expendable, if the consequences of a disastrous military appreciation by the German High Command were to be salvaged. Moltke, in his account of the operation, put the blame squarely on his *bête-noire* Frederick Charles, while conveniently forgetting that he had delegated full freedom of action to the commander of Second Army.[52] But it was Moltke's refusal to reconsider his main strategy in the light of the information reaching him on the 14th and 15th, and his bland assumption (again attributed by him to Frederick Charles) that 'serious fighting with the French was no more to be anticipated on the Moselle', which hazarded the entire campaign.

On the 16th, Steinmetz's First Army was still on the right bank of the Moselle south-east of Metz acting as a pivot and flank-guard for Frederick Charles,[53] while far to the south the Crown Prince was dragging his feet in pursuit of MacMahon's disordered Army of Alsace. Thus the task of intercepting Bazaine and bringing him to battle fell to Second Army. It will be recalled that while Moltke's order of the 15th to Frederick Charles had given him only the vaguest direction as to the main thrust of his advance, it had been delivered in the form of a blank cheque — 'the commander of the Second Army is entrusted with this operation which he will conduct according to his own judgment and with the means at his disposal, that is, all the Corps of his Army.'[54] Convinced, despite the evidence of reports from 5th Cavalry Division, that whatever their problems the French must by now be well on their way to Verdun, Frederick Charles had left III Corps (less its Corps artillery) to cross the Moselle at Novéant and engage Bazaine's presumed rearguard on the main road about Vionville and Mars-la-Tour, while launching Second Army on a wide left-hook westward to the Meuse; in other words, marching all but one of his Army Corps directly away from the enemy.

52 *See* p. 108.

53 Towards evening — by when Moltke's lack of judgment had been redeemed by Bazaine's lack of resolution — a single brigade of VIII Corps made a costly intervention on the Gravelotte plateau.

54 On the evening of the 17th Moltke was to demonstrate a similar lack of precision, and on the following day Frederick Charles was to repeat his faulty judgment with near-fatal results.

This tactical decision was to have a domino effect on the administrative efficiency of Second Army. Once the main thrust of the pursuit had been indicated by Frederick Charles, the formidable machinery of the German supply organization was channelled through Pont-à-Mousson, with its excellent — and uncontested — river-crossings. Had the tactical appreciation of the situation been based on the available evidence and not on a wrong assumption, German staff expertise would have ensured more than adequate support for a westward advance on a wide front. But the master-plan at once foundered, as Kluck's plan was to founder nearly fifty years later, on a combination of complacency and arrogance. Few commanders have been offered so striking an opportunity to turn their opponent's error to their own decisive advantage as was Bazaine on the morning of the 16th; and none, it may fairly be said, so wantonly cast a victory away.

The bill for Frederick Charles's indiscretion was picked up by Alvensleben. The flank-march of III Corps at dawn on the 16th was always likely to be hazardous. A force numbering some 30,000 men and 6,000 horses with all the apparatus of supply and sustenance had to be passed across the Moselle by way of a single road bridge and a hastily assembled pontoon. It is inexplicable why Bazaine, for all his problems in Metz, did not, even as early as the 14th when the decision to retire on Verdun had been taken, cut the nearest permanent crossings upstream from the fortress at Ars and at Corny/Novéant. The former certainly was covered by the great guns at Forts Queleu and St Quentin and was not used until after dark on the 17th. But the failure to destroy the bridge at Novéant (let alone occupy the village) meant that Bazaine was actually inviting the very fate that was to obsess him; the turning of his left flank and the cutting of the communications with his main base. Indeed, when the Germans found the crossing intact and undefended on the 15th they at first suspected a deliberate trap. Little did they know Bazaine.

Thus Alvensleben marched away to the north-west up the narrow defiles leading to the Gravelotte plateau, ignorant of what lay before him, each hour carrying him farther from effective contact with X Corps on the westerly road through Thincourt, his single supply artery vulnerable and congested. His resources were adequate if, as Frederick Charles's order of the 15th had vaguely indicated, he was 'likely to come up with some of the enemy tomorrow morning'. A head-on collision with the entire Army of the Rhine was something rather different.

We have already seen how, as the true situation began to dawn on Alvensleben during the forenoon, he decided to bluff his way through a desperate predicament. In a sense, he was fortunate. The axis of his advance narrowed the front on which Bazaine, had he been remotely so minded, could have brought his massive superiority in numbers to bear. Thus for most of the morning the battle was fought between the German III Corps and Frossard's 2 Corps; the former reinforced towards noon by

Lehmann's four battalions from Thiaucourt; the latter, driven out of Vionville and Flavigny, replaced by Picard's Grenadier division; while Canrobert — Bazaine's supine centurion — watched from the sidelines.

The unexpected scale of the morning battle, fought by Alvensleben at, as it were, a long arm's-length from his source of supply at Novéant, is strikingly reflected in many ways which German accounts — perhaps out of deference to Frederick Charles and Moltke and to the verdict of history — largely gloss over. What, we may wonder, was it like that morning in the eye of the storm?

From the first moment that Alvensleben called Bazaine's bluff, III Corps was critically short of men, and certain so to be until mid-afternoon. And as the day wore on the expenditure of ammunition, both artillery and infantry, fast began to exhaust the ability of even so skilled a commissariat to sustain the fire-fight. Alvensleben had a simple option: to defend or to pretend. He never hesitated. He pretended.

But battles are not only about bullets. They are about men and morale; about dust and heat; about dying and defying. Mars-la-Tour was such a battle. The men of III Corps had cooked an early meal before dawn and, piously Protestant, had received the blessing of their padres. Not for many hours were they to enjoy another meal beyond the iron rations in their packs;[55] and by the day's end many would be beyond further benediction.

It was a day of burning heat and swirling dust, as both men and horses came into action after exhausting marches up steep and narrow roads to the bare and arid uplands. Buddenbrock's division, for instance, went straight into action at Vionville after covering 15 miles in 5 hours. Before night fell upon this burning battlefield, the infantry of X Corps would achieve even greater feats of stamina and endurance — and pay a dreadful price for the privilege.

More critical was the shortage of water as the morning wore on. German march-discipline strictly regulated all drinking from water-bottles (many old soldiers, like those before and since, contrived to carry something more stimulating), but on a morning of fierce heat and fiercer fighting and with water-carts lagging in the rear to make way for ammunition-carriers, men and horses alike suffered acutely under a pitiless sun. Thus even the brackish pond at Vionville became a pearl of great price.[56]

Most melancholy of all was the fate of the wounded. The scale and bitterness of the fighting as the morning wore on had been totally unexpected, and the mounting casualties (on both sides) soon over-

---

55   German pack-rations, according to regimental returns, consisted chiefly of bread, biscuit and sausage, and variations on the theme of salt pork, ham and pickled herring. Coffee, too. But there were no coffee-breaks on this day of battle.

56   The horses, under saddle from dawn to dusk, suffered not only from a shortage of fodder and water. On the baked ground many of them cast shoes, and with no respite in the fighting, farriers could only improvise. Thus a large proportion of horses became unserviceable. Most seriously this affected gun teams.

whelmed the normal medical resources at regimental level. On the German right wing it was possible for walking wounded to make their way down the forest paths to the comparative security of Gorze where the large convent was hastily converted into a field hospital and virtually every house became a dressing-station, staffed by army medical personnel and by devoted Sisters of Mercy. Few stretcher-bearers could survive on the bare killing-ground above the Bois de St Arnould and the Bois de Vionville, but the regimental record of the *48th* notes that more than a hundred men made their way back to the firing-line after treatment of often severe wounds.

But on the left wing there was naught for their comfort. There, in the desperate battle around Vionville and Flavigny, there was no such lifeline for the wounded. Under the burning sun, small salvation came for the dying and the disabled. Tronville, the nearest shelter, was no more than a cluster of farmsteads within range of French artillery. By noon a small *lazaret* or field hospital had been established at Puxieux, a mile or so to the south-west, but throughout the morning evacuation of the wounded from the fire-swept fields was hazardous if not impossible. So it was that men in their hundreds died so close to succour and yet so far from help. There are no statistics available, and in any event they would be meaningless; but it is certain that for every man killed in action another bled or burned to death.

On 20 August, four days after Mars-la-Tour, Archibald Forbes, correspondent of the London *Daily News*, 'traversed the whole of the battlefields of the Tuesday and Thursday [16th and 18th]'. His account spared his readers nothing:

> The outward and visible signs of slaughter more and more convinced me that the fight of the former day had been unquestionably the fiercer and the more hotly contested .... Within an area about six miles in length by four in depth there was not a space so large as Piccadilly Circus that did not bear some token that one or more men had fallen upon it. Now the tokens were dead bodies, sometimes straggling so that several yards intervened, sometimes so close that you could hardly step without treading on the dead [*and this was four days after the first battle*]. They consisted of bloody coats, pieces of linen, helmets, cuirasses with the tell-tale holes, knapsacks riddled by bullets, dead horses all but blown into fragments by the bursting of shells. The lines of demarcation between the German and French dead were in places drawn with almost mathematical accuracy. On one of the roads leading up the steep slope out of Gorze I came on an outlying part of the tableland where the Germans lay very thickly. It looked as if they had advanced in column along the road, for its margin was quite bordered with the dead .... Then I came to this place where the column had struggled into deployment and had got within the fatal 200 yards distance of the

Frenchmen [*the chassepot greatly outranged the needle-gun*]. The latter lay far thicker there than the Germans had lain in the first space. Burial parties were at work at this place, but seemed bewildered where to make a beginning ....

Small wonder. And small wonder, too, that Forbes felt obliged to add that even the strong smell of carbolic could not contain the odour of putrefaction. The quality of Lister's achievement was no match for the scale of human misery.

All was not well on the other side of the hill, but for very different reasons. Bazaine certainly had no shortage of men, even if he spent the morning of the 16th imagining, at Alvensleben's prompting, hostile masses which did not exist; nor, despite his later excuses, did he lack food and ammunition.[57] By dawn on the 16th he had, at the cost of administrative chaos, assembled some 150,000 men on the plateau — the equivalent of nearly 11 infantry divisions, 5 cavalry divisions, and more than 300 guns. He was within ten miles of his fortress base. His troops, in their neatly aligned shelter tents, had enjoyed the benefit of a night's rest. The order to resume the withdrawal at dawn had been given. All should have been well.

But all was not well. Since the reverses on 6 August and the unnecessary battle of Borny on the 14th, a deep contagion had infected the Army of the Rhine. The air was heavy with defeatism, and an army not famous for its discipline already felt itself to have been betrayed by those whose authority it doubted and whose leadership it had good reason to suspect. Certainly even an earlier Bonaparte would have had difficulty in playing the hand of cards which his lack-lustre nephew had dealt to Bazaine. But Bazaine was no Bonaparte, and when with Napoleon's dawn departure he compounded administrative inefficiency with a fatal change of plan, the Army of the Rhine found itself in a crisis of morale from which it was not to recover until its sorry surrender ten weeks later.

It is easy, as a cloud of hostile witnesses would later do, to blame Bazaine for every sin of commission on the 16th. It was not his fault that the massive civilian train which he inherited — nearly five thousand cumbersome vehicles — was already clogging the arteries of escape (indeed, as early as the 14th, he had taken measures to reduce the risk of a thrombosis of supply by arresting the movement of 2000 wagons from Metz). It was not his fault that the locust years since 1866 had left him with a staff well versed in playing games with *goums* in Africa, but totally unequipped to match Moltke's ruthlessly modern model for a continental war of movement. It was not entirely his fault — although his absurd inferiority complex contributed greatly to that end — that he could never impose his will on his subordinates, each one of whom should have occupied a seat in the dock beside him three years later at his

57 *See* Appendix B.

court-martial; that, for example, his lack of control allowed Leboeuf's 3 Corps to leapfrog Ladmirault's 4 Corps on the northern exits from Metz, and thus bring on the fatal decision to halt the march on Verdun.

It is none the less fair to compare Bazaine's preoccupation with lost causes during the morning battle with Alvensleben's brilliant improvisation in turning to account his opponent's errors of omission. For if ever there was a lost cause in the making that morning, it was on the side of III Corps. Bazaine fought the battle in the only way he understood — by personal example. He was that curious and dangerous blend in a leader: a model of physical courage and a moral coward. When he galloped off shouting to Changarnier that he could not be everywhere at once, he was really voicing the thought that he should not have been there at all, that not many privates of the line have the true makings of a Marshal disposing of five army corps in an unnecessary battle. To illustrate this, it is revealing to study the despatch he wrote six days later in Metz (which is printed here at Appendix C, verbatim except for the correction of spelling errors that suggest a very imperfect memory of the battlefield). It is a melancholy document, for, self-justification aside, it tells the reader quite simply that the commander-in-chief of the Army of the Rhine was then no wiser as to the events of 16 August than he had been on that morning when, in Colonel d'Andlau's biting phrase, he had behaved like 'un simple colonel'. If anything in war is certain, it is that, with roles reversed, an Alvensleben would have destroyed III Corps by noon; and that 'an ordinary colonel' was no match for a resolute corps commander.

We have seen the domino effect of Frederick Charles's ill-considered order of 15 August on III Corps' administrative lifeline. No such problems should have worried Bazaine. He had a firm base, so well stocked with provisions of every kind that, given even the most elementary staff organization, the morning march should have proceeded without delay. So well stocked that when the Army of the Rhine fell back to the Amanvillers line on the 17th tons of stores and equipment were burned in the Mance ravine to free wagons for the evacuation of the wounded.[58] So well stocked that an army of 170,000 soldiers and more than 40,000 civilians could sustain a siege of ten weeks in Metz before surrendering.

But a glance at the map on page 149 will show how handsomely Bazaine contributed to the administrative confusion himself; for by 1 p.m. he had crowded together in a small quadrilateral to the east of Rezonville upward of 5 infantry divisions, 3 cavalry divisions and more than 150 guns. This purely defensive mass, together with a clutter of vehicles, lay immobile like some great stranded whale, serving no purpose other than to impede all movement towards the killing-ground where Alvensleben was fighting for his life. In a sense it could be said that during the morning battle, the Army

---

58 Even then, more than 5000 French wounded, with their attendant doctors, were left behind on the Gravelotte plateau after the fighting on the 16th. 300 of them were to be burned to death by their own guns two days later in the château at Malmaison.

of the Rhine strangled itself to death when, without risk or peradventure, it could and should have kept its hands free to sweep aside the brave but insubstantial obstacle on the Verdun road. Almost without exception commentators have described the battle of Mars-la-Tour as 'indecisive'. This is not so. It was lost by Bazaine — though not, as we shall see, irretrievably — during the morning hours when, instead of trying to command battalions and batteries, he should have behaved like a Bonaparte and made a monkey out of Moltke. Of all battles, Mars-la-Tour illustrates most vividly that morale is to men as ten is to one.

Thus, beset by very different problems, two very different men brought to battle two very different armies. Alone in physical numbers of every arm were the French superior. Indeed, the two sides may be likened to the matching of an ill-trained amateur heavyweight with a world-class bantam, skilled in ringcraft and strong in stamina.

As we have seen, the German cavalry — after one bloody indiscretion at Spicheren which Steinmetz inexplicably was to repeat with even more dire results on the 18th — operated with extraordinary boldness and flexibility in its true tactical role as the eyes and ears of the Army commander. Forty-eight hours before the first infantry crossings of the Moselle, Rheinbaben had been operating more than fifteen miles to the west of the river. It was not his fault that Frederick Charles ignored the evidence that his intrepid patrols sent back; nor can Frederick Charles be seriously blamed for confusing fact with fiction, even if the unexpected outcome was an unpredictable and potentially disastrous collision.

French cavalry doctrine, on the other hand, was still rooted in the distant past when thundering squadrons rode down and pursued a demoralized enemy. The lesson of Waterloo, however, had been forgotten. Cavalry was no match for determined infantry. By 1870 fire-power had changed the geometry of the battlefield, as MacMahon had learned to his dreadful cost at Morsbronn and at Froeschwiller, disasters of which Bazaine was certainly unaware when at Rezonville he ordered the Cuirassiers of the Guard to their destruction. And there is something infinitely pathetic in the scene at dawn on the 16th, with Forton's division — charged with the protection of a retreating army — comfortably encamped at Vionville under the astonished eyes of an apprehensive German commander, for all the world as if the vital Verdun road were no more than a poplar-lined avenue across the parade-ground at Châlons.

Before the day was out, the cavalry would have its say. But during the morning battle, the cavalry forays had been, in Michael Howard's words, 'spectacular, invigorating and entirely ineffective'.[59]

With the infantry the pattern was set by Alvensleben's consummate skill and determination; nor could he have taken the risks he did without complete confidence in the initiative of both senior and junior commanders

59 Howard: *op. cit.*

(before the morning was out at least three battalions had lost all their officers, yet still held fast under their NCOs) and in the quality of German battle-training. Herein lay the critical difference. The French infantry, ceaselessly battered by the assembled artillery of III Corps, fought with the greatest courage. In the light of later recriminations, it is right and proper to record this fact. The French soldier is (so runs the conventional wisdom) by temperament aggressive, not easily subjected to the disciplines of either peace or war.[60] No army, except the predictable British which had over many years made *débrouillage* into an art form, is at its best in adversity; and on the 16th the Army of the Rhine, all inspiration gone, acquitted itself with pride and honour, and would, two days later, give even more signal proof that it did not care for the odium of defeat. Sadly, while the men believed in victory, their Marshals did not.

And there is a strange paradox here. The French chassepot outranged the German needle-gun by more than 600 yards; yet this apparently overwhelming advantage produced a quite contrary result.[61] This great superiority in range induced a dangerously defensive element into French tactical doctrine, for it substituted for the famous *furia francese* the alien alternative of *noli me tangere*. Nor did it end there. French musketry was, like virtually every aspect of field-training, greatly inferior to that of the Germans — army manœuvres in the great camp at Châlons had been no more than colourful parade-ground exercises, the infantry marching and counter-marching behind its bands, the cavalry in its peacock feathers wheeling and counter-wheeling in great masses, handsome and impressive but totally irrelevant to the harsh imperatives of the modern battlefield. Fieldcraft, the use of ground, the close co-operation between the different arms of the service, the arts of concealment and deployment — none of these was taught or practised in an army which, reflecting the great traditions of the first Bonaparte, mistook arrogance for efficiency and elegance for expertise. Indeed, it is a matter for wonder that these men, under their elderly[62] and often illiterate *troupier* junior officers, gave so brave an account of themselves. Not many of them cared one jot for 'the dynasty'. Not one of them cared other than for France. They deserved a fairer fate than that to which their lack-lustre leaders delivered them.

So, as the morning battle reached its climax and its crisis, the balance between success and failure was dictated by the artillery; and it was here

60   La Gloriette, the formidable cemetery at Verdun, so close to Mars-la-Tour, speaks sombrely for the defence.

61   In the strictly defensive context of the fighting along the Amanvillers Line on the 18th the French chassepots, firing at extreme range, caused havoc not only among the German infantry but also among the exposed German batteries. Thus, for example, the German positions around Gravelotte were rendered almost untenable by French rifle-fire from their distant fox-holes at Point du Jour 1500 yards away (see Map 17).

62   In the 77th Regiment of the Line, there was no company commander under the age of fifty; and two aged over sixty.

that the Germans demonstrated their matchless quality. Throughout the morning — indeed, throughout the day — Bazaine had a numerical superiority in guns of at least two to one; but there his advantage ended. The French muzzle-loaders, virtually unchanged since the days of the Italian campaign of 1859, were outranged, outgunned, and above all outfought by the new Krupp steel breech-loaders. Whereas the French pieces fired only air-burst projectiles with two fuse-settings at 1250 and 2500 yards, the Germans, with flexible range and using predominantly percussion shells, hunted and harried the enemy gunners, forcing them constantly to move position or seek shelter from the great arc of batteries stretching from the Bois de Vionville to the Bois de Tronville with which Alvensleben sustained an otherwise insupportable fire-fight.

For herein lay the decisive difference. Throughout the morning the German artillery was committed to a boldly conceived and brilliantly executed offensive role (the lessons of Sadowa had been thoroughly learned). It was as much a matter of geometry as of good training, for, given the superior range of chassepot and mitrailleuse, the German artillery alone could narrow the gap and, as we have seen, 'beat a path' for their infantry to come to grips, first at Vionville and then at Flavigny. Thus, careless of casualties, Alvensleben's devoted gunners dragged their pieces down the forward slopes towards Rezonville, often leading the way for rifle companies, always in the thick of the fight. In stark contrast, while Frossard's corps was being driven from the vital ground to the south of the Verdun road, Canrobert, to the north, with batteries to spare, did not move until it was too late. The Roman road, whence early he could have launched a counter-stroke, became a moat defensive to a house; and the house tumbled to the impetuous charge of Bredow's brigade.

Reflecting therefore on the morning battle, it may rightly be summed up thus: Faith, hope, and artillery — and the greatest of these was artillery.

****

It was now shortly before 1.30 p.m. On the German right wing Stuelpnagel's division, with no infantry reserve, was pinned down on the northern fringes of the Bois de St Arnould and the Bois de Vionville, outranged by the chassepots of Picard's Grenadiers and of Jolivet's and Lapasset's staunch brigades on the Rezonville ridge, and sustained only by the intermittent fire of eight batteries with a dwindling supply of ammunition. It was a strange situation. Stuelpnagel had only one option: survival. Facing him, with an embarrassment of resources more than sufficient to wipe the slate clean, was Bazaine with only one purpose: survival. Such situations, where a pawn can threaten a king, are the stuff of chessboards, but less frequently of battlefields. When eventually, towards 5 p.m., modest reinforcements from VIII Corps and IX Corps reached the German right wing, Bourbaki, commander of the Imperial Guard, mounted a great battery of 54 guns[63] in the depression running down from the east of Rezonville and threw the Germans back into the woods with bloody casualties, their track marked today by a string of memorials on the bare slopes. Those guns, which by noon could have destroyed Stuelpnagel, had stood idle since dawn. Yet at his trial Bazaine advanced the lame argument that in husbanding his artillery on this wing, and keeping a tight rein on his uncommitted infantry reserves, he had proved his point that 'the battle of Mars-la-Tour' should more properly have been described as 'the defence of Metz'. So, towards 1.30 p.m. the fighting on the German right stuttered to an inconclusive halt. On the left wing, however, the chessboard had assumed a very different and dramatic character.

Here, on a front of more than two miles, Buddenbrock's division had fought its way 1000 yards to the east of Vionville and Flavigny, covered by 100 guns of III Corps artillery, while Lehmann's battalions and the *24th*, emerging from the northern edge of the Tronville copses,[64] had been driven back with heavy casualties by a storm of chassepot and mitrailleuse fire from the higher ground above the Roman road. Every gun was committed. No single battalion of infantry remained in reserve. Losses had been severe, and the exhausted troops had been fighting without respite for nearly three hours. Ammunition was in desperately short supply, while dust-clouds to the north told Alvensleben that at last Leboeuf's 3 Corps was coming into line on Canrobert's right. Despite Caprivi's urgent summons to Voigts-Rhetz at Thiaucourt, no more help could be expected from X Corps for at least two hours. It was Alvensleben's one saving grace that while he was all too aware of his desperate situation, Bazaine plainly was not.

As the enemy fire began to slacken, Canrobert seems to have sensed his opportunity, encouraged no doubt by the arrival of 3 Corps on his right. All morning his long line of guns along the Roman road had been pounding the German left wing, where the artillery of III Corps, heavily outnumbered if not outgunned, could barely hold its ground.

There is much room for argument here. Moltke wrote thus: 'Marshal Canrobert, in the French centre, had discerned the right moment to press forward against Vionville with all his might.' And thus the official French version: 'Canrobert, who had developed [*sic*] a strong line of guns, as well as infantry on the right of Picard's Grenadiers ... determined to attempt the recapture of Vionville and Flavigny. He was led to do so by a belief that the partial cessation of German fire indicated exhaustion and, aided by the whole of his artillery, he certainly delivered a formidable onset carried up to the very outskirts of the two villages.'

---

63   It was the first time throughout the day of battle that French artillery had been used *en masse*.

64   Today the Bois de Tronville is a thick, continuous wood. On the day of battle it consisted of undergrowth and scattered clumps of trees which provided little cover.

Both opinions, for different reasons, are much exaggerated: Moltke's, because he wished to lend credibility to the events which now followed; the French account's, because like so much hindsight, it sought to attach blame by association not to Canrobert but, inevitably, to Bazaine. For at this vital hour, Canrobert — with Bazaine nowhere to be found — discovered himself in the difficult position of having to act on his own initiative. Both men studiously avoided any public comment on their inadequacies at this moment, which may rightly be described as the supreme crisis of the day of battle;[65] and this is why.

Certainly, at or about 1.30 p.m. Canrobert began to edge forward from his central position, which ran north from Rezonville to the Roman road (*see* Plate 8). He moved according to what was called 'the Niel doctrine', with his gun-line leading, and Lafont's infantry following in the intervals between batteries, and in extended order to the rear. This 'formidable onset' carried him, not to 'the very outskirts of the two villages', but only a few hundred yards down the forward slope which 6 Corps had occupied since dawn.[66] There he now received a rude shock.

Alvensleben, well aware that time — 'my only advantage' — had now slipped away, and that he faced a crushing defeat on his thinly protected left wing, took the kind of decision which throughout the morning had escaped his irresolute opponent. 'I had to match the physical inferiority of my numbers by the moral superiority of my offensive action.' He had one last such chance — and he took it with stunning effect.

By 1.30 p.m. the infantry of III Corps was no longer a force capable of the kind of offensive action which had driven Alvensleben to such extraordinary feats of improvisation. All that remained was his cavalry; and it was to his cavalry that he now turned. As he later wrote, he judged that one last bluff would again deceive his opponent into believing that the Germans lay in great and growing strength astride the Verdun road. He had fought a brilliant action throughout the morning. If, as now seemed certain, he had to go down he would go down still fighting. If he failed he would extricate the remnants of his command and, *still* fighting, retire along the main road until he could effect a junction with X Corps around St Hilaire ten miles to the west. When he came to express this view he was not simply being wise after the event; for the event on which he now gambled justified his decision in a way that he could not possibly then have anticipated.

At 1.30 p.m. Alvensleben's only reserve was the cavalry of the 5th[67] and

65 But *see* Appendix C, and Bazaine's *amende déshonorable*.

66 As evidence of Canrobert's cautious advance, no single part of 6 Corps crossed the Verdun road or came within rifle-range of Flavigny.

67 Strictly, 5th Cavalry Division, detached from X Corps, was not under his command, but, as we have seen (and shall see again) Moltke's doctrine of delegating authority paid precious dividends. After all, it was Caprivi, chief of staff of X Corps, who had brought on the dawn battle of III Corps.

6th Divisions, strung out behind the long, thin line of infantry and artillery stretching from the Bois de St Arnould to the Tronville copses. At this hour the only immediately available force was Bredow's 12th Cavalry Brigade assembled behind the Flavigny ridge; and of this brigade there were at hand only two regiments — *7th Magdeburg Cuirassiers* and *16th Altmark Uhlans*. The third regiment — *13th Dragoons* — had been witdrawn during the morning to support Barby's 11th Cavalry Brigade which, as part of Alvensleben's bluff, was covering his left flank to the north of Mars-la-Tour and pretending, with some apprehension, to be a *force de frappe*.

Alvensleben's order to Bredow was brutally simple: to charge and disorganize Canrobert's line of battle to the north of the Verdun road. Both men were well aware of what such an order meant, for it flew in the face of any conceivable cavalry doctrine, and both men had seen the fate of the French Cuirassiers at Flavigny two hours earlier. There were no heroics; no talk of 'sacrificing a regiment'. But it was a wild surmise; and it was to prove a memorable one.

Bredow accepted his order without argument; but he took his time. He first reconnoitred the ground, and detached, perhaps unnecessarily, one squadron from each of his two regiments to protect his flank in the Tronville copses. At 2 p.m. he was ready.

A little to the west of Vionville there was a shallow dip towards the Roman road. It is marked today by a narrow track concealed from the Rezonville ridge (*see* Plate 14). It is not possible to follow this track now without a strong sense of involvement, for it was to lead to what was perhaps the last great cavalry charge in modern war. And the scene which presently confronted Canrobert must have carried his mind back sixteen years to another valley at Balaklava.

At 1.58 p.m. Bredow led his squadrons, 804 strong, in close column up this sheltered approach, the dust and smoke of battle concealing his movement and — more importantly — the modest size of his force. One thousand yards to the north of Vionville, the track drops suddenly into a shallow valley (*see* Map 10 and Plate 16) which lies below the line of trees skirting the Roman road. Here the head of the column wheeled to the right under increasingly heavy fire, forming first into squadrons and then into line of brigade, the Cuirassiers on the left echeloned slightly ahead of the Uhlans; and the order was given to charge.

Remarkably, surprise was almost complete (a tribute to Bredow's carefully reconnoitred plan of attack), and the German horsemen, galloping up the slope, first overrode Canrobert's gun-line, cutting down gun-crews and teams, and then fell upon Lafont's infantry lined up a few paces to the rear, before a single volley could be fired. Amid scenes of wild confusion, Bredow's squadrons charged on over the Rezonville ridge, scattering the second line of infantry and guns; but by now all control and cohesion had been lost. The German troopers had covered more than 3000

Plate 14   The approach taken by Bredow's brigade. On the skyline, the Roman road, and to the right, the position occupied by Canrobert's gun-line

Plate 15   The Bois de Tronville, covering Bredow's left

Plate 16   The shallow valley up which Bredow's brigade charged

yards, and with their horses blown and their ranks thinned, like Ponsonby's Union Brigade at Waterloo, they found themselves irresistibly driven to inevitable disaster. In total disorder, they were struck by four regiments of Forton's cavalry division lying a little to the north of the Roman road, and eager to redeem their lost virtue at Vionville when Körber's batteries had put them to flight at the first onset. The cavalry combat was brief and brutal as Cuirassiers and Uhlans, assailed on every side, cut their way back to a safe haven through Lafont's infantry. Not many lived to tell the tale; and strangely, not many tales have been told. Here is one revealing gloss: 'Our losses were comparatively small, for our horsemen, using the point, struck home where front and rear cuirasses joined and below the helmet-guard, while the Germans, using the cutting-edge and the pistol, wounded many of our horses but few of our men.'[68]

It lasted twenty minutes; and precious they were to prove. The survivors battled their way home and assembled behind their infantry supports at Flavigny. Of the 804 men who set out in the charge fewer than 400 returned, and when, on the following morning, King William surveyed the battlefield, the track of the so-called *Todtenritt* was marked with melancholy precision by the white tunics of the fallen Magdeburg Cuirassiers.

'This charge of Bredow's brigade has been severely criticized by many

---

68   Bonie: *La Cavalerie française.*

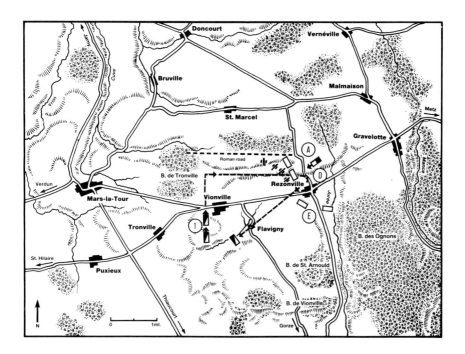

KEY

1 12 Cav. Bde, 7th Cuirassiers followed by 16th Uhlans

D Gun line and infantry of Canrobert's 6 Corps

A Forton's Cavalry division. E Part of Imperial Guard.
   Other dispositions as in Map 9

Map 10 Bredow's charge at 2 p.m., 16 August

writers.'[69] It is difficult to see why. At 2 p.m. the situation on Alvensleben's left wing was so perilous that his only wrong decision would have been indecision; and his only hope of survival was that one last bluff would succeed. The answer to those critical purists of the cavalry school lies in the extraordinary success of a desperate gamble. On the German side, it provided a brief but vital breathing-space for the infantry and artillery of III Corps, and an opportunity to hurry forward every available round of ammunition. There was little enough on hand to sustain the battle; but the second — and more important — result of Alvensleben's gamble was as unforeseen as it was decisive.

Throughout the morning, as we have seen, Bazaine had swallowed every bait that Alvensleben had offered to him, convinced that his escape route — if, indeed, escape was a serious option — was barred by a formidable opposition. Thus Bredow's six squadrons assumed for him the character

69 Hohenlohe-Ingelfingen: *Letters on Cavalry.*

171

not of a dying fall but of a dangerous assault. Canrobert, no less a moral coward, assumed the same with much less right or reason.

When the remnants of Bredow's squadrons, outnumbered by so many that figures are irrelevant, turned for home down the long slope from Rezonville to Flavigny, there was no pursuit — or, in the words of the official account, '*la poursuite exercée par notre cavalerie fut très molle, et opérée seulement par quelques fourrageurs*'. A 'feeble' pursuit, when the full weight of the Army of the Rhine stood ready to exact a terrible price for Alvensleben's final fling. The chance would come once more; and once more would be cast away.

At this momentous hour Bazaine was nowhere to be found; but six days later, in his despatch from Metz, he revealed himself in his true light:

> The fire of his [Alvensleben's] guns had nearly ceased, and he was evidently [*sic*] making preparations for a new effort. Completely reassured as to my right by the entry into line of the first troops of my 3 Corps, I ordered Marshal Leboeuf to maintain firmly his position with Nayral's division.[70]

There speaks the moral coward. There speaks the born loser. Small wonder that when the veteran Changarnier presently came upon his commander-in-chief and urged him to press his attack on the right wing Bazaine rode off shouting, 'I can't be everywhere all the time!' Canrobert was happy enough to await superior orders; so, seemingly, was Leboeuf, whose 3 Corps had spent a whole morning manœuvring within the untroubled two miles which separated him from St Marcel and the Roman road. And thus it was that Bredow's charge, a sharp harpoon delivered into the belly of a wallowing whale, threw the French centre into confusion. From this single stroke the French never recovered; and Canrobert's 6 Corps, shaken but in no sense shattered, took no further part in the battle. Eight hundred horsemen had against every probable event drawn the enemy's teeth; and, equally improbably, eliminated one army corps and halted a second in its tracks.

****

But it was no moment for euphoria. III Corps had achieved no more than a moment of repose. Bredow's charge had bought a little time and had wrecked whatever plan of attack Canrobert may have been projecting. A strange silence fell upon the battlefield while one side contemplated its failure and the other its incredible fortune. On Alvensleben's right the fragile stalemate continued. Here Jolivet and Lapasset clung bravely to the

---

70 A division which Bazaine contemplated moving to his absurdly overstocked left wing later in the afternoon.

higher ground. Here Stuelpnagel maintained the foothold he had gained during the morning along the forest fringes. The fire-fight had now dwindled to occasional artillery exchanges, while to the east of Rezonville Bazaine still kept his pointless padlocks in place, his sole new disposition, the result of a congestion of his own making, being to move the Voltigeur division of the Guard astride the road running south from Gravelotte with a battalion of Chasseurs thrown forward into the Bois des Ognons, watching and waiting for an imagined attack where none such threatened.

In the centre, to the south of the main Verdun road, the men of Buddenbrock's 6th Division still held the ground they had won to the east of Vionville and Flavigny, their flank secured at least for the moment by the collapse of Canrobert's attack and by the failure of the French to pursue Bredow's battered squadrons. Here less than 1000 yards separated the German line from Picard's Grenadiers. Here too there was a sudden silence, broken only by occasional rifle-fire as both sides sniped warily at each other. Alvensleben, at Tronville, waited and watched his left wing, measuring the minutes to an attack which he knew, his last card played, must put not only III Corps but the entire Second Army in peril. Bazaine, at Gravelotte, waited and watched *his* left wing, his mind fixed on Metz, his eyes averted from the true battlefield where victory and Verdun beckoned. The 'morning battle' was over. The 'afternoon battle' was about to begin. It was to prove a very extraordinary passage of arms.

****

When, at 2 p.m., Alvensleben ordered Bredow's charge as an act of desperate defiance he was concerned not so much by Canrobert's manœuvre to the east of Vionville as by the massive threat to his left wing as first Leboeuf's 3 Corps and, farther still to the west, Ladmirault's 4 Corps began to change front and overlap his weary battalions in the Tronville copses. At this critical moment the 'available' (the word is important) French superiority on this flank was of the astonishing order of nearly ten to one. That it was never used to button up the 'afternoon battle' in a single, co-ordinated stroke is as much a commentary on the two corps commanders as on their commander-in-chief, six miles remote in Gravelotte, and, as subsequent events were to show, either unwilling or unable to impose his will either upon a stricken opponent or — more importantly — upon his hesitant subordinates. Not once during the afternoon did Bazaine, so ready to lead battalions and site batteries during the morning, venture forth to see for himself the prize which was there for the taking. And it is important to the understanding of this day of battle to compare the striking difference in the conduct of both sides.

The news that III Corps was involved in a major battle did not reach Frederick Charles at Second Army HQ, 15 miles away at Pont-à-Mousson, until nearly 1 p.m. At that hour there was nothing he could do to influence the outcome of the battle. The crisis, which had been brought about by his own rash assumptions, could be averted in one of three ways: the folly of his opponent; the quality of his men; and, above all, the initiative of his subordinates. It was the last of these which saved the day and salvaged Second Army. It may properly be said that during the battle the balance between both sides hung upon the nice distinction between errors of commission and omission. The reader may judge for himself. And should he be in doubt, the events of the 'afternoon battle' will presently provide an improbable answer.

It was the quality of Frederick Charles's subordinates which turned the scale, right down to battalion and battery level. The whole thrust of Moltke's training for war had been based upon a single premise: once battle had been joined, there was little that the higher command could do to influence the immediate outcome. Success or failure was then in the hands of lesser leaders, freed from all rigid restraint, both self-reliant and — as the day of battle positively proved — inter-reliant. For example: the order to open fire on Forton's camp had been given by the chief of staff of X Corps, standing alongside the commander of III Corps; Colonel Lyncker's covering detachment on the Moselle, a part of X Corps, went into battle without hesitation with Stuelpnagel's 5th Division; and at noon Lehmann's battalions of 37th Brigade (X Corps) marched to the sound of the guns from Thiaucourt with neither instruction nor permission.[71] And in the afternoon which lay ahead the pattern was to be repeated again and again.

The news that III Corps was fighting for its life seems not to have addressed itself to Bazaine. On the contrary, he spent the morning behaving like the *troupier* he was, rallying his men around Rezonville (when that evening he decided to pull the Army of the Rhine back towards Metz, the cynical word went round among his disheartened men that he would surely be rewarded with the title of 'Duc de Rentre-en-Ville'). For most of the morning he had been separated from his staff, and from the outset he had treated Jarras with studied indifference. This would have been a matter for less concern if Bazaine had, like his opponents, delegated responsibility to his subordinates; but that was not the French way. Even when war had become inevitable, there had been no attempt in Paris to analyse and apply the lessons of Prussia's victory at Sadowa. *Débrouillage*, not delegation, remained the order of the day. Such doctrine for war as existed was fatally infected, first by Niel and then by 'professors' like Frossard, with the defeatist contagion of defence which ran entirely counter to both history and temperament, and to a volatile people who had greeted the war, when it came, with the cry: '*À Berlin!*'

71 The line between initiative and disobedience is a narrow one; but it is not possible to imagine a single French brigade commander acting as Lehmann did.

But defeat had been early in the air. Had not Bazaine himself left for Metz in July with the bleak comment that France was heading for a disaster? And had not the reverses at Spicheren and Wörth — neither of them irreversible, and both reflecting serious flaws in the machinery of Moltke's plan — been compounded by an ailing Emperor with one blinkered eye on the battlefield and the other on the politicians in Paris? That was no way to fight a war. It is said that, as Napoleon took his leave of Bazaine at Gravelotte on the 16th, he murmured: '*Songez au Prince Impérial!*'[72] It sounds a little unlikely; but it may well have been so, and Bazaine cannot possibly be blamed for being caught in the crossfire of *débrouillage* and dynasty. He was the victim of the one and the servant of the other.

That cannot be said of his subordinates, who throughout the day of battle waited upon orders because *Système D* had long since stultified initiative and subordinates had taught themselves (for the system had given no other instruction) that safe inaction was wiser than risky adventure, and that errors of omission were more easily justified than sins of commission. It has rightly been observed that Second Empire paladins were not a band of brothers.[73] Thus throughout the day Bazaine's corps commanders waited upon Bazaine; and Bazaine waited on events. It was to prove Frederick Charles's salvation.

****

The 'morning battle' had been almost entirely confined to the Verdun road and to the area to the south and west of Rezonville, and serious fighting on this flank was not resumed until 5 p.m. when elements of VIII and IX Corps reached the battlefield[74] from the Moselle valley. Now the action moved to the north of the main road, and to Alvensleben's seemingly doomed left wing, where III Corps's precarious position was sustained by six batteries of artillery, six hard-pressed infantry battalions in the Tronville copses, and farther west, covering Mars-la-Tour, Barby's cavalry brigade of 5th Cavalry Division with two additional regiments attached. Against this tiny buttress the French, with maddening deliberation, had started to develop the outflanking movement which they could have delivered with crushing effect at least two hours earlier.

Around noon Bazaine had 'proposed' to Leboeuf that he should change front and bring 3 Corps into line on Canrobert's right along the Roman road (it was the dust-cloud of this evolution which alerted Alvensleben and led to Bredow's charge). In fact 3 Corps was by no means the

72 D'Andlau: *Metz: op. cit.*

73 Guedalla: *The Two Marshals.*

74 32nd Brigade, *11th Grenadier Regiment* of 36th Brigade, and a part of 49th (Hessian) Brigade.

sledgehammer that it should have been, for Bazaine had already switched Montaudon's division to upholster his left wing, and Metman's division[75] was still struggling to make its way out of the traffic jam in Metz. This left Leboeuf with Clérambault's cavalry division aimlessly directed on Bruville to the north-west and with two infantry divisions, those of Aymard and Nayral,[76] available to extend Canrobert's line. But Bazaine was careful to tie one hand behind Leboeuf's back by his message suggesting that his new position was 'to be maintained at all costs'. Thereafter Bazaine, far away at Gravelotte and increasingly concerned with his absurd obsession about the threat to his left, allowed victory to go by default on his right. Had he ventured even to send a staff officer to that flank he would have learned something to his advantage; and this is why.

During the course of the morning Ladmirault's 4 Corps, driven to take the more northerly road from Metz by Woippy and St Privat, had climbed to the plateau, and by 1 p.m. his cavalry division (Legrand) had reached Doncourt, closely followed by his leading infantry division (Grenier). If Bazaine was aware of this there is nothing in his subsequent — and conflicting — recitals of events to show it, beyond a bland assumption that a commander of Ladmirault's experience would by training and instinct march his men to the sound of the guns. It was an assumption which throughout the day was repeatedly demonstrated by German commanders even down to brigade level, and with striking effect; and it is to Ladmirault's credit that although his nerve failed him at two critical stages of the afternoon battle, he shrugged aside the silence of his incompetent commander-in-chief and by a show of aggression came close to achieving the victory which Bazaine did not deserve. And it is further to Ladmirault's credit that, alone of the paladins of the Army of the Rhine, he spoke firmly in Bazaine's defence at the subsequent court-martial when, of all the five corps commanders, he had the most reason to censure him.[77]

Shortly after Bredow's charge at 2 p.m., Leboeuf and Ladmirault met a little to the north of the Roman road. That of itself was unusual during a day when mutual co-operation was not the most signal feature of the conduct of affairs on the French side. Neither man had the remotest idea of the situation south of the Verdun road, but here on the right flank it was now plain that German resistance was weakening as Canrobert's gun-line along the Roman road enfiladed the Tronville copses and Leboeuf's chassepots and mitrailleuses took a heavy toll of Lehmann's battered battalions as they struggled to hold the northern perimeter of the woods.

75 In fact this division only reached the Gravelotte plateau in time to provide a rearguard to cover Bazaine's withdrawal to the Amanvillers position.

76 Incredibly, at the crisis of the 'afternoon battle' Bazaine sent for Nayral's division to join the battalions massed around Gravelotte, but seemingly was dissuaded by Leboeuf from so ill-judged a course of action.

77 At the date of Bazaine's trial three years later, Ladmirault was Military Governor of Paris.

To the west, the artillery of Grenier's division had driven Barby's flank guard to take refuge behind Mars-la-Tour and du Barail's cavalry, patrolling cautiously to the south of Bruville, reported no enemy opposition. Alvensleben's left flank had been turned. It was 3 p.m.

****

There now began, with a caution in marked contrast to the bold offensive spirit which had animated Alvensleben's every action, the first and only concerted French attack throughout this long day. Since battle was joined in the early morning, the French had fought bravely and well, but every aggressive movement and every counter-stroke had been purely defensive in purpose and strictly limited in intention. A joint attack by Frossard and Bourbaki from the strong Rezonville position would have thrown Stuelpnagel's division back into the Gorze defiles long before it could have established a foothold on the plateau; an hour later, the combined divisions of Frossard and Canrobert — let alone the passive reserve formations grouped around Gravelotte — could have crushed the German left flank. By 1 p.m. the battle could and should have been decided, III Corps destroyed, Second Army thrown into total confusion, and — possibly, although not probably — the course of history significantly changed. But none of these things happened. And a single desperate attack by 800 horsemen an hour later had stopped Bazaine in his tracks and stood history on its head. There can be few more singular examples in the long catalogue of war when the action of so small a parcel of men succeeded in throwing so great a body of the enemy into such absolute disarray. Bredow had saved Buddenbrock. But it was 2.30 p.m., and despite Caprivi's urgent calls to his corps commander, Voigts-Rhetz, no significant help could reach III Corps for at least one hour. Of this Alvensleben at Tronville was acutely aware. Of this Bazaine, at Gravelotte, was not.

Nevertheless, shortly after 3 p.m. Leboeuf and Ladmirault summoned up the courage to launch a combined attack with as its objectives the village of Mars-la-Tour and the Verdun road to the west of beleaguered Vionville: in other words, the wide outflanking movement which Alvensleben had for several hours expected and feared. There is no evidence that the two corps commanders sought Bazaine's permission or even informed him of their intentions, and Bazaine's subsequent despatch,[78] carefully designed to justify his preoccupation with his left wing, equally carefully saddles Ladmirault with the blame for not having forced the issue to a decisive conclusion. Hindsight can be a useful devil's advocate.

The French advance towards the Verdun road extended Canrobert's gun-line and Tixier's division of 6 Corps in this fashion: on the left, Nayral's division of 3 Corps; in the centre, opposite the Tronville copses,

78 *See* Appendix C.

Aymard's division of the same corps; on the right, overlapping the copses, Grenier's division of 4 Corps. At a conservative estimate, the French had in line and in immediate reserve a force of some 30,000 men on a front of less than two miles. Facing them, crowded into the copses, were the survivors of the German *20th* and *24th* and of Lehmann's four battalions of 37th Brigade — discounting casualties, about 4000 effectives. West of the copses, after the withdrawal of Barby's cavalry brigade, there was not a single German soldier between Bruville and Mars-la-Tour. The tidal wave began to break upon a desolate shore. Let Moltke take up the story.

> At three o'clock, four [*in fact, three*] of their divisions advanced upon the Tronville copses. Barby's cavalry brigade, watching the western verge, had to retire before the enemy's fire, and the German infantry occupying the wood also had to yield to so superior a strength. The batteries which were in action between Vionville and the copses were assailed in rear from the west through the glades of the copses, and were likewise forced to retire. But not until the lapse of an hour did the French succeed in overcoming the obstinate resistance of our few battalions. At the subsequent roll-call near Tronville, it was ascertained that the *24th Regiment* had lost 1000 men and 52 officers, and that the second battalion of the *20th Regiment* had lost all its officers. The 37th demi-Brigade,[79] which of its own accord had been fighting valiantly in support since noon, took possession of [*more correctly, retired to*] the village of Tronville and prepared it for an obstinate defence.

The rout had been complete. By 3.30 p.m. Alvensleben's flank had been turned and the only Germans remaining north of the Verdun road were two companies of the *20th* which clung grimly to the south-west corner of the copses. Mars-la-Tour was in flames; and at this most propitious of moments, the French lost the battle.

While Leboeuf consolidated his position in the copses, Grenier's division on his right, accompanied by Ladmirault, advanced towards the main road without opposition. Farther south Alvensleben gathered his scattered remnants — infantry, cavalry and guns — around Tronville, resolved to buy what time remained or, if necessary, to die in the last ditch. Such resolution was not shared by his opponents.

Inexplicably, when his solid lines of infantry were less than 1000 yards from the Verdun road, and when both Mars-la-Tour and Tronville were there for the taking, Grenier hesitated. Not for the first or for the last time, a French general faltered at the spectre of success. It had been so at Spicheren. It had been so at Borny. It had been so at Rezonville. And it would be so again two hours later on this same field. Grenier's subsequent

79 Lehmann's battalions, which had suffered over 1200 casualties.

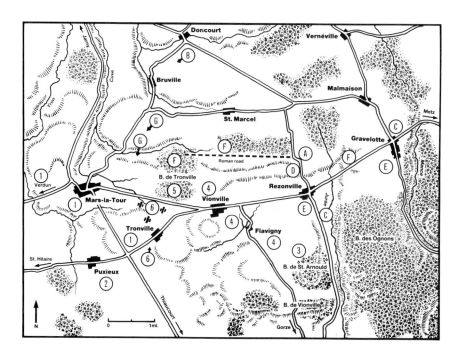

KEY

FRENCH

A. Cav. Div Forton
B. Cav. Div Barail moving on Bruville
C. 2 Corps
D. 6 Corps
E. Imperial Guard
F. 3 Corps
G. 4 Corps, Grenier's division leading Cissey's

GERMAN

1. 5 Cav. Div
2. 6 Cav. Div
3. 5 Inf. Div
4. 6 Inf. Div
5. 37 Inf. Bde
6. 20 Div, X Corps approaching Tronville

Note
Corps Artillery of X Corps already in action on main road. Corps Artillery of III Corps as in Map 8

Map 11   Situation at 3 p.m., 16 August

explanation for his sudden loss of nerve was his conviction that the enemy had regrouped in considerable strength to the south of the main road and that, in his own words, 'precipitate action' would be unwise until 4 Corps was fully deployed. (It must be remarked again that throughout the day the French were persuaded that they were faced by most, if not all, of the German Second Army. Canrobert had earlier gone so far as to 'identify' in front of him both the Guard Corps and XII (Royal Saxon) Corps — both at least a day's march away to the south; both, if they had indeed been present, plainly identifiable by their distinctive uniforms.)

There followed an absurd discussion between Ladmirault and Grenier. Before them they could see the burning buildings of a deserted Mars-la-Tour. Their left was solidly buttressed by Leboeuf's infantry, now in almost complete occupation of the Tronville copses. On their right Barby's brigade had been driven from the field, and a mile to the north a great mass of French cavalry stood ready to advance and roll up the German left. Time enough, said Grenier. Within half an hour the second infantry division of 4 Corps (Cissey) would be on hand to join in a victorious assault.

But half an hour is a long time in a day of battle. And even while Ladmirault and Grenier were engaged in their semantic argument (to stand today where they then stood is to be like a spectator at a bull-fight where two matadors discuss the relative methods of dispatching a dying bull), the German ranks around Tronville began to thicken. It was a little after 3.30 p.m. And it was enough to satisfy Ladmirault that caution, that most dangerous of military counsellors, might be the proper wisdom. And so, as Voigts-Rhetz's X Corps began to arrive piecemeal on the battlefield, he called Grenier's dismayed soldiers back to the Bruville slopes to await events. It was an act of surrender; and it was not the last.

****

We last left X Corps marching westward from Pont-à-Mousson in accordance with Frederick Charles's orders of the 15th. Those orders,[80] it will be remembered, ignored the contrary evidence of Rheinbaben's patrols and spoke of 'the supposition that the enemy's advanced troops on his retreat may be already approaching Verdun'. The direction given to Voigts-Rhetz was Thiaucourt−St Hilaire−Fresnes-en-Woëvre, a quite different axis to that which Moltke had laid down in his earlier instruction and one which would carry X Corps to the west instead of the north-west, and on a course parallel to and 12 miles to the south of the main Metz−Verdun road. Certainly, Moltke had given Frederick Charles complete freedom of action, and the latter cannot be blamed, as the official German history was quick to do, for his failure to guess the full measure of French incompetence or the true nature of Bazaine's irresolution. None the less, his error of judgment could and should have had fatal consequences as the two corps forming the right wing of Second Army marched steadily away from each other, inviting destruction in detail; for while Frederick Charles was bound for the Meuse, Bazaine remained bound to Metz, and the plateau which should have been the scene of disaster for the one became the setting of defeat for the other.

Late on the 15th, the three leading corps of Second Army had anticipated Moltke's decision to press forward beyond the Moselle and all had started to cross to the left bank: III Corps at Corny/Novéant; X Corps at Pont-à-Mousson; and the Guard Corps a few miles upstream at Dieulouard. We have seen the events which followed upon Alvensleben's

80 *See* p. 108.

flank-march towards Mars-la-Tour. It is now time to follow X Corps.

In the van was 19th Division (Schwarzkoppen), and the leading brigade (Wedell's 38th) bivouacked for the night of the 15th at Thiaucourt, where it was joined by the Dragoon Brigade of the Guard Corps from Dieulouard.[81] This is yet another example of Moltke's doctrine of flexibility and mutual support, and this attached cavalry brigade was to play a significant part during the second crisis of the afternoon battle. The second brigade of this division (Lehmann's 37th, less Colonel Lyncker's detachment at Novéant) halted during the evening about four miles to the east on the Thiaucourt road. Meanwhile 20th Division (Kraatz-Koschlau) spent the night on the left bank of the river at Pont-à-Mousson.

The whole of X Corps was early on the move on the 16th, and throughout that day of burning heat it was to achieve astonishing feats of endurance on the line of march. (38th Brigade, for example, would cover more than 27 miles in under ten hours and 20th Division nearly 25 miles in eight hours, both going straight into action without a cooked meal and with only the briefest rest-period. Moltke would later comment sternly not on the stamina of his infantry but on the 'unacceptable' number of stragglers who fell out on the line of march. During this same day the greatest distance covered by any infantry of the Army of the Rhine was 12 miles — Cissey's division of 4 Corps — and indeed almost the whole of Bazaine's army had spent the night of the 15th encamped *under canvas* on the battlefield of the morrow.

Wedell's Brigade with the Guard Dragoons set out from Thiaucourt at dawn in the direction of St Hilaire, twelve miles to the west on the main Metz–Verdun road; in other words, following the thrust of Frederick Charles's march-order to intercept the enemy's retreat at or near Verdun. It had been on the road for three hours when the sound of Rheinbaben's cannonade reached it from the north-east. Judging — wrongly, as we now know — that this was the modest rearguard action which Frederick Charles had expected, it hurried on its westward way. Already, on a cloudless morning, the fog of war was closing in.

The four remaining battalions of Lehmann's Brigade also set out at dawn in Wedell's tracks and reached Thiaucourt shortly after 10 a.m. There the rising thunder of the guns, and Caprivi's urgent warning from Tronville, reached Lehmann, and instinctively he turned aside, and marched his men, with a small cavalry escort and two batteries, towards the sound of battle. As we have seen, he reported himself to Alvensleben near Puxieux at noon, and without pause or preparation fed his weary battalions straight into the Tronville copses. To Bazaine, sitting apprehensively on the ridge at Rezonville, this sudden apparition assumed the character of a major attack upon his powerful right flank. Thus it is that, when a fearful leader

---

81   It should be remembered that the cavalry division of X Corps (5th) was on detached duty to the north-west, where it came under the temporary command of III Corps.

becomes the victim of his own obsessions, and when a tiny trumpet-call assumes the crack of desperate doom, battles are quickly lost and fortunes are cast away. So it was that Lehmann, during the morning battle, made of four battalions a brave, bold and brilliant bastion on Alvensleben's empty left flank. Perhaps he saved the day.

So much for 19th Division, marching both *into* battle and *away* from battle. Let us now return to 20th Division.

This division had left Pont-à-Mousson at 5 a.m., following the westward path to Thiaucourt, and thence towards Verdun. It marched incuriously, its eyes fixed on the Meuse, 40 miles beyond its horizon. It had no contact of any sort with III Corps working its way to the north-west. Indeed, it had little contact with 19th Division pressing forward on the single road that lay ahead. At dawn on 16 August, its objective was Verdun. By noon, its duty lay elsewhere. For by noon Second Army was fighting for its life.

****

During the latter part of the morning the commander of X Corps, Voigts-Rhetz, reached Thiaucourt, where he received an urgent message from his chief of staff, Caprivi. This informed him that III Corps, far from being involved in a rearguard action, was engaged in a full-scale battle with most, if not all, of the Army of the Rhine; that supplies of ammunition were critically low; and that Alvensleben was in imminent danger of being overwhelmed by a massive turning movement round his left flank. Even at this advanced hour, Caprivi seems to have been alone, with Rheinbaben, in accepting — and understanding — the true peril in which not only III Corps but also the whole German Second Army was placed. Alvensleben, the great gambler, was well aware that this was no rearguard action; but his right wing was holding its ground above the Gorze defiles, 6th Infantry Division had stormed and captured Vionville and Flavigny, Lehmann's brigade and Buddenbrock's *24th* and *20th* had secured the Tronville copses; and Bazaine's listless response might even mean that the main body of the Army of the Rhine was withdrawing on the central *chaussée* through Doncourt and Étain. In other words, that he had struck not a rearguard, but a strong flank-guard. It was not a particularly educated guess, and by noon even the adventurous Alvensleben had come to terms with the grim reality of the situation.

Voigts-Rhetz, with the thunder of battle echoing down to him from the north, was undecided. His orders were to hasten westward to intercept the main body of the enemy at or near Verdun. But the urgency of Caprivi's warning, and Lehmann's bold decision to march to the sound of the guns, were enough to convince him that a crisis was at hand. He sent four messages: the first, to Frederick Charles at Pont-à-Mousson (this was the earliest intimation to reach Second Army HQ that III Corps was involved in a battle for survival); the second, to Schwarzkoppen, marching 38th

Infantry Brigade and the Guard Dragoon Brigade westward to St Hilaire, to halt there and turn back at once along the Verdun road to Mars-la-Tour; the third, to Kraatz to halt the head of 20th Division at Thiaucourt and to take the Chambley road to Tronville with all speed; and the fourth — and most interesting — an instruction to hurry his corps artillery forward *across country* and to come into action ahead of Kraatz's marching infantry to the west of the Tronville copses. The most interesting, because it reflected precisely the way in which Alvensleben had handled *his* corps artillery in the early stages of the battle. It has been said before, and it should be emphasized again: the battle of Mars-la-Tour was, like every battle, a destructive infantry encounter; it was, like not many battles, marked by a series of resounding clashes of cavalry; but, like almost no other battle, it was dominated, sustained, and won by an artillery which though outnumbered by at least two to one demonstrated throughout the day the simple equation that quantity is no substitute for quality, and that energy is no answer to expertise. When in later years the war artists came to record this battle and the bloodbath of 18 August, they painted the long lines of poplars, the bloody scenes at Flavigny, at St Privat, and at St Hubert, the great swirling hosts of horsemen. But they did not come close to the true heart of the battle — the grandeur of the guns.

So, with the sound of those guns rumbling southward to him, Voigts-Rhetz set off from Thiaucourt. There he met Alvensleben near Tronville shortly after Bredow's charge and saw for himself the parlous state in which III Corps stood, and the long lines of Ladmirault's infantry advancing on Mars-la-Tour. And he at once recognized that the conduct of the next — and probably decisive — phase of the battle was now largely in his hands.

****

20th Division began to reach the battlefield in strength a little after 3.30 p.m., at the very moment that Ladmirault and Grenier were deciding that perhaps discretion was after all the better part of valour. The half-hour that Grenier had proposed as a comfortable cushion to allow Cissey to bring his division into line on the right was wasted time while the minutes slipped away; for at 3.48 p.m. the corps artillery of X Corps, hastening forward from Thiaucourt, opened fire in close order from positions just to the south-west of the Tronville copses. Ladmirault needed no further prompting. This sudden show of aggression was enough to convince him that fresh German forces 'in considerable numbers' were already being deployed to the south of the Verdun road; indeed, that a serious threat to his own right flank was about to be mounted. Without even attempting to test the opposition, he at once summoned Grenier's division back to the comparative security of the Bruville slope.[82]

82 This — to Voigts-Rhetz — inexplicable decision was in the event to lead to an equally unexpected disaster on the German side.

As 20th Division marched up the long, dusty road from Chambley, Voigts-Rhetz surveyed the battlefield from a vantage-point to the west of Flavigny. He did not care much for what he saw. Alvensleben's infantry of the 5th and 6th Divisions was stretched in a single diminishing line from the Bois de St Arnould to the Verdun road. It had, in every sense, borne the heat of the day since early morning. Men and horses were exhausted. Ammunition was low. Only the devoted gunners manning their red-hot pieces buttressed this beleaguered corps.

Voigts-Rhetz could not possibly have known the mind of Marshal Bazaine at this moment. But his instinct and experience were enough to warn him that the entire battle — even the entire campaign — hung in the balance. He reasoned thus, as he later wrote.[83] The main threat to the German position that afternoon lay on the left flank beyond Tronville and Mars-la-Tour; and it was there that X Corps could render the most necessary service. But if Bazaine were to summon up his numerous reserves from Gravelotte and deliver a concerted attack from Rezonville, III Corps, lying chiefly to the south of the Verdun road, and no longer capable of organized resistance, would be swept away, and in the debris of defeat, the *right* wing of X Corps would be fatally compromised. He therefore took a brave and interesting decision. As the leading brigade (39th) of 20th Division arrived upon the battlefield he detached three battalions and fed them into the critical junction point between 5th and 6th Divisions at Flavigny. He did not consult with Alvensleben before doing so. He did not need to. The unexpected appearance of this stimulating reinforcement was no more lost on Picard's Grenadiers than had been the arrival of the artillery of X Corps before the hesitant Grenier.

****

Ladmirault's decision to call back Grenier's division shortly before 4 p.m. had a knock-on effect on Leboeuf; for now Aymard's division of 3 Corps, having cleared the Tronville copses, found itself dangerously exposed to the artillery of X Corps, and then to Kraatz-Koschlau's infantry as it reached the Verdun road.

The reader may care to reflect here, with special reference to Maps 5–15, on the crucial part played by these copses throughout the day, lying as they did at the very centre of the battlefield, skirted to the south by the vital Verdun road, and sharply dividing the morning and the afternoon battles. As has been suggested, Mars-la-Tour was an extraordinarily 'geometrical' battle, enclosed within a clear rectangle, split from east to west by the Verdun roads,[84] the morning and the afternoon fighting broadly

83   Voigts-Rhetz: *Briefe aus den Kriegsjahren 1866 und 1870–71.*

84   The southerly through Mars-la-Tour; the central through Doncourt; the northerly through Briey.

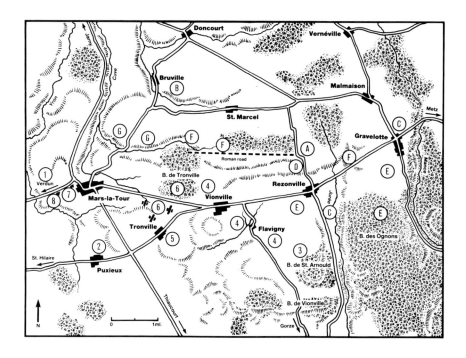

Map 12   Situation at 4 p.m., 16 August

divided by these blood-soaked bushes and scattered trees.

The swinging pendulum may be summarized thus: when Rheinbaben's guns opened up on the morning of the 16th the copses lay in the tranquillity of a summer's day, the nearest German infantry deep in the southern defiles, the nearest French innocently encamped at Vionville 500 yards away; between 9 a.m. and noon. When even the most elementary precaution should have advised either Frossard or Canrobert to occupy these empty acres, they remained virginal and vacant, while no fewer than four French divisions watched and waited at a discreet distance. Plate 7 will show how short a step was needed to grasp this prize. Map 12 will show how lamely it was lost.

By noon the scene had greatly changed, as the pendulum began to swing. Alvensleben had by then pushed his reserve battalions of the *20th* and *24th* into the copses, soon to be followed by Lehmann's battalions from X Corps, and these troops, despite the close attention of Canrobert's batteries along the Roman road, soon reached the northern fringes of the woods. Beyond that point, outranged by Leboeuf's chassepots on the higher ground between St Marcel and Bruville, they could make no progress. At this point in the battle the copses formed a fragile salient projecting into the heart of Bazaine's ponderous left-wheel, thinly covered to the west by Barby's cavalry brigade near Mars-la-Tour. Yet the mere presence of the German infantry in these woods had been enough for Bazaine to propose to Leboeuf that he should mark time until Ladmirault's corps was ready to extend an already powerful right flank. And it was to relieve the intolerable pressure on the Tronville copses that Alvensleben ordered Bredow to charge Canrobert's guns at 2 p.m.

There followed a pause. Then at 3 p.m. the pendulum swung again as Leboeuf and Ladmirault began their fatally delayed advance towards the Verdun road. Overborne by numbers, exhausted by hours of burning sun and bitter battle, decimated by casualties, and with little ammunition left, the Germans broke and fled '*au pas de course*'. By 4 p.m. the Tronville copses were almost entirely in French hands (for the first time). By 4 p.m. the debris of Alvensleben's infantry had rallied around Tronville. And at 4 p.m. the pendulum swung again.

****

After the briefest of rests, Woyna's 39th Brigade (less the battalions earlier detached by Voigts-Rhetz to bolster Stuelpnagel's thin battle-line at Flavigny) was pushed straight into the Tronville copses under cover of X Corps guns now reinforced by the artillery of 20th Division. Twenty minutes later it was followed by 40th Brigade (Diringshofen). As throughout the morning, so now. Not a single battalion was kept in reserve. As with Alvensleben, so with Voigts-Rhetz. Everything was hazarded on a show of aggression and on a pretence of strength.

Ladmirault's decision to recall Grenier's division had uncovered Leboeuf's right flank, and the copses, which had earlier formed a narrow German salient, now in turn became a potential death-trap for the French. Mindful of Bazaine's earlier proposal to maintain his former position 'as strongly as possible' and apprehensive of the true strength of the newly arrived enemy,[85] Leboeuf ordered the withdrawal of Aymard's division from the Verdun road. Despite the fatigue of their long march, the German infantry pressed forward until, shortly before 5 p.m., the copses

---

85 Kraatz's total available force consisted only of 8 battalions, 4 squadrons, and 4 field batteries.

were once again in their hands; and now, in the most dramatic fashion, the pendulum swung once more.

As we have seen, Voigts-Rhetz before leaving Thiaucourt had sent an urgent message to the commander of 19th Division, Schwarzkoppen, then marching westward with his second infantry brigade (Wedell's 38th)[86] and the Guard Dragoon Brigade to halt his column at St Hilaire and to hasten back to Mars-la-Tour. The Dragoon Brigade arrived shortly after 4 p.m. and took up station a little to the north-west of the village, covered on its left by Barby's cavalry brigade. Half an hour later Wedell's Brigade reached Hannonville to the south-west, where for all their legendary stamina on the march, the exhausted men were obliged to halt for half an hour's rest. The scene was set for an epic passage of arms.

Voigts-Rhetz, still imbued with the offensive spirit which had dictated every German action since dawn, had made a bold but hazardous decision. The withdrawal of Grenier's division and the recapture of the Tronville copses led him — understandably, perhaps — to misjudge both the strength and the intention of the enemy. It seemed, as he later wrote,[87] that the French were vulnerable to an immediate attack against their right flank. It was a dangerous speculation, which a brief reconnaissance would have shown to be unwise. There was no reconnaissance. Had there been, a dreadful error would not have been made.

While Leboeuf was pulling Aymard's division back from the copses, Ladmirault had completed the deployment of 4 Corps. A little to the west of Bruville there is a deep ravine which, running due south for a mile, turns east opposite the hamlet of Ville-sur-Yron. While it is not so striking a feature as the Mance ravine,[88] which was to be the setting for an even greater disaster on the 18th, it provides an important flank protection and a formidable obstacle to any infantry attack; and of its existence Voigts-Rhetz and Schwarzkoppen were unaware. In the angle formed by this ravine Cissey had drawn up his division on Grenier's right, his centre resting on the strong-point of Greyères (spelt Grizières on some maps). Thus two virtually intact divisions were deployed facing the road between Mars-la-Tour and Tronville, and supported to the north-west by an uncommitted mass of 12 regiments of cavalry. It was 5 p.m.[89]

Voigts-Rhetz's order was for an immediate attack towards Bruville. While 20th Division was to press forward against Leboeuf from the copses on the right, Wedell's 38th Brigade, exhaustion notwithstanding, was to take the French in flank from the left. For reasons nowhere explained the

---

86   This was a Westphalian brigade, consisting of the *16th* and *57th* Infantry Regiments. One battalion of the latter was left to secure the main road at St Hilaire. It would presently have cause to count itself lucky.

87   Voigts-Rhetz: *op. cit.*

88   *See* Plates 21-22.

89   At this moment, too late to influence the course of events, Frederick Charles reached the battlefield from Pont-à-Mousson.

Plate 17   The wooded ravine as seen by Wedell's brigade (38th) as it advanced from Mars-la-Tour

Plate 18   The ravine — scene of the destruction of Wedell's brigade

order seems not to have reached 20th Division. Thus 38th Brigade advanced unsupported to its doom.

The brigade moved across the main road[90] in extended order, facing a little to the north-east, the three battalions of the *16th* echeloned ahead of the two battalions of the *57th*. Then, as the lines of infantrymen breasted the gentle slope, they were greeted with a storm of mitrailleuse and chassepot fire from both front and flank, while before them lay the unsuspected ravine (Plate 17). Wedell's men had blundered into the very centre of the French position.

With exemplary fortitude the Westphalians pressed ahead. Despite heavy casualties, the front ranks of the two regiments reached the ravine and climbed down the southern edge to the rock-strewn bottom (Plate 18). They did not get beyond.

> Not a man reached the further side; the French chassepots brought them to a dead halt. The troops who reached the bottom ... crouched there, too exhausted and terrified to move. For perhaps ten minutes the French fired into this inert mass; then roused by their officers and their drummers, they hurled themselves shouting into the valley and pursued the fleeing Prussians up the corpse-strewn slopes beyond ... . Fugitives poured back over the road, horses bolted, and in Tronville Caprivi ordered all X Corps documents to be burned. Now, if ever, was the moment for the French cavalry to charge. Now was certainly the moment for Ladmirault to attack.[91]

Such was also the picture seen through German eyes:

> At some 90 to 100 yards from the ravine our line came to a halt and tried to answer the enemy's fire. From this moment the attack came to a standstill. The men lay on the ground, but that gave them no cover. Two-thirds of their officers were down and the body, thus deprived of its soul, gave way. They held their ground for a time, then turned and bolted.[92]

Wedell's Brigade had gone into action 95 officers and 4546 men strong. Of these the *16th* lost 49 officers and 1756 men, the *57th*, 23 officers and 786 men. The only wonder is that so many survived.

'Now was certainly the moment for Ladmirault to attack.' But as he had done earlier in the afternoon, so Ladmirault hesitated again. It is impossible to understand why. The destruction of Wedell's brigade and the

90 The German account improbably records 'at the double'.

91 Howard: *op. cit.*

92 Hönig: *Gefechtsbilder aus dem Kriege 1870–71.*

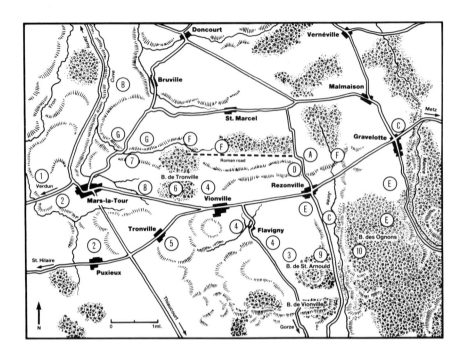

Map 13   Situation at 5 p.m., 16 August

desperate situation to the south of the Verdun road had caused the
pendulum to swing violently again and had compelled Voigts-Rhetz once
more to summon back 20th Division — his only remaining battleworthy
infantry — from the long-disputed Tronville copses. Even in the presence
of his Army Commander, the temptation to surrender his left wing and
draw closer to Alvensleben on his right, and there to protect the positions
so painfully secured during the morning battle, must have been overwhelming. He was short of men, short of ammunition, short of medical
facilities, short of everything except the will to win. That will was still in

190

strong supply. Like Alvensleben four hours earlier, he had one remaining card, and this he was presently to play.

None of these considerations should have caused Ladmirault to hesitate. Indeed, a more resolute commander would have pressed his manifest advantage home. His opponent, by a gratuitous error of judgment, had unlocked a door which since early in the day had been swinging on uncertain hinges. His eager men, having savoured victory, were pressing forward to feast upon the fruits of their good fortune. And at that moment the founding father of the feast hesitated.

History is hindsight. It is easy to sit in remote judgment on men who can no longer fight their corner or describe their doubts and indecisions. The art of war is the art of weighing in the balance the discreet distinction between the improbable and the impossible, the narrow divide between moral certainty and moral cowardice. It was such a divide that separated the two sides on the day of battle. And now it was to decide the day.

Ladmirault chose the contagious line of moral cowardice which had pursued the Army of the Rhine since Napoleon's departure; if not, indeed, before. Perhaps he could not believe his luck. Certainly he did not perceive his opportunity. Incredibly, as he had waited upon Cissey at the first crisis of the afternoon battle, so now he waited upon his *third* division, Lorencez's, four hours' march away to the east and quite incapable of influencing a battle in which minutes, not hours, counted. Six days later Bazaine was to write: 'General Ladmirault recognized that Tronville [*no mention of Mars-la-Tour*] was too strongly occupied to be taken with two divisions, and he contented himself (*sic*) in occupying temporarily the enemy, and in establishing himself on the ground he had gained.'[93] This absurd distortion of the truth tells us more about Bazaine than about Ladmirault.

No such elegant excuses exercised Voigts-Rhetz. To him minutes mattered: with his infantry in disarray and his artillery forced to fall back to the protection of the low ridge behind Tronville, he turned to his last resort as Alvensleben had done four hours before.

Sixteen years earlier Bosquet, looking down on the charge of the Light Brigade at Balaklava, is credited with saying: 'It is magnificent, but it is not war.' He would have thought no differently now. Brandenburg's Guard Dragoon Brigade, attached with typical foresight to Wedell's westward march, now stood east and west of Mars-la-Tour, its purpose protective, its role reservist. But as Wedell's brigade came tumbling back in panic and disorder, Voigts-Rhetz called forward his cavalry. Three squadrons of 1st Guard Dragoons on the right, two squadrons of the 2nd on the left,[94] rode out through the smoke and dust of battle and fell upon Ladmirault's

93 *See* Appendix C.

94 Many German accounts wrongly reverse the order of advance of these regiments. The two surviving memorials tell the true tale.

infantry as it pressed forward from the ravine in pursuit of Wedell's fleeing Westphalians.

In life nothing succeeds like success. In war nothing succeeds like surprise. Thus as the long lines of French infantry in their thick thousands bore down on the Verdun road, they were struck by a furious phalanx of some six hundred horsemen. It is inconceivable that so small a demonstration could have achieved, as Bredow had earlier done, so decisive an effect. The whirling squadrons of Brandenburg's Dragoons fell upon the leading brigades of Grenier's and Cissey's divisions and threw them into momentary confusion. The advancing lines of Frenchmen, startled and surprised, faltered and fell back, clustered around their standards, seemingly convinced that this desperate charge presaged the German turning movement that had haunted Ladmirault throughout the afternoon. The time was 5.30 p.m.

Why should this have been? When Voigts-Rhetz ordered forward Brandenburg's squadrons his only hope — a slender one — was that this diversion would provide a few precious minutes to enable the remnants of Wedell's brigade to disengage and rally to the south of Mars-la-Tour. He could not have imagined, for all his offensive spirit, that so modest a force could stem, let alone reverse, the advancing tide of 4 Corps infantry. Certainly the cavalry attack took the French by surprise. In the dust and smoke of battle a hundred horsemen can seem like five hundred, five hundred like a thousand. The charging Germans,[95] big men on powerful horses, caused panic in the leading files of Frenchmen and suddenly the dead hand of doubt rippled along the ranks. The headlong pursuit stuttered and stopped. The unequal combat raged for a brief period until the Guard Dragoons drew off, their duty done and half their number dead or wounded. Brave as the charge had been, it should not have been enough to stop the enemy from resuming his advance. But it was enough for Ladmirault. For the second time during the afternoon he sent for Grenier and Cissey to recall their bewildered men behind the protection of the ravine.

Ladmirault was to justify this wanton decision by claiming to have identified 'a whole new army corps' confronting his victorious troops. That this corps existed only in his imagination cannot be explained by the apparition of five squadrons of German cavalry. The answer is more simple. Like Bazaine since dawn, like Canrobert since the early afternoon, Ladmirault had lost his nerve. His eager infantry was buttressed by sixteen batteries and by a great assembly of cavalry lying no more than a mile to the north-west of the battlefield. His left flank was secured by Leboeuf. The swinging pendulum had brought the Tronville copses back within the French fold. It is not possible to imagine a more sure and solid platform

95 Two of Bismarck's sons took part in the charge. The eldest, Herbert, was seriously wounded, and the youngest, William, brought a fallen comrade out of action on his horse.

from which to launch a final and conclusive blow. It is not easy to excuse Ladmirault's tame surrender not only of the initiative, but of the very prospect of victory.

In every battle there have been moments when a single stroke, fortuitous or foreseen, has turned the day; when bravado has outfaced bravery. Moreover, battles are not like the intellectual exercises of wargames. They are about sound and fury, about death and destruction, about triumph and tragedy. It is the singular quality of a great commander to keep a cool head when all about are losing theirs. It is a quality called 'leadership': Marlborough at Malplaquet, Wolfe at Quebec, Wellington at Mont St Jean, Smith-Dorrien at Le Cateau. It is a quality which Alvensleben and Voigts-Rhetz demonstrated hour by hour during the day of battle. And it is a quality that was fatally lacking among French commanders during a day when even modest resolution would four, five, even six times have brushed aside a brave but beaten opponent.

For the French rank and file it is possible to feel only pity. It is fair to say that while they fought for a cause in which they believed, they died for a dynasty which they had reason to deride. While Napoleon hurried on his way to Châlons, the army which he had left battled bravely and well; and despite the bitter disappointments of Mars-la-Tour, would acquit itself with yet greater gallantry at Gravelotte and St Privat. The soldiers of France have every reason to be proud of their day of battle. They have less reason to be proud of the leaders who let them down.

****

It was 6 p.m. when Ladmirault recalled Grenier and Cissey to their former positions on the Bruville slope. A stillness fell upon the scene, presage of the truly Wagnerian finale which would presently ring down the curtain here on the western flank. Meanwhile it is time to return to the morning battlefield and to the further fortunes of III Corps.

After Bredow's charge had thrown Canrobert's corps into disarray to the north of the Verdun road, Buddenbrock's 6th Division maintained the positions it had reached earlier to the east of Vionville and Flavigny, exhausted by long hours of fighting and driven at last to abandon any thought of further offensive action. Facing it, in a tight arc around Rezonville, stood Picard's Grenadiers of the Guard in the same purely defensive posture which they had adopted since replacing Frossard's 2 Corps at noon. Thus the centre of the line lay in a curious state of armed repose, the Germans still covered by Alvensleben's steadfast artillery,[96] the

---

96 Remarkably, Körber's four horse-artillery batteries were still occupying the positions at Tronville from where they had opened their account at 9 a.m.; and where they would remain until the long day's end.

French seemingly ready to wound and yet afraid to strike, when a single blow would have been enough to break the deadlock.

On the German right where, during the afternoon, Kraatz's three battalions had been diverted from the line of march of 20th Division to stiffen Stuelpnagel's thinly stretched ranks, the morning battle had similarly become, as it were, stagnant. Here 5th Division's line ran from the northern fringes of the Bois de St Arnould to Flavigny, also under the watchful eye of Alvensleben's guns. And here, by afternoon, Bazaine's padlocks were thickly strung on the slopes south of Rezonville, chassepot and mitrailleuse replying without answer to the outranged needle-gun, the German breechloaders alone able to sustain the fire-fight.

Here the French line ran from right to left: Picard's 3rd Grenadiers; Montaudon's division of 3 Corps, lately removed from St Marcel; Lapasset's brigade, still astride the Rezonville—Gorze road; the left flank secured by Deligny's Voltigeur division of the Guard with its Chasseur battalion thrown forward into the Bois des Ognons; and as if such solid strength might not be enough to resist a spectral attack on the French left flank, Sorval's division of 6 Corps lay listlessly along the Verdun road east of Rezonville; beyond it at Gravelotte the roughly handled divisions of Frossard's corps, and farther north six brigades of cavalry. Thus as the afternoon wore on Alvensleben's III Corps, covered at last by the arrival of Voigts-Rhetz's infantry and guns on its empty left flank, stood facing half the Army of the Rhine: nearly six divisions of infantry, 200 guns, and an immobile mass of cavalry. The position at this moment may best be likened to a boxer, with a small opponent on the ropes, leading defensively with his left when one solid right-hook would settle the issue. There can be few more striking examples in the long catalogue of conflict of the wanton waste of a victorious advantage. Nor, on this southern flank, had the day's surprises run their course. Let us therefore leave for the moment the architect of victory, Alvensleben, and turn to Gravelotte, and to the architect of defeat, Bazaine.

We last left Bazaine at noon at Rezonville, urging on his battalions, siting his batteries, behaving like 'an ordinary colonel', and in imminent danger of capture by Redern's harrying hussars. As figures on a flickering film, he and his small entourage, which included two of his nephews, disappeared for a long while from the screen. Bazaine was enjoying himself in the eye of the storm. 'He was happily commanding some guns when a member of his staff discovered him at last. *"Ah, ça"*, he remarked cheerfully, *"ces bougres-là vont me laisser seul en l'air"*.[97] It was splendid stuff, richly reminiscent of Algeria and of the heady air of Mexico; but it was not the way to command a retreating army of 140,000 men, or the way to defeat a very professional opponent who had rashly dropped his guard.

It was nearly 3 p.m. before he made a reappearance at his HQ at

97 Guedalla: *The Two Marshals.*

Gravelotte, and by then, as his proposal to Leboeuf to stand on the defensive once 3 Corps had completed its change of front suggests, it seems beyond argument that he had abandoned any intention he might earlier have had of clearing the enemy obstacle astride the Verdun road. Bredow's charge and the resulting disorder in the ranks of Canrobert's corps convinced him — for such a conviction suited his supine purpose — that the obstacle facing the Army of the Rhine was no small shadow but a force of serious substance. This conviction is underlined by the total failure of Forton's and Valabrègue's cavalry divisions to pursue the remnants of Bredow's brigade as they struggled back across the road towards Flavigny.

Bazaine did not leave Gravelotte again until after midnight, by when he had issued orders for the withdrawal of his whole army to the Amanvillers line. The man who had spent the morning in the thick of things now retired into a shell of introspection, his thoughts concentrated on Metz and on his obsessive fears for his left flank, haunted by the spectre of a defeat at the hands of an enemy who himself was desperately fighting for survival. Such was the strange military paradox as the centre of gravity of this long day of battle shifted to the west.

From Gravelotte, Bazaine could see nothing except the gratifying spectacle of soldiery which he had crowded into the narrow triangle Malmaison−Rezonville−Bois des Ognons. Here, apart from the defensive screen which commanded the southern approaches from Gorze, he could survey with satisfaction, if not pride, something of the order of six infantry divisions, three cavalry divisions and an ample artillery. From Gravelotte, he could not even see Rezonville, let alone Vionville and the Tronville copses and the critical battlefield beyond. He did not ride the short distance to St Marcel to consult with Leboeuf. He did not trouble to acquaint himself with the progress of Ladmirault's corps at Doncourt and Bruville. He did not even send a single staff-officer to that beckoning flank, either to give orders or bring back information. By mid-afternoon Bazaine, silent on his private peak in Darien, seems to have opted out of battle. And about the same hour, his opponent unwittingly — certainly unintentionally — provided him with a slender justification for his *idée fixe*.

When news reached Frederick Charles of the critical plight of III Corps he at once set out for the battlefield on the heels of Voigts-Rhetz. But before leaving Pont-à-Mousson he sent an order to Manstein, commanding IX Corps, to make all haste to push the head of his column across the river and to march at once to the aid of Stuelpnagel's embattled division still hanging on grimly to the forest fringes below Rezonville. The shortest route would take this relief force through Gorze, already encumbered with traffic and with a growing welter of wounded.[98]

98 The reader may reflect again on Bazaine's failure to occupy this vital village during the wasted hours of the 15th.

IX Corps had not reached the river until noon. In the van was the *11th Grenadier Regiment* (36th Infantry Brigade of Wrangel's 18th Infantry Division) followed by 49th Brigade of 25th (Hessian) Division. Progress across the congested river approaches was slow; and it was accompanied by yet another example of the instinctive improvisation which had marked — not always wisely — Moltke's great westerly wheel since Saarbrücken.

It will be remembered that, after the battle of Borny on the 14th, Steinmetz's First Army had been halted to the east and south of Metz, its function to serve as pivot and flank-guard to Frederick Charles as he pressed forward across the river, and to protect the right wing of Second Army against the possibility of a sortie by Bazaine to the south of Metz. At noon on the 16th the left-hand corps of this Army, Goeben's VIIIth, lay around the village of Frontigny on the right bank of the river. Here throughout the morning the sound of battle on the Gravelotte plateau could be clearly heard, although the escarpment concealed any view of the fighting.

There is no evidence of any communication between Frederick Charles and Steinmetz before the former left Pont-à-Mousson, nor did Steinmetz, who had been sulking since his reprimand after Spicheren, issue any order to the commander of VIII Corps. But as at Spicheren and at Borny, so now the ingrained doctrine of German battle-training — to march to the sound of the guns — anticipated any formal instruction. And shortly after 1 p.m. 32nd Brigade (Colonel Rex)[99] of 16th Division (Barnekow), accompanied by three batteries and three squadrons of cavalry, filed across the bridge at Corny, below Novéant, and headed up the steep defile to Gorze, where it halted. The time was 3.30 p.m., and the column of IX Corps from Pont-à-Mousson was still on the march from the south.

Rex reported his arrival to Stuelpnagel and at once sent his three batteries with their cavalry escort to join the depleted artillery of III Corps on the Flavigny ridge. And shortly before 5 p.m. the *40th*, followed by two battalions of the *72nd*, debouched on to the plateau above the Bois de St Arnould. At almost the same moment, Wedell's brigade was advancing to its destruction eight miles away to the west. Much the same fate awaited Colonel Rex, and the *11th Grenadier Regiment* following in his wake, for the French lay in overwhelming strength on the upper slopes, and by nightfall this diversionary column had lost 119 officers and 2466 men.[100] Even then, the most northerly of the many memorials on this bitterly contested slope is that of Rex's *72nd*. It stands near the site of the former farm called Maison Blanche; and it is less than 2000 yards from Rezonville.

The thunderous battle raging beyond the Tronville copses has obscured

---

99   This brigade consisted of *40th Fusilier Regiment* and *72nd Infantry Regiment.*

100   49th (Hessian) Brigade, arriving from Pont-à-Mousson as darkness fell, attempted an ambitious flank movement through the Bois des Ognons but was easily repelled by the Voltigeur division of the Imperial Guard.

the true cause and effect of the renewed fighting on the French left. Most German accounts either pay scant attention to the intervention of VIII and IX Corps or present their entry on to the battlefield as a concerted effort to take Rezonville by storm before darkness fell. This was certainly not the German intention. By early afternoon the battle had assumed an entirely different pattern and its axis now ran broadly east to west. With the deployment of the French 3 and 4 Corps and the arrival of Voigts-Rhetz's X Corps it had become clear that if a decision were to be reached it would be here, on the German left. The battle of Mars-la-Tour would end, as it had begun, as a fight for survival on one side and an unco-ordinated effort to secure the southerly lifeline to Verdun on the other. That, at least, was the German purpose. In the light of events it was arguably not Bazaine's.

By early afternoon, the picture, though not an inviting one, was plain to Alvensleben and to Stuelpnagel on the German right. By then the true imbalance of forces was only too evident, the French response less so. Since 10 a.m. Alvensleben had sought survival in a series of brilliant bluffs, culminating in Bredow's charge and Canrobert's weak withdrawal. Every French riposte on this wing had been doubtful and defensive. Even Bazaine's single sally by the Cuirassiers of the Guard had been accompanied by an explicit admission of defeat — 'It is absolutely necessary to *stop* them!'

So, as the battle ebbed away to the west, Frederick Charles sent his column of IX Corps north from Pont-à-Mousson with no other intention than to relieve the pressure on Stuelpnagel. So also went Rex's brigade from VIII Corps. Their joint purpose was not the turning of the French left flank or, certainly, a *coup de main* against the solid defensive wall covering Rezonville. Frederick Charles's mind was fixed on Mars-la-Tour; and his purpose was to hold Bazaine's mass of manœuvre tightly tied to the main road from Metz. It was to prove a costly operation; but it succeeded beyond every expectation. And this is why.

By mid-afternoon Bazaine's mind was made up — or more precisely, firmness had given way to fantasy. He had no idea what was happening in and beyond the Tronville copses; certainly no conception of the victory on that flank which his massive superiority invited, indeed demanded. Instead he turned his back on one battle, and in his imagination dreamed up another one. By his irresolution, he was to lose both.

It was about this hour that Bazaine — *'notre glorieux Bazaine'*[101] — finally decided that the full weight of the German thrust was to cut him off not from distant Verdun but from nearby Metz; from the comfort of the fortress (far from fully fortified) and the consolation of a place of refuge which, two months later, he was ignominiously to surrender. Every kind of base motive has been attributed to Bazaine, as we shall see when we reach

101   The phrase was that of Thiers, the veteran Orléanist. It was a phrase which was to bring Bazaine to a supreme command which he had never sought, and to an inglorious end which he surely did not deserve.

the end of this melancholy road. He had no motive. He was the least treasonable of men. He fought, so far as he was able, a good fight; but he remained not a commander-in-chief presented with a god-given opportunity to drive the enemy from the field but a former private of the line who when the chance came was incompetent to turn it to his advantage. For that he has been neatly erased from the French historical record. For that the French people have much to answer.

So, when towards 5 p.m. Frederick Charles's modest relief column began to emerge from the woods above Gorze, Bazaine's reaction was immediate. This was surely the great German effort to turn his left flank and to sever his communications with Metz. It was, of course, nothing of the sort. But it was enough for Bazaine to claim in due course that his hourly apprehension of just such an effort to cut him off from Metz was fully justified. It was an absurd assumption. With his great gallery of divisions and guns stacked up around Rezonville and Gravelotte, no such danger existed. Indeed, it was a ripe moment for a great counter-stroke. No such stroke came. And unwittingly, as has been earlier suggested, a minor demonstration on the German right pinned down Bazaine's last mass of manœuvre. It was 5 p.m.; and Bazaine did not know that while he was stifling the small assault upon his left, he was losing a major battle on his right.

****

Beyond the Tronville copses, as the day slipped away, both sides had cause to feel apprehensive about their vulnerable flank to the west, although the clear advantage lay with the French, with their vastly superior numbers, provided that Ladmirault acted with the same resolution and dispatch which his opponent had already demonstrated; for not only did he have two scarcely scarred infantry divisions in the line but also, a little to the north beyond the Jarny road, a great phalanx of cavalry — Legrand's division, de France's brigade of the Imperial Guard, and the remaining regiment of Chasseurs d'Afrique of Barail's reserve division,[102] a total of more than 3000 horsemen. To his left lay Leboeuf, and at Bruville Clérambault's cavalry division of 3 Corps. Faced by this formidable array, Voigts-Rhetz had concentrated his artillery and the battered battalions of 20th Division and Wedell's brigade behind the shallow ridge running west from Tronville. His only flank protection was provided by six regiments of cavalry: Barby's brigade from Rheinbaben's division, *13th Dragoons* from Bredow's brigade,[103] *10th Hussars* from Redern's brigade which had

---

102   De France's brigade had escorted the Emperor from Gravelotte at dawn as far as Jarny, where it had handed over its duty to two regiments of Chasseurs d'Afrique. This latter brigade, Margueritte's, was to charge to its destruction two weeks later at Sedan.

103   This regiment had not taken part in Bredow's charge at 2 p.m.

provided the escort for Körber's batteries nine hours earlier at Tronville, and *16th Dragoons*, the divisional cavalry of 20th Division. This force lay to the south and west of Mars-la-Tour. It was 6.30 p.m.; and not a single German soldier stood north of the Verdun road. The scene was set for the epic encounter by which the battle of Mars-la-Tour is chiefly — and quite superficially — remembered. The reader will have seen by now why the Germans describe the day of battle as 'Vionville', and the French 'Rezonville'. There is nothing like a mighty cavalry encounter to put a romantic gloss on history.

****

Ladmirault pondered his options. The first — and most obvious — was to summon up a great infantry assault in concert with Leboeuf and to drive Voigts-Rhetz from the field by sheer weight of numbers; and in so doing put paid to Alvensleben's heroic defence of a cause which should long since have been lost. His second option — more cautious, because it would leave his infantry intact — was to launch his cavalry around the open flank and roll up the German left. At this hour he had no knowledge of the state of play far to his left at Rezonville where Frederick Charles's relief column had stumbled up the wooded slopes from Gorze. He had no need to concern himself with that flank. The decisive arena lay before him here. He chose the second option; and he was wrong.

****

It is the fate of generals to display their follies in open court when silence might be more sensible. Three years later, at Bazaine's trial, Ladmirault revealed both his weakness of intellect and, more critically, his weakness of resolve:

> At this moment, I wished to exploit my advantage. My corps had suffered some 2,000 casualties [*fewer than Wedell's single brigade*]. I had only two divisions in the line: Cissey's, which had taken part in the earlier attack, and Grenier's which had been fighting throughout the afternoon. My third division, Lorencez's, which had left Metz on the 15th, had not arrived. I sent aide-de-camp after aide-de-camp to urge him to expedite his arrival on the battlefield. He did not arrive until 10 p.m.[104]

Until 10 p.m. Until night had fallen on the battlefield. Until the darkness of defeat had fallen on the Army of the Rhine. For an hour later, at

---

104 *Procès Bazaine.*

Gravelotte, Bazaine was wearily dictating, by the light of a single candle, the order to retire on Metz.

****

Now came still evening on. To the west of the Jarny road there lies a swell of downland, bordered by the road and by the hamlet of Ville-sur-Yron. Nature could not have designed a more perfect jousting-ground for a cavalry encounter; and just such an encounter it now entertained.

It is impossible at this remove in time to conceive the collision of 5000 horsemen on this empty upland. To stand on the bare battlefield today (*see* Plates 19-20) is to tax the most subtle imagination and the most vivid vision. There had been comparable cavalry encounters before. There would not be another such again. And it came about in this fashion.

At 6.45 p.m. Ladmirault chose his second option. He ordered his massed cavalry to advance and roll up the German left wing.

At 6.45 p.m. Voigts-Rhetz chose his only option. He ordered Rheinbaben to advance and roll up the French right wing.

The two great masses of horsemen — 49 squadrons in close order — met with a clash that echoed east to Vionville and north to Bruville, and grappled together under a giant cloud of dust which obscured the view not only of observers but of the combatants themselves (thus, for example, a regiment of Legrand's division, mistaking the sky-blue uniforms of their own lancers for the enemy, fell upon them with fearful effect). Within moments all control was lost as squadron after squadron on both sides charged into the great cauldron of milling men and horses. To one eye-witness the scene resembled 'some vast chemical reaction as the different elements fused, separated, and fused again — in every sense a kind of mercurial mêlée'.

> A mighty cloud concealed the various phases of this hand-to-hand encounter of 5,000 horsemen, which gradually declared itself in favour of the Prussians. General Montaigu, severely wounded, was taken prisoner, and General Legrand fell while leading his Dragoons to the assistance of the Hussars.[105]

On the German side, four regimental commanders were killed or disabled. Yet in a cavalry combat of this magnitude sheer numbers ceased to have much meaning. Crowded together in inextricable confusion, men could only strike blindly at each other, and it is significant of the nature of such hand-to-hand fighting that on both sides the horses suffered many more casualties than their riders.

This — the last great cavalry battle of modern times — lasted no more

105 Moltke: *op. cit.*

Plate 19 The scene of the great cavalry battle looking north towards Ville-sur-Yron

Plate 20 The scene of the great cavalry battle, looking south towards Mars-la-Tour

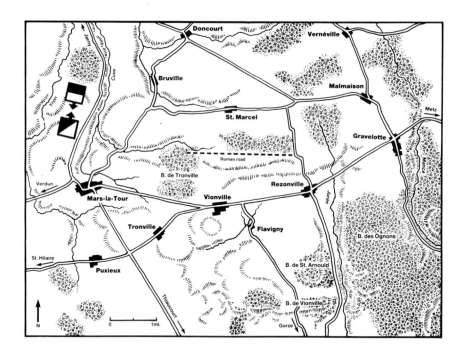

KEY

French Cavalry mass :

German Cavalry mass :

Remaining positions as shown on Map 13, except that ⑦ and ⑧ had been driven
to take refuge to the south of the main road at Mars-la-Tour

Map 14   The cavalry battle at 6.30 p.m., 16 August

than fifteen minutes. Ladmirault's infantry, massed beyond the ravine,
could only stand and stare. Only Clérambault's five uncommitted cavalry
regiments near Bruville could have intervened, perhaps decisively. But
Clérambault hung back, awaiting word from his corps commander,
Leboeuf; and when at last he sent Maubranche's brigade cautiously
forward, it was too late, and his men were thrown into disorder by
Legrand's fleeing Dragoons as they advanced.

Legrand's fleeing Dragoons? If neither side could claim a decisive result,
the Germans at least more than held their ground. The French account
speaks of a bugle sounding the rear rally and of a deliberate disengagement. That was not the picture from where Ladmirault stood, nor the
experience of Maubranche's brigade as it rode forward from Bruville. And
Barby's brief pursuit was halted not by the French cavalry but by Cissey's
infantry occupying the stronghold of Greyères in the angle of the ravine.

The battle has been fairly summed up thus:

The Prussian cavalry rallied on the plateau which they had won, and then retired into the line of battle of their infantry, who had in the meantime reformed near Tronville, and were prepared for fresh resistance. Darkness fell upon this phase of the combat.

This cavalry action has been called, by critics who condemned it, an unnecessary cavalry duel. But it was by no means without result. The Prussian cavalry had the advantage ... The enemy did not suffer a severe defeat, but he was driven back in the end and the Prussians held the field of battle. The result was that we obtained all that we wanted to obtain. The combat was restored and night fell without the enemy having dared to advance again. If any cavalry must be blamed it is General Clérambault's five regiments which took no part in the charge. They might have converted the Prussian victory into a defeat.[106]

And so indeed it proved. With the end of the great cavalry encounter, the curtain fell on the afternoon battle. There was to be an unexpected epilogue, but that would fill the centre stage.

As Barby's horsemen retired to Mars-la-Tour, 4 Corps found itself occupying the very same ground on which it had stood at 3 p.m. Twice since then Ladmirault had ventured forth; twice he had stood on the threshold of success; and twice he had lost his nerve. Now he decided that he would hold what he had or at least await the arrival of Lorencez's division. But there is no doubt that he had abandoned all thought of a fourth and final effort to clear the Verdun road. Certainly the hour was late; certainly he had no idea of the situation on the French left; certainly his commander-in-chief, seemingly deaf to entreaties and blind to opportunity, offered him naught for his comfort. By now the contagion of defeat had spread from Gravelotte to Greyères. But on the other side of the hill, it was quite otherwise.

****

It was shortly after 7 p.m. that Frederick Charles decided to stake his own claim to some of the day's laurels. He had been on the battlefield since mid-afternoon, but beyond his instruction to IX Corps before leaving Pont-à-Mousson, he was too late to influence the course of what had long since become a battle for survival. It is possible that he wanted to redeem his error, which had put the whole Second Army at risk. It is likely that he genuinely felt that one last effort might set the seal on the brilliant bluff and heroic endeavour with which his two corps commanders had conducted the long day's action. It is certain that, at this hour, he was almost alone in grasping Bazaine's predicament and realizing the measure

106 Hohenlohe-Ingelfingen: *Letters on Cavalry.*

of French irresolution. He therefore ordered a final attack on the French centre, its objective the capture of Rezonville and the severing, not of Bazaine's lifeline with Metz, but of his grossly unbalanced left and right wings. It was rash, impetuous, but — as we shall see — quite unexpectedly effective.

Frederick Charles has been universally condemned by German sources for this decision, although it was no more than a rather grandiose extension of the repeated offensive stance which Alvensleben and Voigts-Rhetz had so successfully adopted throughout the day. The wonder is that the Germans could, at so late an hour, summon up the reserves of men, material, and morale to sustain so desperate a venture. Moltke, whose deference to royalty was matched only by his distaste for the Red Prince, did not even give him the benefit of the doubt:

> Thanks to the valuable assistance of X Corps it was possible to carry on the battle through the afternoon on the defensive, but only by the most resolute counter-attacks by the cavalry, and by the unflinching tenacity of the artillery.
>
> It was clearly most inadvisable to challenge by renewed attacks an enemy who still outnumbered the Germans; which action, since no further reinforcements could be hoped for, could not but jeopardize the success so dearly bought. The troops were exhausted, most of their ammunition was spent, the horses had been under the saddle for fifteen hours without fodder; some of the batteries could only move at a walk, and the nearest Army Corps on the left bank of the Moselle, the XII,[107] was distant more than a day's march.
>
> *Notwithstanding all these considerations,*[108] an order from Prince Frederick Charles's HQ, issued at seven o'clock, commanded a renewed and general attack on the enemy's positions. X Corps was quite incapable of answering this demand [*small wonder*]; and only part of the artillery went forward on the right followed by some infantry. The batteries indeed reached the much-disputed plateau south of Rezonville, but only to be exposed on both sides to the fire of infantry and artillery. Fifty-four guns of the French Guard alone, in positions on the farther side of the valley, were taking them in flank.[109] The Prussian batteries were compelled to retreat to their previous positions, but two brigades of 6th Cavalry Division still pressed forward. Scarcely able to discern in the increasing darkness

---

107 Not so. The nearest corps of Second Army was IX. And whose fault was that if not Moltke's?

108 Author's italics.

109 Bourbaki was several hours too late.

where their proper [*sic*] line of attack lay, they came under very sharp infantry fire, and withdrew with great loss.[110]

Moltke, writing twenty years after the event, skates nimbly over a very slippery surface. When Frederick Charles — rightly or wrongly — decided to bring the issue to a head Moltke was far away beyond the Moselle, at least as much concerned with the impetuous Steinmetz on his right as with the stuttering progress of the Crown Prince's Third Army through the Vosges passes on his left. He knew that MacMahon had made his escape towards Châlons. He knew that First Army was standing watch and ward to the south of Metz. He knew that the whole thrust of his strategic plan lay with Second Army, and that he had given Frederick Charles his head on the 15th. Of the true state of affairs on the plateau on the evening of the 16th he knew nothing.

It is at least arguable that Frederick Charles took his cue from Alvensleben and Voigts-Rhetz. Throughout the day the two men had contrived to avert a series of impending disasters by their resolute and sustained offensive action. It seems not to have occurred to the Red Prince that success had been achieved at a daunting cost and that III and X Corps — horses no less than men — were totally exhausted. Certainly, with hindsight, Moltke was probably right in his view that, with no further support available until the next day except on the French left wing, the chief objective — the cutting of Bazaine's main line of retreat — had been secured and that a further demonstration of aggression might have hazarded a prize so dearly won.

So much for hindsight. It was not the view of Frederick Charles as he surveyed the scene on the evening of the 16th.[111] Along their whole line the French now stood on the defensive. The danger to his own left wing which had haunted both his corps commanders throughout the day he now judged to have been cauterized. One final attack on a hesitant and demoralized enemy might drive him at last from the vital Rezonville position and set the seal of victory on a day of fluctuating fortunes. It is beyond argument that this proud and arrogant prince decided, with little thought of the consequences, that he would be a headline in history and not a mere footnote. So, shortly after 7 p.m., he ordered an advance from Vionville and Flavigny against the French centre, preceded by a cannonade in which every serviceable gun fired every round of its slender remaining supply. It was a flamboyant gesture. Even twenty years later Moltke still thought it futile and reprehensible. Reprehensible, perhaps; futile it was not. For its unexpected effect was to concentrate Bazaine's mind most wonderfully and most cravenly.

110   Moltke: *op. cit.*

111   Frederick Charles: *op. cit.*

Frederick Charles's order was absurdly ambitious. In effect, it was for an assault on Rezonville by both Alvensleben *and* Voigts-Rhetz. The latter, as Moltke noted, was quite unable to comply.[112] The attack was therefore mounted by the weary infantry of Buddenbrock's 6th Division and by part of 10th Infantry Brigade from 5th Division. The Brandenburgers went forward with exemplary courage and made some progress against Lafont and Picard on either side of the Verdun road, but a thousand yards from their objective they were taken in flank by the assembled batteries of the Imperial Guard to the east of Rezonville and the attack was broken up, the retreating ranks being pursued by a hail of chassepot and mitrailleuse fire to their former positions in front of Vionville and Flavigny.

It was now nearly dark, and it might be thought that enough blood had flowed. Frederick Charles had other ideas. His infantry was spent, his artillery silent. But his cavalry remained. It almost seems that he was determined to ensure that no part of his force should be denied its own battle honour.

Apart from an ineffective intervention during the morning battle, 6th Cavalry Division had spent the day to the west of the Flavigny road covering Stuelpnagel on the German right. Now Frederick Charles decided that there was still time for it to share in the day's renown, and ordered that most hazardous of military manœuvres — a night attack by cavalry against a solidly held enemy position. Thus Grüter's 14th Brigade and Rauch's 15th rode out into the darkness and fell upon the French centre. There was no objective. There was certainly no object. The outpost line was taken by surprise — as well it might have been — and tumbled back in panic into Rezonville; but losing all cohesion in the gloom, the German horsemen were met by a murderous fire from the solid ranks around the village and fled the field in disorder.[113] Grüter was dead; and more than 700 casualties was the sum of Frederick Charles's arrogant folly.

Yet, arrogant though it may have been, was it also foolish? Moltke thought so. But Bazaine did not. The appearance of small bodies of troops from VIII and IX Corps on his left flank during the late afternoon had been enough to convince him that his fears of a turning movement on that wing were fully justified (he neither knew nor seemingly greatly cared about the situation on his right); and now the unexpected evening advance and the night attack by the German cavalry against his centre confirmed what he had always *wished* to believe: that the Army of the Rhine was, and always had been, opposed by a greatly superior enemy. That this was not so, had never been so, and would not be so for another forty-eight hours is

---

112   In fact two of Lehmann's battalions — originally from X Corps but under Alvensleben's command since noon — joined in the advance.

113   It is a measure of this extraordinary night-charge that the memorial to the 3rd or Ziethen Hussars of Rauch's brigade stands at the centre of Canrobert's position on the Rezonville ridge (*see* Plate 7).

irrelevant. When a commander abdicates supreme responsibility and allows a resourceful opponent to dictate his course of action, figments of imagination become useful substitutes for true facts.

It is for this reason that Moltke was wrong and Frederick Charles — for all the wrong reasons — was right. As it had been with Alvensleben, as it had been with Voigts-Rhetz, so was it now with him. It may, in Moltke's phrase, have been 'most inadvisable to challenge by renewed attacks, an enemy who still outnumbered the Germans'. But numbers are nothing where will is wanting. Repeatedly throughout the day Bazaine and his subordinates had been wanting in will, while their men had been willing only to win. When Frederick Charles made his final flamboyant gesture he could not have dreamed that Bazaine would gratefully take the bait and surrender for the last time the initiative which he himself had so gratuitously handed to him so many hours ago. Metz, which Bazaine had been so loth to leave, now beckoned him back. He needed no more bidding; and it is a majestic irony that when on the 17th Bazaine set up his new headquarters at Plappeville, he found himself looking down on his ancestral home, the tiny village of Scy.

****

So towards 9 p.m., this long, burning day of battle reached its end. It had started twelve hours earlier on a modest swell of ground near Tronville; it had caught fire, as a fuse-paper takes light, in the woods and uplands above Gorze, and had spread westward to the critical villages of Vionville and Flavigny; the flame had passed north through the Tronville copses and away to Mars-la-Tour, to the blood-soaked ravine below Bruville, and to the great cavalry encounter above the Yron; as the day lengthened, the fighting flared again above the Gorze approaches; and as darkness fell it ended in a desperate encounter, within killing distance of where it had started, between two brave and steadfast opponents. With nightfall, both sides sniped warily at each other. But the day was done, all passion spent. A silence fell upon the scene.

****

When the day's fighting ended the French outpost line ran from the Bois des Ognons westward to Rezonville. Thence it inclined north-west to the Roman road, and turning again passed along the Bruville slopes above the Cuve ravine, its right resting on the wooded area north of Ville-sur-Yron. The German line followed the northern fringes of the Bois de St Arnould and the Bois de Vionville, passing in front of Flavigny and Vionville and so along the Verdun road to Mars-la-Tour. Almost as a mark of mutual respect the Tronville copses on which the battle had hinged were left as no-man's-land, occupied only by the dead and dying, both French and

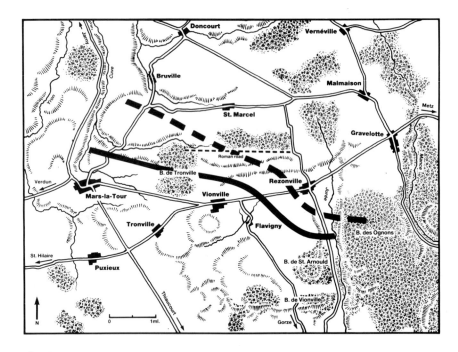

French outpost line :
German outpost line :

Map 15   Situation at nightfall, 16 August

German. Thus, as a glance at the different battle-maps will show, an action which had opened on an east-west axis ended with the opposing sides facing each other roughly north and south.

What then is the verdict on this memorable, if little-remembered, day of battle? Neither side claimed an outright victory; and in the short term this is probably true. But battles have been called the punctuation marks of wars, and if that is so, then Mars-la-Tour represents the first full-point in the Franco-German conflict. Without Mars-la-Tour there would have been no Gravelotte or St Privat two days later, and no chapter-ending at Sedan on 1 September.

On the eve of battle, Bazaine had at his disposal 201 infantry battalions, 126 cavalry squadrons, and 76 batteries, but of these 52 battalions, 15 squadrons, and 15 batteries took no part in the action. Consequently the effective strength of the Army of the Rhine on the 16th was 149 battalions, 111 squadrons and 61 batteries, including 10 of mitrailleuses, a total (allowing for the defective strength of many units) of perhaps 140,000 men.

To these the Germans opposed — and then only when the day was far advanced — 60 infantry battalions, 87 cavalry squadrons, and 37 batteries, a total of 76,000 men. Even at the day's end, therefore, Bazaine had a superiority of two to one, but throughout the morning battle and until the arrival of X Corps towards 4 p.m. he could, *had he been so minded*, have brought to bear an advantage of four or even five to one.[114] There can be no question where the moral victory lay.

So too in tactical terms. At dawn on the 16th the German objective had been to intercept the retreating Army of the Rhine before it could reach the comparative safety of Verdun. That in the event Bazaine's main lifeline was cut as far east as Vionville and Mars-la-Tour was a matter of luck rather than good judgment. That Frederick Charles' error could and should have been swiftly punished has been amply demonstrated. That it was so improbably turned to advantage against such overwhelming odds is due as much to French irresolution as to German pride and professionalism. History may record that Bazaine surrendered the Army of the Rhine in Metz on 27 October. In fact his act of surrender came here on the Gravelotte plateau on the evening of 16 August. Nor did he accept moral defeat at the end. He had invited it from the beginning. The key to the day of battle is to be found in his order postponing the retreat after Napoleon's dawn departure, before a single shot had been fired. 'We shall probably resume our march during the afternoon.' By the afternoon the door had been slammed in his face. Not only a battle but a whole war had been thrown into the discard.

****

114   For details of casualties incurred on both sides, *see* p. 210.

THE AFTERMATH
Wednesday, 17 August

As night fell on the field of Mars-la-Tour both sides bivouacked on the positions which they held, and counted the cost. On the German side there was more cause for relief than rejoicing, for they had sustained in casualties a staggering 22 per cent of their effectives. French losses were also savage, but a significant part of the Army of the Rhine had not been involved in the day's fighting, and Bazaine still had a potentially decisive numerical superiority.[1] On the other hand, time — a much more important asset — was fast running out for him. It is entirely in keeping with his character that he again squandered both advantages.

If Bazaine was not aware of this, Moltke certainly was. Despite the efficiency of his administrative organization, he was faced by serious supply and medical problems, and it would be the best part of a day before he could deploy any substantial reinforcements on the Gravelotte plateau. He did not yet have the true measure of Bazaine, and could therefore only proceed on the assumption that his opponent would no longer make a virtue of lost opportunities. On one of his celebrated staff-rides before the war he had allowed himself a rare excursion into irony: 'It has been my experience in war that there are always three courses open to an enemy, and that he invariably takes the fourth.' Now he could only wait until morning to see what Bazaine would do. He could not have imagined that many a true word indeed is spoken in jest.

Reflecting on the situation some time later, one of Moltke's most able generals had this to say:

---

1 Details of casualties on both sides are as follows:

	Killed	Wounded	Missing	Total
German	4,421	10,402	965	15,788
French	1,367	10,120	5,472	16,959

In addition the Germans lost no fewer than 1,300 horses.

If we think what would have been the result if Bazaine had struck a blow with his reserves and had at 4 a.m. on the 17th attacked the Prussian troops who had already been engaged on the 16th, and had forced them back on the defile Gorze−Thiaucourt, we must admit that the blockade of the Marshal in Metz, and the entire annihilation of his whole army, which took place at a later date, would in no circumstances have been possible.[2]

****

But at Gravelotte that night, Bazaine was carefully hedging his bets. A full-scale attempt to break out the following morning was not one of them. As we shall presently see, so contradictory, even inexplicable, are his orders, telegrams, and subsequent statements that it would be charitable to suggest that he had already decided to throw in the towel. He had convinced himself — if only because it suited him to do so — that the enemy now lay before him in great and growing strength, and that the non-existent threat to his left which had dominated his every action during the day was indeed the reality which it had never been, and still was not.

In one of his very few comments on Bazaine's conduct of affairs, Moltke wrote:

Supposing that the Marshal was determined above everything to effect his retreat, he could do so only by fighting hard for his right of way . . . It is not easy to discern, from a purely military standpoint, why this course was not resorted to. There was the full certainty[3] that only part, and probably only a small part, of the German armies could as yet have reached the left bank of the Moselle, and when during the course of the day [*the 16th*] the divisions detained about Metz reached him, he had an overwhelming numerical superiority. But it seems that the Marshal's chief concern was lest he should be forced to relinquish his touch with Metz; and he gave almost his whole attention to his left wing, constantly sending fresh reinforcements opposite the Bois des Ognons, whence an attack was exceptionally improbable. One is tempted to assume that political reasons alone thus early actuated Bazaine in his resolve to cling to Metz.[4]

Although he did not know it (and could scarcely have believed it), on the night of the 16th Moltke hit upon the truth of his own dry comment. Metz was indeed Bazaine's 'fourth option'.

2 Hohenlohe-Ingelfingen: *Letters on Cavalry.*

3 Certain, that is, to Moltke; but not to Bazaine.

4 Moltke: *op. cit.*

Towards 10 p.m. Bazaine assembled his staff and informed them of his intention of taking up a new position the following day on the line Rozérieulles−St Privat. He then added a breath-taking afterthought: 'If any of you can think of something better to do, I am prepared to listen. If not we must save the army, and to do that, we must retire on Metz.'[5] There was a stony silence. In other circumstances Jarras might have offered a suggestion, but having been treated with studied indifference by Bazaine ever since the 13th, he preferred now to leave him to work out his own salvation.

At 11 p.m. Bazaine telegraphed to the Emperor at Châlons:

> At 9 o'clock this morning the enemy attacked the head of our columns at Rezonville. The battle lasted until 8 o'clock this evening. It was an extremely bitter engagement; despite considerable casualties we have held our ground. Our main problem now is that our expenditure of ammunition and supplies has been such that we should have difficulty in getting through another such day. I therefore feel obliged to fall back to the line Vigneulles−Lessy to replenish my stocks.[6] The wounded have been evacuated to Metz.[7] According to the information I have regarding German troop concentrations, I think that I shall be obliged to take the northern route to Verdun [by Étain].

Then, at 4.28 p.m. on the following afternoon, he telegraphed to the Emperor, and to Palikao in Paris (the message to Palikao is subtly different and demonstrably untrue):

> I had the honour to inform your Majesty yesterday of the battle lasting from 9 a.m. to 8 p.m. with the Prussian army which attacked our positions between Doncourt and Vionville.[8] The enemy was repulsed and we spent the night in our conquered [sic] positions. Shortage of supplies and ammunition have obliged me to retire on Metz to replenish stocks as soon as possible. I have deployed the Army of the Rhine on the line Saint Privat−Rozérieulles. I hope to be able to resume our march the day after tomorrow [the 19th] by the more northerly route.

Neither of these messages seems to have reached Châlons, for on the

5 *Procès Bazaine.*

6 But *see* Appendix B.

7 This was not true. More than 5000 were left in German hands.

8 As the preceding narrative shows, this was clearly — and perhaps deliberately — inaccurate.

evening of the 17th a nervous Emperor telegraphed to General Coffinières de Nordeck, the Military Governor of Metz:

> Have you any news of the army? Reply urgently to His Majesty at the camp at Châlons.

Coffinières replied (and his message was uncomfortably close to the truth):

> Yesterday, the 16th, there has been an extremely serious engagement near Gravelotte; we have won the battle [*sic*] but our casualties are heavy. The Marshal has re-grouped near Metz and is encamped on the high ground about Plappeville. Please supply food and ammunition. Metz is virtually blockaded.

This is the language of panic. It must also have been unintelligible at Châlons. 'Conquered positions'? 'Won the battle'? Since when does a victorious army quit the field and submit itself to a 'blockade' by the beaten enemy?

Eventually on the 17th Bazaine managed to pass an officer through enemy lines, carrying copies of his two previous messages, and adding the following (the wording matches the flat tones of his speaking voice):

> We are going to make every effort to re-equip ourselves so that we can resume our march in two days, if that is possible [*sic*]. I shall take the Briey road [*to the north-west, viz: away from Verdun*]; we shall lose no time unless my calculations are upset by renewed fighting.

If Coffinière's language was that of panic, Bazaine's is the language of fantasy, hedged about as it is with doubt and indecision.

What Bazaine's intentions were on the night of the 16th and during the 17th we shall never know for certain; for the two public statements which he was later to make flatly contradict each other.

To the Commission of Enquiry in 1871 he said:

> It seemed to me that by fighting one or perhaps two defensive battles in positions which I felt to be impregnable [*inexpugnable*] I would wear down my adversary's strength, forcing him to sustain heavy losses which ... would weaken him enough to allow him to let me pass without serious opposition.

But at his court-martial two years later (by when Napoleon conveniently was dead) he declared (and his exact words are important):

> *Je croyais, et l'Empereur croyait également, qu'en donnant le temps*
> *à l'armée de Châlons de se former, elle pourrait atteindre un effectif*

considérable qui lui permettrait de venir nous dégager.[9]

So much for *arrière-pensées*. Bazaine's real intention is best summed up in his weary words to his staff at Gravelotte: *'We must save the army, and to do that we must retire on Metz.'* There could not have been a man present who did not know that with those words Bazaine was launched upon a road from which there would be no returning.

****

Frederick Charles spent the night of the 16th at Gorze amid the debris of the day of battle. He was under no illusion that his position was not still one of great peril. His right wing had survived (by courtesy of his opponent) against the most improbable odds, but he had only to look around him to realize that the storm had by no means blown itself out, and that a rising wind at dawn would inevitably sweep away the broken remnants of III and X Corps before he could summon any substantial reinforcements to their aid. Meanwhile, five miles away at Gravelotte, Bazaine was taking a decision which would have allowed the Red Prince to sleep more soundly.

The situation of Second Army that night was a direct consequence of Frederick Charles's order of the 15th to press forward to the Meuse and to bring Bazaine to battle at or near Verdun. Mars-la-Tour, which should have been a minor episode, had become a dramatic dénouement. What should have been a by-play had become, centre-stage, the heart of the action, with more than half the cast waiting in the wings.

On the left of Second Army, IV Corps had crossed the Moselle on the 16th at Marbache and, covering the Crown Prince's right, had made an unsuccessful demonstration against the fortress of Toul, thirty miles south of Metz.[10] It could therefore in no way be counted on to support the concentration of the German forces on the killing-ground of the 18th. Next in line came the Guard Corps farther downstream, which had crossed the river at Dieulouard and by nightfall on the 16th was bivouacked at Beaumont and Bernécourt, a full day's march (22 miles) from Mars-la-Tour.[11] During the morning of the 16th, XII (Saxon) Corps had crossed at Pont-à-Mousson and was bivouacked on the left bank. IX Corps was already on that bank, and one regiment of 18th Division and a brigade of the Hessian Division were already in action that evening on the fringes of

9   'I believed, *and so did the Emperor*, that by giving time to the army of Châlons to form, it would reach a great enough strength to allow it *to come and relieve us.*'

10   Toul, at the time of mobilization, had been the main artillery park for the Army of the Rhine. Thus IV Corps' demonstration played an unwitting part in the final disaster at Metz.

11   As we have seen, the Guard Dragoon Brigade had played a crucial part in the afternoon battle of the 16th.

the plateau. Finally II Corps, the last to have detrained on the frontier, was pressing forward by forced marches to Pont-à-Mousson.[12] Thus by midnight Frederick Charles could count on three more army corps to reach the battlefield by the 17th, and a fourth by the following day. But what if the Army of the Rhine returned to the attack in strength at dawn? It was with some apprehension that he passed the night at Gorze.

To Moltke, who had established an advanced headquarters at Pont-à-Mousson during the evening of the 16th, the situation presented itself in a very different light. The fighting during that day, indecisive or not, had produced at least one conclusive result. The southerly of Bazaine's three available escape routes to Verdun had been cut, and even if he were to decide to batter his way through Mars-la-Tour early the next day, the initiative had now changed hands and the Army of the Rhine would be increasingly vulnerable to being attacked in flank by the uncommitted corps of Second Army. Time, that most precious of military commodities, was no longer on Bazaine's side. It had been wantonly wasted at Borny and fatally squandered in the hours that followed.

There was something else. With a shrewdness which had escaped Frederick Charles, Moltke had correctly 'read' the battle of Mars-la-Tour and had rightly interpreted Bazaine's preoccupation with his left wing as an obsession, not with escaping to Verdun, but with clinging close to Metz. Certainly there were still several options open to Bazaine, but each of them offered Moltke an opportunity which he had never envisaged when he had given Frederick Charles his head on the 15th. The Meuse no longer mattered. A chance encounter battle, a child of error, had become father to the possibility of an undreamed-of strategy: the containment and destruction of the Army of the Rhine. 'The more enemy opposing III Corps,' he wrote, 'the greater the success will be tomorrow when we can deploy against it X, III, IX, XII, VIII,[13] VII[13] and even II Corps.' (He did not add, as well he could, the Guard Corps.) Thus Moltke issued his orders that the French were to be pursued 'up to the Luxembourg frontier, and eventually on to the territory of that country'. So, towards midnight, both First and Second Armies were set in motion. To their deployment we shall return. But when his instruction went out Moltke could not possibly have foreseen the unexpected — and nearly disastrous — result.

****

At this same hour Bazaine was also issuing his orders for the following day. The Army of the Rhine would fall back at dawn to the Amanvillers line.

The ground to the east of Gravelotte is in striking contrast to the gently

12 It covered 81 miles in under six days.

13 Both of First Army. Moltke was no longer thinking in terms of Frederick Charles alone, but of the total involvement of all his available resources.

Plate 21 The Mance ravine, looking north from the causeway

Plate 22 The Mance ravine, looking south from the causeway

Plate 23 The Metz–Verdun road near St Hubert, where the descent into the Mance ravine commences. On the skyline: left, Gravelotte; right, Bois des Genivaux

undulating plateau on which the battle of the 16th had been fought. The main feature is a broad hog's back running north from Rozérieulles for some eight miles to the village of Roncourt. On one side this secondary plateau falls steeply away to the narrow valley of Châtel St Germain, which is overlooked by the forts of Plappeville and St Quentin, the two main western outworks of the defensive perimeter of Metz. On the side of Gravelotte the small Mance rivulet — now as then no more than a trickle — starts on its way to join the Moselle at Ars in the Bois des Genivaux near Malmaison. As it runs south it enters a formidable ravine whose thickly wooded sides are separated by a narrow stretch of meadowland (see Plates 21 and 22) and turns east into the river valley at the Bois de Vaux.

The road from Metz to Gravelotte — the lifeline which so exercised Bazaine throughout the 16th and again the 18th — winds up the escarpment until it emerges on the central plateau above Rozérieulles. As it reaches the farmstead of Point du Jour on the crest it turns due west, forming a sharp elbow (the '*coude*' of French accounts) and leaving the buildings of St Hubert on its right, runs in a long straight line to the Gravelotte crossroads, descending into the Mance ravine, which it crosses on what was then a narrow causeway. To stand on the causeway today is to stand at the heart of one of the bloodiest disasters in the history of German arms. It is not difficult to see why.

This long hog's back is a defensive position of great natural strength;[14] and in the light of Bazaine's apparently snap decision on the night of the 16th, it is arguable that it had always been his intention to fight his decisive battle there. The southern end, protected by the Mance ravine, resembles a monk's tonsure, the bare uplands fringed by plunging woods, and broken by quarries and gravel-pits. It dominates the valley approaches to Metz; and more significantly, it stands astride the elbow of the main road and commands the ravine and the plateau to the immediate west. If it is possible to describe any defensive position as impregnable by nature and by artifice combined, this was such a position; and so it was to prove.

As the ridge runs north from Point du Jour, and as the Mance ravine peters out in the Bois des Genivaux, the contours soften and the westerly slope resembles the glacis of a seventeenth-century fortress with wide and distant fields of fire. Here the line passes through the solid farm buildings of Moscou and Leipsic[15] on the exposed hillside and thence, by the château of Montigny-la-Grange, to Amanvillers, a fortress village tucked into a curious fold in the ground and linked by a secondary road with the valley behind it.

From Amanvillers the ridge runs on to the northerly escape route from Woippy to Briey, flanked on its left by the tiny hamlet of Jérusalem and on its right by the massive masonry of St Privat, a quiet complex of sturdy Lorraine stonework and garnished garden walls, which was presently to be the scene of an epic encounter.[16] A mile away, a mile too far away, lay Roncourt.

Such then was the Amanvillers line to which Bazaine summoned the Army of the Rhine at nightfall on the 16th. It may not have been a very distinguished decision. It certainly did not commend itself to his brave and disillusioned men, who expressed their feelings in widespread looting and other forms of indiscipline. Marshals who cannot command respect abdicate the authority of command. And so it was as the day of the 16th turned wearily into the dawn of the 17th. Bazaine had chosen a formidable rampart on which to oppose a formidable enemy. He had also made a formidable error of judgment; and for this he was presently to pay a formidable price.

*** *** **

14   The set-piece battle of the 18th — the first of the August campaign — is referred to in French accounts as 'The Defence of the Lines of Amanvillers.' The Germans call it 'The Battle of Gravelotte—St Privat.'

15   A dramatic irony indeed that these two immemorial farms should have celebrated in name the road to ruin of another Bonaparte.

16   It has often been observed that these farms and villages seem to have been like small fortresses. And so, in the light of past history, they were.

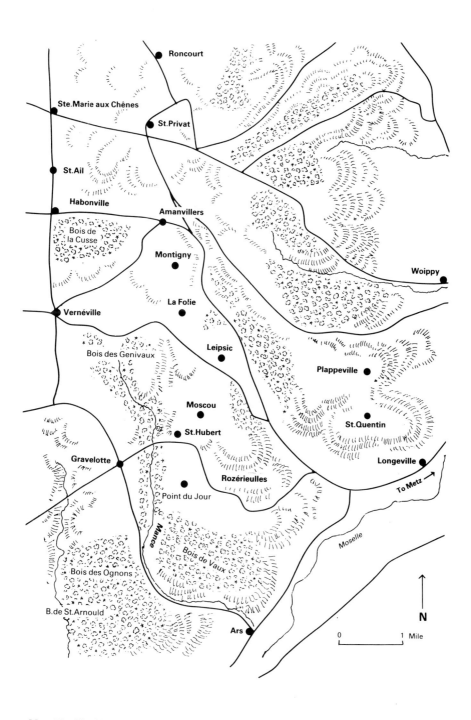

Map 16 The Line of Amanvillers, 18 August

Roncourt

Ste.Marie aux Chênes

St.Privat

St.Ail

Habonville

Amanvillers

Woippy

Bois de
la Cusse

Montigny

La Folie

Vernéville

Bois des Genivaux

Leipsic

Plappeville

Moscou

St.Hubert

St.Quentin

Gravelotte

Longeville

Rozérieulles

To Metz

Point du Jour

Moselle

Mance

Bois de Vaux

Bois des Ognons

B.de St.Arnould

Ars

N

0   1 Mile

Not until the next morning could Moltke be sure of Bazaine's intention; but he wasted no time, and shortly before midnight orders went out to Frederick Charles and Steinmetz. They were as follows.

The Guard Corps and XII Corps were to march at 3 a.m., the former by Chamblay to Hannonville a mile to the west of Mars-la-Tour, the latter by Thiaucourt to Puxieux and Mars-la-Tour itself.[17] In fact the respective corps commanders, Prince Augustus of Württemberg and the Crown Prince of Saxony, anticipating Moltke's intention, had already set their heads of columns on the road so that, with typical German march-discipline and stamina, XII Corps reached its concentration area by noon on the 17th, and the Guard by 3 p.m. Their arrival serves to emphasize in the most striking way the magnitude of Bazaine's folly in countermanding the order for withdrawal at dawn on the 16th; for, III Corps notwithstanding, the bulk of the Army of the Rhine would have long since reached Verdun and thence have linked with MacMahon's army at Châlons. The massive French memorial at Mars-la-Tour stands as mute testimony to an army that was left to drown in open sea and within sight of land.

Next in line stood IX Corps. Part of this corps was already on the left bank, and the remainder was now ordered forward to covered rendezvous positions to the west of the Bois de Vionville.

On the right stood First Army; and here Moltke moved with circumspection. He was little concerned with any risk of a bold initiative by Bazaine from Metz; but he had no illusions about the impetuous Steinmetz (his fears were to be bloodily confirmed on the 18th) and accordingly, while hastening Frederick Charles on his way to the plateau, he kept a tight rein on his right wing.

I Corps was ordered to stand fast in its bivouac area to the south-east of Metz. VIII Corps, whose 32nd Infantry Brigade had been fighting on the plateau since the evening of the 16th, was now pushed across the river by five pontoon bridges on either side of Novéant and assembled in the wooded country around Gorze. More importantly — and to Steinmetz's ill-concealed anger — its command and control was retained by the King (*aliter* Moltke). The idea was wise. Not so the unpredictable result.

Finally, VII Corps (Zastrow), which had so nearly precipitated a disaster at Spicheren, was fed across the Moselle at Ars under the nose of Fort St Quentin during the hours of darkness, and bivouacked astride the Mance ravine in the Bois de Vaux and the Bois des Ognons. Its orders were explicit. In no circumstances was it to engage the enemy by direct action. It was to adopt 'an expectant stance' and act as a pivot for the grandiose manœuvre which Moltke was carefully stage-managing.

Thus throughout the night two German armies marched purposefully forward. What might be required of them, only dawn would tell.

---

17   In the event these routes and destinations were, by a staff error, transposed so that when the order to advance was given on the 18th there was serious confusion in Mars-la-Tour as the two columns crossed each other.

****

Meanwhile, in another part of the forest ... To understand the implications of Bazaine's decision to fall back on the Amanvillers line, it is necessary to return to the situation of the Army of the Rhine as the day of battle ended.

At nightfall the army was facing south. On the extreme right, 4 Corps; then 3 Corps; then 6 Corps; then a massive conglomeration of the Imperial Guard, detached divisions, cohorts of cavalry, and the battered parts of 2 Corps to the north of Gravelotte. To launch an offensive at dawn from such a platform was, leaving aside Bazaine's lame excuse about material shortages, as inviting as it was obvious. To summon back this far-flung battle-line to the Amanvillers plateau required a manœuvre which would have taxed even Moltke and his disciplined staff. Bazaine was no Moltke; and his staff was long since demoralized.

Consider, therefore, Bazaine's redeployment of his army as it marched miserably back to the walls of Metz. As has been suggested earlier, the detail of the French dispositions on the Amanvillers line suggests strongly that it was a preconceived plan. It could not possibly have been worked out in the bare hour between the staff meeting at Gravelotte and the issue of the order itself. The 'planned' withdrawal, timed to start at dawn and covered by Metman's tardily arrived division of 3 Corps, required that the Army of the Rhine must pivot on its left through a complete right angle, exchanging an east-west front of seven miles for a north-south line of roughly the same length — a difficult exercise rendered the more dangerous by the proximity of the enemy. There was no time to work out march-tables, and Jarras's task was made impossible by the appalling congestion on the roads, particularly around Gravelotte,[18] and by Bazaine's eccentric choice of defensive sectors for his Army corps.

Common sense, if not simple prudence, dictated that the various formations should have fallen back in sequence, left to right, from the positions which they occupied at midnight. There was always going to be a problem of passing several thousand men and several hundred wagons across the narrow Mance causeway, and indeed it is interesting to speculate, with hindsight, what might have occurred if Steinmetz had mounted a strong attack with VII Corps from its covered positions south of Gravelotte during the early hours of daylight on the 17th.

This then was Bazaine's chosen order of battle: on the extreme left at St Ruffine astride the main road, Lapasset's brigade; occupying the Rozérieulles plateau at Point du Jour and extending as far as the elbow in the road, Frossard's 2 Corps with advanced posts in the quarries and woods of the eastern face of the ravine; here the line was taken up by Leboeuf's 3 Corps, which held the long crest from St Hubert through the farms of Moscou and Leipsic to La Folie, with a brigade thrown forward into the

18 *See* Appendix B.

Bois des Genivaux; in the centre stood Ladmirault's 4 Corps holding the strongpoints of Montigny and Amanvillers, but with no covering troops in the important area of the Bois de la Cusse to the immediate west; and on the right Canrobert's 6 Corps astride the road at St Privat with its flank resting on Roncourt and with a strong advanced guard at Ste Marie-aux-Chênes.[19] The cavalry was posted — or, more precisely, crammed — into the narrow Châtel valley, with Forton on the left and Barail on the right. Still obsessed with his left wing, Bazaine placed his reserve, the Imperial Guard, and the artillery reserve, in the Col du Lessy between the two great forts, and this was to prove a crucial and, in the event, a disastrous decision. The natural strength of the commanding ground on this flank rendered the position truly *inexpugnable*. The one weakness of the Amanvillers line lay on the right, where 6 Corps was vulnerable to a turning movement. It was there that the Guard and at least part of the reserve artillery should have been posted (Canrobert was still short of guns, and lacked even a single battery of mitrailleuses). It is easy to be wise after the event, but when on the evening of the 18th the German Guard Corps battered itself to near-destruction on the defences of St Privat, a determined counter-attack here by Bazaine's ample reserves would arguably have sealed a famous victory.

Meanwhile the Marshal established his headquarters behind the left wing at Plappeville, six miles from St Privat and remote from all contact with Canrobert. There he spent the 17th, as his army struggled back, preoccupied with such trivia as promotions and decorations; and there he remained throughout the 18th, his only communication with his corps commanders a bleak instruction to fortify their positions as strongly as possible. It is difficult to believe that this was the same man who had spent the morning of the 16th encouraging his men by his example (and confounding his staff by his absence).

While the chaotic procession threaded its way across the causeway and the bonfires burned in the ravine, Bazaine's arbitrary allotment of assembly areas was causing all manner of confusion to the north of Gravelotte. Two examples will suffice. As 6 Corps marched away from Rezonville towards Vernéville its track crossed that of 3 Corps as it followed the easterly road from St Marcel towards St Hubert and Moscou on the far side of the ravine. The resulting traffic-jam in turn halted 4 Corps on its way from Bruville to Amanvillers. Secondly, Montaudon's division, which since midday on the 16th had been detached from Leboeuf to protect the southerly approaches from Gorze, collided with Metman's division of the same corps as it attempted to deploy as the covering force around Malmaison and Gravelotte. It seems not to have occurred to Jarras

---

19 6 Corps had originally been directed on Vernéville, but Canrobert had complained, with every justification, that this left his right flank *en l'air*. Bazaine, never one to argue with his social superiors, readily agreed to the alternative position at St Privat.

that, by a simple adjustment, the roles of the two divisions could have been reversed and an inevitable thrombosis avoided.

Equally inevitably, discipline began to deteriorate. Many men had had no proper meal for twenty-four hours. They could not understand why, after their brave exertions, they were retreating towards Metz when even the most illiterate of them — and that included many elderly junior officers — could see that Bazaine had snatched defeat from the jaws of victory. It is a very singular fact that in spite of everything the morale of the Army of the Rhine did not finally break; that any sort of cohesion was maintained in the retreat; and that on the 18th this greatly ill-used army gave a moving and magnificent account of itself.

And here is another equally singular fact. It was after nightfall on the 17th that the Army of the Rhine finally reached its defensive positions. Some units had taken all day to cover as little as three or four miles. Yet by midnight they had pitched their little shelter-tents in tidy lines, and when day broke German patrols, cautiously scouting across the Gravelotte plateau, were astonished to see an army in repose, as if it were on military manœuvres at Châlons. But this was not all. This nonchalant army had been at work. As each corps reached its allotted position it began to dig in, to construct rifle-pits, covered trench-works, camouflaged gun-sites, every farm and outbuilding loop-holed and prepared for doughty defence. All except one. On the distant right wing Canrobert's 6 Corps had reached St Privat with no engineer park and no entrenching tools. Here, where the French needed to be at their strongest, they were therefore at their most vulnerable. Canrobert relied upon the stout walls of his fortress village. Six miles away Bazaine relied upon his superior philosophy of *inexpugnance* and continued to prod around with his pen and his promotions. A short ride to St Privat would have given him some cause for reflection. His every reflection was concentrated elsewhere.

There has been much argument about the time-scale of the French defensive preparations on the Amanvillers line; that such extensive defence works could not possibly have been completed between the morning of the 17th and noon on the 18th. Quite simply, they were. Quite simply, there was no way that Bazaine could have otherwise converted a cautious retreat to Verdun into a defiant defence of Metz in so short time, and with such slim resources. It remains a minor miracle; and it came close to achieving a major miracle.

****

The Germans were early astir on the 17th. While First and Second Armies were wheeling up to the plateau to join III and X Corps, Frederick Charles left Gorze at 4 a.m. and from a vantage point near Flavigny surveyed the enemy lines to the north and east. After a curiously — perhaps prophetically — chilly night, it was to be another day of burning heat, and this, if nothing else, ensured that the newly arriving corps from Pont-à-Mousson and Dieulouard would not be fit to fight a major battle on that day; nor, as the corpse-strewn battlefield made all too clear, would III and X Corps.

At 6 a.m. King William, with Moltke and his staff, joined Frederick Charles from Pont-à-Mousson. Let Moltke take up the story:

> At sunrise the French outposts were observed still occupying the sweep of front from Bruville to Rezonville. Behind them were noticed a stir and much noise of signalling, which might be the indications equally of an attack or a retirement.[20]

Moltke did not yet know that all this activity in fact signalled an army attempting to sort out the indescribable confusion of a hasty retreat. Uncharacteristically, he did not attempt to take the temperature of the water, although cavalry patrols at dawn had reported only stragglers on the central Verdun road towards Étain. But his tidy mind told him to hold his hand until the concentration of his force on the plateau was complete. He goes on:

> Reports sent in from reconnoitring cavalry were somewhat contradictory [*and were to remain dangerously so during the next twenty-four hours*]. They left it uncertain whether the French were concentrating towards Metz, or were pursuing their retreat by the two still open roads through Étain and Briey. By one o'clock the head of VII Corps had reached the northern skirt of the Bois des Ognons, over against which the French subsequently abandoned Gravelotte.[21]

At one o'clock, Steinmetz could have told him. For at one o'clock VII Corps, from its covered position in the Bois de Vaux and the Bois des Ognons, could see the neat tent-lines of Frossard's 2 Corps and Leboeuf's 3 Corps stretching away from Point du Jour towards Amanvillers. This was not an army breaking out to the north or west. This was an army preparing to give battle on a position of quite exceptional defensive strength. Steinmetz, still sulking since Spicheren, contemplated this interesting prospect, and kept his counsel. He was a foolish man. By the evening of the 18th he had successfully destroyed First Army, and was duly rewarded with the Governorship of distant Posen.

****

---

20 Moltke: *op. cit.*

21 Moltke: *op. cit.*

Moltke wisely ignored Steinmetz. He continues:

In making the dispositions for the impending battle of 18 August, two possibilities were foreseen and had to be provided for. To meet both, the left wing was to be sent forward in a northerly direction through Doncourt towards the nearest of the routes still open for the retreat of the French. If the enemy was already retiring, he was to be at once attacked and detained while the right wing was hurrying up in support.... In case the enemy should be remaining about Metz, the German left wing was to swing eastwards and outflank his farthest northern position, while the right was to hold his left closely engaged until this movement was accomplished.[22]

It was a classic concept of the tactic of encirclement. And it went dreadfully wrong.

****

22 Moltke: *op. cit.*

BLOODY THURSDAY
18 August

Thursday, like Tuesday, dawned bright and clear. It was to be another day of dust and stifling summer heat; and it was to be marked by an even bloodier passage of arms.

By midnight on the 17th, the Army of the Rhine had made its painful way back to the Amanvillers line. There it had cooked its meals, pitched its little tents, dug its defences, and now awaited an uncertain dawn. At Plappeville Bazaine retired to bed, content with the dispositions he had made but which he had studiously avoided visiting. Jarras was one day to have the last word:

> Having no firm plan of action, he [*Bazaine*] was reduced to vague improvisation, in the hope that events would provide, if not an answer to his army's predicament, at least a justification for his personal conduct. Had not luck so far been on his side? Whether or not, he now decided to leave everything to chance, the last infirmity of men who have lost faith in themselves.[1]

It was a bitter, perhaps extravagant, verdict; but by midnight on the 17th Jarras had reason to be bitter.

****

At 2 p.m. on the 17th, King William had issued his orders for the following day at his battle headquarters near Flavigny:

> Second Army will get under arms tomorrow morning at 5 a.m. and advance in echelons between Ville-sur-Yron and Rezonville. VIII

1   Jarras: *Souvenirs*.

226

Corps will follow this movement on the right [*of Second Army*]. VII Corps will at first be charged with the task of warding off any attack the enemy might undertake from Metz. The King's further orders will be determined by the measures taken by the enemy....

The King then returned with Moltke to Pont-à-Mousson while Frederick Charles and Steinmetz repaired to their respective headquarters at Buxières and Ars.

It will be seen that these orders were designed to meet two contingencies. If the French were to attempt to resume their withdrawal by the central or northern roads to Verdun, they were to be attacked and detained while the German centre and right wing hurried up in support. If, on the other hand, Bazaine decided to give battle on the Amanvillers line, then the left wing of Second Army would wheel eastward and attempt to outflank the enemy's position.

Curiously, Moltke made little effort to keep in contact, and the official German account is highly critical of the inept handling of the cavalry on both the 17th and 18th. Certainly, the Uhlan brigade of the Guard and a Saxon brigade had scouted westward towards the Meuse and north as far as Conflans on the central road, and had predictably reported that the enemy was nowhere to be found in those two directions. But no attempt was made to keep the Army of the Rhine under observation as it made its disordered way towards Metz. Steinmetz had already seen the large French encampment stretching north from Point du Jour on the far side of the Mance ravine, and this scarcely suggested that Bazaine was contemplating a dash for freedom. The 17th had come and gone, and with it the escape 'window' as the remaining bulk of Second Army arrived on the plateau. But Moltke was not minded to pay much attention to Steinmetz. It is probable that he had divined Bazaine's intention as early as the morning of the 17th (when the expected dawn attack had not materialized), and he was taking no chances by giving Steinmetz any opportunity to precipitate an early battle at the wrong time and in the wrong place. He was playing for much higher stakes.

****

At 4 a.m. on the 18th Frederick Charles was back at Flavigny, and an hour later he issued his verbal instructions for the advance:

Second Army continues its forward movement today with the view of cutting off the enemy's line of retreat to Verdun, and of attacking him wherever he may be encountered.

The army would advance in echelon, XII Corps on the extreme left taking the direction of Jarny, the Guard Corps on its right marching on Doncourt.

Farther to the right, IX Corps would set off an hour later between Vionville and Rezonville, leaving St Marcel close on its left; and finally VIII Corps — still at the King's personal disposal — followed the echelon pattern and was directed on Gravelotte and Malmaison. Strict — and repeated — instructions were given to Steinmetz by Royal headquarters that VII Corps would act as pivot for this magisterial movement, and would in no circumstances engage the enemy closely without written permission (it was to prove a pious hope). Finally, the second line would follow the main advance thus: X Corps and 5th Cavalry Division would march behind XII Corps on the left, and III Corps with 6th Cavalry Division would occupy the centre between the Guards and IX Corps.[2]

Frederick Charles's order ended with these words:

> The advance will not be made in columns of march. Divisions are to move in concentrated masses, the corps artillery occupying the intervening spaces.

It was a remarkable decision, the more so since it was based on guesswork. No one on the German side yet knew Bazaine's true intention, or indeed the exact whereabouts of the Army of the Rhine. In the event this cavalier attitude was to have the most dire consequences, and for this Moltke was at least as culpable as Frederick Charles.

This extraordinary manœuvre merits closer inspection; and to understand both its nature and its implication the reader should study the diagram on pp 230-231, which represents a bird's eye view of the Gravelotte plateau on the morning of the 18th as the German armies advanced to battle.

They moved in solid phalanxes on a front of some eight miles. It was not so much a mass of manœuvre as an exercise in military geometry as some 200,000 men marched, inclined to the north-east, across the face of a still formidable foe. There had been nothing like it before; and there would certainly never be anything like it again. These phalanxes advanced, like soldier-ants, straight across country, ignoring roads and brushing aside obstacles, with a final objective still undefined. From such a march formation, Frederick Charles could not possibly have deployed to meet a determined flank attack from Amanvillers. Perhaps he knew this. Perhaps he believed that so blatant a display of physical power would stun the enemy into submission. Certainly, the French made no move. From their shelter-tents and rifle-pits on the Amanvillers ridge, they watched this tidal wave advance across their front. At Plappeville, Bazaine confined himself to the infinitely delicate matters of promotions and decorations. When his staff told him that there was the sound of gun-fire to the west, he replied:

2   An urgent order had already been sent to Fransecky, commander of II Corps, far in rear, to hurry forward from Pont-à-Mousson to the plateau. Thus, early on the 18th, eight German army corps were either in position or on the march.

'It is nothing — just a matter of advance-guards.' A short ride across the valley and up the hill would have given him cause to think again. Instead, he ordered a dish of veal and onions and returned to his contemplation of the kind of intelligence that he should convey to Châlons.

****

The battle of Mars-la-Tour had fallen, for reasons which need no further rehearsing, into two complementary halves — the morning and the afternoon; for it was a chance encounter which grew from a minor cannonade to a major climax. Out of this encounter — the decisive engagement of both the campaign and the war, as it proved — proceeded the battle of Gravelotte–St Privat. It differed in every way from the action of the 16th.

First, it was a deliberate confrontation, a combat *à outrance*, and as such it was the first 'pitched battle' of the August campaign. Secondly, it was an engagement in which both sides fought with fronts reversed, the French with their backs to the Rhine and the Germans with their backs to Paris. Thirdly, the Germans for the first time in the campaign brought to bear on the Army of the Rhine the massive superiority of numbers which they had always threatened to deploy, but which they had failed to deliver on the battlefield.[3] Finally, the Germans, who had so bravely held the pass on the 16th, now learned to their cost the price of a frontal assault against a well-prepared and stubbornly defended position on which the entrenching-tool played at least as great a part as chassepot and mitrailleuse. They learned another lesson: that not even the most meticulous attention to military detail can account for arrogance, ineptitude and plain human error.

****

Because of the wide sweep of the German advance on the 18th and the uncertainty regarding the dispositions of the enemy, it was essential to Moltke's master-plan that there should be no premature engagement on his right, where the two sides were narrowly separated by the Mance ravine. The strictest instructions were issued to Steinmetz that VII Corps (Zastrow) was to remain in its covered positions in the Bois de Vaux and the Bois des Ognons and was to restrict its activity to artillery fire against Frossard's stronghold at Point du Jour, with the sole object of pinning down 2 Corps and preventing any movement designed to buttress the French centre and right. Until the early afternoon the only battle here was a battle of wills — Moltke against Steinmetz. The winner was to be

---

3 The opposing strengths on the 18th have been the subject of dispute, since there must always be some argument about numbers 'engaged' or 'available'. A fair estimate of troops 'engaged' would be: *German*, 230,000 and 720 guns; *French*, 126,000 and 520 guns.

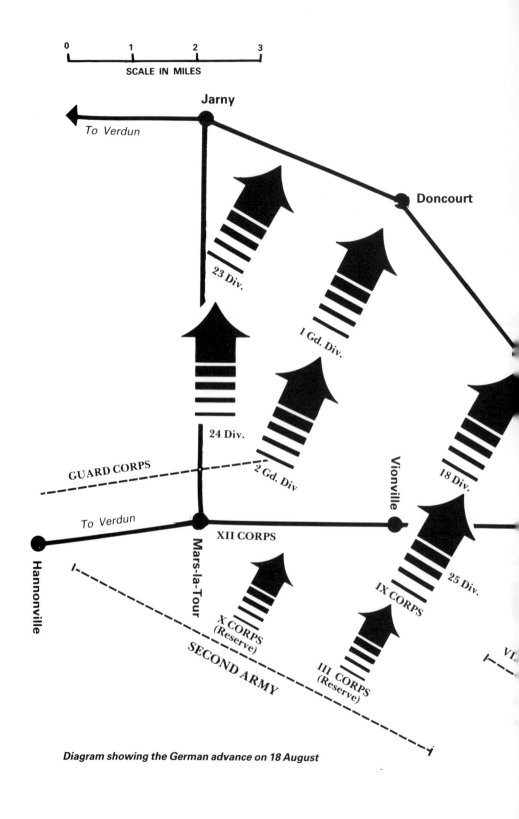

SCALE IN MILES
0 1 2 3

To Verdun

Jarny

Doncourt

23 Div.

1 Gd. Div.

24 Div.

2 Gd. Div

GUARD CORPS

Vionville

18 Div.

To Verdun

Hannonville

Mars-la-Tour

XII CORPS

25 Div.

X CORPS
(Reserve)

IX CORPS

III CORPS
(Reserve)

SECOND ARMY

VI.

Diagram showing the German advance on 18 August

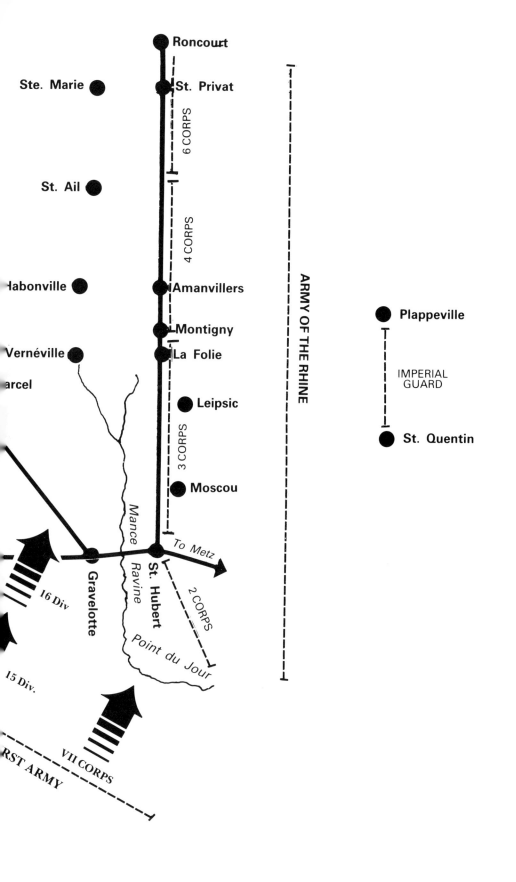

Steinmetz, with terrible consequences for both First and Second Armies.

So, too, during the morning VIII Corps (Goeben) moved forward to its allotted area between Gravelotte and Malmaison. It will be remembered that Moltke, ever mindful of Steinmetz's capacity for mischief, had reserved this corps to the King's personal discretion. It was a wise idea. But battles have an uncomfortable habit of standing wisdom on its head; and so it was presently to prove.

In the German centre IX Corps (Manstein) had been directed on Vernéville while the Guard Corps and XII Corps continued their long flank march to the north. Moltke's version of events which now brought on the battle of Gravelotte−St Privat is particularly interesting since it contrives, by subtle inference, to pin the blame on Frederick Charles. It has been said that the paladins of the Army of the Rhine were no band of brothers. There was not much love lost on the other side of the hill either. Here is Moltke, blandly ignoring the fundamental truth that time spent on reconnaissance is seldom wasted:

> First Army was not to begin its frontal attack until Second Army should be ready to co-operate .... In obedience [sic] to those instructions Prince Frederick Charles ordered IX Corps to march towards Vernéville and, *in case*[4] the French right wing should be found there, to begin the action by bringing a large force of artillery into action. The Guard was to continue its advance by way of Doncourt to support IX Corps as soon as possible. XII Corps was to remain at Jarny for the present.
>
> A little later fresh reports came in which indicated that IX Corps, should it proceed in the manner ordered, would not strike the enemy on his flank, but full on his front. The Prince, *in the discretion of his high position*,[4] therefore determined that IX Corps should postpone its attack till the Guard Corps should have been brought to bear on Amanvillers. At the same time XII Corps was to push on to Ste. Marie-aux-Chênes.
>
> But while these orders were being expedited, there was heard from Vernéville at twelve o'clock the roar of the first cannon shots.[5]

Thus, by a blunder altogether greater than Wedell's extravagant attack on the 16th, Manstein, obedient to his master's voice, brought on the battle of Gravelotte−St Privat. It was high noon. By nightfall much blood had been shed. By nightfall a German disaster had become an irreversible French defeat. By nightfall the doomed Army of the Rhine was filing back towards the sombre siege of the fortress from which it had set out in equal disarray four days earlier, and whence, within two months, it would go ignomi-

4 Author's italics.

5 Moltke: *op. cit.*

niously into captivity. The surrender of the Emperor at Sedan on 1 September has been longer remembered, for it symbolized the fall of one Empire and, within weeks, the rise of another. But the true tragedy of this unnecessary war is indelibly stamped here, on the bare uplands of Lorraine and in the martyrdom of Metz.

****

The battle of Gravelotte–St Privat suggests, by its name, that the day's fighting was concentrated on the two extreme flanks of Bazaine's position; but the French description — the defence of the Amanvillers line — is more strictly accurate, for it was here, in the centre, that Frederick Charles's ambitious plan almost foundered before it had started to develop. In accordance with a new order issued at 10 a.m., IX Corps was directed on Vernéville and La Folie with instructions that if it came in contact with the enemy thereabouts, action was to be joined in the first instance by a strong force of artillery. Ever since dawn the Germans had inexplicably assumed that Bazaine's defensive position extended no farther north than Montigny or — at most — Amanvillers, for no better reason than that this fitted neatly into the geometry of an outflanking movement later in the day by the Guard Corps and the Saxons as they wheeled into line at Habonville and Ste Marie-aux-Chênes.[6] It was a classic example of the wish being father to the thought. Not even the most elementary reconnaissance was carried out. And as with Wedell on the 16th, so now with Manstein.

As the artillery of IX Corps pushed forward from Vernéville, it could see the lines of tents on either side of Amanvillers, and was received with a brisk ripple of rifle-fire. What it could not see, however, was the great mass of Canrobert's 6 Corps ranged to the north around Jérusalem and St Privat (see Plate 26). Manstein had struck not the French right wing but its solid centre. More seriously, in accordance with his orders, he had sent his artillery on ahead without infantry support. The whole German master-plan was suddenly in danger of collapse.

Ladmirault, in the few hours available to him, had added artifice to nature and had created a position of formidable strength, as indeed had the French corps commanders on his right and left. There is reason here for reflection. Between them, Moltke and Frederick Charles had offered every kind of hostage to fortune in seeking a decisive victory. The reader should look again at the diagram on pp 230-231, as the great German phalanxes marched across the face of the Army of the Rhine.

And the commander of that Army? While the enemy marched upon its

6   4 Corps was deployed thus: on the right, a little to the north, and inclusive of Amanvillers, Cissey's division; on the left, extending as far as Montigny, Grenier's division; in reserve, above and behind the village, Lorencez's division. Foolishly, the French did not occupy the Bois de la Cusse 1000 yards to their front.

uncertain way, Bazaine pondered his own uncertain future at Plappeville. A wasted forenoon had come and gone. He had resolved — if resolution is a quality which can be attributed to him — to invite the enemy to batter himself to death on the Amanvillers line. His only order to his corps commanders had been at once passive and negative: to dig in and stand firm. It did not occur to him now or at any time during the day to go forward and see the situation for himself, or indeed to send a single staff-officer to report at first-hand on the progress of the battle. The same apathy which had lost him the afternoon opportunities at Mars-la-Tour was now to lose him the chance of a comprehensive victory against an enemy whose consecutive errors were to invite the most summary punishment.

Ladmirault ran true to form. He dug in and prepared to stand firm. When during the early afternoon Manstein had hazarded the whole German centre, and when the initiative — that rare and priceless military advantage — had passed to the French, to the point when a strong counter-attack would have split the German First and Second Armies and cut Moltke's dangerously extended lifeline with the Moselle crossings, Ladmirault sat tight on his defensive line with its formidable fields of fire (see Plates 24 and 25). As we have seen, he had not occupied the Bois de la Cusse to his immediate front; nor had he put strong outposts in the small but solid farm buildings at Champenois, L'Envie and Chantrenne. Had Manstein been denied these *points d'appui*, it is quite possible that the battle of Gravelotte–St Privat would have ended in disaster for the Germans long before Steinmetz's notable contribution to that end, and equally long before Frederick Charles could have redeemed a seemingly lost cause on the French right.[7]

* * * * * * * *

The battle of bloody Thursday may best be described in three phases: win, draw and defeat. It could, and should, have had a very different result. That it did not was due once more to Bazaine's apathy and ineptitude, reflected first in his refusal to allow his subordinates to pass to the offensive when repeatedly that opportunity presented itself; and secondly his failure, until the day was far advanced, to reinforce Canrobert at St Privat with the Imperial Guard and the reserve artillery. The men of the Army of the Rhine, although outnumbered on this field by two to one and massively out-gunned, fought with exemplary bravery. On their left wing they gave not an inch, and hurled Steinmetz's First Army back in panic-stricken rout across the Mance ravine not once but three times. On their right they held fast until, late in the evening, they were overborne, but not before they had left the sombre slope below St Privat strewn thickly with the dreadful

7   There is an irony here. Cissey's division on Ladmirault's right and the Hessian division of IX Corps on Manstein's left met astride the uncompleted railway cutting which would have been Bazaine's secure link between Metz and Verdun.

debris of the German Guard Corps. So close did these men come to a memorable victory that towards 6 p.m., when the German right hand had long since lost contact with its left, the order went out from the King's headquarters near Gravelotte to clear the Moselle crossings from Ars to Novéant for a retreat which would, as darkness fell, have become a sensational shambles. But it did not happen; and this is why.

The battle began in the centre; and it began, as it was to continue, with the first of many German errors.

It will be remembered that during the morning news reached Frederick Charles that the French right wing, far from lying around Montigny and Amanvillers, was reported to extend at least as far north as St Privat.[8] But his order to arrest IX Corps' engagement of the enemy until the left wing of Second Army had completed its wheel arrived too late. Manstein, with the same enthusiasm which Alvensleben had shown on the 16th, hurried his artillery forward well in advance of his infantry and, without caution or reconnaissance, pushed nine batteries onto a long shoulder of ground facing obliquely *south-east* from the Bois de la Cusse. There his 54 guns suddenly found themselves exposed at short range not only to the full weight of fire of Ladmirault's corps on either side of Amanvillers, but also enfiladed by the unsuspected mass of 6 Corps to the north at St Privat and Ste Marie-aux-Chênes. It was noon precisely. And it is a measure of Manstein's precipitate action that at the moment when his guns opened up on what the German account describes as 'a camp in negligent repose' his own negligence is underlined by the fact that the nearest infantry support (18th Division) was an hour's march away beyond Vernéville. It was an hour which the French could have turned to greater advantage than they did.

When Manstein's guns began to fire, 4 Corps stood to arms. It is inconceivable that Ladmirault could have been taken by surprise, for the Amanvillers position, with its long fields of fire, commands the whole plateau to the west, and throughout the morning the corps commander could have watched the dust clouds of a massive army as it marched in serried columns across his front. Yet at noon Grenier's division was pleasantly occupied in cooking its midday meal, when prudence dictated that a strong force should have been pushed forward to occupy the Bois de la Cusse and the three outlying farmsteads, and to prepare a royal reception for an unwitting enemy. Instead, 4 Corps occupied the shelter-trenches and rifle-pits which it had dug, and brought up its guns and mitrailleuses behind the garden walls and solid masonry of Amanvillers and Montigny. No more meals would be cooked that day; and when Manstein's guns began to fire it did not occur to Ladmirault to inform Bazaine that he had a battle on his hands.

---

8   Not for several hours did Second Army headquarters discover that Canrobert's right wing in fact rested upon Roncourt.

XII CORPS

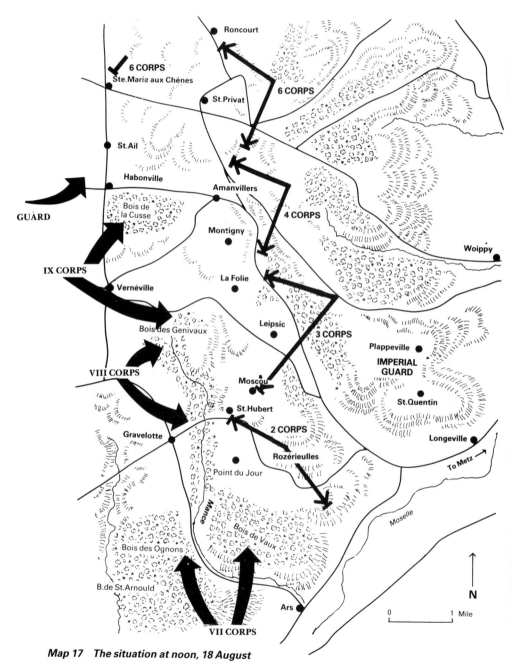

Roncourt

6 CORPS
Ste.Marie aux Chênes

6 CORPS

St.Privat

St.Ail

Habonville

Amanvillers

GUARD

Bois de
la Cusse

4 CORPS

Montigny

Woippy

IX CORPS

La Folie

Verneville

Leipsic

Bois des Genivaux

3 CORPS

Plappeville

IMPERIAL
GUARD

VIII CORPS

Moscou

St.Quentin

St.Hubert

Gravelotte

2 CORPS

Longeville

Point du Jour

Rozérieulles

To Metz

Moselle

Bois de Vaux

Bois des Ognons

Meuse

B.de St.Arnould

Ars

N

0   1 Mile

VII CORPS

Map 17   The situation at noon, 18 August

IX Corps was at once in deep trouble. On its left — and well in rear — the Guard Corps and XII Corps were still moving on the outside arc of Second Army, unaware that the French line extended as far north as Roncourt.[9] Thus Manstein found himself in a salient of his own making, with the greater part of his artillery with neither cover nor support, and open not only to a frontal attack but to the concentrated fire of Leboeuf from its right, and even to a strong flank attack by 6 Corps on its left.[10] In some sense, his position was not unlike that of Alvensleben at noon on the 16th; but this time there were to be no cavalry heroics.

It was not long before the only heroics were, once more, to be the unhappy lot of the incomparable German gunners. Pushed recklessly forward within range of chassepot and mitrailleuse and of the eager French batteries, they at once provided the kind of target practice which rarely comes a defender's way. For an hour they withstood a storm of shot and shell, but as the casualties to men and horses mounted, Manstein called his batteries back, leaving eight guns to protect his withdrawal in a sheltered corner of the wood. As the Germans retired, manhandling their guns 'through an avenue of slaughtered horses', Grenier's men rushed forward, seized two abandoned pieces, and triumphantly hauled them back to Amanvillers. It was bold and brave; but it was an empty gesture. Not only was the Bois de la Cusse left in German hands; so too were the strongpoints of Champenois, L'Envie and Chantrenne. Trophies are to be treasured; but battles are not to be counted in single batteries. Ladmirault, as has been suggested, ran true to form. As he had drawn back to Bruville on the afternoon of Mars-la-Tour, so now he took to his trenches and awaited his opponent's next move. It was not long in coming.

Manstein had no time to lose. With his corps artillery virtually out of action and his infantry (18th Division and 25th (Hessian) Division) not yet deployed forward of Vernéville, IX Corps was as vulnerable to a counter-thrust by 4 Corps from the Amanvillers position as X Corps had been at Mars-la-Tour. Indeed, had Ladmirault maintained a strong presence in the Bois de la Cusse[11] and in the three farmsteads, IX Corps

9   As will be seen, 3rd Guard Brigade was diverted *en marche* at Habonville to relieve the hard-pressed Hessians opposite Amanvillers. It thus largely escaped the fate which awaited the rest of the Guard Corps towards evening.

10   3 Corps and 6 Corps were disposed thus:
a) *3 Corps*: On the right, Montaudon's division at La Folie and in the upper corner of the Bois des Genivaux; Nayral's division at Leipsic and in the eastern part of the woods; Metman's division between Leipsic and Moscou; and Aymard's division entrenched between Moscou and St Hubert, with outposts on the eastern declivity of the Mance ravine.
b) *6 Corps*: Tixier's division on the right with the 9th Regiment, offering a refused flank from the Bois de Jaumont to Roncourt; in the centre, Lafont's division between Roncourt and St Privat, with four battalions thrown forward to Ste Marie; and on the left, connecting with 4 Corps, Sorval's division astride the road between St Privat and Jérusalem.

11   This feature is misleadingly named, for it consisted only of scattered clumps of trees and afforded little cover. But while it was commanded to the east by the Amanvillers trenches, the low ridge on which it stood made all movement to the west between Vernéville and Habonville extremely hazardous.

would have been effectively neutralized and lateral contact between the German right and left wings virtually severed. More seriously, since it was now well past noon, the already tight time-scale of Moltke's master-plan would have been seriously compromised.

The reader may reflect yet again upon Bazaine's Olympian detachment. He had already — albeit fortuitously — deceived his opponent by the distance to which his own right wing had been extended through St Privat to Roncourt (Canrobert's decision, not Bazaine's). Had he accepted the formidable natural strength of his own left wing on the dominating heights above the Mance ravine and trusted Frossard and Leboeuf to make that massive redoubt *inexpugnable* (as indeed they did), and had he come forward during the forenoon to Amanvillers, whence (for the first time) he could have seen not only the small fortress of St Privat to his right but the inviting flank of Second Army as it marched across his front, it is conceivable that he might have been encouraged to teach Moltke and Frederick Charles a salutary lesson.

He was not so encouraged. He did not even communicate with Ladmirault and Canrobert. Instead he sat inertly at Plappeville, surrounded by the élite reserve which could, and should, have turned the day; and there is an element of tragi-comedy in the fact that the running commentary on the battle of the 18th was conveyed to him by telegraph from watchers on the cathedral tower in Metz. It is a curious commander-in-chief who chooses to fight a decisive battle by remote control.

Manstein, quick to see the error of his ways, plugged the gap by pushing 18th Division forward on his right to occupy the farmsteads and the northern fringe of the Bois des Genivaux; and by sending a brigade of the Hessian Division through the Bois de la Cusse to a position astride the railway cutting. Every available gun — the artillery of both divisions, and even the weary batteries of III Corps from the reserve line behind Vernéville — was hurried up. At 2 p.m., as 3rd Guard Brigade with three batteries came forward from Habonville, the first crisis was averted. The German centre, if not secure, was stiffened. IX Corps (*see* Plates 24 and 25) could make no further progress. Outranged by chassepots from Amanvillers and from Leboeuf's commanding positions at La Folie and Leipsic, Manstein's men bravely took their punishment.[12] But, as the many memorials now show, they died in their tracks. Here, by mid-afternoon, the battle stuttered and stopped, with both sides exhausted and the killing-ground more than adequately stocked. The stalemate here in the centre continued until dusk, when the collapse of the French right wing compelled Ladmirault to pull 4 Corps back.

****

12   Casualties in IX Corps during the afternoon of the 18th were 4816.

Plate 24 Amanvillers, looking east. The scene of the unsuccessful attack by 25th (Hessian) Division

Plate 25 Amanvillers, looking east. The scene of the attack by 3rd Guard Infantry Brigade

Plate 26   Looking north-east to St Privat from IX Corps position opposite Amanvillers.
Centre left, the corner of the Bois de la Cusse

Meanwhile on the German right wing, on either side of Gravelotte, a very different kind of battle had begun. However else it may be described, it was not to be a stalemate. Instead, it came close to being a German disaster on a Wagnerian scale.

It is important here that the reader should have a clear picture at the outset of the curious conduct of the German high command throughout this day. In a sense, it was a mirror-image of Bazaine's tactical folly of a policy of remote control, quite literally on the other side of the hill.

At 6 a.m., as the two German armies were set in motion, Royal Headquarters were established 'on the height south of Flavigny' (all orders were issued in the name of the King, but the voice was that of Moltke until, late in the evening, he decided to distance himself from his master's miscalculations). Towards noon, when the sound of gunfire began to echo down from Vernéville, the royal entourage moved forward to Rezonville. There, while it could see little of its right wing and nothing of its centre and left, it was at least more accessible. Little did that profit the high command; for while Canrobert was later to comment drily on Bazaine's inability 'to command an army of 140,000 men', the Great General Staff, Moltke's finely tuned instrument, now showed that for all its expertise it was powerless to keep control of a force nearly twice that size in which events had overtaken both army commanders and — more critically —

both army commanders had precipitated quite unforeseen events. In mid-afternoon the King rode forward to Malmaison with his staff in time to be a horrified spectator of the panic-stricken flight of First Army across the Mance ravine. In time, too, to be driven back himself to Rezonville by the long-range fire of Frossard's *fantassins* at Point du Jour.

The official German account is nicely ambivalent about the conduct of the high command. It speaks of a constant flow of information from Frederick Charles about the progress of Second Army in the centre and on the German left. This is not true. When Frederick Charles rode forward to Vernéville about 2 p.m. his mind was wonderfully concentrated by the situation which confronted him. IX Corps and 3rd Guard Brigade, supported by every available gun, were holding a tenuous line under the remorseless fire of Ladmirault's solidly entrenched divisions. Away to the north-east and in Ste Marie, Canrobert's corps stood unexpectedly astride the line of the flank-march which had been so complacently assumed at dawn that day. There is no evidence of any kind that Frederick Charles communicated during the afternoon of the 18th with the King, whether at Flavigny, Rezonville or Malmaison. And it is the most dramatic *trouvaille* of this day of high drama that when, towards midnight, the German high command had accepted a crushing defeat on its right, word came at last that St Privat had been captured and that the French had been outflanked and driven from their line of last resort.

****

When at noon the guns began to speak at Vernéville, First Army was disposed as follows. On the extreme right at Vaux, facing Lapasset's group posted at Jussy and St Ruffine, stood 26th Infantry Brigade of 13th Division (VII Corps) with a single battery of artillery. To its left, astride the Mance ravine in the Bois de Vaux and the Bois des Ognons, were the remainder of 13th Division and the two brigades of 14th Division. Farther north, 16th Division of VIII Corps lay around Gravelotte with, on its left and in tenuous contact with Wrangel's 18th Division at the Bois de Genivaux, Weltzien's 15th Division. This last division, not yet seriously engaged in the campaign, was presently to receive a bloody baptism of fire. Finally, at Malmaison was 1st Cavalry Division, which had crossed the river at Novéant early on the 18th, and part of which was also soon to be ruthlessly sacrificed on the altar of Steinmetz's insensate arrogance.

Facing First Army within chassepot range across the ravine stood 2 Corps and the left wing of Leboeuf's 3 Corps,[13] astride the highway to Metz. 2 Corps lay thus: from St Hubert and the elbow of the road to the farmsteads at Point du Jour, Vergé's division with Jolivet's brigade on the right; thence, on the crown of the plateau facing south-west, the division of

13 *See* footnote p. 237.

Bastoul (formerly that of Bataille, killed in action at Vionville) linking with Lapasset's group near Rozérieulles.

Today the topography of what we may call the Point du Jour plateau has changed significantly, but on that distant Thursday it was a true *redan*, bare fields sloping upward to a commanding crest and dominating the westerly plain from Gravelotte to Vernéville. Below it, as a moat defensive to a house, ran the deep and thickly wooded Mance ravine. It is not possible to imagine a position of greater natural strength.

To nature, Frossard added the expertise of an engineer. The infantry of 2 Corps was dug in on the slope in a series of terraced trenches, rifle-pits and covered supports one above the other, with protected gun-emplacements and with the exposed farm buildings traversed and loopholed. This must be said again. It is difficult to understand how, in the hours available to him and with the limited materials at hand, Frossard contrived to convert what he would have called *une position magnifique* into a position that was truly *inexpugnable*. And so it proved. For despite everything that Steinmetz hurled against Point du Jour, despite every desperate attempt by First Army to storm the heights, 2 Corps gave no ground. And on a day of bloodshed which left the Mance ravine packed thick with German dead, the total casualties of 2 Corps were 621. The pity is that Bazaine had long since distanced himself from any personal involvement in a battle of his own choosing. While great and glorious things were happening at Point du Jour, he kept his counsel a mere gunshot away at Plappeville. In the evening, the Germans broke and fled. Jolivet (who seems alone to have sensed victory) later wrote: 'I did not think I should pursue them, having been ordered to stay on the defensive.' 'Such an army', observes Professor Howard drily, 'does not deserve victory.'[14] Amen to that.

****

Moltke's orders for the 18th had closely enjoined Steinmetz to restrict his activity on the right wing to artillery fire until Frederick Charles had completed his long flank march and inward wheel. Not until then was an infantry attack on Point du Jour to be contemplated.

As we have seen, the plan began to founder from the very outset when, for want of adequate reconnaissance, IX Corps blundered prematurely into the centre of the French line at Amanvillers. Thus by 2 p.m. the tidy geometry of a set-piece engagement had been knocked askew and Manstein, far from buttressing the flank attack of Second Army, found himself in serious danger of being driven off the middle ground; and this situation created an equally serious — and equally unforeseen — problem for Frederick Charles.

14   Howard: *op. cit.*

It is easy to start a battle. It is impossible, once the forward gear has been engaged, to put a vast military machine into reverse. In his philosophy of war — and war is a dangerous playground for philosophers — Moltke has recorded his opinion that once great armies have been set in motion in both a strategic and a tactical sense, a supreme commander can only influence the outcome of events by the resolute employment of his reserve (as Moltke had discovered at Sadowa, and as Bazaine failed to grasp at Gravelotte−St Privat). It had been so, even as recently as the Napoleonic wars, but then the scale of battles had been such that a Bonaparte at Wagram and a Wellington at Waterloo could still *personally* play the role of actor-manager. Once battle was joined, so ran Moltke's received wisdom, the result was in the hands of subordinate commanders, and success or failure was dependent on their expertise, on the quality of the fighting-men, on that indefinable essence called morale — and on luck. Throughout this day, Moltke's philosophy was to be put under a most searching microscope. The first subject for scrutiny was to be Steinmetz.

****

When Manstein began the battle at noon, Steinmetz brought his own guns into action. And at once a profound flaw in Moltke's philosophy was revealed. It will be remembered that the King had, presumably on Moltke's advice, reserved Goeben's VIII Corps of First Army to his personal command. But at noon Royal Headquarters was still some miles away at Flavigny, and Steinmetz, smarting under the implied criticism of his competence, seems to have decided that distance not only lent enchantment to the view but released him from the restraints upon his own freedom of action. It is a strange fact that nowhere in either official or unofficial German accounts is there mention of or comment upon the fact that from noon onward Steinmetz reassumed command of VIII Corps. How, during the remaining hours of daylight, he squandered his precious resources, leaves Moltke's tidy philosophy in tatters.

By 1 p.m. the corps and divisional artillery of First Army — more than 120 guns[15] — had been deployed on either side of Gravelotte. It was by no means a strong position, for here the two opposing sides were so closely engaged across the Mance ravine that Steinmetz's batteries were within range not only of Frossard's artillery, but even of his chassepots and mitrailleuses at Point du Jour.[16] The reader will recall how, during the morning of the 16th, Alvensleben's gunners had 'beaten a path' for the

---

15   The German account states that by 3 p.m. First and Second Armies had 246 guns in action between Gravelotte and Ste Marie. And by 5 p.m., more than 400 guns.

16   The German artillery line was also well within range of the fortress guns of St Quentin beyond the Rozérieulles plateau, but there is no evidence that the siege guns of this fort, only partly armed, contributed to the French defensive fire.

infantry of III Corps to press forward beyond Vionville and Flavigny. Here, in the early afternoon of the 18th — and in circumstances quite different — Steinmetz decided that he must at all costs push his batteries forward to the edge of the ravine; and that his *infantry* must 'beat a path' for his *guns*. It was a reckless thing to do. And in plain defiance of Moltke's orders, he set the infantry of First Army in motion to storm the heights of Point du Jour and Moscou. It was to prove a formidable error of judgment.

****

About 1 p.m., Moltke, then still at Flavigny, sent one last restraining order to Steinmetz:

> The fighting which can be heard from the direction of Vernéville does not on any account mean that First Army is to engage in a general offensive action. It will remain under cover and restrict its activity *for the time being*[17] to counter-battery fire preparatory to a full-scale assault on the enemy positions *in due course*[17].

Moltke was too late, for Steinmetz had already slipped his leash.

In fact, Steinmetz was not solely to blame. Since it takes two to fight a battle, and since battles do not conform to even the best-laid plans, the agents responsible for the premature involvement of First Army's infantry were Ladmirault and Leboeuf. When Manstein deployed his 18th Division opposite the French positions between Montigny and Leipsic, his right flank rested on the northern fringes of the Bois des Genivaux. Here, and in the three farmsteads on the lower ground, the German infantry was caught in a potential death-trap. Thus the pressure had somehow to be taken off 18th Division; and to achieve this it became imperative for the Germans to occupy the woods and to draw off Leboeuf's fire between La Folie and Moscou. Thus Goeben's VIII Corps, barely in contact with Manstein's right, was irresistibly drawn into the battle. It was a little after 2 p.m.

****

It is proper to reflect here briefly on the problem confronting even a General Staff of the quality which Moltke had for so many years perfected, and to recall his own comment that 'the best training for war is war itself'. It is a pleasant cliché. It is also true.

A student of modern warfare — that is, of our own century — will take in his stride the sophisticated means which are available today to a

---

17 Author's italics. It should be added that Steinmetz had been present at the meeting of Supreme HQ on the 17th, and was perfectly well aware of the master-plan for the following day.

commander to move his pieces round the chessboard. And the quantity and quality of the available intelligence to justify or frustrate those moves. In 1870, although the electric telegraph had provided a new strategic dimension, communications on the battlefield itself were still restricted to verbal messages (visual contact could, and did, lead to some fatal misjudgments). Indeed, the very scale of the battle area on and around the Gravelotte plateau — more than sixty square miles — and the sheer number of formations involved meant that information from the fighting-line was slow in reaching the high command (Royal headquarters did not move forward from remote Flavigny until the afternoon) and was out of date when it did so. Thus Moltke, in particular, had to fight this great set-piece as it were by instinct; and his instinct was of a very different order to that of Steinmetz and Frederick Charles.

Moltke was a highly gifted child of his times. Bazaine was an untalented product of a decadent military system. Yet for all the gulf that separated these two men — symbolized perhaps by the daunting Mance ravine — their problem was the same: to fight a blindfold battle, and to trust a not always trustworthy subordinate command to wave a wand and make a warlike wish come true. The reader may fairly feel that this narrative has been — and will yet be — harsh on Bazaine. It does not award too many marks to Moltke either.

****

At 2 p.m., while Steinmetz was deploying his artillery in line on either side of Gravelotte, Weltzien's division[18] of VIII Corps had pushed forward into the southern edge of the Bois des Genivaux with the object of clearing the wood and joining hands with Manstein's 18th Division on its left. This involvement of the infantry of First Army is nowhere explained. However reckless and disobedient Steinmetz was presently to be, he does not seem at this stage to have initiated any order to Goeben, the commander of VIII Corps; and certainly, in the confusion caused by the failure of IX Corps in the centre, there could not possibly have been time for any *coup de main* to have been organized from Flavigny, where the King, in theory, was still reserving VIII Corps to his own command. We have seen why Moltke had proposed this over-optimistic restraint on Steinmetz, and it is possible that if Royal Headquarters, on hearing the cannonade from Vernéville at noon, had sent its chief of staff forward to Gravelotte the consequent debacle might have been avoided. But it cannot be emphasized too strongly that, as early as 2 p.m., the German general staff had lost control of the battle of Gravelotte–St Privat.

Moltke's subsequent 'disclaimer' is particularly interesting, not so much

18   29th Brigade, 30th Brigade and *8th Jäger Battalion*. The commander of 29th Brigade was the brother of the Wedell whose own brigade (38th) had suffered so severely on the 16th.

for what it says but for what it — not too subtly — implies:

> The sixteen batteries [*of VII and VIII Corps*] were drawn up right and left of Gravelotte .... Their fire was ineffective because they were too far distant from the enemy; and furthermore they suffered from the fire of the French tirailleurs nestling in the opposite woods. It became necessary [*sic*] to drive these out, and thus there occurred here a premature infantry fight. The French were cleared out from the eastern declivity of the Mance ravine, and the artillery line, now increased to twenty batteries, was able to advance closer up to the western brink and now direct its fire against the main position of the enemy.
>
> But the battalions of 29th Brigade pushed the attack further. They pressed on leftward into the southern section of the Bois des Genivaux, but were unable to obtain touch of IX Corps in possession of the northern portion of the forest, since the French firmly held the intervening ground. On the right sundry detachments took possession of the quarries and gravel-pits near St Hubert.[19]

****

When Goeben pushed forward into the southern half of the Bois des Genivaux he found the main part of the wood occupied by a strong force of Metman's division. In the short time available to them, the French had cut down trees to create abatis and had blocked the few paths leading to the eastern edge with solid fieldworks. 15th Division on Goeben's left could make no progress on that flank, and the leading battalions were subjected to a murderous fire from the commanding heights around Moscou and St Hubert. There was no going back; and thus the infantry battle which Moltke had so expressly forbidden on this wing was joined in earnest. By nightfall it was to suck in the whole of VII Corps and VIII Corps, part of 1st Cavalry Division, and towards dusk II Corps of Second Army which, as it arrived at Rezonville, was diverted to Steinmetz's command and recklessly squandered on a futile final assault on the unshaken French positions at Point du Jour and beyond. By nightfall, the German right wing would have suffered a bloody defeat. By nightfall a lack-lustre Bazaine at Plappeville would have cast away a crucial victory.

Steinmetz watched this unexpected development from Gravelotte. He had still been given no authority to issue orders to VIII Corps, although he had put his own interpretation on the 'expectant stance' which had been enjoined on him. Now, as the fighting flared up, he threw both orders and caution to the wind. From shortly after 2 p.m. until darkness put an end to his wanton arrogance, no restraint was put upon him by Royal Headquar-

19 Moltke: *op. cit.*

ters and no directive was given; not after the bloody disaster of his second attack; not even after the panic-stricken rout which followed his third attack and brought Moltke to the brink of a humiliating retreat across the Moselle; and when, in the late evening, II Corps[20] arrived upon the battlefield the King lamely consented to Steinmetz's request to launch the Pomeranians into one last attack across a long-since impassable causeway over the ravine, a stupendous folly which, as we shall see, led to yet another dreadful disaster. At no point on this wing does Moltke seem to have been consulted. It is not always easy to play second fiddle to an elderly warrior-king; and Moltke was later to distance himself from any taint of responsibility:

> It was six o'clock, the day was nearly at an end, and it was imperative [*not to Moltke*] that the decisive result should be precipitated. The King [*sic*] therefore ordered First Army to make a renewed advance in support of which he [*sic*] placed II Corps, just arrived after a long march, at the disposal of General von Steinmetz .... It would have been more proper if the Chief of Staff of First Army, who was personally on the spot at the time [*so was Moltke*], had not permitted this movement at so late an hour of the evening. A body of troops, still completely intact, might have been of great value the next day; but it could hardly be expected on this evening to effect a decisive reversal of the situation.[21]

The student of military history should always be extremely cautious of the latter-day reflections of military magnates. The student of this particular battle should particularly bear in mind that, while Steinmetz was busy filling the Mance ravine with German dead, Moltke had not the remotest knowledge of the progress of events six miles away on his left flank, the very flank where his own master-plan had predicted the turning movement which would roll up the Amanvillers line and drive Bazaine back on his final bastion at Metz. Gravelotte—St Privat was, first and last, a soldiers' battle. If it reflects little credit on Bazaine, it adds nothing to the exaggerated stature of Moltke.

****

It is time to return to Goeben and VIII Corps, and to Steinmetz's disobedient intervention. It was 2.30 p.m., and to escape the increasing attentions of Leboeuf at Moscou there was no alternative for the Germans but to cross the ravine and establish a foothold on the edge of the plateau under whatever cover Steinmetz's gun-line at Gravelotte could provide.

20 The *9th Colberg Grenadiers* of this corps was Moltke's old regiment.

21 Moltke: *op. cit.*

The objective was the farmstead of St Hubert. Against this strongpoint the whole of 15th Division and 31st Brigade of 16th Division were launched.

St Hubert stands below the crown of the ridge running from Point du Jour to Moscou, a little to the west of the elbow of the main road, a hundred yards from the woods which cover the steep eastern face of the Mance ravine, and with a commanding view of the western plateau. Here the road bends slightly to the left and descends through a cutting, flanked by quarries and gravel pits, to the then narrow causeway which crosses the flat, grassy bottom of the ravine. Thence the road rises in a straight line to Gravelotte beyond (see Plate 23). It was then a much more substantial complex than it is today, comprising a large stone-built farmhouse, solid outbuildings, and walled gardens. It was a formidable obstacle to any frontal assault on the main French position with its terraced trenches and covered emplacements on the bare slopes behind it and on either side, and its capture — the sole and excessively bloody victory for the Germans throughout the day on this flank — was the key to any *coup de main* against the great *redan* of Point du Jour. By noon on the 18th it was occupied by seven companies of the 80th Regiment of Aymard's division (3 Corps), with a skirmishing line thrown forward into the woods and undergrowth on the eastern face of the ravine.

Steinmetz's order for the attack on St Hubert was a wild surmise. On the left, 15th Division was sent forward across the ravine on either side of the causeway, followed closely — too closely — by 31st Brigade of 16th Division which pressed up the wooded slope below Point du Jour. Into this confused mass the French poured a hail of shells and bullets, and within minutes the ravine became a shambles as the Germans struggled to make their way up the further side. Thus the official account:

> Companies, already weakened by dreadful losses, became inextric-ably confused in the thick undergrowth, and the remnants of these groups, all their officers dead or wounded, were driven back to such shelter as they could find in the bottom of the ravine. South of the causeway elements of 29th and 30th Brigades which had managed to work their way up the further slope and to occupy the gravel-pits below Point du Jour were halted in their tracks. Thus, by 3 p.m. some thirty companies — or what was left of thirty companies — were left clinging to the brow of the ravine. The division was by now in a parlous state and at the mercy of a strong counter-attack ...

No such counter-attack came.

The efforts of the German infantry had, however, one immediate result, for by engaging the attention of both Frossard's and Leboeuf's batteries on the further ridge it enabled Steinmetz to advance his own considerable artillery to the western edge of the ravine, and from there his guns could bring an overwhelming fire to bear on St Hubert at almost point-blank range.[22] Soon the buildings were ablaze and half the small garrison of 750 men were out of action; and shortly before 3.30 p.m., as the French withdrew in good order to their support line, the *8th Jäger Regiment* and five companies of the *28th* and *67th* rushed forward from the quarries and captured the farm. It was soon to prove a hollow victory.

****

To Steinmetz, from a vantage-point a little to the north of Gravelotte, the capture of St Hubert was not an episode but a climax, and with a ridiculous sense of melodrama he reported to the King that 'the heights have been stormed and captured, with drums beating and bugles sounding'. He was to be swiftly disabused. Had he gone forward across the ravine he would have found a very different picture, for St Hubert, far from being a haven, was a hornet's nest. Frossard and Leboeuf had, within the short time available to them, put the entrenching-tool to formidable use, so that the long crown of the Rozérieulles plateau was covered by an intricate pattern of terraced rifle-pits and gun emplacements. To stand today and look at this bare hillside, dominating every approach from the wooded ravine far below, is to be witness to the revolution in weaponry and defensive tactics which were to be so dreadfully demonstrated on the first morning of the Somme battle 46 years later. Point du Jour and the Schwaben Redoubt have much in common. Thus any attempt by Goeben's exhausted infantry to press forward from St Hubert was met by a storm of fire from Point du Jour and Moscou. VIII Corps may have reached the protection of the walls of St Hubert. It had also run into a brick wall beyond which it could not move without inviting instant destruction.

This was not the view of Steinmetz, his head full of the sound of drums and bugles. Casting aside every restraint so rightly but so ineffectively placed upon him, and overriding Goeben's protestations, he set in train a series of cumulative disasters. The French were later to parade Bazaine before a court-martial. The Germans might well have applied the same medicine to Steinmetz.

Towards 4 p.m. there was a lull in the fire-fight. Around St Hubert, the Germans licked their considerable wounds and sheltered behind the garden walls and in the quarries, unable to venture forth towards either Point du Jour or Moscou. Already the ravine and its narrow causeway were crowded with the debris of the first attack, and VIII Corps had been fully committed except for Rex's Brigade of 16th Division in reserve at Gravelotte.[23] About this time the French artillery along the Point du

22 It is a measure of the confused pattern of fighting on the far side of the ravine that the German shells caused appreciable casualties to their own infantry.

23 It will be remembered that this brigade had been roughly handled on the evening of the 16th at Rezonville.

Jour—Leipsic ridge fell silent. This was partly in order that the busy batteries might replenish their ammunition, but more certainly to conceal the location of their covered gun-emplacements from the long line of German artillery on the further side of the ravine.

Steinmetz, despite Goeben's warning that, far from the heights having been 'stormed', VIII Corps had only gained a fragile foothold on the eastern edge of the ravine — and that, too, at crippling cost — was stubbornly determined to convert an imagined victory into a decisive rout. He was later to justify his subsequent actions by claiming that the slackening of French fire was adequate evidence either that the enemy was withdrawing or was transferring strong forces to his vulnerable right flank. Goeben protested that such a delusion could hazard the entire First Army. 'Captain Seton, an Indian Army officer who was present, noticed the violent gestures and rapid talk of the older man because they offered so strong a contrast to the quiet coolness of the younger. At that moment the Army Commander was expounding opinions and issuing orders which were to bring on one of the most destructive episodes of the battle.'[24]

What Steinmetz now designed was a home-thrust on Frossard's virtually unscathed position at Point du Jour.

His first move was a diversionary attack from Ars by 26th Brigade of 13th Division against Lapasset's group which was covering the main road below Rozérieulles. This foray, supported by only a single battery, succeeded in occupying the villages of Vaux and Jussy, but an attempted advance across the road at St Ruffine was easily beaten off, and here the fighting petered out. If this demonstration achieved anything, it was to confirm — if such were any longer necessary — Bazaine's apprehensions about the threat to his communications with Metz. Neither now nor as Steinmetz stumbled from one disaster to another did it once occur to him that his opponent might have put his own much more tenuous lines of communication with Novéant and Pont-à-Mousson in jeopardy.

On the left of 26th Brigade, the rest of VII Corps (Zastrow) was deployed astride the ravine with 25th and 28th Brigades in the Bois de Vaux and 27th Brigade posted south of Gravelotte as corps reserve and as protection for the gun-line. Zastrow, as he had already demonstrated at Spicheren, shared Steinmetz's capacity for precipitate action. From where he stood near the crossroads, he could see the black smoke billowing up from the blazing farmsteads at Point du Jour and Moscou. Like Steinmetz, he watched the enemy infantry evacuating the buildings, and, like him, assumed that this signalled a general retreat. But it meant no such thing, as Goeben on the left, with the broken remnants of his own infantry huddled desperately round St Hubert, knew only too well. Frossard, the expert engineer and disparagingly styled 'professor' of defensive tactics, had done his work well, and 2 Corps, far from retreating, had fallen back a short way

24 Hooper: *The Campaign of Sedan.*

to occupy the untouched trenches and rifle-pits terraced one above the other on the higher slope and on the crown of the ridge. On his right Leboeuf had similarly withdrawn from the burning shell of Moscou to his prepared positions along the ridge, and had given added strength by bringing forward his reserve division from the reverse slope. It was a classic case of *reculer pour mieux sauter*. And this Steinmetz now discovered, to the bitter cost of First Army.

It is difficult to justify or even understand Steinmetz's conduct throughout this bloody Thursday. As we have seen, he had been present when the King issued his orders to the two army commanders on the previous day. As we have also seen, repeated *written* instructions were sent to him during the morning of the 18th to hold his hand and to restrict his activity to artillery fire until Second Army had found Bazaine's right flank and completed the inward wheel of the Guard Corps and XII Corps.

It is even more curious when it is remembered that at all times a highly trained member of the General Staff was attached to each Army headquarters, and that these officers were answerable direct to Moltke; and that at no point during the day was Goeben's VIII Corps placed under Steinmetz's authority. Perhaps Goeben may be blamed for letting his heart rule his head and for being drawn into a premature infantry engagement in the Bois des Genivaux. He may surely be blamed for allowing his superior to represent the bleak success at St Hubert as a comprehensive victory over Bazaine's *inébranlable* left wing. By nightfall, all that First Army had to show for its endeavours was 6000 casualties — many of them self-inflicted in a final catastrophe — and the remnants of forty-three companies from seven different regiments hanging on the brink of the ravine whence hundreds of their comrades had fled in panic.

Almost alone of the senior commanders on either side, Steinmetz kept his counsel and never committed himself to print. Indeed, there seems to have been a conspiracy of silence, both in the official record and in the pyramid of prose which later kept the presses busy. Perhaps it was left to one man, by inference, to salvage the wrecked reputation of this brave but reckless old[25] soldier; and that, by pinning the ultimate responsibility where it belonged — on Moltke and on the King.[26] No such obloquy was to attach to Prince Frederick Charles and to Prince Augustus of Württemberg for their dreadful errors on the German left wing and for the destruction of the Guard Corps. But then St Privat was to prove a victory, and princes are privileged persons.

****

25 He was seventy-four, and had commanded V Corps in the Sadowa campaign in 1866.

26 Hönig: *Twenty-four Hours of Moltke's Strategy*.

Wheresoever the blame lay, it was by now a matter past all redeeming. Zastrow's two brigades pressed forward across the ravine and worked their way up the further slope towards the southern flank of Frossard's position. But as the leading lines of skirmishers (*77th* and *55th*) broke cover, they were received with a storm of artillery and chassepot fire from the quarries bordering the main road and from the rifle-pits and covered emplacements beyond. A few groups of resolute men clung to the fringes of the woods, but the rest were driven back in disorder to the comparative shelter of the bed of the ravine, carrying with them in indescribable confusion the company columns climbing up behind them. Within a few minutes all control had ceased,[27] and a thick pall of smoke shrouded the battlefield.

It is charitable to suggest that this smoke-cloud deceived, if it did not unhinge, Steinmetz. There can be no other rational explanation for what now occurred. It will be remembered that during the morning of the 18th, 1st Cavalry Division had crossed the river and had assembled at Malmaison a little to the north of Gravelotte. Now, shortly after 4 p.m., with VII Corps thrown back in confusion from the further plateau, Steinmetz ordered his cavalry 'to cross the defile at Gravelotte and to throw themselves on the retreating enemy. The artillery of VII Corps will follow on behind.'

To have risked a single squadron to prove his point — that the enemy was in full retreat — might have had some slim justification (by now *both* his corps commanders could have disabused him of any such fancy); but to launch a whole cavalry division and an entire corps artillery down a single road in full view of the enemy, across a narrow causeway already cluttered with all manner of transport, and up a steep defile beyond (*see* Plate 27) was an act of such criminal folly as to make Balaklava seem a minor error of judgment. The infantrymen huddled in the comparative security of St Hubert could only watch in horrified disbelief as the inevitable disaster took its course.

Only one cavalry regiment (*4th Uhlans*) and four batteries succeeded in crossing the causeway; and as they emerged onto the open plateau beyond they were struck at close range by a hail of fire. Within minutes the Uhlans, attempting to deploy to the right of the road, were cut to pieces, and the survivors tumbled back down the gravel-pits to the bottom of an already blood-soaked ravine, having lost more than half their number. Moltke's dead-pan reference to this catastrophe deserves to be recorded:

> The foremost regiment of cavalry bent to the right at the gallop on leaving the hollow way, and advanced [*sic*] towards Point du Jour, but the enemy, being completely under cover, offered no mark for an attack. Clearly there was no field here for the utilization of this arm,

27 One battalion of the *77th* was forced to make good its escape by crossing to the north of the road and taking shelter with the assorted companies clustered around St Hubert.

Plate 27 Looking east towards Point du Jour from the memorial to *8th Jäger Battalion.* It was up the main road to the right that *4th Uhlans* were sent to their destruction

so the regiments withdrew across the Mance ravine under a heavy fire from all sides .... The result of the ill-success of this attempt was that swarms of French tirailleurs now poured down from Point du Jour and drove the Prussian detachments still remaining on the bare plateau to the skirts of the woods.[28]

Meanwhile the artillery fared little better. Only four batteries succeeded in threading their way across the cluttered causeway — no mean achievement, however ill-advised. As the first two reached the open plateau, they were met by a withering fire from Vergé's division on either side of Point du Jour and, virtually decimated, were driven back through the debris of the Uhlans down the rough paths and gravel pits to join the broken units of VII Corps cowering in the bottom of the ravine. The third battery (Capt. Hasse), emerging from the defile opposite the elbow of the road, somehow succeeded in unlimbering its six guns in the wooded fringe where, despite desperate casualties, it gallantly maintained itself in action for more than two hours. Finally the fourth battery (Capt. Gnugge) under cover of the thick pall of battle-smoke turned aside and deployed behind the solid

28 Moltke: *op. cit.*

garden walls of St Hubert where, although caught in the French cross-fire from Point du Jour and Moscou and eventually reduced to a single gun, it remained in action until nightfall.

Shortly after 4.30 p.m. the fighting died down again. The French had good cause to be pleased with their performance on this flank. In their covered positions they had withstood the pounding of a greatly superior enemy artillery and had easily beaten off Steinmetz's extravagant abuse of both his infantry and cavalry. All that First Army could show for the reckless insubordination of its commander was a tiny and perilous salient at St Hubert. And Steinmetz had by no means exhausted his capacity for dealing in disaster. He still had two such cards up his sleeve.

If the French had cause for satisfaction, their commander-in-chief was not aware of it. Ever since battle was joined on the Amanvillers sector of the line, and — more critically — throughout Steinmetz's first attacks on Frossard and Leboeuf, Bazaine had remained in his headquarters at Plappeville, passive to the point of indifference, still brooding over the imagined threat to his left flank and not troubling to go forward to the plateau where a commander even of his limited imagination would have seen that the Germans were battering themselves to death on the rock-like defences between Point du Jour and Moscou. Certainly, after the fall of St Hubert, he had ordered Bourbaki to send a Voltigeur brigade of the Guard to support Frossard. Bourbaki had remonstrated that this was neither the time nor the place to commit the reserve corps in penny packets (he could foresee, if Bazaine could not, that while the battle might be won here on the left flank, it could more surely be lost six miles away on the right where Canrobert's 6 Corps was increasingly vulnerable to Frederick Charles's swinging left hook). Bazaine's reply to Bourbaki, his military subordinate but social superior, speaks for itself: 'You may either recall it [*the brigade*] or leave it there, as suits you best'; and at his trial he advanced the novel theory that Bourbaki, as commander of the reserve corps, was entitled to use it where and when he thought proper.

This calls into question whether the timely use of the Imperial Guard might have turned the day in favour of the French, for had it been placed on the right wing behind Canrobert's corps, it is arguable that Frederick Charles's turning movement which so nearly foundered on the ramparts of St Privat would have been frustrated at least until the onset of darkness; and that failure on this flank might have had a decisive effect on both the Vernéville and Gravelotte sectors of the German line.

And there is another interesting speculation which seems nowhere to have been discussed. By mid-afternoon virtually the whole of Steinmetz's VII Corps was irrevocably committed against the main French position and confusion reigned in the Mance ravine and on the causeway (the small diversionary attack by 26th Brigade on the extreme right had been firmly checked by Lapasset at St Ruffine). II Corps, the rearmost formation of Second Army, had set out from Pont-à-Mousson at 2 a.m., and by 1 p.m.

had halted at Buxières to rest and cook a mid-day meal. From there its commander, Fransecky, had ridden forward the few miles to Rezonville to report to Royal Headquarters, and there the King had decided to place II Corps under command of *First* Army. The reason for this decision was simply one of time and space. Fatigued by yet another of those memorable marches which the German infantry had made since the night of the 15th/16th, there was no way that the Pomeranians could reinforce the German left wing before dark. Logically, the King might have listened to Moltke's advice to reserve the newly arrived corps under his own hand; but Fransecky was eager that his men, after their exertions, should have their share in the day's blood-letting, and at 2.30 p.m. Steinmetz had yet to demonstrate his appetite for useless slaughter. He did not, in the event, disappoint Fransecky, as the memorials to the men of II Corps bear melancholy witness.

Thus by mid-afternoon all but one corps of First and Second Armies were assembled on the Gravelotte plateau and dangerously exposed towards their rear and the narrow supply-lines winding up the escarpment. That corps, I, was still on the right bank of the Moselle around Courcelles, watching out for any French sortie from Metz, but under the heavy guns of the two southerly outworks at Queuleu and St Quentin. Fifteen miles upstream from Metz, the main German supply artery at Pont-à-Mousson was now too far removed from the battlefield seriously to influence the outcome of a waning day. But closer to the fortress, and crucial to Moltke's master-plan, were the river-crossings at Ars and at Corny/Novéant. Here the only defensive cover consisted of two infantry battalions, four bridging companies and an assortment of L of C troops. Here indeed was an invitation to a resolute commander to strike.

Such a commander was not on stage but standing idly in the wings. Around him in the overcrowded area between Plappeville and Lessy were the Imperial Guard, 2½ cavalry divisions, and the whole reserve artillery. Between this force and the river stood only the 26th Brigade of VII Corps at Jussy, too weak to serve as more than the decoy duck which Steinmetz had intended it — beyond all expectation — to be.

But what if Bazaine — so long solicitous of his left flank — had sallied forth in mid-afternoon to secure the vital river-crossings to the south? The fortress guns of Metz and a sortie by Laveaucoupet's garrison division from the town would have stifled any counter-demonstration by the German I Corps on the right bank, and by a single stroke the Army of the Rhine might thus have left an over-ambitious enemy shipwrecked beyond salvation in open country.

We know that at the third crisis of the battle of Gravelotte, and before the first crisis at St Privat, Royal Headquarters had sent to clear those same vital river-crossings, thinking that the day was lost. But we know something else. At no moment during this day of make-or-break did it once occur to Bazaine to profit by the successive errors of his opponent, if indeed he was ever aware of his lost opportunities. As on the 16th, so now on the 18th. Then he could have turned the German left flank long before the arrival in strength of X Corps. Now he could have turned the German right to even more decisive advantage. He had already shown his hand. On the 17th, with the complacency of a man who was master of his own fate, he had advised the Emperor at Châlons that within a couple of days he would take his refurbished army on the north-western road to Verdun by Briey to effect a junction with MacMahon. He had no such intention. For to the Commission of Enquiry in 1871[29] he had said that his plan was to invite the enemy to dash himself to pieces on a rock-like defensive position and so, presently, to let him pass. What he did not tell the Commission was that the failure was not one of concept but of execution; or, more precisely, his personal failure to impose his authority on the battlefield. Between noon and 7 p.m., the enemy did in fact dash himself to pieces on the Amanvillers line: first in the centre, then on the great southern redoubt, and finally on the ramparts of St Privat.

The plan was good, but it was fatally flawed in two respects. First, it left nothing to the initiative of the subordinate commanders — indeed, it expressly forbade any but the most strictly *defensive* counter-attacks; secondly, it left in limbo the powerful reserve which could either have strangled First Army on the left or slammed the door on Frederick Charles's Second Army on the right. When, about 6 p.m., Ladmirault called urgently for help (Canrobert's earlier messengers had gone unheeded), Bourbaki dispatched the Grenadier division of the Guard and the reserve artillery up the narrow track and through the thick woods towards Amanvillers. He was too late. As he emerged onto the plateau he could see stragglers streaming away along the Woippy road. Angrily he called his men back. Wisely he left a great battery of artillery in the huge quarry which lies between Amanvillers and St Privat. And, as darkness came on, covered by these guns, 4 Corps and 6 Corps withdrew towards the protecting ramparts of Metz. They retired in good order, angry and disillusioned. They had fought a magnificent fight against the most professional army in Europe. They had covered the long, bare slopes that stretch away from Point du Jour to Roncourt with a harvest of German dead and wounded. Given a man to match their mood, the battle of 'Bloody Thursday' would have surely ended otherwise. Towards 7 p.m. Bazaine emerged from his self-imposed solitary confinement. He rode up the hill to the fort at Plappeville and there, for the first time, he saw the signs of disintegration. Jarras was with him, and Jarras records: 'He looked at the lines of stragglers coming back from the front and he said: "What can one do with men like that?" ' It may well be argued that the stragglers had good cause to wonder what they could do with a commander so remote from their own sense of duty.

29 *See* p. 213.

****

It might be supposed that after the disastrous failure of his second attack Steinmetz would now have proceeded with some caution. On his left — although he seems neither to have known nor cared — IX Corps was barely holding its own on the open slopes below Montigny and Amanvillers. Of the progress of the Guard and XII Corps farther north there was no word. Across the ravine, French fire had slackened, and Bazaine had made no attempt to exploit Frossard's striking success.

Towards 4.30 p.m. the King, innocently believing that VIII Corps had 'stormed and captured the heights'. rode forward from Rezonville with a numerous retinue to a swell of ground between Gravelotte and Malmaison. He arrived in time to have a grandstand view of a very different dénouement.

It is difficult to explain the sequence of events which now followed. The scenes of chaos in the ravine and on the further slope, the jetsam of Steinmetz's scattered squadrons, the cluttered causeway, told the same story. This was not the scenario of success but the making of a major defeat. Moltke's master-plan had never envisaged a decisive solution here on the southern redoubt, but a battle of containment while Frederick Charles completed the great inward wheel which the King's order of the 17th had projected. It did not happen. Only rarely in war do the best-laid plans not stumble at fences unforeseen.

'The whole course of the struggle had conclusively [sic] proved that the French left flank, almost impregnable by nature and art, could not be forced even by the most devoted bravery and the greatest sacrifices.'[30] Why then did the architect of this massive project stand aside while the whole foundation on which his reputation had been staked disintegrated before his eyes? Of this there is no question. When Royal Headquarters came forward to Malmaison in the course of the afternoon, there was a feeling of elation. 'We could see the smoke and flames rising up from the farmsteads on the further plateau. To our artillery fire, the French gave no reply.'[31] Such euphoria was short-lived. It did not take Moltke long to see that First Army was in disarray and that the crisis here on the right, by its domino effect on the centre and left, might gravely compromise the entire German position. Yet from now until nightfall, despite his deep misgivings,[32] he made no effort to intervene as one disaster followed upon another. Why should this have been? He enjoyed the full confidence of his royal master (though not, as events were later to prove, of the devious Bismarck who, with Roon, was present at Malmaison). Ever since Spicheren — and

30 Moltke: *op. cit.*

31 Verdy du Vernois: *With the Royal Headquarters*.

32 *See for example*, p. 260.

certainly since the 17th — he had taken every precaution to keep Steinmetz out of mischief. The evidence of his failure to do so was now all too clear. It can only be supposed that at this critical moment he decided to give his feckless army commander enough rope to hang himself. In this at least he was successful.

Steinmetz had some scores to settle. Ever since his formal reprimand by Moltke on the 6th, he had played the part of sulking Achilles. During the battle of Borny on the 14th, he had adopted an attitude of studied indifference. And he had shown his resentment when the orders for the great set-piece battle were issued on the 17th at Flavigny, and he found himself relegated to a supporting role while — supposedly — the hero's laurels were handed to Frederick Charles.[33] It was now 5 p.m. and the day was fast dying. II Corps, despite its devoted exertions, could not reach Gravelotte for two hours. Time enough, however, for Steinmetz to commit the greatest of all his successive blunders, in every sense a *folie de grandeur*. Ignoring his corps commanders, Goeben and Zastrow, without reference to Moltke or his own chief of staff, Sperling, he appealed direct to the King for permission to mount a 'final' attack across the ravine 'to regain the heights which had been carried, but then lost'. To the bitter end, Steinmetz maintained the fiction that the lodgement at St Hubert and the lull in the subsequent fire-fight had signified the collapse of French resistance at Point du Jour. By now he knew — at bloody cost — that this was not so. If by this hour Second Army had reported the successful turning of Canrobert's open flank, then there might have been some slim justification for one more concerted effort by First Army against the French redoubt beyond the ravine, if only to prevent the movement of men and guns to bolster their more vulnerable right wing. But no such report reached Malmaison; and this is not surprising, for had Frederick Charles sent word of any kind, it would have been the sombre news that the Guard Corps had just suffered a disaster in front of St Privat on a scale incomparably greater — and potentially more perilous — than all the assembled horrors of the Mance ravine; and that it had done so in a matter not of hours but of minutes. To this we shall presently address ourselves.

For whatever reason — and it is difficult to think of a single cogent one — the King gave Steinmetz his head.

The sun had begun to set as the two reserve brigades — 32nd and 27th of VIII and VII Corps — together with the last three uncommitted battalions advanced stoically into the ravine and, with such bodies of infantry as could be gathered into some semblance of cohesion amid the shambles on either side of the causeway, attempted once more to fight their way up the

33 Steinmetz had the last laugh; for towards evening, six miles away, Prince Augustus of Württemberg, commanding the Guard Corps, launched a premature and disastrous attack on St Privat for no better reason than to steal the thunder of the Crown Prince of Saxony on his left.

eastern face and thence to the plateau beyond. From Point du Jour the French watched and waited, while farther to the west they could see the thick columns of Fransecky's II Corps as they hastened forward from Rezonville. As the Prussians attacked, the whole firing-line sprang into life, and Steinmetz's last onslaught was met by fire at point-blank range.

> The German infantry reeled back; in the ravine some of the horses crammed on the narrow road began to bolt; and suddenly the tension which had sustained the Germans snapped altogether. Squadrons of cavalry, teams of gun-horses went careering back through Gravelotte, and the infantry, too long patient under the French shells, ran shrieking with them in a ragged howling mass out of the ravine, through the flame-lit village streets under the astounded eyes of their Supreme War Lord, shouting 'We are lost!' Staff officers, the King himself, weighed in cursing with the flat of their swords, but the flood of men swept on to Rezonville before it halted. The panic swept round the German rear; a line of retreat was reconnoitred for the King.[34]

Almost without exception, commentators have been strongly critical of the French failure to exploit this German rout; for here, on a scale vastly greater than Wedell's disaster at Mars-la-Tour, was an invitation to punish a rash opponent for his successive acts of folly. That the contagion of defeat had infected the royal entourage itself is sharply underlined by the order, as repulse turned to rout, to clear the lines of escape across the Moselle. Yet on reflection, there are four likely reasons why the Germans survived so spectacular a disaster on this wing.

First — and the reader may well be wearied by such infinite repetition — Bazaine, despite his later protestation that it had been his plan so to exhaust the enemy in 'one or perhaps two defensive battles' along the Amanvillers line that serious resistance to a resumed withdrawal on Verdun would be broken, had no such intention, as a cloud of witnesses — Canrobert, Bourbaki, and Jolivet[35] among them — later testified. To the end he held MacMahon responsible for the plight of the Army of the Rhine by his headlong retreat after the battle of Wörth on the 6th;[36] and since dawn on the 17th (if not before) his purpose, as he had told his corps commanders after Mars-la-Tour, was 'to save the Army and, to do that, we must retire on Metz'. There he would feel secure; and there he could detain a major proportion of the German field armies until, like some knight-errant, MacMahon, Marshal of France and Duke of

---

34 Howard: *op. cit.* (quoting Hönig and Verdy du Vernois).

35 *See* p. 336.

36 *See* p. 334.

Magenta, could ride to his rescue with the Army of Châlons. By a curious irony, had he made proper use of his reserve on the 18th, he might well have achieved the very victory he did not really seek.

A second reason was a matter of time. When, towards 7 p.m., First Army broke and fled through Gravelotte, the light was fast fading. By then Bourbaki had set out belatedly with the Grenadier division of the Guard and the reserve artillery to buttress Ladmirault at Amanvillers. By then Canrobert's brave but unavailing defence of St Privat had been broken, and though neither Bazaine nor indeed the German high command knew it, the French right wing had been turned. Even then a determined counter-attack from Point du Jour might have swept away such resistance as remained on this flank and left Frederick Charles with a hollow victory and a severed lifeline on his hands. But a night pursuit of a broken enemy — as the Crown Prince had discovered after Wörth — is the most difficult of military manœuvres, and one for which the French army in 1870 and its leadership was neither morally nor physically prepared. Cavalry — then the classical arm for such a counterstroke — was available in useless profusion behind the great redoubt, for in such terrain and with the onset of darkness there was no way in which it could have been deployed.

Thirdly, like a latter-day Blücher, Fransecky and his II Corps arrived *in medias res* on the battlefield. Whatever other verdict may be passed on the conduct of the German high command and on its two army commanders throughout this day, there can be no question that the decision to hasten this corps forward was as prudent as it was provident. That the King had earlier consigned it (no other word is appropriate) to Steinmetz's command is comment enough. That, when the litany of disaster during the afternoon could no longer be drowned by excuses, he did not assume direct command of his last reserve is beyond explanation; and that Steinmetz, even under Moltke's disapproving eye, marched the eager Pomeranians forward to yet another sordid sacrifice: all this is melancholy history. Yet II Corps was 'a fleet in being'. By its unexpected arrival on the battlefield, it served, by its very presence, as a deterrent to any concerted initiative by Frossard and Leboeuf.

There was a final reason; for towards 7 p.m., when Steinmetz's third attack disintegrated, the bed of the ravine was thronged with dead and wounded, with wagons and horses, with those behind crying 'Forward!' and those in front crying 'Back!' The clinical efficiency of French defensive fire thus had an untoward result; for while the ravine remained an impassable barrier to the Germans, by a grim irony the very debris of destruction provided no less an obstacle to any counter-attack from Point du Jour. There can be few more singular examples of a victorious defender defeating his own hard-won opportunity by the very measure of his success.

Such then was the situation on the German right as II Corps reached Gravelotte amid scenes of indescribable panic. It was nearly dark, and the long lines of the French rifle-pits and trenches on the further plateau were picked out in rippling flashes of light as guns, mitrailleuses and chassepots plied their steady trade.

It is difficult to imagine what Steinmetz, surrounded by the evidence of defeat, thought he could achieve at this late hour. 'People', said Bismarck later, 'are fed up with Steinmetz's butchery.' Yet it could have been stopped by a single word, whether from the King or from Moltke, or from the butcher himself. No such word came. And down into the ravine marched 3rd Division of II Corps.

There was no time — and certainly no space — to deploy into any kind of battle formation. The division simply advanced in a thick column down the main highway, dividing left and right as it reached the causeway, and followed in close order by 4th Division. *Nos morituri salutamus.*

What then followed has been covered by a decent veil of obscurity. No one had told Fransecky of the position on the far side of the ravine. Thus, as his men began to climb the eastern face in the darkness they were greeted by fierce fire from the scattered German companies clustered around St Hubert, imagining themselves to have been taken in rear by the French; and in turn the men of 3rd Division fired back into the dark mass before them. For twenty dreadful minutes the mutual slaughter continued[37] until the distraught garrison around the farmstead could stand no more and 'poured to the rear in a wild panic, rushing, shouting, and quite out of their senses, to an extent indeed which has seldom happened in the history of war.'[38]

Fransecky, following his assault battalions, ordered the cease-fire to be sounded to stop the carnage. And the weary French on the ridge beyond, hearing the German bugles, though unaware of the brutal truth, laid their own weapons down.

It was nearly 10 p.m. when fighting finally ceased on this southern flank apart from some desultory sniping. On either side of the highway little more than 100 yards separated the two sides, neither knowing — or much caring — what had been the day's outcome farther north.

But shortly after dawn on the 19th the men of 4th Division of II Corps[39] crept cautiously forward from their outpost line along the eastern face of the ravine, only to find that the French had slipped away in the night, leaving behind their dead and wounded and the empty trenches and rifle-pits of Point du Jour. They had gone, not because they had been driven from the ground which they had held with such resolution throughout the previous day, but because six miles to the north at nightfall

37   In the short time during which II Corps was in action it suffered casualties of 58 officers and 1,258 rank and file.

38   Hönig: *op. cit.*

39   At midnight Fransecky had relieved his 3rd Division which had occupied St Hubert and the quarries below after the tragic error and mutual slaughter three hours earlier.

St Privat had fallen, and with its capture the whole Amanvillers line — impregnable, had Bazaine so willed it — had collapsed. Now the Pomeranians looked down from the Rozérieulles plateau whence they could see the French shelter-tents clustered around Plappeville and St Quentin. Bazaine had had his way. The Army of the Rhine had retired on Metz.

****

A day which had ended on the brink of total disaster for First Army had not started propitiously for the Second either.

When, during the night of the 16th/17th, Moltke ordered Frederick Charles and Steinmetz to hasten their respective corps forward to their concentration areas on the Gravelotte plateau he broke one of his own primary rules: 'More haste, less speed.' His fault was understandable, for he had every cause to be apprehensive of the danger to Second Army, in particular if Bazaine should attempt a break-out to the west at dawn on the Wednesday. IX Corps, already partly committed on the previous evening, lay around Novéant and had a short, if difficult, march through Gorze; XII Corps was farther upstream at Pont-à-Mousson; and beyond, at Dieulouard, was the Guard Corps.[40]

The speed was implicit; the haste unfortunate. For instead of directing the Guard on Mars-la-Tour and XII Corps, with a head-start, to a bivouac farther to the west, the march tables, through a staff error, were reversed and the Guard took the outside route which brought it to Hannonville on the Saxons' left. This should have had no tactical significance, for the two corps of Second Army's left wing had been delivered on time to the wide front on which the great advance was to be launched. But such a deployment seemingly gave pride of place to XII Corps, and pride can be a dangerous military counsellor. The Guard, although it alone of the thirteen federal German army corps was recruited not from local military districts but from all the member states of the Confederation,[41] considered itself heir to the Prussian traditions of Frederick the Great; and Prussians had not forgotten that the Kingdom of Saxony had fought on the Austrian side at Sadowa.

When, therefore, Frederick Charles issued his own orders at 4 a.m. on the 18th he directed XII Corps on Jarny and the Guard Corps on

---

40 On both sides the Guard held a special position. To the Germans, it was an élite which claimed a prescriptive right to be in the forefront of the battle. To Bazaine, it was the jewel in the Imperial crown and so not lightly to be compromised or cast away. These two equal and opposite aspects of the last romantic concept of war were to be starkly demonstrated on the 18th.

41 Curiously, the commander of the Guard Corps was Prince Augustus of Württemberg, a small state which was not even part of the Confederation and which had provided only a single division to the Crown Prince's Third Army opposite Strasbourg.

Doncourt, apparently unaware of the actual bivouac areas which the two formations were occupying. As a result the Guard had to mark time until XII Corps had cleared Mars-la-Tour on the Jarny road before it could put itself *en marche* towards Doncourt; and in the process it lost two valuable hours.

Two valuable hours. By such narrow margins battles have been won and lost. This had been spectacularly demonstrated on the 16th when Bredow's charge had bought valuable time for Alvensleben around Vionville. And Gravelotte−St Privat, a planned battle rather than a sequence of improvisations, hung to the very end on the simple fact that the sun rises in the east and sets in the west; and that between the one and the other there is small room for error.

Leaving aside the gratuitous follies of Steinmetz which amounted to self-inflicted wounds, Frederick Charles contributed formidably to the problems of Second Army by one major and unwarranted assumption which he took no steps to corroborate until the morning was largely spent, by when it was too late to countermand the original order to XI Corps in the centre. The assumption had certainly originated with Moltke on the 17th: that the French right wing extended only as far as Montigny or at most Amanvillers. This — as it proved — false premise can only be explained either as an over-hasty judgment or a dangerous guess.[42] But once Second Army was set in motion, it was Frederick Charles's responsibility 'to seek out and find the enemy' and 'to attack him wherever [*sic*] he may be encountered'. This he singularly failed to do. Certainly, he sent out cavalry patrols to the north and west but not to the east, where the most cursory glance at a map — or even an inquiry of Steinmetz — must have convinced him of Bazaine's true intention, if not of Bazaine's greatly extended position. It was left to Manstein to pay the price for so cavalier an attitude to elementary reconnaissance.

Frederick Charles was well aware of the time factor. Whereas on the 16th night could not come too soon for Alvensleben and Voigts-Rhetz, now even a long summer's day might prove too short for the deployment of a whole army on an extended front and for the mounting of a set-piece attack against an entrenched enemy in a position of formidable natural strength. This explains the singular — and potentially dangerous — decision to launch the whole army across country in solid divisional phalanxes rather than in conventional march formation. In war, time is no respecter of convention.

Had Frederick Charles's false assumption that the French right extended no farther than Amanvillers been correct, the wasted hours while XII Corps and the Guard crossed tracks need not have been as critical as they were to prove. The tidy tactic had been to hold the presumed French right

42 In fact, Moltke nearly guessed right; for Bazaine originally directed 6 Corps on Vernéville, and it was only as a result of Canrobert's protestation that the French right wing was pulled back to St Privat astride the Woippy−Briey road.

wing tight at Amanvillers until the early afternoon and then to wheel the two corps of the outer arc inward from Ste Marie-aux-Chênes and roll up Bazaine's open flank. It was a classical manœuvre in the true tradition of Bonaparte; and it went very wrong. For shortly after 10 a.m. word reached Frederick Charles that the French right wing extended as far north as St Privat (not until 3 p.m. did he learn that Canrobert's flank actually rested on Roncourt). By then it was too late to warn Manstein; and the tidy tactic was in tatters.[43]

****

As we have seen, the failure of the German high command in general (and Frederick Charles in particular) to establish with reasonable certainty the true extent of Bazaine's defensive position before committing Second Army to a set-piece battle came close to a disaster for IX Corps; but more seriously it put at hazard the whole of Moltke's master-plan.

Certainly, it convinced Steinmetz — who needed little persuading — that the sound of the cannonade to his north at noon signalled that Second Army had found Bazaine's flank, and that the main action had been joined; and without waiting for either clarification or permission, he had set in train the premature infantry attack by VIII Corps, the results of which it is not necessary to rehearse. But Moltke, rightly judging the immense natural strength of the French position opposite Gravelotte, had never sought a decision here on the right wing. The whole thrust of his order on the 17th, however imprecise its wording, had postulated a holding action by First Army while Frederick Charles attacked Bazaine's centre with IX Corps and then enveloped his open flank with the Guard and XII Corps. Even Steinmetz's insubordination need not have fatally comprom-ised this plan. The flaw lay elsewhere; and the true fault lay in a serious — even complacent — misreading of Bazaine's hand; for when Manstein, pushing his unsupported artillery forward beyond the Bois de la Cusse, discovered the unsuspected presence of Canrobert a mile farther north at St Privat, an already tight time-schedule was abruptly disjointed. Already the hours lost in the early confusion at Mars-la-Tour assumed a new significance. Already a long summer's day began to seem dangerously short. And to this new situation Frederick Charles reacted with some confusion. As the head of the Guard reached Habonville, he detached 3rd Brigade to support the hard-pressed Hessians in front of Amanvillers and then pushed his columns to the left on the narrow road towards St Ail and Ste Marie, while to the Crown Prince of Saxony he sent an urgent order to fetch XII Corps from Jarny in a wide arc towards the valley of the Orne and the villages of Montois and Roncourt. It was at best an improvisation;

---

43   The reader may reflect again on the failure of communications to match the geometry of the 1870 battlefield.

at worst an abortive manœuvre. Above all, it had become a race against time.

****

St Privat and the small farm of Jérusalem lie on either side of the road from Woippy to Briey, the northerly of Bazaine's three escape routes to Verdun. Here, seven miles north of Point du Jour and — more importantly — seven miles away from Bazaine's headquarters at Plappeville, the long Amanvillers ridge begins to fall gradually towards Roncourt and the Orne valley beyond.

The village stands squarely on this ridge, still curiously ominous because of its association with the epic events of that distant afternoon. It was then a virtual fortress of solid grey houses built of locally quarried stone and surrounded by walled gardens; and it is inexplicable that Bazaine should have traded in so formidable a bastion for the indefensible alternative of Vernéville in his original order to Canrobert on the night of the 16th.

To the east of the village the ground falls sharply and, buttressed by the Bois de Jaumont, provides a strong, covered reserve position. Here, where it could have little or no influence on an attempt to outflank St Privat from the direction of Roncourt, stood du Barail's single remaining regiment of Chasseurs d'Afrique, reinforced by a brigade of Forton's cavalry division.[44] Here, where the Germans finally and most bloodily decided the day, the presence of the Imperial Guard and the reserve artillery of the Army of the Rhine might have swung the balance. Early in the afternoon, Canrobert saw clearly both the danger and the opportunity; and we shall presently see the bleak indifference with which Bazaine ignored his repeated calls for help and left him and his resolute soldiers to their fate.[45]

To the west, whence the main enemy attack must come, Canrobert could contemplate the strength of his position with more confidence; for here, in a wide arc from St Ail to Auboué, the ground falls gently away like the glacis of some medieval fortress (*see* Plate 28). These bare slopes, innocent of any cover except the poplars and ditches which then lined the Briey road, provide an exceptional field of fire extending over more than 3000 yards. The contrast with Frossard's redoubt at Point du Jour, protected by

44   About 6 p.m. a half-hearted attempt was made to mount a cavalry attack from this quarter, but by then XII Corps had deployed a massive line of guns to the north of Ste Marie and the manœuvre was still-born. Three hours earlier it might well have thrown the Saxons into disarray.

45   The reader should bear in mind that when the Army of the Rhine fell back during the night of the 16th/17th, the Imperial Guard, then concentrated near Gravelotte, could only follow the main road across the Mance ravine on the French left. None the less, there was more than enough time to have redeployed the main reserve during the morning of the 18th from its cosy quarters around Plappeville to succour and sustain 6 Corps on the right.

its great natural moat, could not be more striking, or the defensive strength at either end of the same battlefield more mutually complementary. Here, surely, if the Army of the Rhine was to fight a decisive battle, was Bazaine's *position inexpugnable*. But it was not; for it contained a fatal flaw which Bazaine himself even more fatally compounded. And for this there are two main reasons.

Due west of St Privat, a little over a mile away and dominated by the Amanvillers ridge, lies the village of Ste Marie-aux-Chênes. This village posed a problem for Canrobert; it also dictated Frederick Charles's tactical plan, once he discovered the extent of his original error. Canrobert could not afford to leave Ste Marie unoccupied, yet with his limited resources he could not spare more than two and a half battalions (of the 94th) as an outpost to his main position; and these, with a single artillery battery, he sent forward during the morning of the 18th, but too late to put the village into any proper state of defence. He was well aware that so small a garrison could not survive a concerted attack by the overwhelming force which would shortly be delivered against it. But he was watching the sun climb across the sky; and he was playing for time.

Frederick Charles, faced by the daunting prospect of the long, bare slopes that rose towards St Privat and mindful of the same sun which Canrobert was watching, was also playing for time. He had sent the Crown Prince of Saxony on a long detour to the north-east which added seven miles and several hours to the grand manœuvre.[46] Thus, beyond all expectation, Ste Marie became not a buttress to the German left but a critical *point d'appui* to the assault on St Privat. And Ste Marie was now the focus of German attention.

But Canrobert's main concern lay elsewhere; for it is an axiom of war that there is no defensive position so strong that, given the necessary physical superiority on the side of the attacker, it cannot be turned.[47] Of such a superiority Canrobert was aware as he watched the dust-clouds to the west and — more significantly — to the north-west. At St Privat, he rightly felt himself to be impregnable against even the most formidable attacks from the direction of St Ail and Ste Marie. But the first flaw in the argument lay beyond St Privat where, without benefit of an available, but uncommitted, reserve of infantry and (above all) artillery, 6 Corps was open to a turning movement which it could not hope to contain. In fact, it came close to doing so, for a single French brigade — Péchot's, of Tixier's division — resisted nearly 20,000 Saxons until, as darkness fell, it was driven out of Roncourt.

46 The original plan would have brought XII Corps into line at Ste Marie by 2 p.m., ready to strike in on Amanvillers. The unexpected intelligence of the true French position was to cause a dramatic shift in the time-scale of this flank march.

47 A classic exception is the so-called 'race to the sea' in September 1914 and the first battle of Ypres where, gallantry apart, the German attempt to turn the Allied flank was halted by natural and improvised water barriers.

And herein lies the second flaw; it was in Bazaine's deployment on the Amanvillers line. The reader will recall that at nightfall on the 16th, the Army of the Rhine, facing south, read thus from left to right: 2 Corps, Imperial Guard, 6 Corps, 3 Corps, 4 Corps. By the morning of the 18th the line ran, south to north, 2 Corps, 3 Corps, 4 Corps, 6 Corps, with the Guard behind the *left* flank around Plappeville. A glance at the map on p. 219 will show that this manœuvre, always difficult given the deficiencies of French staff work, depended on Bazaine's true intention. And to understand this we must return to the candlelit room at Gravelotte as the fate of the Army of the Rhine was decided by its commander-in-chief.

There is no transcript of that meeting with the corps commanders. But we know that this brave but bewildered man, his mind obsessed with defeatism — 'We must save the Army, and to do that, we must retire on Metz' — had eyes only for his left flank. From the evidence of his conflicting telegrams and despatches to the Emperor at Châlons and from his equally conflicting published accounts of events, the certainty that the Germans, with the immense superiority in men and guns which they had assembled on the Gravelotte plateau by the 17th, would seek to turn his right seems not seriously to have entered into his calculations. How else to explain his vague indication to Canrobert that 6 Corps might usefully occupy itself in putting the indefensible Vernéville into a state of defence? If he did not convince Canrobert, he came close to deceiving both Moltke and Frederick Charles.

6 Corps was unlucky. It had always been the lame duck of the Army of the Rhine since the beginning of the campaign; for when, after the reverse at Spicheren, it had been summoned back to Metz from Châlons, it had left behind its cavalry division and all but one regiment of its fourth infantry division. Much more seriously, it was critically short of artillery[48] and lacked its entire engineer park. On the morning of the 18th it had not a single battery of mitrailleuses which, in the last analysis, might well have saved the day. It was therefore the least equipped of Bazaine's five corps to stiffen the sinews of his right hand. And when, as the day wore on, the commander-in-chief left it to fend for itself against overwhelming odds, it put him to shame by one of the bravest and most moving passages in the history of French arms.

The positions to be occupied on the Amanvillers line by 3 and 4 Corps were dictated less by any deliberate choice than by the grave confusion which had been occasioned after the engagement at Borny on the 14th, and from which the Army of the Rhine never recovered. When fighting ended on the 16th, the head of Lorencez's division of 4 Corps had only reached Habonville, a mile to the west of Amanvillers, while Metman's division of 3 Corps bivouacked for the night around Malmaison. It might be thought

---

48 When, late on the 17th, it eventually reached St Privat, it had fewer than 60 pieces of modest calibre, to which Bazaine belatedly added a single battery of 12-pounders.

that once Bazaine had abandoned all idea of a renewed attempt to break out to the west at first light on the 17th while time and numbers were still on his side, the logical sequence of withdrawal from his centre and right wing would have been 6 Corps, 3 Corps and 4 Corps. But when at midnight he wearily announced his intention to fall back on Metz, with the pathetic afterthought that he was open to any alternative suggestion, only Canrobert[49] chose to speak, and then only to object (with good reason) that at Vernéville 6 Corps would be '*en l'air*' and proposing, with even better reason, to retire farther to the little fortress-village of St Privat. '*Bien entendu*,' was Bazaine's credited reply.[50]

So it was that the Army of the Rhine, so close to victory on the 16th, stumbled back to defeat on the 18th; for 3 and 4 Corps were directed on their respective laggard divisions (Metman's was given the unenviable task of covering the disorderly retirement from Gravelotte across the Mance ravine).

The return to Metz matched in every way the bleak departure on the 15th — but with a significant difference. The men had then been disappointed. Now they were angry. They had good reason to feel that they had done more than enough to outface a redoubtable enemy at Mars-la-Tour, and they did not understand why they were now having to retrace their steps (and in the process leave a large proportion of their wounded behind). Discipline had never been a signal feature of the army of the Second Empire, and as the ill-organized columns made their way back, the troops gave vent to their sense of betrayal in loud recriminations and looting, saved from breaking-point by the steadiness of their brave, elderly, illiterate *troupier* junior officers. Yet remarkably these same men were to recover their pride and their composure, make ready in the few hours left to them a defiantly defensive wall, pitch their little white tents with a splendidly Gallic insouciance, and then come close to the decisive victory which irresolute leadership had denied them two days earlier. Of all the charges against Bazaine — and many are at least open to argument — the one that sticks most tellingly in the mind is his alleged comment on the evening of the 18th as he saw the crumbling debris of his right wing. 'What can one do with men like these?' It is a question which would not have occurred to the King of Prussia as he surveyed the stricken field at daybreak after that bloody Thursday.[51]

So it was that Bazaine's plan was fatally flawed, and that mindlessly he directed his weakest corps to protect his most sensitive flank; and that deliberately he kept his decisive reserve in an absurd vacuum, where it was

49   'He was seven years my senior,' said Bazaine at his trial; and that tells us more about Canrobert than about Bazaine.

50   D'Andlau: *op. cit.*

51   Thus in a telegram to Queen Augusta: 'Our soldiers performed prodigies of valour *against an equally brave enemy* who defended every foot of ground.'

not needed to buttress a natural redoubt, but where it could not influence elsewhere the outcome of a battle for survival. To the exchanges between Canrobert and Bazaine, as the sun climbed towards the west, we shall presently return. But meanwhile, there were premonitions of disaster on the other side of the hill.

****

It was 2 p.m. Had Moltke's premise on the 17th gone accordingly to plan, this was the hour when the Guard and XII Corps should have struck in from Habonville and Ste Marie and rolled up Bazaine's right flank. But with Canrobert's wise precaution of occupying St Privat and the wasted hours as the two left-hand corps of Second Army crossed tracks at Mars-la-Tour, a very different scenario now presented itself.

When, in mid-morning, Frederick Charles discovered that the French position extended well to the north of Amanvillers, he halted the flank march (a decision which was to cost him another precious hour) and rode forward to Vernéville. There he met an anxious Manstein. IX Corps, committed in accordance with the dawn order, had collided with the strongly organized French centre before its forward movement could be arrested and was in serious difficulties. Its artillery, boldly if rashly exposed, had been so roughly handled that it had been driven to find cover to the rear. On the left, the Hessian Division in the Bois de la Cusse was pinned down by heavy crossfire from Amanvillers and St Privat. On the right 18th Division had fought its way into the farm buildings at L'Envie and Chantrenne and was clinging precariously to the northern fringes of the Bois des Genivaux under Leboeuf's guns strongly established on the eastern ridge at La Folie and Leipsic. Between the two there was a gap of more than half a mile, a — literally — open invitation to Ladmirault to divide and conquer. It was an invitation which, to Frederick Charles's good fortune, was not accepted before he plugged the gap with 3rd Guard Brigade.

The scenario, however, had changed not only on the front of Second Army but also, unknown to Frederick Charles, on the German right. Even as he was contemplating an urgent change of plan at Vernéville, Steinmetz at Gravelotte was preparing to throw his hat prematurely into the ring. Thus at the very moment which Moltke had chosen for his Cannae, a combination of the unexpected, of tactical ineptitude, and of insubordination, reduced a tightly conceived plan to a dangerously extended improvisation.

In a project which Moltke had prepared during the winter of 1868-9 as a working model for war with France (in the event the model became, with only minor variations, the strategic plan) he permitted himself a number of intellectual excursions into the art of warfare and the function of supreme command. One of these he now had reason to reflect upon. 'The primary object of an operation is to seek out the enemy's main force and, *when found*, to attack it.' The project did not dwell upon the situation which now confronted him. Nor did his intellectual excursions play upon the dangerous premise that war is a strictly human extravagance and that it is a game played by characters as different as Frederick Charles, Steinmetz and Bazaine. Or, for that matter, Moltke himself.

A small but significant example will illustrate how the changing scenario in the forward area was reflected in the higher echelons towards the rear; and how a command structure, even as carefully tuned as the German general staff, began to crack as it became apparent that the battle-plan for the 18th had not accounted for two contingencies: the complacency of one army commander and the disobedience of the other.

When the great *Aufmarsch* was set in motion at dawn, Royal Headquarters, absurdly swollen by an unnecessary infusion of blue-blooded 'observers', was located rather grandly on the nearest available eminence. Moltke's order, issued at 1.45 p.m. on the 17th, in the King's name, read: 'The King's further orders will be determined by the measures taken by the enemy. Reports for His Majesty are to be sent, in the first instance, to the heights south of Flavigny.' In fact, throughout the 18th, the only orders which the King sent to anyone were repeated instructions to Steinmetz (which went unheeded) and to Fransecky to hasten II Corps from Pont-à-Mousson to Gravelotte to shore up the crumbling German right wing.

It was shortly after 1 p.m. that the royal retinue moved forward to Rezonville across fields littered with the debris and the dead of the earlier battle. The sound of gunfire from the direction of Vernéville was gratifying. Clearly Second Army must have found Bazaine's flank, and the turning movement was therefore on schedule. A further precautionary order was sent to Steinmetz, and, in the insalubrious surroundings of what Verdy du Vernois described as 'a large Lazarett', luncheon was served. It was the last untroubled hour that Royal Headquarters would enjoy until nearly midnight, for all was far from well at Vernéville; and Steinmetz, within the hour, would ensure his own first contribution to a growing crisis.

During the morning a verbal message had reached the King from Frederick Charles that there was evidence that the French line extended some way north of Amanvillers. The official German account is ambivalent about this critical piece of intelligence, and it must be assumed that Moltke's advice was to rely on the commander of Second Army, with five corps at his disposal, to use his professional judgment and make the necessary adjustment to his original plan. That adjustment, in fact, far from being cosmetic, degenerated into a major (and quite separate) battle the nature and consequences of which could only be a matter for uneasy speculation on the German right, where by early afternoon Royal Headquarters had lost all semblance of control.

About 4.00 p.m. the King and his staff rode farther forward to a swell of ground just south of Malmaison. There, like Bazaine at Plappeville, they were remote from sight or indeed knowledge of events at St Privat; but there, unlike Bazaine, they were spectators — the word accurately underlines the extent to which the function of supreme command had been abdicated — of the fate of First Army; of the panic in the ravine; and were driven to take shelter that evening in Rezonville again as the fire of the unshaken French at Point du Jour swept either side of Gravelotte. 'Chassepot bullets even reached the position of the Royal Commander-in-Chief and his personal staff', recorded Moltke, adding with a certain dry satisfaction, 'and Prince Adalbert's horse was shot under him.'

The narrative of events on the 18th has thus far concentrated almost exclusively on the German right wing, for this reflects the extent to which the premature involvement of First Army and Steinmetz's false claim of early success so preoccupied the attentions of Royal Headquarters that it found itself locked into the wrong battle in the wrong place. Of the critical situation in the centre facing Amanvillers, news was scant and sketchy; and of the dramatic developments on the German left where Moltke's turning movement had been pre-empted by Canrobert at St Privat, no word came until after nightfall. And it is there, while an anxious high command pondered the possibility of having to salvage something from the wreckage of Steinmetz's errors, that the action now turns.

****

It was 2 p.m. If IX Corps was to be saved from the predicament in which it found itself opposite the French centre and unexpectedly taken in flank from St Privat, then the original turning movement had assumed a new and urgent dimension. There was still no certainty how far north the French position had been extended, or the exact strength in which that position was presently held. Much of the Army of the Rhine had not yet been accounted for. That St Privat was occupied by 6 Corps was an obvious assumption. That the Imperial Guard possibly also stood on the French right, where, as the day slipped away, it could and should have decided the issue, was a more serious speculation. But too many hours had already been wasted in speculation on the German side. All now hung on the fate of St Privat — and with it the fate of Second Army. And of the battle itself.

In this confused situation, Frederick Charles acted with an authority which he had not notably demonstrated during the morning of the 18th. His earlier order to the Crown Prince of Saxony to swing XII Corps on a wider arc from Jarny towards Auboué had been largely dictated by a conjunction of time and space. In the improvised plan which he now set in train, he, unlike Bazaine, committed the Guard. It was to prove a necessary, momentous and murderous decision.

The first objective was the capture of Ste Marie-au-Chênes, held in uncertain strength by the enemy but essential as a *point d'appui* between the Guard and the Saxons and as a springboard for an infantry assault up the long, bare fields which led to the frowning fortress on the ridge beyond. Frederick Charles was well aware that only a small part of XII Corps[52] was in a position to support the preliminary attack. The main thrust must thus come from the south, and it must come quickly; first, to distract Canrobert's attention from the Hessians in the Bois de la Cusse but more surely to seek a decision here on the German left before darkness restored the initiative to Bazaine.

It will be recalled that the various corps of Second Army had been set in motion after dawn in solid masses marching across country and with the artillery occupying the spaces between infantry divisions. The Guard, the largest of the five corps on the German centre and left, numbered, even without its cavalry, more than 30,000 men and 90 guns. This highly unconventional — and highly dangerous — march formation was now to prove the salvation of Second Army, and its deployment from the tidy geometry of a parade-ground into a hastily improvised battle-order a considerable technical feat.

As with Alvensleben on the 16th, so now with Prince Augustus. As the head of 1st Guard Division reached Habonville, the divisional artillery was pushed on ahead and came into action facing north-east on a shoulder of ground running towards the village of St Ail. There, however, it found itself between two fires — from Canrobert's guns at St Privat and from the chassepots of the 94th in Ste Marie — and was driven to take cover on the reverse slope where it was joined by the corps artillery. So, within the hour, some 72 guns of the Guard had been deployed in an arc stretching from Habonville to St Ail.[53] And behind this screen the infantry attack on Ste Marie was launched.

It was never possible that so small a nut could long resist so massive a sledgehammer. The French garrison in the village numbered fewer than 1500 men and a single battery of guns. Against it the Germans deployed successively, from the south, the whole of 1st Guard Division, and presently, from the north-west, a Saxon brigade, supported on both flanks by a growing concentration of artillery. Yet for an hour the French stood their ground. For an hour, even with odds of twenty to one against, chassepot silenced needle-gun.[54] The official German account speaks of heavy casualties among the leading regiments of the Guard. It does not

---

52 47th Infantry Brigade (24th Division) and, in the first instance, 6 batteries (36 guns).

53 When, at 7 p.m., the final assault on St Privat was made, the village was subjected to the concentrated fire of 208 German guns. Small wonder that Canrobert's last message to Bazaine — a pencil note — ended with the words: '*Son artillerie a dominé la mienne à tel point que je ne pourrai plus tenir.*' At that hour the reserve artillery of the Army of the Rhine was standing silent six miles away.

54 Throughout this day, as throughout much of the fighting on the 16th, the superior power and range of the chassepot held the attacker at arm's length. Had this superiority been even nearly matched at any point by French gunnery, a very different tale might have been told.

speak of the precious time which Colonel de Geslin's resistance afforded to Canrobert. And when it describes the evacuation of the village as 'a disorderly flight', it plays with words. The 94th, covered by its reserve companies, retired without interference up the long slope towards St Privat; and indeed when the Saxon brigade ventured in pursuit beyond the village it was taught a salutary lesson by a brisk counter-attack by Tixier's 100th Regiment and driven from the open ground. If there was disorder, it was in the roughly handled ranks of the Guard as, 'with loud hurrahs', they occupied Ste Marie. The time was 3.30 p.m.

* * * * * * * *

Canrobert had watched the German progress across his front, and since noon he had given artillery support to Ladmirault as Manstein's attack foundered before Amanvillers. He was well aware of the strength — and weakness — of his position; of his fortress village with its formidable fields of fire across the empty approaches from the west; but also of the equally empty flank on his right, and of his desperate shortage of artillery. And since the battle which would finally decide the day was presently to be fought on these bleak uplands, it is proper to reflect upon the man who came so close to a success in the event denied to him by his superior.

Canrobert was something of a French phenomenon — a national hero in a society which had for a long time distanced itself from the military *métier*. At sixty-one he was the senior, though not the oldest, of the serving Marshals of France, and had given distinguished service in Africa, the Crimea, and in the Italian campaign of 1859. More significantly, perhaps, he had been in command of the troops who had buttressed Napoleon's *coup d'état* in 1851, and thus was considered politically suspect by radical and royalist opinion in Paris. Yet when on 12 August the Emperor at last decided to abdicate command of the Army of the Rhine, this servant of Empire had declined the honour — and responsibility — of taking over, and had stepped aside in favour of '*notre glorieux Bazaine*', the man of the people.[55] There is no question whatever of Canrobert's motive. After the reverses at Spicheren and Wörth on 6 August (he himself did not arrive in Metz with 6 Corps until the 9th), this wily and experienced soldier rightly read the signs of impending disaster and chose to play Pilate in the face of the enemy. The tears he shed at Bazaine's court-martial three years later were rather those of relief than of compassion.

We have seen his strangely ambivalent attitude throughout the morning of the 16th when resolute action by 6 Corps would have driven Alvensleben from Vionville and reopened the road to Verdun; and how, after Bredow's charge, he had virtually opted out of battle. Yet his conduct then — and the weasel words he resorted to at the trial — are evidence

---

55 *See* p. 99.

enough that he sought that the stigmata of defeat should be squarely placed upon the man set, by his own act of moral cowardice, in authority over him.

Yet there is no hiding-place on battlefields. And thus it was that Canrobert's day of disgrace at Mars-la-Tour was now to be redeemed by eight heroic hours at St Privat. Certainly, when Bazaine had sought the opinion of his subordinates at Gravelotte on that now distant-seeming night, Canrobert had not spoken up for a dash for freedom at the next dawn. Certainly he had saved his superior from the suicidal occupation of Vernéville. Now the two men were separated by six miles of space. But between them there was a deeper gulf — that of mutual distrust. It was to prove an expensive exercise in human relationships.

****

Towards 1 p.m. Canrobert sent an officer to Plappeville, warning Bazaine of the developing threat to his position and asking for further supplies of ammunition and of infantry reserves.[56]

'Tell Marshal Canrobert,' replied Bazaine, 'that I have ordered General Bourbaki to send him a division of the Guard, *in the event that the attack on his position becomes more serious.*[57] I have given orders for a battery of 12-pounders to be sent to him. Tell the Marshal that if he wishes to restock with ammunition, the reserve park is located here.'

At 2.30 p.m. — by when Canrobert's earlier message had still gone unheeded — he sent a Captain de Chalus to Bazaine with an explicit request for the support which he had been promised. Chalus flits across this sombre stage like the Messenger in a Greek tragedy. He reached Plappeville shortly after 3.30 p.m., at almost the exact moment when the Germans captured Ste Marie; and *on a map* he indicated the situation facing 6 Corps. This should have been of some interest to Bazaine since, as the Commission of Enquiry recorded in due course, he himself had no map of the country around St Privat. He seems, for whatever reason, not to have cared; whether because he believed that Canrobert was crying before he was hurt, or — which is more probable — because he was no more concerned with his right wing than he had been on the 16th. Certainly it did not for one moment occur to him to ride down one slope and up the next and see for himself the stoutness of his defence and the growing disorder of

56 The reader should bear in mind that because of Bazaine's decision to establish his headquarters behind Point du Jour, at least three hours passed between the dispatch of a message from St Privat and — if Bazaine was so minded — the receipt of a reply.

57 Author's italics.

his opponent. Instead, he instructed the luckless Chalus to conduct a column of four *caissons* (perhaps 500 rounds) to St Privat; warned Bourbaki to hold the Guard 'at readiness'; and then rode back up the hill to St Quentin, where he diverted himself by personally laying four pieces of siege artillery to cast a few rounds into the Moselle valley around Ars. From now until nightfall he left Canrobert to fend for himself; but he found time to address a few words to his anxious Emperor at Châlons. At 2 p.m. he signalled:

Canrobert's corps is very likely to be attacked at St Privat.

At 4 p.m. he advised:

General attack along the whole line. The King of Prussia is in personal command. Our men are holding their positions well but our artillery has been obliged to cease firing.

And at 7 p.m., when his left wing had brilliantly succeeded and his right was broken:

I have returned from the plateau [*which plateau*?]. The attack has been intense. At this hour, 7 p.m., firing has ceased. Our men have held all their positions.

In fact 'at this hour' firing had not ceased. The battle, which Bazaine should have won, had been irretrievably lost. This he did not know. And this he did not tell his Emperor.

****

With the capture of Ste Marie, the German left wing lay thus: 3rd Guard Brigade of 2nd Guard Division at Habonville, detached to IX Corps; 4th Guard Brigade halted at St Ail; 1st Guard Division in Ste Marie itself, reorganizing after the assault on the village.[58] To the north 47th Saxon Brigade rejoined XII Corps as it continued its hesitant flank march to the north-west; for even at this late hour the Crown Prince of Saxony had not yet succeeded in identifying the true extent of Canrobert's position beyond St Privat, not even when two of his squadrons made an unopposed foray down the valley of the Orne and successfully cut the French rail and telegraph connections with Thionville at Maizières, six miles due north of Metz. By 4 p.m. however, a massive array of guns had been deployed on either side of Ste Marie, even though its fire was so ill-coordinated that the

---

58   X Corps stood in reserve at Batilly, a mile to the west of the Guard Corps. Only its corps artillery was called forward after the capture of Ste Marie.

artillery of the Guard was concentrated on Jérusalem to the south of St Privat and that of XII Corps on Roncourt to the north, thus leaving Canrobert's main bastion largely unscathed. Behind this screen of fire a dreadful disaster was in the making.

Frederick Charles was ever more anxiously watching the already declining sun. So also was Prince Augustus, the Guard Corps commander. Neither knew nor much cared about the crisis on the German right which Steinmetz had so obstinately engineered. Both were well aware that Manstein was no more than holding his own against the concentrated resistance of Leboeuf and Ladmirault along the Amanvillers ridge. Both were watching with growing concern the slow progress of the Saxons in their search for Canrobert's flank. And together, since time and tide wait for no man, they took the option which Canrobert had been expecting.

****

It was shortly after 4.30 p.m. There have been many arguments why the Guard Corps was launched against St Privat at this critical moment. To stand today on the road that runs from St Ail to Ste Marie and to look at the empty ground that stretches upward for a mile towards St Privat is a heart-stopping experience. And to stand at St Privat and look down upon this doomed land is to invite a suspension of belief.

There are two propositions. First, that Frederick Charles, seeing the *day* slip away, ordered an ill-prepared assault on St Privat. Second that Augustus, seeing his *authority* slip away, determined that, if there were laurels to be won, they would be his and not those of the Crown Prince of Saxony. So it is in war that military measures are so often dictated by private prejudice. The truth is more simple.

It was now or never. Frederick Charles, despite his earlier complacency, and despite the laggard Saxons on his left, was minded of Moltke's injunction to attack the enemy 'wherever found'. And so, when Augustus urged a frontal assault upon St Privat, bleak uplands notwithstanding, he agreed. It was, at that hour, and in the circumstances of the moment, a proper decision. Had his opponent, Bazaine, troubled to pre-empt so obvious an attack, then much might have been changed. But Bazaine, deaf to all warnings and entreaties from Canrobert, held his own Guard in check at Plappeville.[59]

The attack of the Guard Corps was launched in succession, right to left. At 4.45 p.m., 3rd Brigade was pushed forward through the Bois de la Cusse and on the right of the 49th Hessian Brigade which, since early afternoon, had been pinned down in its exposed position astride the railway cutting. This movement had a double purpose: to buttress the Hessians and to divert the attention of Cissey's division on the right of 4

59 But see p. 274.

Corps from the main attack on St Privat farther to the north. In both objects it succeeded, but at a terrible cost; for as the thick lines of infantry emerged from the woodland onto the bare fields beyond, they were struck by a devastating fire — artillery, mitrailleuses, and chassepots — from Ladmirault's terraced and covered positions at Amanvillers. Thus the German account:

> A storm of bullets struck the leading battalion [*Garde-Schützen*]. Major Fabeck, the commander, was instantly killed and with him fell most of the company commanders. In the firefight which followed the battalion lost all its officers, and the command of the few survivors passed to a young cadet. The two battalions of the *1st Grenadiers (Emperor Alexander's)* which extended the line to the right fared no better, and their losses were such that one company was left in the hands of a sergeant.

The same fate awaited the *3rd Grenadiers (Queen Elizabeth's)* on the left; and within minutes the attack was reduced to a bloody shambles.[60] It had been brief. It had been brave. But it was only the prelude to a greater drama.

****

At 5 p.m. the main attack was launched on St Privat, despite a warning from the commander of 1st Guard Division at Ste Marie that the Saxons on the far left were in no position to co-operate in the planned outflanking movement against Roncourt. But with less than three hours of daylight remaining, Augustus persuaded Frederick Charles that any further delay would be fatal. In the event — by courtesy of Bazaine — this precipitate decision turned the day, but at a savage price. For by nightfall, when Canrobert's gallant but forsaken men had been driven from the burning wreckage of their fortress village, the Guard Corps alone had suffered 8230 casualties.[61] There were to be few blacker days in the history of German arms.

The assault opened with the advance of 4th Guard Brigade[62] which passed through the gun-line south of St Ail and, behind its skirmishers, moved in close order up the long, empty slope beyond. It is a measure of this hasty deployment that the men went forward across nearly 3000 yards of open ground with full packs and equipment weighing nearly 100 pounds;

---

60 The limit of the progress made by 3rd Brigade is marked today by the memorials to the two Grenadier regiments (*Emperor Alexander's* and *Queen Elizabeth's*).

61 Killed—2440; wounded—5611; missing—179. By far the greatest part were incurred in the space of 40 minutes.

62 *2nd* and *4th Grenadiers.*

and it is a measure of this incomparable body of soldiers that, in the old Prussian tradition, they advanced at the double, with drums beating and colours flying. It did not last long. The chassepots at St Privat soon saw to that. Here, if anywhere, the romantic age of war died a prosaic and bloody death.

The objective of 4th Guard Brigade was the farmstead of Jérusalem, lying in the angle of the Briey road and a shoulder of ground running thence to the south-west towards Habonville. Here, on the French side, Canrobert had disposed Lafont's division in terraced rows 'like', as one witness recorded, 'the auditorium of a theatre'. Here too, astride the road, were the four French batteries which had survived the long cannonade of the Guard artillery.

A strange silence fell upon the field as the Guard hastened forward and the chassepots waited for them. And as they waited, a most curious misery occurred. As the Guard advanced, a flock of terrified sheep rushed across their front. The French *tirailleurs*, thinking this to be a squadron of enemy cavalry, opened a rapid fire and mowed down each single wretched animal. It was a grim foretaste of things to come.

The range narrowed as the Guard, in two thick ranks of half-battalions, advanced across the open ground. Inexplicably the attack was not supported by the long line of German guns deployed between Habonville and St Ail,[63] and it can only be that for once a German commander allowed events to overtake his professional training. On the far ridge the defenders were left undisturbed to measure their target — and wait.

Then, at their extreme range of 1500 yards, the chassepots opened up from behind their solid stone defences and, in the bleakest words, a wall of men was struck down by a wall of bullets. 'It was', recorded one survivor, 'as if a whistling wind was blowing, as the hail of fire cut great swathes in the advancing battalions.' 'Within moments', says the official account, 'the *4th Grenadiers* were torn to ribbons, their ranks decimated and every field officer killed or wounded. A company of the *1st Grenadiers* [3rd Brigade] on their right, hastening to their aid, was instantly wiped out and two batteries of guns, hurrying forward from St Ail, were shot down even before they could unlimber.'

So began the twilight of the Guard. On the afternoon of the 16th Wedell's brigade had battered itself to pieces on Ladmirault's bullets and bayonets, but that had been an act of blind impetuosity. Here, before the ramparts of St Privat, a deliberate attack foundered on a defiant defence. And here too, both the geometry and arithmetic of battle were of an altogether different order. The statistics of war can often be misleading; but here, on the afternoon of bloody Thursday, they were quite explicit, even if the lessons were all too soon forgotten.

63 In his *Letters on Artillery* which describe this action, Hohenlohe-Ingelfingen, the exceptionally able commander of the artillery of the Guard Corps, offers neither comment nor explanation.

Consider the arena; twice the area of Waterloo, one-fiftieth of that the first morning of the Somme. An empty expanse with neither cover nor contour to conceal the attacker's approach. On the German side, three infantry brigades numbering — if it were possible to deploy them all — perhaps 18,000 men. On the French side — if it were possible to bring every rifle to bear — perhaps half as many. On the German side, an infantry weapon unable effectively to engage above 700 yards. On the French side, the chassepot with twice the range. And not only twice the range, but with an average rate of fire of five rounds a minute. Thus it may be estimated that the defenders could deliver upward of 40,000 rounds of rifle-fire a minute, and during a period when the German needle-gun could provide no response. There had been no such previous military equation; and as the minutes passed, so the scale of the equation grew.

It was now 5.20 p.m., and the Grenadiers, their battalions reduced to companies and companies to broken remnants, halted and lay down in such small cover as the swell of ground offered while the French continued to fire down into the inert mass 800 yards to their front. There remained of all the field officers of the brigade only a single major. There they cowered, exhausted; lesser soldiers would have broken and fled, as had the Westphalians at Mars-la-Tour, and as at this very moment Steinmetz's infantry was fleeing in disorder in the Mance ravine; but, for all the carnage and confusion, these men held their ground. It may be that there was in the air a faint echo of Frederick the Great's wrathful words to his own Grenadiers: '*Hunde, wollt' Ihr ewig leben?*' ('Dogs, do you wish to live for ever?').

From St Ail, Prince Augustus watched the destruction of the 4th Brigade. General Pape, commander of 1st Guard Division at Ste Marie, had warned him that the Saxons were dragging their feet and were in no position yet to support a frontal attack on St Privat, and it may well be argued with hindsight that an hour's delay would have saved many lives and achieved the same final result. But Augustus had thrown his cap into the ring and the Guard was left to pay his princely price.

The official German account describes the setting:

At 5.45 p.m. General Kessel [commander of the 1st Guard Brigade][64] advanced from Ste Marie and attempted to cross the open slope which led upwards to the French positions. This slope is surmounted by a kind of terrace which stretches for about 500 yards to the west of St Privat, and the north and west faces of which are covered by several enclosures with high walls. At various points the French had constructed covered trenches [*this, in fact, is not so, since Canrobert had no entrenching tools*]. Thick ranks of marksmen manned these terraced buildings, behind which, like a natural

---

64 *1st Foot Guards* and *3rd Foot Guards*.

fortress, stood the village of St Privat, almost entirely surrounded by walls, and with every house manned to the rooftops by French soldiers.

Such, then, was the nut that Augustus determined to crack.

1st Brigade, as it moved forward from Ste Marie, was forced to take station some 500 yards to the north of the Briey road in order to avoid the debris of the *Grenadiers* on its right. Then, wheeling into line and led by the *Fusilier* battalion of the *3rd Foot Guards*, the solid ranks advanced upon their formidable objective (*see* Plate 28). They were at once received with an even more murderous fire from the massed chassepots on the farther ridge, and within moments the attack was reduced to a bloody shambles. Undaunted, two more battalions pressed forward, only to founder as much on the ramparts of their dead and wounded comrades as on the hail of French bullets. 'The slaughter', records the German account, 'was indescribable. This whole action of the 1st Brigade had lasted no more than half an hour. Towards 6.15 p.m. four and a half battalions of the brigade lay in total disorder some 700 yards from their objective.'

But there was no going back. Between the 1st and 4th Brigades on either side of the main road there lay a wide gap; and into this the commander of 1st Guard Division now despatched all but one battalion of his remaining infantry.[65] With extraordinary resolution these men doubled into action, 'bending forward as if in the teeth of a gale'. And the gale blew them also into broken fragments. Within minutes — for this doomed passage of arms was, in a sense, mercifully short-lived — all but a handful of officers were casualties and Bismarck's bland equation of 'blood and iron' had been brutally demonstrated. A French eye-witness watched the slaughter:

> From where we stood we could see, through a screen of riderless horses, a kind of whirlpool of men which resembled for all the world an anthill into which a stick has been thrust; and upon this scene of wild confusion the chassepots continued their deadly work. All that remained at this horrific moment was a final act of destruction, for the Germans themselves expected at any moment an irresistible counter-attack to sweep aside the shattered Guard and recapture Ste Marie.

That counter-attack never came; and this is why.

****

It will be remembered that during the forenoon (that is, even before Manstein's artillery began the day's action opposite Amanvillers) Can-

65 2nd Guard Brigade, consisting of *2nd Foot Guards* and *4th Foot Guards*.

Plate 28 St Privat, looking east from Ste Marie-aux-Chênes, the scene of the disastrous attack by 1st Guard Division. On the right skyline, the road from Metz to Briey

robert had sent the first of many messages to Bazaine asking for reinforcements to bolster his right wing. His sole concern was defensive, for he had already identified Frederick Charles's intention to outflank his apparently strong but actually precarious position between St Privat and Roncourt. Above all, he was, with every justification, anxious about his severe shortage of artillery. About 12.30 p.m., Bazaine had sent a verbal promise of a division of Bourbaki's Imperial Guard in the event that the situation of 6 Corps were to become 'more serious'. In fact, the only support to reach Canrobert during an afternoon in which the initiative was fast slipping away from the Germans was a couple of batteries and four caissons of ammunition. And the Imperial Guard, that powerful reserve which far from simply protecting the right wing might, if properly and timely deployed, have rolled up the German left and so decisively have turned the day?

At his trial Bazaine advanced the startling theory that, as commander of the reserve, Bourbaki had sole discretion as to the time and place of its employment, although he appeared to have forgotten that about mid-afternoon he had sent him an express order not to move from his concentration area near Plappeville. Thereafter there is no record of any

281

communication between the two men; and when eventually Bourbaki decided to act on his own initiative, he was too late and he marched in a lost cause.

In his account of the battle, and despite his knowledge of the true facts, Moltke wrote: 'When Bazaine received word that the Germans were stretching out in constantly increasing extension with intent to outflank his right, he at 3 p.m. ordered Picard's Grenadier division posted at Plappeville to march towards the threatened flank.' This is patently untrue, and can only be explained as wishful thinking — namely, that the savage resistance of the French 4 and 6 Corps could only have been sustained by the arrival of substantial reinforcements. Certainly in mid-afternoon Moltke himself was at or near Rezonville and had no knowledge of the growing crisis facing IX Corps and the Guard. The facts are otherwise,[66] and explain why, at the opportune moment, Canrobert had neither the reserves nor the resources with which to complete the destruction of the Guard.

At 6.00 p.m. two officers arrived at Bourbaki's headquarters — not from St Privat but from Amanvillers; for Ladmirault, while aware of the situation on his right, felt — not without reason — that a sustained attack on his own front might not only relieve the pressure on Canrobert but might punch a hole through the German centre in the direction of Vernéville. Bourbaki hesitated. The hour was late, and the sight of men straggling back from St Privat was disturbing evidence of the true situation. None the less, he set out with his Grenadier division and a major part of the reserve artillery, taking the narrow wooded valley which lay to the east of the main French position. Progress was slow and the head of the supporting column did not emerge onto the plateau near Amanvillers until dusk had fallen. By then, so too had St Privat. And Canrobert's retreat down the Woippy road had uncovered Ladmirault's flank. Any thought of a counterattack against the German centre could be dismissed; if there were to be any heroics, they would now be those of survival.

An angry Bourbaki decided to retrace his steps, leaving two regiments of Grenadiers and the reserve artillery, deployed in the great quarries near the Woippy road, to cover the withdrawal from Amanvillers. But there was no pursuit. Darkness and exhaustion combined to discourage any further action by the enemy; and the Imperial Guard, which could and should have played a decisive role, lamely quit the stage.

****

Meanwhile XII Corps on the far left of the German line had at last completed its long flank march and was disposed thus: 45th and 48th Brigades near the villages of Auboué and Montois to the north-east of St

66 *Procès Bazaine.*

Privat; 47th Brigade in the woods facing Roncourt; 46th Brigade a little farther west at Coinville. It was shortly after 6.30 p.m. At St Privat Canrobert, isolated, and forsaken by Bazaine, sent his final message to Plappeville[67] and prepared to sell his life dearly.

Late though the hour was, Frederick Charles was taking no more chances. While the Saxons first occupied Montois before the assault on Roncourt from the north-west, the entire artillery of the Guard and of XII Corps, supported by six batteries of the reserve corps (X) from Batilly, formed up in a great arc on either side of Ste Marie and for forty minutes smote the defenders of St Privat 'with a torrent of shells which tore great gaps in the solid masonry and lit the evening sky with a fiery glow that matched the blood-red sun as it set in the west. Thus began the last martyrdom of the embattled village.'[68]

To this holocaust Canrobert, his guns disabled and his ammunition exhausted, could offer no reply other than his own indomitable spirit and that of his courageous soldiers. Certainly some elements of 6 Corps broke under the intolerable pounding and began to stream away along the Woippy road (it was these fugitives whom Bourbaki had met as his relieving column approached Amanvillers, and who drew from Bazaine his contemptible reproach). But by far the greater part of 6 Corps stood their ground in the burning wreckage of St Privat, doughty and determined defenders of a doomed cause.

It must be repeated, especially in the light of what was said — and left unsaid — at Bazaine's trial three years later, that throughout this long day, from Point du Jour to Roncourt, the soldiers of the Army of the Rhine conducted themselves with the most exemplary fortitude. And this is all the more remarkable, for these soldiers were for the most part unprofessional peasants, inexpertly trained, and by this time deeply disillusioned with a leadership which had led them into a wanton war and then, not once but twice, denied them the opportunity to fashion victory out of vacillation. St Privat, small, squat and sinister on its hillside, bids fair to rank with Verdun as one of the grander memorials to French military valour; and it is a singular commentary on the irony of history that these two honoured places, fifty miles apart in space and almost fifty years in time, have come to be associated in the long chronicle of French arms with two of the least honoured names among the Marshals of France.

****

It was 7 p.m. To the north of St Privat, Péchot's brigade was still offering stout resistance in Roncourt. Had even the single division of the Imperial Guard which Bazaine had long since promised been on hand at this

66 *Procès Bazaine.*

67 See p. 275.

juncture, the precious daylight hours might well have been denied to a hesitant opponent. 'The enemy did not come himself', said Canrobert at Bazaine's trial, 'but as it was shells instead, we could not hold on. Péchot warned me, and we were obliged to retire. We did so by moving in echelon from the centre, and in good order — I emphasize the phrase — we gained the wood of Saulny.' The German account confirms that their withdrawal was conducted with exemplary skill and discipline, but the final collapse of the French right wing was a great deal more dramatic than the bare record suggests.

Faced by three parts of XII Corps, Péchot pulled his brigade back to the forest of Jaumont to cover the vital escape route to Metz, and as he did so the Saxons entered Roncourt. The flank, so late discovered, was turned at last. And this was the signal for which Prince Augustus had been impatiently waiting.

The Guard, for so long pinned down by French rifle-fire, now roused itself and, storming up the slope, forced its way into the battered and burning village, while from the north the Saxons attacked with their two leading brigades. A generation of artists was to spill much paint in depicting the scene, but not even the liveliest imagination could capture on canvas the true savagery of the fighting. In St Privat, glowing like a furnace and in the eerie light of a deepening dusk, Prussians and Saxons hunted the French defenders from street to street and from house to house. The Guard had a score to settle and a humiliation to avenge; the French, faced by overwhelming numbers and inevitable defeat, had little left to lose except their pride. It is in such a situation that even the most disciplined of men are driven to imitate the action of the tiger and to fight with inhuman ferocity. So it was, as darkness fell on St Privat, that bloody Thursday reached its end. The crowning irony of this day of ironies is that as Canrobert went down to a twilight defeat at St Privat, Steinmetz, six miles away, was presiding over an equally critical disaster at Gravelotte. It is one of the more paradoxical passages of arms. It was not until nearly midnight that word reached the King and Moltke that the Amanvillers Line had been successfully turned, and that the prospect of defeat for the First Army had been, at the last hour, salvaged by the Second.

Meanwhile, little more than a gunshot away to the east, Bazaine had folded his tents and departed quietly. He had never grasped the opportunity that Frossard and Leboeuf had provided. He had certainly not responded to Canrobert's early warning of the threat to his right wing. He was at no moment aware of the bold chance that faced Ladmirault at Amanvillers. Thus, while he had manufactured a marvellous defensive position during the daylight hours of the 17th, it is absolutely evident that his true intention, as it had been from first light on the 16th, was to summon the Army of the Rhine back within the safe-seeming security of Metz — and there to await events. There is no doubt that all his ills stemmed from MacMahon's defeat at Wörth on 6 August and his

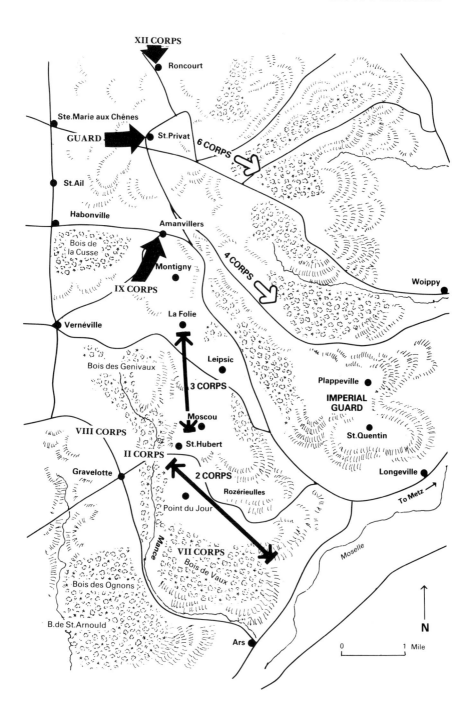

Map 18   The situation at nightfall, 18 August

subsequent flight, and that one of his remaining options now was that, by engaging the attention of two entire German armies around Metz, he would give time for a major relief operation to be mounted from Châlons.[69] In a purely negative sense, he was right; but by choosing a course of passive resistance when a surprised opponent presented him with repeated opportunities to win successive battles on his own account, he was decisively wrong. So it was that the Army of the Rhine, so bravely named and so grossly mismanaged, retired sullen and subdued into the snail-shell of Metz, there to be sent two months later into surrender and servitude. Milton's words would be a proper memorial:

> I cannot praise a fugitive and cloistered virtue, unexercised and unbreathed, that never sallies out and seeks her adversary, but slinks out of the race, where that immortal garland is to be run for, not without dust and heat.

2 Corps was the last to quit the Amanvillers line. Frossard's men had bloodily repulsed every effort by Steinmetz to dislodge them from their great redoubt and had enjoyed the — in the event, empty — satisfaction of seeing a German army reduced to panic-stricken disorder. By dawn the gun-pits and shelter-trenches at Point du Jour had been evacuated and the Army of the Rhine, with a nonchalance which would be touching if it were not ludicrous, had once more pitched its little shelter-tents under the guns of the fortress. The enemy watched cautiously and made no attempt to interfere. They had no need to; and Moltke had more pressing business — with MacMahon and the Army of Châlons a hundred miles to the west.[70]

In a sense, it can be said that Bazaine never really abandoned the fortress; for had he not said on the night of the 16th 'We must save the army and to do that, we must retire on Metz'? Thus he clung to his 'fortress' concept of warfare until, inevitably, what had long ceased to be a source of strength became instead a pathetic prison. His apologists (and they are not notable for their number or, with one exception,[71] their distinction) have argued that by retreating into Metz he immobilized for two months an investing force of 200,000 Germans who would otherwise have been available for operations in the heart of France and before Paris itself. That is to ignore the order which he disobeyed, the failure of his leadership, and the irresolution which cast away so many glittering opportunities. He did not betray France. But he most surely did betray his brave and bewildered men, and in so doing gravely compromised his

---

69 See p. 213.

70 It is an eloquent comment on Moltke's 'Prussianism' that the 'Army of the Meuse' which he at once formed to pursue MacMahon and bring him to battle included, despite its savage casualties, the Guard Corps.

71 Bonnal: *La Manœuvre de Saint-Privat*.

reputation. It is a measure of his disgrace that alone with Pétain — who in the end *was* a traitor — of all the Marshals of France, his name is nowhere celebrated today in his country.

As we have seen, bloody Thursday was the first set-piece battle of the campaign, and in its peculiar ferocity and in its demonstration of the stunning effect of modern fire-power it cast a long shadow forward into the future of positional warfare. The casualties speak for themselves.

On the German side 20,160, of whom no fewer than 5237 were killed, including a quite exceptional proportion of officers of every rank. On the French side 12,275, of whom 4420, listed as 'missing', were taken prisoner. There are other melancholy signposts. It is the first battle in which commentators resorted to the descriptive word 'front', and the first 'front' to have extended across a positional defence as great as seven miles. Except for the criminal sacrifice of the *4th Uhlans* at Gravelotte, cavalry for once took no part in the battle. The scale and nature of the fighting created formidable new administrative problems, logistical and — more especially — medical, for which even a general staff as professional as the German was wholly unprepared, while the difficulties of command and control on both sides over a battlefield on which the geometry had so strikingly changed have already been remarked upon.

There remains one other lesson which students of the American Civil War should have more profitably absorbed. In such a confrontation, the entrenching-tool had become as potent a weapon of defence as the chassepot; and against the concentrated fire-power of breech-loaders the simple alternative for attacking infantry was dispersal or destruction. When, within fifty years, great armies clashed once more, these forgotten lessons had most painfully to be learned again. By then, at least, no vestige of the romantic concept of war remained. Idealistic, it may still have been; drab, impersonal and inexpressibly dreadful it had become. If it were possible — or necessary — to mark the great divide between battles old and new, then these uplands of Lorraine, suitably illuminated by a pitiless sun, are a grandiose and grisly setting for that nineteenth-century *verismo* which simultaneously invaded the national cultures of the time.

There are many — not least King William — who thought that the battle of St Privat–Gravelotte was the critical victory; that all that went before and all that followed after were, in dramatic terms, prologue and epilogue. That is a tidy view, but a simplistic one. Certainly it marked, at whatever cost on the German side, the beginning of the end for France, in both a physical and a moral sense. Within two weeks one-third of her regular field armies would, with their broken Emperor, be led away, like latter-day Israelites, into captivity at Sedan; within twenty days a new Republic would have risen defiantly from the ashes of the old Empire; within two months the Army of the Rhine would have capitulated — 173,000 strong — in the fortress-prison to which it had been condemned by a dreadful conjuncture of ineptitude and impotence. Yet it was not until May 1871 that the final peace treaty was signed and the future of Europe, then dimly perceived, had been irrevocably changed. And to these profound events we shall briefly return.

But the true tragedy had already been played out on another neighbouring stage — at Mars-la-Tour, Vionville, Rezonville, call it what we will. And it was played out between two men, anti-hero and hero. The key, the crux of this whole — and wholly forgotten — crisis of history lay first in Bazaine's decision early on the morning of 'the day of battle' to reverse the Emperor's instruction to make all haste on the road to Verdun. It lay, secondly, in the extraordinary resolution and tactical skill of Alvensleben in opposing a single widely dispersed corps to the full weight of a vastly superior opponent. By noon on the 16th, when he had so improbably captured Vionville, he should have been fighting, if at all, with his back to Verdun. By dusk on the 16th the real crisis had come and gone; and all that followed was, however climactic, anti-climax — whether it be Steinmetz at Gravelotte, Manstein at Amanvillers, or the Guard at St Privat. It is difficult to think of a great passage of arms in which one critical day of battle was so strangely — and so soon — underscored by another. Nor was that to be the end of the story.

****

THE MOUSETRAP

It had never been part of Moltke's master-plan to become involved in the investment of Metz. When early in August he had launched his three Armies in a great swinging movement through Alsace and Lorraine, his best hope had been to bring the enemy to battle in open country or to drive him back to the gates of Paris.

The unexpectedly summary collapse of the French right wing at Wörth and Froeschwiller, and MacMahon's flight by Lunéville to Neufchâteau and thence to Châlons had opened up a wholly new prospect for Moltke; for suddenly the Army of the Rhine, already separated from the Army of Alsace by the Vosges massif, had become the prime objective of the main German thrust; and Moltke's orders on the 15th had been designed to intercept Bazaine's withdrawal on Verdun and to prevent the junction of the two French armies beyond the Meuse. How Bazaine's irresolution and Alvensleben's brave gamble had swung the day of battle on the 16th, and how bloody Thursday had hung in the balance until nightfall, we have seen. But while it is not within the province of this narrative to pursue the war in detail to its bitter end, a tale has yet to be told.

****

The mountains which had so clearly dictated Moltke's strategic dispositions (and the vulnerability of the French to defeat in detail) had also proved to be MacMahon's temporary salvation; and indeed he had demonstrated considerable skill in extricating his army and in assembling his scattered divisions by road and rail to the open plain of Champagne at Châlons.[1] There, on the 16th, he had been joined by the Emperor, and by the newly

---

1   1, 5 and 7 Corps.

formed 12 Corps from Paris.[2] In theory, MacMahon had been placed under Bazaine's command on the 12th, but in practice there was no effective communication between Metz and Châlons after the battle of Borny (14 August), and thus both armies stumbled separately to disaster and defeat.

The Crown Prince, perhaps surprised by success, had been slow to react after his victory on the 6th (his two cavalry divisions, for example, which should have led the pursuit, were a day's march to the rear of his infantry after the battle), and thus the German Third Army had moved forward with unusual circumspection through the narrow passes of the Vosges, uncertain of MacMahon's intention and even of the direction of his flight.

Moltke was cautious too. There was always the possibility that MacMahon might use the still available railway link between Nancy and Metz to join hands with Bazaine in Lorraine; or, an even less likely possibility, that Bazaine might strike south from Metz at the flank of the Third Army as it emerged from the mountain passes. This explains the apparent failure of the Crown Prince to maintain contact with MacMahon, and the seemingly wasted week on the German right and centre between the battles of Spicheren and Borny, a week which saw the appointment of Bazaine as commander-in-chief on the 12th and the subsequent failure of the Army of the Rhine to make good its withdrawal to Verdun. Thus it had not been until the 15th that Moltke saw his way clear; and even then he should have been too late. How and why his caution had been rewarded by the errors of commission and omission on the part of his chief opponent, we have seen in melancholy detail.

****

If there were proof needed of Moltke's exceptional strategic flair and of the extraordinary efficiency of his small but finely tuned general staff, we need look no further than the morning of the 19th and of the twelve momentous days which followed. For consider the situation at nightfall on the previous day.

To the south, Third Army had by-passed Strasbourg and Toul,[3] and was across the Meuse on the line Commercy–Bar-le-Duc–St Dizier, with cavalry patrols thrown forward to Vitry-le-François and in contact with MacMahon at Châlons. At Gravelotte, Royal Headquarters had come close to accepting defeat after Steinmetz's successive disasters in the Mance ravine. Only a last-minute reprieve with the fall of St Privat had turned the day. By the forenoon of the 19th, Bazaine had pulled the Army

---

2 From Paris had also come an ill-organized division of Gardes Mobiles under the able General Trochu. But these battalions had proved to be so insusceptible to discipline that they had been swiftly returned to the capital, where Trochu was installed as Military Governor.

3 The former was invested by the Baden division; the latter, first by a Bavarian brigade, and later by 17th Division (originally part of IX Corps), hurried forward from the Baltic coast on 12 August. Toul surrendered on 23 September, and Strasbourg on the 28th.

of the Rhine back within the perimeter of the fortress defences of Metz. Against every possible prediction, Moltke now found the greater part of the French field army locked into a prison of its own making. He acted with incredible speed and authority. 'Under the altered conditions, the regular investment of Metz was now necessary and this involved a radical alteration of the existing arrangements throughout the whole army.'[4]

Accordingly, an investing force was formed under Frederick Charles consisting of I, II, III, VII, VIII, IX and X Corps of the former First and Second Armies, together with 3rd Reserve Division and 1st and 3rd Cavalry Divisions (Steinmetz had been summarily despatched to a distant corner of provincial Germany where he could do no more mischief). This force was concentrated in a wide arc of 28 miles on the west bank of the Moselle with I Corps supported by the Reserve Division in broadly its old position on the right bank. It was a formidable array, and given Bazaine's track-record unnecessarily lavish — to the point where apologists were later to advance the lame argument that the last service of the Army of the Rhine to France, if not to the Emperor, was to immobilize 150,000 Germans in Lorraine, and thus prolong the country's agony.

There remained MacMahon; and to him and to the Army of Châlons Moltke simultaneously addressed himself. While the investing force around Metz was being given its several stations, a new Army — the Army of the Meuse — was formed, consisting of the Guard (casualties notwithstanding); IV Corps (then to the west of Toul at Commercy on the Meuse); and XII (Royal Saxon) Corps; together with 5th and 6th Cavalry Divisions which had played so great a part on the 16th. Surprisingly, the command of this Army was given to the Crown Prince of Saxony and not — perhaps as a royal rebuff — to the Guard commander, Prince Augustus. The Saxons were assembled at Conflans on the road to Étain, the Guard at Mars-la-Tour, and IV Corps directed on Verdun.

'All these orders received the approval of the King, and were dispatched to the commanding officers by eleven o'clock on the morning of *the 19th*.'[5] That so radical a change of plan and so detailed a reallocation of resources was achieved in less than half a day — and after two bloody passages of arms — is barely credible. That it proceeded, with all the profound administrative complications which it involved, with assured efficiency explains as nothing else can explain the true genius of Moltke — that withdrawn man of whom it was said that he could be silent in seven languages — and the dangerous quality of the German military machine when it lets slip the dogs of war.[6]

****

4 Moltke: *op. cit.*

5 Moltke: *op. cit.* Author's italics.

6 On 22 August the strength of the Crown Prince's Third Army is given as 137,622; and that of the new Army of the Meuse as 86,275.

At Châlons deep doubt and confusion reigned. There MacMahon found himself saddled, as Bazaine had earlier been, with a demoralized Emperor, lacking the will to lead and with the authority of his office fast ebbing. The situation around Metz was clouded by conflicting reports and garbled messages. One thing was certain; and it was summed up in a throwaway line by Bazaine to his staff. '*Notre situation n'est pas brillante.*' It was a formidable understatement. And it could equally have done duty for MacMahon as he wrestled with his uneasy options a hundred miles to the west.

MacMahon's military instinct was at all costs to disengage from an indefensible position on the open plain at Châlons and to fall back to the west. His army, numbering some 150,000 men, was ill organized and ill equipped. If the Army of the Rhine was indeed beleaguered far away in Metz, then he had a double duty: to preserve the remaining field army of the Empire, and to cover Paris. That there was presently imposed upon him a quite different obligation was not his fault. In Paris the dynasty was at stake, and his military instinct was overruled by his political masters.

It is an apocalyptic picture. At Châlons, MacMahon playing host to his Emperor, his Emperor's cousin Prince Napoleon, and to the sad little Prince Imperial, unaware that his nominal chief, Bazaine, was beyond both hope and recall within the walls of Metz; certain that his first duty lay in preserving his own army and protecting Paris.

But in Paris? There all eyes were fixed on Metz. On the 19th, the last day on which he was still in direct communication with Châlons and the capital, Bazaine had briefly — and misleadingly — reported the events of bloody Thursday and had stated his vague intention to 'resume' his westward march 'in a couple of days' by way of Montmédy or, if pressed by the enemy, by the last available route south of the Belgian border through Sedan and Mézières. But there was a not very subtle difference in his messages.

To MacMahon, who had been subordinated to his command since the 12th, he carefully delegated the right to act as he thought best 'in the circumstances', in words strikingly similar to those he had used to Bourbaki at a critical moment on the 18th. To Palikao, his political chief, he proposed to stand his ground until MacMahon could assemble a sufficient force to march to the relief of the Army of the Rhine. Thus this simple soldier, perhaps more sinned against than sinning, hedged his bets. Little good did it do him. For this much is sure, regardless of all later recriminations and imputations: on the morning of the 19th, when Moltke was busy with the prospect of a crushing victory, Bazaine was absorbed with the political implications of a crushing defeat. He had not the slightest intention of fighting his way to freedom. The man who had clung to Metz when the road to Verdun was his for the taking; who had invited the enemy 'to batter himself' on the Amanvillers line and had weakly watched while that battered enemy was allowed to salvage security from disaster; that

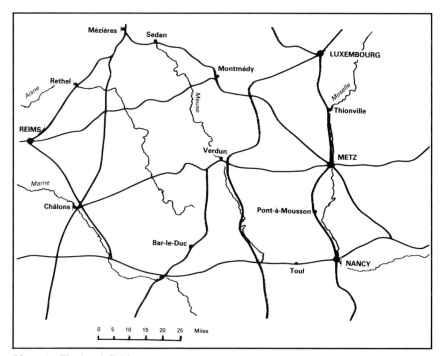

Map 19   The battlefield moves west

man was now comfortably installed in an elegant villa at Ban St Martin, playing billiards, and surrounded by his few close confidants. And waiting.

But in Paris? The Empire was at stake. The Empress, Palikao and the Council of Ministers, little knowing but shrewdly guessing, rightly interpreted the messages from Metz. If the Army of the Rhine went down to total disaster, with it would go the dynasty. That the Emperor was still with the Army of Châlons was no longer a matter of military concern; that he was still there was more surely a formidable political problem. From Paris there went forth to MacMahon a simple — and in the event doom-laden — direction: '*Il faut sauver Bazaine.*' And thus the final disaster came about.

****

MacMahon was not so easily moved. He knew — as his masters in Paris did not — that the Germans were closing in on him; from the south, the Third Army of the Crown Prince, 150,000 strong and not greatly injured by the frontier battles at Wissembourg and Wörth; from the east the three corps of the new Army of the Meuse (Guard, IV and XII). He thus ignored the immediate implication of Palikao's message, and on the 21st moved the whole of his army north-westward to Reims. There at least he could win some breathing-space before committing himself to an irrevocable decision; and thither on the 22nd came the president of the Senate, Rouher, with a copy of Bazaine's final, and fatally delayed, message of the 19th with its false promise of a break-out towards Châlons. In retrospect, it would have served France (and MacMahon) better if the message had failed to arrive. It would not have changed the inevitable outcome of the war, but it would have averted the catastrophe of Sedan, and possibly — just possibly — it would have preserved the dynasty. But the dynasty was bent on self-destruction. The order which Rouher brought with him may be summed up thus: 'The Regency and the Council of Ministers require you unconditionally to effect your junction with Bazaine's army, else there will be a revolution in Paris.' It was to prove the only accurate forecast among the shifting sands of hopes and fears.

At this moment of dilemma, the Emperor stood aside. 'He did not approve, he did not oppose; but he shared, as a sort of interested spectator, in a venture determined by political motives and devoid of any sound military basis.'[7] MacMahon took his leave of Rouher with these words: 'I shall find myself in a most difficult position and experience a disaster which I desire to avoid.' And on the morning of the 23rd, unable to take the direct route to Metz by Stenay on the Meuse, he turned to the north-east towards Rethel on the Aisne, where, from the magazines in that small fortress, he could restock and rearm his makeshift army. And as he marched away, the weeks of stifling heat turned, by a grim twist of chance, to days of unrelenting rain.

* * * * * * * *

Royal Headquarters was at Bar-le-Duc. Moltke moved with innate circumspection. He had, at whatever cost, neutralized a major part of the French field army and locked it tidily away in a feeble fortress where it could do no harm. MacMahon was a problem, only in so far as his intention was not clear. By the 21st, on a wide front of 56 miles, the Germans had available 8½ army corps and (which were to prove a trump card) four thrusting cavalry divisions. Against this formidable host MacMahon could oppose only four army corps and two cavalry divisions, deficient in *matériel* and, more importantly, defective in morale.

The arrival of the Army of Châlons at Reims still left MacMahon with his original option of retiring on Paris, and Moltke with no sound reason for changing his own order of march towards the west. But by the 24th the picture had changed dramatically. From — of all sources — the Paris newspapers, reinforced by a telegram routed through London, it was learned at Bar-le-Duc that MacMahon had quitted Reims and was marching eastward to the relief of Bazaine; and on the 25th it became clear

7 Hooper: *The Campaign of Sedan.*

that the Army of Châlons, plainly seeking to by-pass the Crown Prince of Saxony's army as it closed up on the Meuse below Verdun, had taken a route to the north of Stenay which, while directed on Montmédy as a notional junction-point with Bazaine, would carry it perilously close to the Belgian frontier.

That Moltke still hesitated is not to be wondered at. He was aware, as MacMahon and his masters in Paris were not, of the formidable force which he disposed; and he was confident, as MacMahon and his masters were not, that Bazaine was neither willing nor able to make a desperate dash for freedom from Metz. But his purely military instinct refused to accept that any commander could embark on so hazardous a flank march with so insufficient an army and so tenuous an administrative organization.[8] It was left to Moltke's Director of Operations, Podbielski, to suggest that MacMahon's extraordinary manœuvre was inspired not by any military magic but by political pressure from the capital; and that by uncovering Paris he had created the condition for a new and totally unforeseen Cannae. And so, at 11 p.m. on the 25th, Moltke acted.

> In war [he later wrote] it is for the most part with probabilities only that the strategist can reckon; and the probability is that the enemy will do the right thing .... It could not be anticipated that the French army would uncover Paris and march along the Belgian frontier to Metz. Such a move seemed strange, and indeed somewhat venture-some ....[9]

Venturesome it surely was; and, finally convinced, Moltke ordered his two Armies to wheel to the right, and in so doing to drive MacMahon inexorably into what he was to call his 'mousetrap'.

****

The events of the final week which now led to the encirclement and surrender of the Emperor and the entire Army of Châlons were played out within a tidy quadrilateral bounded to the west by Aisne, to the east by the Meuse, and to the north by the Belgian frontier. This area, roughly 40 miles by 30 miles, is shown on the outline map on page 293 which excludes roads and minor tributaries.

Between the two rivers lie, at the southern end, the thickly wooded Argonne and at the north near Sedan, where the Meuse forms a sharp loop before turning south towards Verdun, the lower slopes of the great forests

---

8   If MacMahon's bid to rescue Bazaine stood any chance of success, then the securing of the right bank of the Meuse was vital; yet the Army of Châlons set out on its forlorn adventure without even a single bridging column; and this was to prove its ultimate undoing.

9   Moltke: *op. cit.*

of the Ardennes. It was difficult country, with an indifferent road-system made more hazardous by incessant rain; but it was to prove no great obstacle to Moltke's boldly handled cavalry which were to act as beaters driving their game steadily to the north-east, or to his infantry which had long since demonstrated their stamina and exemplary march-discipline. By comparison, the French stumbled eastward by short and ill-coordinated marches,[10] their cavalry, as usual, making no attempt to screen their movement or to reconnoitre the right flank whence an eager enemy was hastening to bring them to decisive battle. It was Vionville once again, but on a very different scale.[11]

****

When, late on the 25th, Moltke ordered the right-wheel and the pursuit of his 'venturesome' enemy, he disposed his two armies thus.

Four cavalry divisions were pushed forward, the Argonne notwithstanding, to keep close watch on French movements on the line Vouziers––Buzancy–Stenay (their hourly reports are a striking example of the classical use of cavalry in a pre-aviation war of movement, and a melancholy commentary on the French obsession with the glamorous function of the mounted arm, an obsession to be nobly and uselessly demonstrated by Margueritte's division on the fields of Floing above Sedan as the final trap was sprung on 1 September).

The right-wheel sent a strong brigade-group of the Army of the Meuse to occupy Stenay on the right bank of the Meuse, thus blocking MacMahon's direct route to his likely junction with an unenthusiastic Bazaine at Montmédy; and — a typical piece of finesse by Moltke — the two reserve corps of Frederick Charles's investing army around Metz were put on stand-by at Briey and Étain in case their presence might be needed on the Meuse.[12]

Meanwhile, the Crown Prince of Saxony's three corps (less the force sent to Stenay) were transferred across the Meuse at Dun (no fewer than six pontoon bridges were laid above and below the town) and the two Bavarian corps were detached to the Saxon command. Beyond the Argonne, and slightly inclined to the north-west, the rest of Third Army moved forward, covering Reims and the escape routes to Paris.

By the 27th MacMahon's headquarters were at Le Chesne, midway between the Aisne and the Meuse. This he judged — in the event correctly

10 On the 28th, for example, the train of Failly's 5 Corps stretched nine miles to the rear; and the corps covered less than five miles.

11 It may be remarked yet again that when, each night, the various corps of MacMahon's army bivouacked, they carefully erected their shelter-tents; even as late as the 29th at Beaumont, when a major battle was pending on the morrow.

12 So sure was Moltke of his successful plan that these two corps were stood down a day later.

— to be the point of no return if he were to avoid the disaster of which he had spoken earlier, for he was now aware both of the German force astride his direct road to Montmédy and of the much more serious threat to his right flank. He reverted therefore to the decision which he should never have changed at Reims; and at 8.30 p.m. he sent a telegram to Palikao informing him that he was turning aside and proposed to resume his original withdrawal to the west by way of Mézières and thence to Paris 'as events dictate'.

If MacMahon thought that this proposition would be readily accepted in the capital he was swiftly disabused, for at 1.30 a.m. the following morning he received a reply which the devious Palikao addressed in the first instance to the Emperor, thus imparting to it an unmistakable political gloss. A copy of this reply, timed a little later, presented MacMahon with — as the Marshal well knew — a wholly erroneous picture of the present German dispositions and a dangerously distorted estimate of the time-scale. On the most important issue of all — the activity and intention of Bazaine — the message was silent. It ended thus:

> Everyone here is convinced of the necessity of extricating Bazaine and your proposal has been greeted with extreme anxiety. Therefore in the name of the Council of Ministers I require you [*je vous demande*] to succour Bazaine, profiting by the thirty hours' start which you have over the Crown Prince of Prussia. I am directing Vinoy's Corps[13] on Reims.

MacMahon hesitated — and was lost. Before dawn he had countermanded his order and had directed his weary and disillusioned army to the north-east on the permanent crossings of the Meuse at Mouzon, Villers and Remilly, a move that would bring him within eight miles of the Belgian frontier. This decision was taken despite strong protests from the Emperor, who reminded the Marshal that the Minister of War had no authority to issue orders to commanders in the field and urged him to prosecute his planned retreat while there was still time.

This much must be said for Napoleon. From the day of the successive reverses at Spicheren and Wörth, he had shown an appreciation of the *military* situation which was considerably wiser and more accurate than that demonstrated by his senior captains. He was well aware of the *political* risk to himself and to the dynasty of a full-scale retreat into the interior and on the capital itself, and of the surrender of great areas of France to the enemy without even token resistance. But he rightly judged that the preservation of his crown could be secured, if at all, by the preservation of

13   This was the newly formed 13 Corps, and Palikao's decision to send it forward was a foolish form of blackmail. In the event, so disorganized was the rail-system, the corps barely reached Mézières by the date of the surrender at Sedan, and thus was just in time to make good its own escape.

the army, and he had long been under no illusions about the shortcomings of that army if opposed *en rase campagne* to the formidable German military machine. When both Austria and Italy hung back after war was declared, his only remaining allies were time and space, and thus it was that he had urged Bazaine to make all haste on the road to Verdun when he took his leave on the morning of the 16th at Gravelotte.

Bazaine had disobeyed, with disastrous consequences; and the Emperor had been dismayed when the Army of Châlons had been interrupted in its withdrawal at Reims. Now he made one last attempt to save what remained of the professional armies of France, but to no avail. MacMahon seems no longer to have felt himself subordinate to the command of his imperial fellow-traveller. More critically, he felt an acute sense of guilt that his failure at Wörth had seriously compromised Bazaine's situation at Metz (as indeed it had done), and that he was duly honour-bound to redeem his reputation and rescue his fellow-Marshal. It was a brave sentiment, but an act of military folly; and since there is no place for sentiment on a battlefield, it resulted neither in redemption nor in rescue, but in humiliating defeat.

****

At Royal Headquarters, MacMahon's decision to resume his march to the Meuse was greeted with something akin to pity. William Russell of *The Times*, attached as correspondent to the Crown Prince's headquarters at Third Army, records in his diary a conversation with Blumenthal, the chief of staff:

> He took me into a room in which was a table covered with a large map on a scale of an inch to a mile.[14] 'These French are lost, you see,' said Blumenthal. 'We know they are there, and there, and there — MacMahon's whole army. Where can they go to? Poor foolish fellows! They must go to Belgium, or fight *there* and be lost.' And he put his finger on the map between Mézières and Carignan.

The point which Blumenthal indicated was a small, insignificant fortress, lying on a loop of the Meuse, called Sedan.

****

Events moved quickly; but Moltke, relieved of the insubordinate presence of a Steinmetz, held his two armies carefully in check and gave repeated

14 The French, as has been earlier observed, had virtually no maps of France. And it is a striking fact that a comparatively new main road from Mézières to Paris had been marked on German maps, but not, ridiculously, on those of the French, the latest of which was dated 1862.

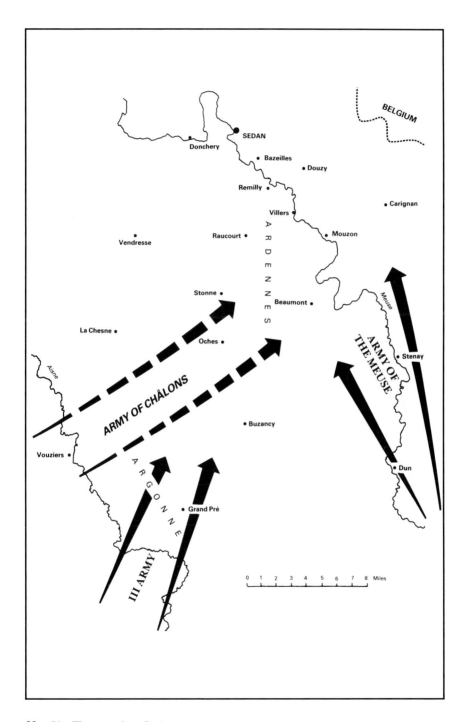

Map 20   The pursuit to Sedan

299

instructions to the two Crown Princes that they were in no circumstances to bring on a major battle until he was ready and able to spring his trap. Thus, as MacMahon edged away towards Mouzon, the German cavalry followed his every movement, and the German infantry closed up through the difficult country of the Argonne until, on the 28th, it had reached the line Vouziers−Buzancy−Stenay.[15]

When an army is moving without flank cover across the face of an organized enemy, it must expect the unexpected; and so it now turned out. On the morning of the 29th, MacMahon had sent a Captain de Grouchy — a name to conjure with as a messenger of doom — with instructions to Failly to conform with the new direction of the army on the downstream crossings of the Meuse. Grouchy was captured by a German cavalry patrol, and with him the Marshal's detailed march-orders. That was a notable coup for the Crown Prince of Saxony, pressing forward on the left bank of the Meuse. It was a savage misfortune for Failly, for as he marched innocently towards his original objective at Stenay, he was intercepted by the advanced guard of the Saxon XII Corps at Nouart, and a sharp encounter was brought on. There is little doubt that Prince George of Saxony[16] could have won a decisive battle at that point, but Moltke by now had learned the lesson of Gravelotte, and held the Saxons back. He was not concerned at this moment to win battles; his single and all-embracing purpose was to win a war; and with his eyes firmly fixed on Sedan, he no longer doubted how and where the final curtain would fall. 'I decided', he later wrote, 'that a lesser success now would, with patience, yield a much more significant decision in the mousetrap into which I was directing Marshal MacMahon.'[17] And he was right.

Towards evening on the 29th, Failly fell back north-east towards the Meuse. He did not get far. On the 30th, he was intercepted again at Beaumont by the German IV Corps, and by mid-afternoon, after bitter fighting,[18] 5 Corps broke off the battle and at nightfall two divisions had struggled across the river at Mouzon, the third turning aside towards Villers. On that same day Douay's 7 Corps was attacked by the Bavarians at Raucourt and only with difficulty made its way back to the Meuse, part crossing to the right bank at Remilly, the remainder making for the shelter of Sedan. To Moltke, the pieces of his elaborate jigsaw were falling into place.

****

15   On the 27th, French cavalry had made a desultory reconnaissance to the east and had reported no German presence in Stenay. That afternoon, German cavalry from Stenay had scouted to the west and had reported the French to be in some strength near Buzancy. The moral needs no other emphasis.

16   Commander XII Corps.

17   Moltke: *op. cit.*

18   German casualties amounted to 3500 men; French, 4800, including more than 3000 prisoners of whom the greater proportion were unwounded.

By midnight on the 30th, with the Crown Prince of Saxony's army pressing hard on his heels on both banks of the river, and with the German Third Army swinging north across an increasingly narrow escape gap, Mac-Mahon was driven at last to take the decision which he had honourably but wrongly reversed at Reims on the 23rd and again on the 28th. His army was in disarray. Of his four army corps, 1 had reached Carignan on the railway line to Metz and 25 miles north-west of Montmédy; the other three — 5, 7 and 12 — were in an indescribable confusion, each with its divisions scattered on either bank of the Meuse between Mouzon and Remilly. The men were without food or sleep, and stragglers in their hundreds had fallen into German hands during the day.

The Emperor was at Carignan with MacMahon.[19] The Marshal, with an optimism that does more credit to his sang-froid than to his military virtue, decided to gather his scattered flock at Sedan and on the high ground which lies in a wide arc to the east of the town between Bazeilles and the Belgian border. Metz — with the Saxons in great strength across the Montmédy road — was no longer the absurd objective which it had always been; MacMahon, even at this hour, was still thinking of heroic adventures elsewhere. Early on the 31st he sent for Lebrun, commander of 12 Corps. 'We have had a difficult time,' he said, 'but the situation is not hopeless. At the most the German army before us cannot [sic] exceed in numbers sixty or seventy thousand men. If they attack us, so much the better; we shall be able, no doubt, to fling them into the Meuse.' With such ridiculous bravado, MacMahon, Duke of Magenta, marched his army (such as it now was) into Moltke's meticulous mousetrap.

With him went Napoleon, sick in mind and body. MacMahon urged him to follow his son and make good his escape through Mézières. But it was too late. The Emperor was brave to the bitter end. If the dynasty was to go down, then it was better that a Napoleon should die with his soldiers than offer an imperial hostage to the Paris mob. That — so his Empress and his miserable ministers had urged upon him throughout the August days — was his duty to France. It was not. But at this hour, and to his great credit, he conceived it so to be.

****

And what, at this critical moment, of Bazaine and the Army of the Rhine, closeted within the fortress guns of Metz?

In what was his last credible message to Paris and Châlons on the 19th, he had spoken of his intention 'within a couple of days' to break out towards a junction with MacMahon. He had vaguely suggested a direction

---

19 During the day the young Prince Imperial had — not before time — been put on a train bound for Avesnes and thence to Belgium while the so-called 'Ardennes' railway-line was still open. It is sufficient commentary on the state of play that this train, with the Prince's baggage, escort and suite, effectively delayed Vinoy's relieving column at Mézières for several hours.

based on Montmédy — even a wider swing by Sedan and Mézières — towards Châlons. It is inconceivable that anyone could have taken him seriously. MacMahon did not; but, as we have seen, MacMahon was compelled to subject his military judgment to political imperatives.

At his villa headquarters at Ban St Martin, Bazaine involved himself in a series of empty arguments with his corps commanders. There were those — Canrobert and Leboeuf — who counselled caution until word came from Châlons; Ladmirault, who felt that a quick break-out to the north was a sensible course; and Bourbaki, who proposed a silly excursion to Château-Salins in the south, whence, as he confessed, 'our next movement would be imprecise'. Old Soleille, the doom-ridden commander of artillery, announced — quite wrongly — that the available resources in Metz were sufficient only for a single day's battle; and Coffinières, the military governor of Metz, complained that if the army ventured forth, then the fortress could no longer defend itself, and must swiftly fall to the investing army of Frederick Charles. Bazaine listened; said nothing; and did nothing. It was now 23 August.

Two days later a delayed message was passed through the German lines. It spoke vaguely of a flank march by MacMahon towards Montmédy and, by implication, invited Bazaine to conform with this movement by making a sortie in strength from Metz in order to effect a junction of the two armies. Thus, with little enthusiasm, a substantial force was collected on the right bank of the Moselle, and on the 27th, the day before MacMahon's decision to press forward to the Meuse crossings rather than retire on Mézières, Bazaine set his army in motion towards Thionville. He did not get far. It was a day of torrential rain which soon dampened any spirit of adventure, and the leading column had barely reached the German outpost line at Grimont when the advance was halted; and after a short discussion with his corps commanders, Bazaine, deciding that discretion was the better part of valour, cancelled his orders, and withdrew his bedraggled troops — no strangers by now to *marches et contre-marches* — to their original cantonments within the fortress. There the semantic arguments were resumed.

On the 29th — quite possibly with the connivance of Frederick Charles — another much-delayed message reached Bazaine. This spoke of the arrival of 1 Corps (Ducrot) at Stenay on the Meuse and 7 Corps (Douay) farther upstream. 'These positions', so ran the message, 'should be reached on the 27th.' With hindsight, we know better. Bazaine, however — for the first and only time — threw caution to the winds, and on the afternoon of the 31st issued orders for 3, 4 and 6 Corps to assemble on the right bank, then at dawn on the following day to attempt a break-out in strength. The first objective was to be the village of Ste Barbe, scene of heavy fighting on the 14th (a date that now seemed an eternity away), and the advance was to be followed on an inner arc along the river by Frossard and Bourbaki. The French preparations were closely observed by Frederick Charles, and by the evening of the 31st part of IX Corps had been sent to reinforce the right bank, to be followed early next day by the rest of that corps and by X Corps.[20]

On the morning of 1 September there was a thick fog which made progress difficult and slow. The forenoon passed without serious incident and the French halted before Noisseville to cook their midday meal, the smoke of their fires neatly defining the disposition of their various corps. At 2.30 p.m., Bazaine ordered a general attack, but it was not until nearly two hours later that battle was joined by the opposing artillery. In the centre Leboeuf made slow progress, and by nightfall had occupied Noisseville and Servigny, a little to the north. But it had been a wasted day. A decisive break-out had not been achieved, and when the fog lifted on the morning of the 2nd the Germans had deployed a formidable ring of guns on the rising ground to the east. Battered into submission, Leboeuf and Ladmirault fell back under the guns of the fortress, and with little resistance the Germans reoccupied Noisseville. It had been a brief but bloody affair;[21] and Bazaine had had enough. Towards 2 p.m. he gave the order for a general withdrawal; and at almost the precise hour at which a defeated Emperor was driving out from Sedan to meet the King of Prussia at Frénois, the Army of the Rhine re-entered its prison in Metz.

The impending disaster at Sedan sealed Bazaine's doom (it may fairly be argued that his conduct on 16 and 18 August had already sealed MacMahon's, a verdict with which his judges at the Trianon would unanimously agree three years later). There were two more minor forays — on 28 September and 7 October — before, as we shall see, on 28 October, Metz capitulated, and the Army of the Rhine, 173,000 strong, joined the Army of Châlons in captivity.

****

Meanwhile the crisis of Sedan was at hand. On the morning of 1 September — even as Bazaine, with tragic irony, was at last making his move at Metz — the Army of Châlons was holding (or was, more precisely, locked into) a confined triangle centred upon Sedan and running from Floing and Illy in the north down to Bazeilles in the south and concentrated on the right bank of the Meuse. No attempt had been made to destroy any of the permanent bridges; and this even led to an element of black farce.

On the 31st a train had been sent from Sedan to Donchery a few miles to the west, bearing a company of engineers with instructions to blow the river bridge at that point. The engineers duly alighted at the station; but the driver, not caring greatly for the close attentions of German cavalry

20   When fighting ended on the 2nd the Germans had opposed to Bazaine 73,800 men and no fewer than 290 guns, while the French had deployed more than 130,000 men.

21   French losses were 3547, including four generals. German casualties were 2976.

patrols, decided to proceed upon his way to Mézières, carrying with him all the explosives and demolition equipment. No less seriously, he carried with him 800,000 rations which had been stored in the train at Sedan. Luck, that valuable ingredient of war, wore no French favours throughout that month of misfortune.

The events of that day were also to carry an unexpected footnote. On the 28th, a General de Wimpffen had visited Palikao in Paris and had suggested to him that the Emperor's presence was an embarrassment to MacMahon (as indeed it was), and that the Marshal's judgment was no longer to be trusted (which was more rightly a fair criticism of Palikao). 'Send me to the Army,' said Wimpffen. 'I shall impart the necessary boldness and decision.' Thus this egregious officer arrived upon a stricken stage to take command of Failly's shattered 5 Corps. He also brought with him a letter from the Council of Ministers authorizing him to assume supreme responsibility in the event of any accident befalling MacMahon. He would very shortly have cause to regret his arrogant intrusion.

****

By midnight on the 31st Moltke was ready.

> The Army of the Meuse advancing in the east and Third Army from the south were now directly in face of the French Army. Marshal MacMahon could scarcely have realized that the only chance of safety for his army, or even for part of it, lay in the immediate prosecution of his retreat on 1 September. It is true that the Crown Prince of Prussia ... would have promptly taken that movement in flank in the narrow space, little more than four miles wide, which was bounded on the north by the frontier. But on this day the French Army was not yet capable of undertaking a disciplined march involving fighting; it could only fight where it stood.[22]

The Army of the Meuse was ordered to attack the French positions with the object of holding MacMahon fast in and about Sedan, while Third Army, leaving only one corps on the left bank about Donchery, was to press forward to secure the loop in the river and, if possible, to cut the last remaining line of escape. Thus, if MacMahon sought to reach Mézières, he would have to fight his way to comparative safety. So it was that, after long marches over difficult country and in treacherous weather, brilliantly screened and sustained by the cavalry and by — a factor not often remarked upon — the most expert use of the engineers' bridging columns, 200,000 men and more than 500 guns converged upon the Army of Châlons

22 Moltke: *op. cit.*

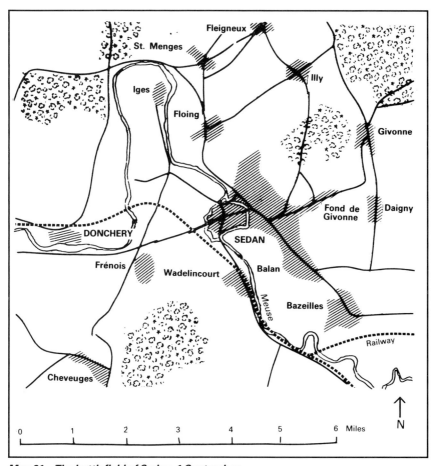

Map 21   The battlefield of Sedan, 1 September

at the precise point which Blumenthal had indicated to William Russell. The trap was sprung.

****

The battle of Sedan opened at 4 a.m. with an attack on Bazeilles by I Bavarian Corps, advancing across the river from the south, supported farther north by elements of XII Corps at La Moncelle and presently by the Guard Corps towards the high ground overlooking the Givonne stream. There followed an engagement of exceptional ferocity, very similar in pattern to the fighting around Rezonville on the 16th. Bazeilles was the key to Sedan in much the same measure that Bazaine had believed Rezonville to be the key to Metz. But now, on 1 September, the arithmetic of battle had changed dramatically. Most significantly, Sedan was the refuge of last resort; and the French — 12 Corps and parts of 1 Corps and 5 Corps — fought like tigers to hold Bazeilles. This has to be said again. In spite of everything, in spite of the miseries of retreat and defeat, ill led and ill fed, the Army of Châlons for the most part went down fighting with wonderful courage, literally in the last ditch. The reader may have good cause to wonder how it was that these men, from the first frontier reverses on 6 August, were so ready to die for so dubious a cause, despite so many disasters. There is no easy answer except the sure belief that, however humble their peasant origin, they sensed the ancient aphorism *Dulce et decorum est pro patria mori.*

****

At 6 a.m. MacMahon was seriously wounded by a shell-splinter near Bazeilles. He had named Ducrot (by no means the next senior general) as his successor; and Ducrot's immediate action was to order a general retreat and to assemble the whole army on the high ground around Illy to the north of Sedan, covered by Lartigue's division to the east, while 12 Corps counter-attacked the Saxons and Bavarians across the Givonne to gain some precious time. Whether such a retreat would have salvaged, even in part, so compromised a cause is a matter for speculation; for at 8.30 a.m. General Wimpffen (in fact Ducrot's senior by several years) produced Palikao's letter, authorizing him to assume command in MacMahon's stead. Ducrot was later to claim that he had strongly resisted the order to hand over to a man with no knowledge of the true circumstances and with a reputation for intemperate decisions. This is unlikely. Ducrot was already unfairly saddled, with the French passion for parading scapegoats, with responsibility for the early reverses at Wissembourg and Wörth in the early August days, and he was well aware of the impending disaster. It is more certain that he was content to allow the flamboyant Wimpffen to reap what he was now about to sow, and with it the personal stigma of defeat. Thus, within three critical hours, the chief command of the Army of Châlons passed through three hands. It is a bleak comment on the cavalier concept of command which had guided the French conduct of the war from the very outset.Throughout August (admittedly a month of hard-won victories) only one senior German leader — Steinmetz — was relieved of his command; and that with abundantly good reason. During the same period — casualties apart — the French replaced ten general officers. And little difference did it make.

Wimpffen's immediate decision was to countermand (by letter, no less) Ducrot's order for a break-out to Mézières on the St Menges road which ran westward between the river loop and the frontier. Instead, he decided on an absurdly dramatic attempt to resume the eastward march on Montmédy through Carignan to effect the junction with Bazaine which he had so airily undertaken in a remote office in Paris. Ducrot (1 Corps) warned him. Douay (7 Corps) warned him. More insistently, since he was already locked in battle, Lebrun (12 Corps) warned him. But Wimpffen brushed his generals aside, accusing them now of lack of moral fibre, and later of cowardice, complicity and disobedience. By the early hours of 1 September the paladins were scarcely on speaking terms; and the soldiers of the Army of Châlons, not knowing and little caring, were duly led, by wilful leaders, to the slaughter.

****

About 6 a.m. the Emperor had ridden out from Sedan as the thick morning mist began to clear. Even at this early hour he had a sure premonition that, before the day was out, the Army of Châlons would no longer exist as a fighting force. Since 12 August he had ceased to exercise any military authority over his generals, or any political influence over the Regency Council in Paris. There can be few historical parallels to this picture of a broken man, stripped within four decisive weeks — indeed, on a single day — of the last vestiges of power and of the final pretensions to a throne which he had usurped. Of few other men is Tacitus' famous aphorism more true: *Capax imperii, nisi imperasset.* Now he seems to have decided to seek a soldier's death rather than face the fury of the Paris mob.

As he made his way to Bazeilles, accompanied by his large imperial suite, he met the wounded MacMahon to whom he expressed his kindly sympathy. From Bazeilles, he rode under heavy fire to La Moncelle and thence — bearer of a charmed life, if little else — to Balan, where he met Ducrot and expressed his mild surprise at the retrograde movement of 12 Corps which he had so recently seen in good heart and holding very strong positions above the Meuse. 'The enemy', said Ducrot, with the silly bravado shared by French generals and the French language, 'is only amusing us at Bazeilles; the real battle will be fought at Illy. I am therefore withdrawing the troops in good order with a view to concentrating the army.' At this hour, neither man knew that the fate of the Army of Châlons had passed into the hands of General Wimpffen. And towards 11 a.m. the Emperor returned to his headquarters in the Sub-Préfecture in Sedan. He would not leave that drab little building until the following morning, and then as the defeated Emperor of a derelict Empire.

****

When Wimpffen countermanded Ducrot's order to retire on Mézières, the Army of Châlons was disposed thus in an inverted triangle measuring some 4½ miles at its longest point and 3 miles at its base.[23] The apex of this

23 *See* Map 21.

triangle running from Bazeilles to Daigny and thence to Fond de Givonne was occupied by 12 Corps, which included two Marine brigades of the first quality; the north-eastern corner from Givonne to Illy and including the Bois de la Garenne was held by 1 Corps; the high ground extending to the west and including the village of Floing was occupied by 7 Corps; and the debris of 5 Corps which had been driven in disorder across the river after the battle of Beaumont was clustered in and around Sedan itself. This triangle was bounded on the west by the Meuse and on the east by the small Givonne stream. It was a neat and tidily defined position. It was also a death-trap.

Wimpffen's decision to resume the attempted break-out towards Carignan resulted in a now familiar confusion on the French side as divisions already committed to Ducrot's intended march on Mézières were summoned back by his successor to the Bazeilles sector. In striking contrast, the two German armies were set in motion with expert precision between midnight and first light. Thus as the morning mist cleared, and brilliant sunshine illuminated the battlefield, the King, his staff, and a glittering company of royal personages assembled on an eminence near Frénois to watch the unfolding drama, each successive act clearly visible as if upon a massive stage. With a fine sense of theatre, Moltke had provided his august audience with the best seats in the house.

Sedan lies in a kind of bowl formed by the valleys of the Meuse and the Givonne; and by noon, true to precedent and practice, the rim of this bowl was crowned, as at Wörth, as at Flavigny, as in the last hours at St Privat, with a formidable ring of artillery — 426 guns in 71 batteries; and true to precedent and practice, the guns had led the way 'to beat a path' for the infantry. The infantry was deployed thus.

On the right the Army of the Meuse, reading from Bazeilles to Givonne: I Bavarian Corps, XII Corps, Guard Corps. On the left, crossing the river at Donchery during the hours of darkness, XI Corps of Third Army followed by V Corps and directed on St Menges and Fleigneux, thus cutting the sole remaining escape-road to Mézières; while the Württemberg Division was held in reserve about Donchery, watching out to the west against the unlikely intervention of Vinoy's hastily despatched 13 Corps. In general reserve, like a stopper in a bottleneck, stood IV Corps and II Bavarian Corps between Frénois and Wadelincourt, and thence along the river to Remilly. Thus Moltke opposed seven army corps and a massive artillery to four (effectively only three) French army corps. The German cavalry waited in the wings. Not so the French, whose horsemen were to win great glory — and the unstinted admiration of the enemy — on a day of humiliating defeat for the Army of Châlons.

****

The battle of Sedan was a modern mirror-image of classical Cannae. It followed two phases, on either side of noon. Moltke's plan — conceived as early as 27 August, when MacMahon's intention to march on Montmédy finally became clear — was brilliantly executed: first, the deployment of his artillery around the stage-setting of his choice to hold the enemy fast;[24] then as the day progressed, two great 'arms' of infantry swung upward and inward so that at 1 p.m. the Guard Corps from Givonne and V Corps from St Menges joined hands at Fleigneux and there closed the circle around a demoralized enemy.

The early fighting was concentrated in the southern apex of the 'triangle' where the two sides were in closest touch. Here Lebrun's 12 Corps was attacked by I Bavarian Corps in accordance with Moltke's prime object of holding the enemy fast on this flank.

MacMahon has recorded that at the time he was wounded near Bazeilles at 6 a.m. he had not yet decided on his course of action. This is hindsight with a vengeance. It is inconceivable that he was still contemplating the option of another break-out towards Bazaine, since on the 31st he had withdrawn all the scattered formations of his army from the left bank of the Givonne into what could only be a purely defensive perimeter. He was well aware of the strength and direction of the German advance across the Meuse below Stenay. He was equally aware of Third Army's activity to the west around Donchery. His last chance to bring the Army of Châlons to any kind of safe haven had been forfeited five days previously. Now, wound or no wound, there is no possible doubt that he had come to terms with an honourable defeat at Sedan.

Not so Ducrot, who learned of his brief — and, it may be surmised, unwelcome — assumption of command at the headquarters of 1 Corps near Illy shortly after 7 a.m. Ducrot, an able and underrated soldier, was not concerned with heroics at such a moment. The road to Mézières by St Menges[25] was still open, although the time factor was already critical as the German Third Army hurried forward across difficult country from Donchery. Thus Ducrot ordered 7 Corps to set out from its position around Floing, followed in echelon by 1 Corps and 12 Corps and covered, so far as it was possible, by 5 Corps and the garrison guns of Sedan. 'It is sometimes necessary in war', he rightly said at Bazaine's trial,[26] 'to sacrifice a fortress to save an army.' So simple a statement of fact must have caused Bazaine to wince. But his good intentions were very shortly to be brought to a halt; for at 9.30 a.m. Wimpffen arrived at the gallop at Illy,

24 This iron ring would have failed in its object without the exceptional expertise of the German administrative staff in maintaining an adequate supply of ammunition across two rivers and 100 miles, over bad roads and in worse weather. During 1 September the artillery of the Guard Corps alone fired 6003 rounds.

25 This was the new road which was shown on German, but not on French, maps.

26 *Procès Bazaine.*

brandishing Palikao's letter of authority. There was a furious argument, variously recorded by both parties. On only one issue both would later agree. 'I will not have a movement upon Mézières,' exclaimed Wimpffen. 'If the Army is to retreat, it shall be on Carignan, and not on Mézières.' Ducrot had been decisively up-staged.

And the Emperor? Wandering between his warring generals, he could still have asserted his imperial will. But by now he had become a pale shadow, flitting among his sullen soldiers, sick in heart and sick in body, seeking, as he was shortly to tell the King of Prussia, a soldier's death. But death could not find him, and he went back, even as the German shells began to fall on Sedan, determined to end the slaughter. It was to take him five more hours of bloodshed before the imperial will prevailed.

****

The morning hours of the battle went thus, against a background of confusion on the French side as Wimpffen tried to redeploy the divisions which Ducrot had earlier directed on the road to Mézières.

There was bitter fighting in Bazeilles, and it was not until 11 a.m., when a turning movement by 23rd (Saxon) Division on the Bavarians' right carried the village of La Moncelle, that Lebrun was forced to withdraw 12 Corps and elements of 1 Corps and 5 Corps (which Wimpffen had summoned to his aid) to a shortened line running along a ridge between Balan and the deep cutting of Fond de Givonne.

Farther north Ducrot had succeeded in pushing Lartigue's division across the stream at Daigny, but the attack was unsupported and was quickly halted by a strong line of artillery and by a timely counter-attack by 24th Division. Fearful of the threat to his left flank and still smarting from Wimpffen's earlier rebuff, Ducrot withdrew to the comparative safety of the Bois de Garenne.

That threat was not long in coming. During the night the Guard Corps had reached Carignan (so much for Wimpffen's boast to the Emperor that he would 'tumble the Bavarians and the Saxons into the river' and resume the march on Montmédy which MacMahon had so rudely interrupted). Here the Crown Prince of Saxony ordered Prince Augustus to march at dawn, the artillery leading, followed by 1st Guard Division.[27] This column, taking the road by Villers Cernay, reached the Givonne valley before 10 a.m. Here the artillery deployed on the high ground to the east of the stream, and an hour later Givonne itself was in German hands. 'There was', an eye-witness reports, 'an air of jubilation. The men cooked a meal, while the bands played as if to celebrate a victorious occasion.' A mile away no bands played, while the French, clustered closely around Illy and

27   Two weeks had been enough for the replacement of most of the savage losses which this division had suffered at St Privat.

the Bois de Garenne, awaited the next onslaught. Already, as the tally of prisoners mounted, French morale, astonishingly resilient in the face of overwhelming enemy attacks, began to break.[28]

Thus, towards noon, Moltke's plan was working like a charm. Here, on the right, despite a stubborn resistance which he had not expected and which drew from him a professional's admiration, twenty-six batteries were in action astride the Givonne, and Ducrot's hard-pressed men were held in a vice as the infantry of the Guard, duly refreshed, began to work their way up the valley towards Fleigneux.

Meanwhile on the western flank the two corps of Third Army (XI and V) were marching round the river loop. As we have seen, the objective of these columns was the new road which led to Mézières, and the villages of St Menges and Fleigneux, the capture of which would seal the trap and prevent any last-ditch attempt of the enemy to break out to the north and find a sort of sanctuary across the Belgian border. Beyond Donchery the country was thickly wooded and ill served with roads, and therefore, wise to the need to keep both encircling wings in close conformity, Moltke had ordered a night march, with XI Corps next to the river and V Corps directed on the village of Vrigne. Few armies would have attempted such a manœuvre, and inevitably there was some delay and disorder.

Yet it is impossible to resist a comparison between the German and the French military mentality; and to reflect on what might have been the outcome of this war if on the night of 15/16 August, and across a plateau with good roads and no obstructions, Bazaine had ordered a night-march on Verdun long before Frederick Charles could have interposed anything more substantial than Rheinbaben's squadrons. It is even possible to wonder whether a physically fit Napoleon might not have had the measure of his mediocre Marshals.

****

Towards 10 a.m., the artillery of XI Corps emerged from the Vrigne defile, and at once ten batteries were deployed on the high ground to the north of Floing, while behind them the infantry of 21st Division pressed round the upper loop of the river and debouched upon St Menges.

Douay found himself caught between two highly incompatible fires; those of Moltke and of his own new chief, Wimpffen. Two hours earlier, in accordance with Ducrot's orders, he had started to withdraw 7 Corps on the road to Mézières, and already Conseil-Dumesnil's division was on its dangerous way from Floing. He did not get far before Wimpffen's order reached him to face about to cover the proposed sortie from Bazeilles.

Douay was later to insist that Ducrot's decision to retreat on Mézières

---

28 By 4 p.m., when French resistance had finally crumbled, the total of French prisoners taken in the Bois de Garenne numbered 110 officers and more than 8500 men.

was the correct one; indeed, that MacMahon should have set this movement in train on the previous day when the escape route to the west was still open, and before the German Third Army had started to cross the river at Donchery. Certainly one, or perhaps two, corps of the Army of Châlons might thus have reached a precarious safety, and have even effected a junction with Vinoy's 13 Corps, already on its way from Paris. But such a manœuvre, given Moltke's moral and physical superiority, would only have resulted in defeat in detail, rather than in the comprehensive disaster at Sedan itself. Now on the morning of 1 September, as the German artillery occupied the dominating ground beyond the river loop in great and growing strength, Wimpffen's reckless decision had made Douay's purpose academic. 7 Corps, halted as it were in mid-stride, found itself stranded in the open country around Floing.

Behind the protective screen of guns, handled on the German side with the same boldness which had been so striking — and indeed decisive — a feature of each successive engagement since the first battles of the campaign, the infantry of XI Corps, followed by that of V Corps, headed eastward, its objective the 'linch-pin' village of Fleigneux. It found only minor opposition in St Menges (Douay's original vanguard on his retreat to Mézières, and now become a forlorn outpost as 7 Corps was summoned back to the battlefield). The village was swiftly captured, and with it the first haul of prisoners, which was to grow at first in hundreds and then, as the day wore on, in thousands.

By 11 a.m., while V Corps moved on Fleigneux, the *87th Regiment* of XI Corps had turned aside to attack Floing. The ground on this northern part of the battlefield closely resembles the Gravelotte plateau — open, undulating fields falling away to a shallow depression through which runs a small stream, and dominated to the north-east by a commanding feature, the Calvaire d'Illy, which was the tenuous point of contact between Douay and Ducrot. Below the Calvaire and extending south almost as far as the outworks of Sedan is the extensive Bois de Garenne. It was on these bare uplands that 7 Corps — or such part of it as Wimpffen had not already ordered away to the Bazeilles sector — stood facing the Crown Prince's Third Army as its columns, not without difficulty, deployed beyond the river loop. The French artillery, caught in the open and critically short of ammunition, stood no chance against the cross-fire of German guns from east and west, as more and more batteries ringed the great amphitheatre. The French infantry could only do and die. There remained, as we shall see in tragic splendour, the French cavalry.

Shortly after 11 a.m. a battalion of the *87th* struck in on Floing. It gained a foothold in the village, but within minutes a vigorous French counter-attack drove it out. Locked together in close combat, from street to street and house to house, so intermingled that neither artillery could intervene, the fight for Floing went its bloody way. The French *fantassins* clung, with a courage beyond all comprehension, to the cliff's edge, as Canrobert's men had, only two short weeks before, shamed Bazaine and died in the last ditch at St Privat.

When, three years later, the assorted marshals and generals of France met to pass judgment upon the chosen scapegoat for the surrender of Metz, the circumstances of Sedan — a subject equally ripe for examination — rated precisely *two* references in all those steepling column-inches of recrimination. The soldiers of France, whose evidence would have gravely embarrassed Bazaine's judges, and not least the new President of the Republic, MacMahon, were not invited to speak. Their mute testimony is recorded in the sombre statistics of dead, wounded, and captive. On their patience in adversity and on their bravery in battle, the Trianon tribunal is shamefully silent.

The battle for Floing lasted until the early afternoon. Three times the infantry of XI Corps, supported by brigades from V Corps, stormed the battered village. Three times Douay's men, Zouaves and Turcos, threw them back at bayonet point. Under a burnished sky, a great cloud of dust and smoke concealed from the royal audience on the hill at Frénois this bitter conflict.

It was nearly 1 p.m. when Douay, remote from Wimpffen and unaware of his decision to break out of the Bazeilles trap towards Carignan, and wise only to the pressure on Ducrot around Illy and the Bois de Garenne, called his men back. 'I believed', he wrote later, 'that if I stayed at Floing, I would not easily bring my greatly disordered divisions back to the Sedan fortress.' And thus, unknown to Wimpffen, 7 Corps retired, in remarkably good heart, their retreat covered by Liébert's division on the gentle ridge which runs above Sedan at Cazal. And as the dust and smoke cleared from Floing, the watchers at Frénois looked down upon a tremendous passage of arms.

****

The cavalry of France was numerous,[29] elegant and élitist, rooted in the old Napoleonic tradition and in the romantic concept of *l'arme blanche*. But in training and temperament it was totally unfitted for modern warfare, and above all, for a war of movement. During the wasted years no single study has been made of the tactical employment of the arm. No senior commander, except the discredited Trochu, had applied the lessons of the American Civil War; more seriously, no one had thought fit to reflect upon the German example. Thus it was that, from the first frontier engagements, the role of the mounted arm on both sides was sharply contrasted.

After a hesitant start, the German cavalry was used with the utmost

29 At the outbreak of war, unlike the infantry, the mounted arm was already formed into divisions; eight attached to the separate Army Corps, and an additional three designated as 'Reserve'.

boldness, scouting far ahead of the infantry masses behind it and screening the axis and direction of Moltke's master-plan. This use of cavalry in its *primary* role was most strikingly demonstrated on the 'day of battle' on 16 August and on a much greater scale during the pursuit of MacMahon to the gates of Sedan. On the one occasion — 18 August — when inexplicably the German cavalry was not used in its role of 'watch and ward' as the massed ranks advanced across the Gravelotte plateau, the result came very close to disaster. Only three times[30] — all of them at critical moments on the 16th — was the mounted arm used in shock action, and then only to save a seemingly lost cause.

On the French side there was no such purpose. Indeed, the mass of horsemen aimlessly grouped behind the divisions of infantry were more an embarrassment than a source of succour. 'Reconnaissance', Bazaine had said on the critical morning of the 16th, 'will be carried out as usual.' It should have been carried out, day by day and hour by hour, from the very moment when the decision was taken to retire on Verdun, and when it was vital for Bazaine to know the intentions and whereabouts of Frederick Charles and the German Second Army. Bazaine, as we know, haunted by fears for his left flank, did nothing to exorcize that ghost, not even to the extent of sending a small search-party to investigate the situation in Gorze. And thus it was that Forton's idle officers had been surprised at breakfast by an uninvited guest.

When Bazaine used the words '*comme d'habitude*', he was merely reflecting the long-outdated French canon that the true function of cavalry was the glorious spectacle of shock action. It was a dream that died hard — and not in France alone, for it recalls the comment of a Viennese cynic as late as August 1914: 'We had the prettiest cavalry in the world. What a pity to have wasted it on a war!' So it had been during this other August. On the 6th the regiments of Bonnemain and Michel had dashed themselves to pieces on the German needle-guns at Froeschwiller and Morsbronn; on the morning of the 16th, Bazaine had, to use his own word, 'sacrificed' a regiment of the Guard Cavalry at Rezonville, and as evening drew on the massed squadrons of Legrand and Barail had joined issue with Rheinbaben in the vast and inconclusive encounter at Mars-la-Tour. It is therefore not inappropriate that the French cavalry should have looked to its traditional laurels as the Germans closed in on Sedan.

****

During the evening of 31 August the scattered French cavalry brigades had been assembled under the command of General Margueritte around Illy

---

30   Bredow's charge; the intervention of the Guard Dragoons; and the great cavalry clash at Mars-la-Tour. The reckless waste of the *4th Uhlans* on the 18th lies solely at the door of Steinmetz.

and under cover in the Bois de Garenne. Margueritte, a brigadier in Barail's reserve division of the Army of the Rhine, had escorted the Emperor from Étain to Verdun on the morning of the 16th with two regiments of Chasseurs d'Afrique.[31] Now he found himself virtually a corps commander with ten assorted regiments and, more significantly, without instructions.

Early in the forenoon, from a vantage-point on the Calvaire d'Illy, he watched the German artillery pounding the open fields to the east of Floing, while farther west the infantry of XI Corps deployed against the village. It was not unlike the situation which had confronted Alvensleben at Vionville, and as with Bredow, so now it was to General Galliffet that Margueritte turned. Galliffet with the three regiments of Chasseurs and two squadrons of Lancers stormed down the slope and fell upon the enemy. But this time there was no surprise. The German infantry protecting their own gun-line watched and waited with impeccable discipline, and then at close range delivered a murderous volley of rifle-fire which threw the charging squadrons into utter confusion. Not one French horseman reached the batteries beyond; and after a short, confused contest at close quarters, the remnants of Galliffet's men galloped back towards the Bois de Garenne. It had been a gallant enterprise. It had achieved nothing other than to underline the lessons of Froeschwiller and Rezonville. But the French cavalry had not yet had its last and most memorable say.

A little after 1 p.m. Floing was in German hands and Liébert's division of 7 Corps had been steadily driven back to the last line of defence above Sedan. Illy had been captured, and as the broken infantry of 1 Corps streamed away towards the fortress, Ducrot turned for the last time to the cavalry. Let Moltke, watching from the hill at Frénois, take up the story:

> Liébert's division, attacked on both flanks and also heavily shelled, at last had its power of resistance undermined; and the reserves of 7 Corps having already been called off to other parts of the battlefield, the French cavalry once more devotedly struck in to maintain the fight.
>
> General Margueritte, with all his remaining regiments, charged to the rescue out of the Bois de Garenne. Almost at the outset he fell mortally wounded, and General Galliffet took his place. The advance was over very treacherous ground and even before the charge was delivered the cohesion of the ranks was broken by the heavy flanking fire of the Prussian batteries. Still, with thinned ranks but with unflinching resolution, the individual squadrons charged on the troops of 43rd Brigade ... and also on the reinforcements hurrying

---

31 The third regiment had remained with Barail, and the fourth, after an adventurous journey from Algiers, had unexpectedly arrived at Mouzon on 30 August.

from Fleigneux. The first line of the former was pierced at several points, and a band of these brave troopers dashed from Cazal through the intervals of eight guns blazing into them ... Other detachments cut their way through the infantry as far as the narrow pass of St Albert, where they were met by debouching battalions. Others again entered Floing only to succumb to the *5th Jägers*, who had to form front back to back. These attacks were repeated by the French again and again in the shape of detached fights, and the murderous turmoil lasted for half an hour. The volleys of the German infantry, delivered at short range, strewed the whole field with dead and wounded horsemen ... and scarcely more than half of these brave troops returned to the protection of the Bois de Garenne ... But this magnificent sacrifice and glorious effort of the French cavalry could not change the fate of the day.[32]

****

It was 1 p.m. when the second and final phase of the battle may be said to have begun. By this hour the two German armies had joined hands at Fleigneux, more than a hundred batteries were in action, while to the north of Sedan the remaining elements of the French 1 and 7 Corps still capable of organized resistance were crowded into an area less than two miles square around Cazal and the Bois de Garenne. Already men were streaming back into the fortress or surrendering in hundreds as the German guns pounded them relentlessly. It was in such circumstances that Wimpffen decided on a *grand geste*.

At 1.15 p.m. he wrote as follows to the Emperor:

I am determined to break through the enemy position facing Generals Lebrun and Ducrot rather than be made prisoner in Sedan. Let your Majesty place himself in the midst of his troops. They will hold themselves in honour bound to force a passage for you.[33]

To this impertinent and futile proposition Napoleon did not reply. Since his return to Sedan during the morning he had at last brought himself to accept the inevitability of defeat. From here on he behaved like an Emperor and not as a military embarrassment to his incompetent marshals and generals. The man who had been so shocked by the slaughter at Solferino eleven years ago now sought only to stop the slaughter at Sedan.

Napoleon's silence was later to be branded by Wimpffen as cowardice and, by inference, his own impulsive decision to lead one last sortie as

32 Moltke: *op. cit.*

33 De Wimpffen: *Sedan*.

'honourable'. The imputation, coming from a man who had deliberately humiliated his Emperor, is as unworthy as it is untrue. Of Napoleon's many defects — early arrogance, political naivety, and finally moral collapse — a lack of physical courage was not one; and Wimpffen's honour rooted in dishonour stood.

Now, even while Margueritte's squadrons were being broken on the fields around Floing, Wimpffen sent a message to Douay, whose one remaining division (Liébert's) was already falling back from Cazal to Sedan, instructing him to cover what he curiously called 'his renewed retreat on Carignan'. He then went into Sedan and collected such troops as he could muster from the rack and ruin of the fortress — the number is given variously as 2000 and 6000 — and led them in a forlorn and final attack on Balan. There the Bavarians, taken by surprise, were briefly driven out of the village. But the Germans were quick to recover, and their artillery around La Moncelle laid down an impenetrable curtain of fire. 'We had not gone a kilometre before the column broke and took refuge in the nearest houses. Looking back, de Wimpffen said: "I see we are not followed and there is nothing more to do. Order the troops to retreat on Sedan." '[34] The battle had at length come to an end. The price remained to be paid.

****

It was 2.15 p.m. In the Sub-Préfecture in Sedan the Emperor, surrounded by the debris of a shattered army, ordered the white flag to be run up. There is no record of the officer who carried out this instruction, but it may be assumed, in the light of subsequent events, to have been Napoleon's personal aide, General Reille. And it is a measure of the near-mutinous atmosphere that Wimpffen's chief of staff, General Faure, personally ascended the citadel and cut down the offending symbol of surrender.

An hour later, when Wimpffen's sortie had ended in predictable failure, Lebrun went to see Napoleon. 'Why does this useless struggle continue?' said the Emperor. 'An hour ago I directed the white flag to be raised in order to demand an armistice.'[35] It was his first expression of imperial will since he had taken leave of Bazaine at Gravelotte on the morning of 16 August.

Lebrun, wiser than Wimpffen and a great deal more loyal, explained that there was a protocol in these matters; it was necessary that a *parlementaire* bearing a letter signed by the commander-in-chief should be sent to his opposite number. Lebrun undertook to seek Wimpffen's

---

34 Lebrun: *Guerre de 1870: Bazeilles−Sedan.*

35 Lebrun: *Ibid.*

signature to such a document, but the latter angrily refused. 'I will not have a capitulation,' was his reply. 'I shall continue fighting.'[36]

By 4 p.m. the situation in Sedan was such that even Wimpffen, sulking in the Croix d'Or inn, could no longer pretend that further resistance, let alone Ducrot's absurd suggestion of a sortie in strength after dark, was possible. There was a semantic argument among the French corps commanders, including the disgraced Failly, while the Emperor waited impatiently for a volunteer to sign the formal letter. Much play was made of the distinction between the words 'armistice' and 'capitulation'. All eyes were turned on Wimpffen (it does not seem to have occurred to anyone to require the signature of the wounded MacMahon in his nearby hospital bed); and Wimpffen's reply, which tells us all we need to know about the man, was to submit his resignation. But the Emperor, driven at last by despair to assert his authority, curtly rejected this unsoldierly offer; and on his orders the white flag was raised again. This time there was no attempt to lower it.

****

At 4.30 p.m., when it was plain that the enemy was ready to parley, the order to cease fire was given by Royal headquarters and an emissary, Colonel Bronsart, was sent to summon the surrender of Sedan. On arrival at the southern gate at Torcy, he was conducted to the Sub-Préfecture 'where', in the words of the official German account, 'he found himself face to face with the Emperor Napoleon whose presence in Sedan had been unknown until that moment'. Armed with this unexpected and — as it was to prove — disconcerting intelligence, but with no effective reply, Bronsart returned to Frénois. The answer, however, soon followed him. Shortly after 5 p.m., General Reille rode out from the fortress, the bearer of a celebrated letter which he handed to the King in person on that eminence of ground whence the royal entourage had watched the dramatic events of the day unfold.

The letter, a personal communication from the Emperor, read thus:

> Monsieur mon Frère,
>   N'ayant pu mourir au milieu de mes troupes, il ne me reste qu'à remettre mon épée entre les mains de Votre Majesté.
>   Je suis de Votre Majesté
>   le bon Frère,
>   Napoléon

This sad, if slightly theatrical, document, with its political overtone, occasioned a quick conference at Frénois. Was the Emperor's letter an act

---

36 Lebrun: *Ibid.* (but not mentioned in de Wimpffen, *Sedan*).

Facsimile of the Emperor's letter of surrender

of personal surrender or was it an unconditional capitulation of both fortress and French Army? Moltke and — more particularly — Bismarck were taking no chances. And thus it was that Reille returned to Sedan carrying the following reply from the King, while Moltke issued a general order suspending all further hostilities until the following morning:

Regretting the circumstances in which we meet, I accept Your Majesty's sword, and beg that you will be good enough to name an officer furnished with full powers to treat for the capitulation of the

319

Army which has fought so bravely *under your orders*.[37] On my side I have designated General von Moltke for that purpose.

****

Meanwhile there had been bitter recriminations at the Sub-Préfecture.[38] Wimpffen accused Ducrot of gross disobedience, and blamed him for his cowardice in ordering the retreat on Mézières. Ducrot threw Wimpffen's offer of resignation in his face. 'You took [the command] this morning when you thought it would bring you honour and profit. You cannot lay it down now. You alone must bear [*endosser*] the shame of the capitulation.' '*Le Général Ducrot était très exalté*' was Wimpffen's subsequent comment. It seems not to have occurred to either man that between them they had gravely compromised, if not betrayed, the wretched men entrusted to their command.

Throughout this unsavoury exchange of insults, the Emperor sat impassively. And when Reille returned with the King's reply, and it was clear that — in MacMahon's fortuitous absence — only Wimpffen would be an acceptable plenipotentiary to negotiate the surrender, Napoleon could have been permitted a wan smile. At this climax of disaster, he had achieved a tiny triumph. He had lost a war; but in the process he had up-staged, by his dignity in defeat, the politicians who had used him so ill, and the generals who had so abused him.

****

At 7 p.m. Wimpffen made his way to Donchery with a small group of officers. He went prepared to play poker with two very professional adversaries. But it is an axiom of the gambler's art that a bankrupt bluffs at his peril. By midnight Wimpffen's bluff had been called; by Moltke, the soldier, who led him to a map — a *German* map — which showed, if nothing else, that Ducrot had been right and Wimpffen recklessly wrong; and by Bismarck, the diplomat, who gave him a brutal lesson in the history of Franco-German relations. 'He gave way at last,' recorded Bismarck, savouring the moment, 'when I showed him that it could do no harm.'

The 'harm' was simply stated. By 9 a.m. — later extended to 10 a.m. — on 2 September, the Army of Châlons and the fortress of Sedan were to be surrendered, lock, stock and barrel. The sole act of clemency — one that was rightly to cause profound indignation — was that officers who were prepared to give a written undertaking to take no further part in the war would be granted parole and the right to retain their arms and personal effects. In all the poker play — and this was to cause Bismarck, in

37 Author's italics.

38 *See*: Ducrot and de Wimpffen, *op. cit.* (*passim*).

particular, dear — there was one curious omission. In the 'Protocol of Capitulation' there is no single mention, in all the six Articles, of the lonely joker in the pack. Thus, when the Emperor left Sedan to meet King William early on the morning of 2 September he did not know, or even consider, that he was driving into captivity; and that he would not see his generals or his soldiers again. It was a foolish German act, and one that does little credit to Bismarck's political judgment. Clever card-players do not throw the joker away; and an angry Moltke began to distance himself that very night from the ambitious Chancellor. When a meeting was held at 2 a.m. at which it was decided by a posse of princes that the castle of Wilhelmshöhe near Kassel in Germany would be a suitably elegant residence for a retired Emperor,[39] Moltke excused himself and retired to bed. He had secured his mousetrap; but he had lost his mouse.

****

At 5 a.m. on 2 September, Napoleon drove out of Sedan on the road to Donchery. His purpose, as he told Wimpffen, was to seek a personal meeting with the King in the innocent belief that, at the royal and imperial level, he might obtain less onerous and humiliating terms. But the man who had so gravely misjudged his enemy when he had acquiesced in embarking on a mad military adventure had still to learn his lesson. Moltke and Bismarck both had scores to settle with France on Germany's behalf. They were the chosen instruments of their King, and there would be no meeting of monarchs until the soldiers had had their say, and the articles of surrender had been signed.

Alerted early, Bismarck set out from Donchery and met the Emperor near Frénois. Together they entered a nearby weaver's cottage, and there for an hour they talked of many things, the political future of the dynasty, the origins of the war. Napoleon, Bismarck recorded, insisted that 'he had been driven into it by the pressure of public opinion'. 'I then asked,' Bismarck added, 'if that were true, who now had authority to make peace?' 'The government in Paris', replied the Emperor in an unconscious gesture of abdication. And when he went on to demand that nothing should be decided until he had seen the King, Bismarck answered that on military matters Moltke alone could speak; and Moltke had spoken. There was nothing left to discuss.

****

39 When, after the capitulation of Metz on 28 October, three Marshals — Bazaine, Canrobert and Leboeuf — joined Napoleon at Wilhelmshöhe, Bismarck cheerfully observed that they would provide a distinguished quartet at whist.

While an anonymous weaver was playing humble host to this distinguished company, the French generals were conducting a pathetic post-mortem in the Sub-Préfecture. At 9 a.m. a Captain von Zingler arrived demanding a decision, and reminding Wimpffen that only one hour remained before Moltke's deadline. Wimpffen protested that he wished first to know the outcome of the Emperor's meeting with the King. 'There has been no meeting,' replied Zingler. 'Nor will it in any way affect the military operations, which can only be determined by the two chief commanders.' And it was left to Lebrun to remark that it was useless to argue with a Captain charged with stating a simple fact. On this note Wimpffen agreed to accompany Zingler on his return to Royal Headquarters.

The last rites were performed at 11 a.m. at the Château de Bellevue near Frénois, whither Bismarck had conducted the Emperor. There, in the presence of Moltke, Wimpffen put his signature to the instrument of surrender. Then, and only then, was he permitted to take his leave of Napoleon. Then, and only then, did the King of Prussia receive the Emperor of the French and, with royal courtesy, commiserate with him on the melancholy fate which, within 30 days, had laid low the armies of France. The two men went their separate ways.

During the battle of Sedan the Germans had lost in killed and wounded 8924 officers and men. French casualties numbered 3220 killed, 14,811 wounded and more than 21,000 captured in the field. The tally of prisoners added to these under the terms of capitulation was of the order of 83,000, and on the following morning these men stacked their arms in Sedan and were marched out into temporary camps within the Iges peninsula to the north-west of the fortress. It had been a famous victory, and a dramatic defeat.

****

Early on 3 September, Napoleon left Bellevue on his way to Wilhelms-höhe. It was a day of thundery rain, very different from that morning of brilliant sunshine when he had set out from Gravelotte. As his carriage journeyed across the border to Bouillon where he took train to Germany, he may have had time to reflect upon his last instruction to Bazaine. 'Put yourself with all haste on the road to Verdun; and above all, no more reverses.' It had always been a pious hope. A handful of days had made of it a mockery and an unparalleled military disaster.

Before he set out into captivity and exile, the Emperor had asked permission to communicate with Bazaine in Metz. His request was refused.

He then asked if he might send a message to the Empress in Paris, and to this his captors agreed. So it was that at 4 p.m. the Regency Council received the following telegram — quaintly enough in cipher.

'L'Armée est défaite et captive. Moi-même je suis prisonnier.'

It was Napoleon's last imperial gesture; and it had a dying fall.

****

There remains one small, vivid postscript which illuminates all that has gone before.

From 5 September, the numerous French prisoners gathered in the Meuse peninsula were sent forward into captivity in batches of 2000. They were marched towards Étain, and thence, by an unforeseen irony, across the Gravelotte plateau to the Moselle crossings around Pont-à-Mousson.

But the irony was not entirely lost on Moltke. The Emperor had asked to send a message to Bazaine. Then his request had been refused. Now it was dramatically delivered. On the morning of 13 September, 500 French prisoners, weakly waving white flags, were driven through the outposts of Frederick Charles's besieging army into Metz. It was a clever, if distasteful, *coup de théâtre*.

****

EPILOGUE

The news of the disaster at Sedan, coming so hard on the heels of the investment of the Army of the Rhine in Metz, was greeted in Paris at first with disbelief and then with an explosion of anger. How could it be that the armies of France — '*prêtes*', had Leboeuf not boasted only six short weeks before, '*aux derniers boutons des guêtres*'? — had been summarily defeated by an army of 'oculists and lawyers'? The time for scapegoats would come later. Now an extraordinary wave of national sentiment engulfed the country.

On 4 September, amid scenes of indescribable emotion, the Second Empire was swept away, and in its place a provisional Government of National Defence was formed, headed by the radicals Favre and Gambetta, and with Trochu as its chief military ornament. Thus, without constitutional authority, but with the implicit sanction of popular opinion, the Third Republic replaced the fallen dynasty. '*Guerre à l'outrance!*' was its watchword. Jules Favre added his own empty infelicity: 'France will not yield one inch of her territory nor one stone of her fortresses.' It was noble stuff; but with Alsace gone, with Lorraine gone, with the field armies of France gone, it was a hollow boast.

It is possible that other men than the brilliant but volatile Gambetta and the romantic patriot Favre — Thiers, perhaps, or even Trochu — might at this moment have struck a bargain with Bismarck which would have bought an early peace with a semblance of honour. But public passions had been aroused; an unpopular Empire had fallen under the weight of its own arrogance;[1] and so it was to be war to the bitter end.

****

1 The Empress had been brought, with difficulty, to the safe haven of Hastings, by the devoted energies of an American dentist in Paris.

Moltke was not one to take chances. 'There could be no doubt', he wrote, 'that the new objective must be Paris, as the seat of the new Government and the centre of gravity, so to speak, of the whole country. On the very day of the capitulation of Sedan, all the dispositions were made for the renewal of the advance.'[2] Two corps were left to guard the mass of prisoners in the Meuse peninsula, and on 4 September the westerly march was resumed.

In Paris preparations to put the city in a state of siege went ahead with a vigour which had been so signally lacking among the French field commanders. On the 12th, Vinoy's 13 Corps, cleverly extricated from its exposed position at Mézières by a series of long night marches, reached the capital, and around this regular nucleus Trochu assembled a defending force of nearly 300,000 men — marines, gendarmes, customs officers, *forestiers*, and Gardes Mobiles — disposed within the massive *enceinte* of fortifications which had been built, with a prophetic wisdom, by Louis-Philippe forty years before; and the elegant parks of Paris presented the strange spectacle of a grazing ground for 3000 cattle, 6000 pigs, and 180,000 sheep. Thus by 18 September the citizens and soldiers stood to arms within a powerfully protected and well-stocked larder. The following morning the two encircling wings of the pursuing German armies joined hands, with some sort of historical propriety, at Versailles. The investment of Paris was complete.

****

Meanwhile most of the committee of National Defence had removed themselves to Tours, there to be joined from Paris in his celebrated balloon on 10 October by Gambetta, Minister of the Interior, Minister of War, the voice — and conscience — of the nation; and while the committee occupied itself with planning *la guerre à l'outrance*, it hedged its bets by sending its most distinguished — and voluble — member to parley with the enemy.

On 17 September Jules Favre presented himself at Ferrières, the Rothschild estate outside Paris. There he proposed, sensibly enough, an armistice to permit the French people to elect an Assembly charged with the task of negotiating an immediate end to hostilities, but adding, absurdly, a demand for the withdrawal of all German troops and the payment of a substantial sum in compensation 'for injuries received'.

The proposal for an armistice was not unattractive to Bismarck, for with the collapse of the Empire it was by no means certain, without free elections, which persons or legislative body had the authority to speak for France. What was, however, certain was that Favre's impertinent demands would receive short shrift. In return, Bismarck, for so astute a politician

2 Moltke: *op. cit.*

who held all the aces, made an extraordinarily mild counter-offer: first, that there should be an armistice to allow the holding of elections; but secondly, that the French should surrender Strasbourg and Toul in order to secure for the Germans the necessary railheads to supply their armies in the interior. The siege of Metz would be maintained, but the surrender of the Army of the Rhine would not be a condition of war.[3] The blockade of Paris would be continued, but if it were raised, the Germans would occupy the main defence-work of Mont-Valérien. Meanwhile the Chamber of Deputies would be permitted to conduct its business at Tours[4] without interference.

A wiser man than Favre would have understood Bismarck's dilemma and turned it to better advantage. But he was carried away by his own excessive eloquence, by the romantic rhetoric of such phrases as 'the immortality of France' and 'the unstained honour of the nation', and by his own ringing declaration — 'not an inch of territory, not one stone of our fortresses'. 'You should know', remarked Bismarck after one such tirade, 'that sentimental outbursts have no part in politics.' And on that note, Favre returned to Paris. An unnecessary war, arrogantly entered upon and wantonly misconducted, was thus, for reasons of pique, false passion and falser pride, unnecessarily allowed to continue to its very bitter and humiliating end.

****

The armistice which Favre could have gained on cheaper terms at Ferrières was not to be won until Bismarck had substantially raised the stakes. The four months through which the war dragged on — the siege of Paris and the provincial campaigns, Loire, Le Mans, Artois and the North, Belfort and the South-East — lie beyond the scope of this narrative, and seem strangely separated in time and space from that August morning when a handful of German guns stopped an entire French army in its tracks at Vionville. It was there — not at St Privat and Gravelotte, not at Sedan, not at Paris, or Orléans, or Coulmiers,[5] or Villersexel, or across the face of France — that the mortal blow was struck.

Throughout October, while Gambetta stirred the pot in the provinces, the Germans, with half their field force standing guard around Metz, had not, for all their expertise, the resources to hasten the end. In this peculiar stalemate, in which the politics of war and the warfare of politics generated a kind of vacuum, the tension showed in a growing friction between

3 The wily Bismarck had already reached the conclusion that Bazaine might well be a valuable bargaining-counter in the event of a Bonapartist revival.

4 When, after repeated postponements, a National Assembly was elected, it removed its seat of office, as it would do 70 years later, to Bordeaux.

5 The battle of Coulmiers on 9 November was the sole French victory of the entire war.

Bismarck and Moltke. It was left to Bazaine to resolve the discord.

In Metz it was raining, day after dismal day. The fate of the fortress had been finally sealed with the fall of Sedan, and since the battle of Noisseville, only two minor sorties had been made — on 27 September and 7 October — and they were no more than foraging expeditions to supplement the dwindling food resources of the place where 60,000 townsfolk were playing unwilling host to three times as many soldiers. They ate their way steadily through the cavalry horses, and dealt as best they could with spreading disease and growing disorder. But the end was inevitable.

Bazaine's enemies were later to claim that from the outset, even as early as the night of 16/17 August, he had been playing for high political stakes; that he had used the Army of the Rhine as a pawn with which to bargain for personal power at the peace table. It was always a silly suggestion. Whatever his military shortcomings, and whatever his private attitude to Napoleon may have been, he was a loyal servant of the Emperor, a professional soldier, and far too naive to have played either conspirator or power-broker.

When, therefore, on 27 October he sent Jarras to seek from Frederick Charles the terms for the surrender of Metz and of the Army of the Rhine, he should not have been — and was not — surprised that they were as ruthless and unbending as those presented to Wimpffen and Napoleon at Sedan. The following day the articles of capitulation were signed; and on the 29th, the Army of the Rhine — its Marshals, Generals and 173,000 officers and men — started on the road to captivity.

****

The surrender of Metz released more than 150,000 troops of First and Second Armies to thicken up the force investing Paris, and to prosecute the war in the interior. Thus while Moltke applied himself to a series of complex military problems, Bismarck addressed his political skills to the achievement of a lifelong ambition.

Ever since his appointment as minister-president, he had been guided by three articles of faith: the humiliation of Austria, the destruction of French imperialism and above all the unification of Germany under Prussian hegemony. Sadowa had achieved his first objective. Now, in November, with the French dynasty overthrown and French military power in disarray, it would not be long until he achieved the second. He therefore judged the hour propitious to complete his ultimate purpose: the creation of a single Empire, embracing all the states of Germany, but not the multi-national Austro-Hungarian[6] conglomerate.

---

6   The so-called 'Dual Monarchy' of Austria and Hungary had been created in 1867.

That such an Empire should be presided over by Prussia, the political dynamo of the North German Confederation and architect of victory, was a *sine qua non*; all the states of the Confederation were already closely linked in a customs union, and Bismarck had only to remind the lesser kings and princes that the historic fragmentation of this great ethnic group had been ruthlessly exploited by the first Napoleon.

South Germany raised some delicate difficulties. Catholic Bavaria, second in size and influence of the Germanic states, took unkindly to the prospect of subordination to Protestant Prussia, and the house of Wittelsbach demonstrated an ancestral distaste to playing second fiddle to the house of Hohenzollern. Bismarck dealt his cards with all his customary skill and patience. In a sense he was fortunate, for his own monarch, William, enjoyed a universal admiration and affection not readily shared by the Bavarian Ludwig. He also indulged in a little curdling of the blood by reminding his opposite number that a French military presence on the Rhine would always pose a threat to the safety and stability of Southern Germany, adding for good measure that 'the protection of Prussia could not be counted upon in every circumstance'.

By the end of December, Bavaria had fallen into line (Baden and Württemberg had offered no resistance). There remained the question of the title to be adopted by the new Head of State. The first proposal was 'Emperor of Germany', but those with long memories and a sense of history recalled the 'foreign' associations of Charlemagne, of Charles V, and of the Habsburg succession — '*Kaiser des Heiligen Römischen Reiches deutscher Nation*' — while others felt that the style implied an unacceptable degree of 'territorial' sovereignty. Thus it was that at Versailles on 18 January 1871, the 170th anniversary of the coronation of the Elector of Brandenburg as the first King of Prussia, the unambitious King William I was unanimously elected 'German Emperor'. The proclamation was read out by Bismarck, now Imperial Chancellor, and it ended thus:

> May God vouchsafe to us and to our successors ever to be increasers of the German Empire, not by warlike conquests, but with the boons and gifts of peace for the national welfare, freedom and civilization.

Posterity was to learn all too bitterly that the road to hell is paved with good intentions — and empty words.

****

Ten days after the glittering ceremony at Versailles, and with Paris on the brink of starvation and civil war, an armistice was signed. It had fallen to Jules Favre to resume the negotiations into which he had entered with such bravado at Ferrières. Now he had not even the bargaining counter of

Bazaine's army in Metz, only the spectre of revolution. Bismarck could not resist teasing him. 'Why should I negotiate with you at all?' he asked. 'Why not with your Emperor?' It was an interesting proposition, and it drew from Favre a final confession of failure: 'I will accept any terms you like, only do not inflict on France, after all her disasters, the dishonour of having to bear the yoke of a Bonaparte.'

The armistice was signed on the 28th, to run in the first instance for three weeks to enable the government of National Defence to hold free elections for an Assembly which would meet in Bordeaux to settle the issue of peace or war. Paris, meanwhile, was disarmed, and the sole concession — one which Favre would presently have cause to regret — was that the National Guard should be permitted to retain their weapons.

If Bismarck had the measure of Favre, he also had no illusions about Gambetta. When news of the armistice reached him, that fiery spark issued a ringing decree which, amid appeals to national sentiment, disfranchised all those who had served under the Emperor. To Bismarck this was a clear breach of the armistice terms. To Favre it was an invitation to civil war. Thus a minister, Jules Simon, was dispatched with all haste from Paris to Bordeaux to demand an instant withdrawal of the decree. Gambetta refused, and with a political agility which would ensure for him a permanent place in the pantheon of French patriots, resigned.

The result of the elections demonstrated clearly that the people had had enough of war. The new Assembly met at Bordeaux on 12 February, and, the representative for Alsace alone dissenting, agreed the terms of the armistice including, despite Favre's brave words, the cession of French soil and French fortresses. On the 17th, Thiers was appointed chief executive, and was commissioned with Favre to conduct the peace negotiations; and to this end the armistice was extended to 12 March.

For a war which had cost both sides so heavily in lives and treasure, the price demanded by the Germans scarcely represented, in legal terms, exemplary damages. The main terms demanded the surrender of Alsace, of northern Lorraine including, symbolically, Metz, and of various fortified places in eastern France; in addition, reparations in the modest sum of five milliards of francs (then about £200,000,000), with a 'rebate' for the value of the railways acquired in the ceded territory, were imposed. In a curious footnote, the fortress of Belfort which held out until 15 February was traded in for an agreement that the German army of occupation should hold a victory parade down the Champs Elysées in the capital.

Full peace negotiations opened in Brussels on 28 March; and on 10 May the definitive treaty was signed in Frankfurt.

****

The nation as a whole had voted decisively for peace; but Paris, where the disastrous adventure had started, was to have the last word.

During his negotiations for the armistice with Bismarck, Favre had proposed that, to preserve internal security, the National Guard — 200,000 of them in Paris alone — should retain their arms. Bismarck had warned him against such excessive trust in an indisciplined body of doubtful political reliability; and Bismarck was swiftly proved right.

With the signing of the armistice, the new government and the National Assembly moved from Bordeaux to Versailles. Almost their first act was to stand the National Guard down, and cease paying them. Thiers, experienced statesman and author of a lapidary study of the first Bonaparte,[7] should have remembered, as Favre had not, the revolutionary origin of France's citizen army. That army now took to the streets.

On 18 March the National Guard elected a central committee of the Republican Federation, or 'Commune,' accompanied by much revolutionary rhetoric and a programme of social and political reforms. The citizens of Paris flocked to the barricades, and when the small force of regular troops still stationed in the capital was ordered to fire on the mob, it at once mutinied; and by the following morning a national disaster had become a bloody civil war.

The German reaction was simple and cynical. 'We could easily have put a speedy end to the matter,' wrote Moltke,[8] 'but what government could allow its rights to be vindicated by foreign bayonets?' The occupying army was duly ordered to seal off any attempt by the Commune to break out of the city centre, and Bismarck, relishing the French passion for self-inflicted wounds, invited the new government at Versailles to summon sufficient of its own soldiers in the provinces to raise the second siege of Paris.

****

Thiers accepted this further humiliation. There were still, as the French account quaintly puts it, enough *'troupes versaillaises'* to crush the insurrection. But who should be entrusted with this distasteful task?

> Baraguey d'Hilliers was too old; Bourbaki was convalescent from his last (second) attempt at suicide; Canrobert was supposed to be a Bonapartist;[9] and Leboeuf was tainted with war-guilt. But [observed Thiers], there was one soldier, *'un qui ferait parfaitement mon affaire. Malheureusement il s'appelle Bazaine.'* So there was nothing for it but MacMahon.[10]

7   Thiers: *L'Histoire du Consulat et de l'Empire.*

8   Moltke: *op. cit.*

9   He was. He had helped to engineer the *coup d'état* in 1851.

10   Guedalla: *op. cit.*

And Bazaine — *'notre glorieux Bazaine'* had Thiers not said? He was presently to learn the same lesson as Dumouriez and Dumont; that the French people greatly enjoy nailing their fallen heroes to the nearest cross.

****

The second siege of Paris culminated in a week of appalling bloodshed — *la semaine sanglante* — between 21 and 28 May. During that time, MacMahon's *troupes versaillaises* fought their way inch by inch into the centre of the capital. There is a dreadful irony in this final vindication of a defeated French army redeeming its 'honour' in the squalor of a mutual slaughter under the impassive eyes of a victorious enemy; and no less an irony that the butcher-in-chief should have been *l'illustre vaincu*, MacMahon.

The Communards went down fighting. On 22 May, they executed 52 hostages, including the Archbishop of Paris. And during the last hours of resistance they set fire to the centre of Paris — the Tuileries, the Hôtel de Ville, the Treasury, the Assembly. On the 27th, as an act of retaliation, 1600 Communards were summarily executed in the cemetery of Père Lachaise; and on the 28th the last barricade, in the Rue de Ramponneau, was carried at bayonet-point.

The final agony of France and its brutal cost may be illustrated in simple, sordid figures: 20,000 killed; 13,500 condemned to death, to deportation, to life-imprisonment, or to exile. The Germans had not managed such comparable casualties in all the bloody fighting on the Gravelotte plateau during those sunburnt days of August.

****

So, as the dust settled on the burning city, and the French came at last to terms with the inevitability of total defeat, the post-mortem began.

How could it be that a great nation, with (give or take a disaster or two) a memorable military tradition, had been so swiftly and comprehensively defeated? The conventional wisdom — and it was to be repeated in almost identical circumstances in 1940 — was very simple and very French. *La France n'a pas été vaincue, la France a été trahie*. And at once the potential scapegoats were paraded for public inspection.

The Emperor? The Republicans, by no means certain that volatile public opinion might not summon back the monarchy, carefully avoided a sitting duck. De Gramont, who had driven Benedetti to dangerous extravagance at Bad Ems? But de Gramont was abroad. Leboeuf, who had promised everything and delivered nothing? But Leboeuf had neatly whitewashed a tarnished reputation. MacMahon, who had commanded the doomed Army of Châlons at Sedan until an honourable wound had relieved him of the ignominy of personal surrender? But MacMahon had saved Paris from the

Commune, and that was enough to establish his credentials. There remained Bazaine. And Bazaine had no credentials, beyond long and distinguished service, and a dangerous loyalty to a deposed and discredited Emperor. Above all, he was a loser — at Rezonville, at Gravelotte and St Privat, and finally at Metz. Here then was a ripe subject for public crucifixion.

****

They went for Bazaine with all the ferocity and none of the subtlety of the bull-ring. The artillery of abuse and innuendo was deployed without regard for truth or even plausibility, for having chosen their object of obloquy, they piled a Pelion of prejudice upon an Ossa of obsession.

Gambetta had started it as far back as October:

> *Metz a capitulé! Le Général sur qui la France comptait, même après l'expédition de Mexique, vient d'enlever à la patrie en danger plus de cent mille defenseurs. Bazaine a trahi …*

The attack was taken up by d'Andlau in his (then) anonymous attack[11] which ran into nine editions within one year, and whose allegations of Bazaine's base ambitions and treasonable activities during the siege of Metz became the received wisdom of the public prints and of the Marshal's carefully rehearsed enemies. It would not be improper to suggest that if half the staff-work that went into the character-assassination of Bazaine had been applied to the military preparations of France in 1870, there would have been no Mars-la-Tour, no Sedan, no Metz — and no court-martial at Versailles three years later.

****

For a while Bazaine, exiled in Switzerland, kept his distance although foolishly filling his empty days with writing an ill-judged book[12] which would presently cost him dear. Old men forget, and are often better counselled not to remember, even in tranquillity. And Bazaine's first essay in apologia is a miserable testament, the rattle of a simple man. The book was not published until 1872, and by then it had been overtaken by events.

But the wounded bull sought, as well he might, the right to answer his critics. When, two years later, he made his final statement before his judges, he resorted to the rhetoric of his rank:

---

11   d'Andlau: *op. cit.*

12   Bazaine, *L'Armée du Rhin depuis le 12 août jusqu'au 29 octobre 1870.*

J'ai sur la poitrine deux mots, Honneur et Patrie, qui m'ont guidé dans toute ma vie militaire. Je n'ai jamais manqué à cette noble devise pas plus à Metz que partout ailleurs pendant les quarante-deux ans que j'ai servi loyalement la France. Je le jure ici devant le Christ![13]

Rhetoric, perhaps. But it is not surprising that it reduced an older Marshal of France, Canrobert, to tears.

****

In September 1871 Bazaine was given permission to return to France. He demanded, as an old soldier, the right to vindicate his honour. And Thiers, the executive head of state, declared himself thus before the Assembly:

Marshal Bazaine has, I am convinced, been cruelly slandered [*calumnié*]; but a government is not enough to destroy slanders. Marshal Bazaine formally demands an enquiry into events at Metz. In general I have no taste for enquiries designed to dwell upon the past and to revive strong feelings. But an enquiry designed to vindicate a noble army and to let the country know whether its commander betrayed it or not — such an enquiry, in my judgment, is an act of justice that cannot be denied to any man. It is for the Assembly to reply.

The Assembly replied without hesitation. It bayed for blood.

****

On 30 September 1871 a Commission of Inquiry was convened '*pour examiner les diverses capitulations consenties avec l'ennemi pendant la campagne douloureuse de 1870-1871.*' The chairman was a superannuated Marshal, Baraguey d'Hilliers, who had been Bazaine's corps commander in Italy and was reputed to be ill disposed towards him. Alone of the field commanders, Bazaine was called to answer for his alleged errors of commission and omission. That should have been a clear warning to him, for the 'capitulations' had been both numerous and 'diverse'. Sedan, Metz, Strasbourg, Nancy, Paris, Belfort, France itself ... But the Commission, stimulated by d'Andlau's[14] recently published philippic, soon lost sight of its terms of reference; for on 12 April 1872 it approved a motion to the effect that

---

13 *Procès Bazaine*, p. 799.

14 D'Andlau's personal qualities may be judged by the fact that ten years later, by when he was both a General and a Senator, he received a stiff prison sentence for trafficking in the distribution of honours.

> *le commandant en chef de l'armée du Rhin était responsable en grande*
> *partie des revers de l'armée de Châlons, et responsable entièrement de*
> *la perte d'une armée de 150,000 hommes et de la place de Metz, sans*
> *avoir fait ce que lui prescrivait le devoir militaire … En outre, plusieurs*
> *blâmes très sévères contre le Maréchal, pour n'avoir pas détruit son*
> *matériel de guerre, pour avoir accepté les clauses de la capitulation de*
> *28 octobre …*

That Marshal Bazaine's oath of allegiance had been (and still was) to his Emperor and not to a *soi-disant* Republic was conveniently ignored.

The findings of the Commission let a large number of apprehensive luminaries off the hook, chief among them MacMahon, who may well have blessed the luck of the Irish. They also provided public opinion with a splendid misrepresentation of history. Certainly, France had not won the war. But if the sole responsibility for the nation's misfortunes rested on Bazaine, then it was not *France* that had been defeated. 'It was comforting to feel that the result was due to a single individual rather than to the French army and to the noble-minded Marshal [*MacMahon*] who was now its leading ornament; and if that individual could safely be identified with the Empire, so much the better for republicans and royalists.'[15]

****

With a stubbornness that does more credit to his injured dignity than to his grasp of history, Bazaine demanded a court-martial. Had he shown the same resolution at Rezonville two years earlier, he might well have escaped the fate which he now invited.

The court-martial was the suggestion of Thiers, who still held Bazaine in high regard, and promised to dismiss any proceedings which might follow. But luck was not on the side of this most unlucky man.

First, *vox populi* intervened when the Assembly ordered a selective investigation into the events at Metz, as if Sedan had been no more than a ripple on an otherwise untroubled water. And in May, Thiers resigned.

This was to be Bazaine's undoing. For now the President of the Republic was MacMahon, who, despite his protestations, was not unhappy to see the old bull transformed into a sacrificial lamb. 'You can rely on me,' he said to Bazaine. 'I have always stood up for you.' 'And so you should', replied Bazaine, 'for you know better than anyone why we fell back on Metz.' After that they did not speak again.

The scales were tilted further. The new Minister of War was Barail, one of Bazaine's cavalry divisional commanders whose main contribution to the battle on 16 August had been to provide two out of his three regiments of Chasseurs d'Afrique as escort to the Emperor on the central road to

15   Guedalla, *op. cit.*

Verdun; while the Military Governor of Paris was now Ladmirault, whose lack of resolution on that distant afternoon had cast away a victory at Mars-la-Tour.

When in October 1873, after sixteen months of semantic argument and with due sense of drama, the government converted the *grand salon* of the Grand Trianon into a court-room, it should have provided at least twenty seats on the *parquet* for those soldiers and civilians who had something to answer for before the bar of justice. Instead, there was a single table which accommodated Bazaine, his improbable defending counsel Maître Lachaud, a criminal lawyer well versed in murder trials, and his faithful aide of many years, Colonel Willette. Since the German withdrawal, Paris had recovered its bread. Now it was to enjoy a profoundly unattractive circus.

****

There were immediate problems. By law a Marshal of France could only be tried by his peers. But since there was a shortage of Marshals — or at least of suitable Marshals — the law was amended, and a court of four generals was convened, with General de Rivière as chief prosecutor. Bazaine had every legal right to object. He did not. He, the former private of the line, was used to accepting orders, if not so capable of giving them. He retired to a small house in the suburbs of Paris and put himself under house-arrest. It was a stupid act of self-abasement; and it tells us more about this strange man and his chronic inferiority complex than all the acres of evidence paraded across the court-room at Versailles. It has been suggested that Bazaine made no attempt to defend himself. That is not true. He was committed on a trumped-up charge of treason. He was not a traitor. He was an incompetent commander-in-chief who hazarded his army because he had thrust upon him a greatness to which he was not equal. He was brave; but bravery is not enough. He was loyal; but loyalty alone does not win battles. He was brought before his judges because he had the broadest pair of shoulders, and was by far the most distinguished of the available scapegoats. It is possible — just possible — that in the end he came to believe in his own guilt.

****

The court-martial started on 6 October 1873. The president was a curious compromise in the person of the Orléanist Duc d'Aumale, who had, like most military men, made a modest reputation in Algeria thirty years before, and who now came to sit in judgment on a former Légionnaire. With him sat the four generals, carefully chosen to ensure their compliance, if not their complicity. A fair trial was impossible, for the Commission of Inquiry had already demonstrated that justification was more important than justice.

The record stands today,[16] more than 800 pages printed in three columns and running, at a conservative estimate, to 1,800,000 words. It is a dreadful document of which every Frenchman should be ashamed, for there is no guilt more criminal than guilt by association. The Assembly had bayed for blood. They got more than they had bargained for.

****

The prosecution, after months of leisurely research, produced 329 witnesses. They made an interesting list, ranging from Canrobert, Leboeuf, Ladmirault, Bourbaki, Frossard, Coffinières, Jarras, Lapasset, down to non-commissioned officers, customs officials, engine-drivers, and even the very foolish proprietress of a *maison garnie* at Metz. Their evidence, *de haut en bas*, was — almost without exception — trite, trivial, tendentious and untruthful. Jarras, whom Bazaine had inherited without enthusiasm as chief of staff on 12 August, and who had a large chip on his shoulder, was quick to set out his stall:

> *Le maréchal m'a tenu dès le commencement systematiquement à l'écarte, sans me faire part de ses projets, qui ne m'étaient connus qu'au moment où il me donnait des ordres pour en assurer l'exécution, de telle sorte que je n'avais pas le temps de les étudier et de proposer ensuite les mesures de détail …*

It is said that not one of the Marshals or Generals who spoke for the prosecution ever looked at the accused. It is also said that whipped dogs will not look at their master.

Bazaine called few witnesses in his defence: 38 soldiers (including the charmingly named Cheval, *cavalier de remonte*), and 9 civilians. He did not feel it proper to involve others in what he considered to be a private crisis. His faithful Willette was at his side; and his counsel, Lachaud, made a fool of himself by quoting a kind and complimentary letter from the Marshal's old adversary, Prince Frederick Charles. Paris was in no mood for Prussian praise.

****

The trial dragged on until 10 December. Then, after 65 days of lies and half-truths, the court took just 4 hours and 20 minutes to deliver its unanimous verdict on François Achille Bazaine, fusilier of the 37th Regiment and Marshal of France:

16 *Procès Bazaine (Capitulation de Metz)*, Présidence de M. le Général de Division Duc d'Aumale, *Paris 1873*.

Condamné à la peine de mort avec dégradation militaire

The judgment further stripped him of his Légion d'Honneur and of his Médaille Militaire;[17] and finally awarded costs against him, an extravagant insult, since he had no financial resources, and dead men tell no tales. He was given twenty-four hours in which to appeal against both verdict and sentence.

****

Bazaine declined the invitation. The man who is alleged to have said at Rezonville 'We must sacrifice a regiment' was not one to plead for his own life. Nor had he need to. For unknown to him (and there is no mention in the transcript of the trial) the court — partly (if Barail is to be believed) from a belated access of conscience, and partly to avert the risk of martyrdom — had added to its verdict a strong recommendation for clemency on the grounds of diminished responsibility (sic), long service and bravery in battle.

This must have relieved MacMahon. As a soldier he was well aware that his own defeat at Wörth had opened the way to Paris and had compromised the Army of the Rhine, although he could — and did — justify the surrender at Sedan as the inevitable price of a gallant effort to relieve the beleaguered Bazaine. (To extend this 'chicken and egg' argument, Bazaine could — and did — claim that but for MacMahon he would not have been in Metz.) But, as President of the Republic, MacMahon felt obliged to play the stern Roman. A verdict was a verdict. There could be no question of an unqualified reprieve. Instead, he commuted the sentence to twenty years imprisonment, but dispensed with the distasteful drama of public degradation. So, on Christmas Day, ex-Marshal Bazaine was taken by train to Antibes, and thence to the grim prison on the Île Ste-Marguerite.

****

His durance was not particularly vile, for he had comfortable accommodation and the company of his wife and his two smaller children. But he was now sixty-three, and he had lived a full and active life. It was the boredom rather than the ignominy of imprisonment that decided him to make a break. The escape was planned with a great deal more skill and resolution

---

17 At the first session of the court on 6 October, the clerk read out Bazaine's record of service, his honours, and his distinctions, which included the Companionship of the Bath and the British Crimea medal. It may also be noted that in the list of Bazaine's wounds in action, no mention was made of the last one, received on 14 August at Borny under the walls of Metz. There were to be no redeeming features.

than any of the abortive sorties from Metz, and on 10 August 1874 Bazaine was in Genoa, a free man.

He spent some weeks (there is no indication where the money came from) travelling aimlessly. First to Germany; then to visit his sons in Belgium whence he addressed a letter to the *New York Herald* in which, for the only time, he permitted himself the luxury of a defence against Aumale's baseless accusations, and a barbed criticism of MacMahon's conduct of the August campaign; and then to Switzerland to meet the recently widowed Empress Eugénie and her 'young Pretender', the Prince Imperial or, as he was now known in 'Court' circles, Napoleon IV. In spite of everything, in spite of the intolerable burden which the Emperor had suddenly placed on him on the eve of the battle of Borny, he remained to the end a loyal Bonapartist even when, in 1879, the pale young Prince Imperial died distantly at the hands of Zulus, and with him died the dynasty.

He finally chose an exile in Spain, where he arrived early in 1875. He spoke the language, his wife Pepita was Mexican, and he had served Queen Isabella — then a child of four — during the Carlist war of the 1830s as a young lieutenant in the Foreign Legion.

He made his home in Madrid; and there he addressed himself to another book, *Episodes de la guerre de 1870 et le blocus de Metz*, which was published in 1883. It was a rambling narrative, better than the earlier *L'Armée du Rhin*, but inaccurate because he relied too much on a failing memory, and because he had no access to the latest source material. Here, if anywhere, he could have stated his case as he had declined to do at Versailles. Here, if anywhere, he could have vindicated himself against the worst excesses of his political and military enemies. But the language is that of the Légionnaire, not of a Marshal of France. Apart from a few caustic asides, he could not bring himself to attack his social superiors for their political malice or military incompetence. He deserved — much more than Dreyfus — a Zola. He chose instead the mild *'Je m'excuse!'* rather than the trenchant *'J'accuse!'* What he really felt about the disasters of 1870 we shall never know. Perhaps Canrobert summed it up best at the trial. 'Not everyone can command an army of 140,000. It is difficult to manage when one isn't used to it.'

****

He died on 23 September 1888. The previous year he had written to his son in France, saying that he was not sleeping well because of the *'trimestre de souvenirs noirs, août, septembre, octobre, 70.'* Metz, which had gripped him during those critical days, still continued to haunt his dreams.

When the Emperor abdicated his military authority on the evening of 12 August, his last instructions to Bazaine had appeared equivocal. 'No more reverses!'; 'Put yourself as soon as possible on the road to Verdun'; and adding, as a bleak afterthought, 'In no circumstances compromise the army!' To Bazaine these orders sowed the seed of doubt and decided him on a course of indecision. Simply stated, he saw the military equation thus. If he could *safely* reach Verdun and effect a junction with MacMahon, then a reunited field army could turn again upon its pursuers on ground of its own choosing between the Meuse and the Marne, and with the arsenals and magazines of Paris at close command. But what if that course of action were contested by a more numerous enemy? What if, in carrying out one imperial order, he failed to execute the other and 'compromised the army'? It was this dilemma which was to prove his undoing.

As we have seen, the fortress of Metz held a fatal fascination for him. The farther he retreated to the west, the more he might distance himself from this illusory source of strength. Metz thus became to him an obsessive symbol of security, long after it had ceased to override the imperative of disengagement. And we have seen how, throughout the daylight hours of 16 August and the two following days, his eyes were fixed on his left flank where little danger threatened, and not on Verdun where prudence beckoned and some sort of salvation lay. So much for the *souvenirs noirs*. An earlier Bonaparte would have made light of the dilemma. A Bazaine was not equal to the opportunity.

Looking back over the shoulder of history, one incontrovertible fact emerges. During the first four weeks of the Franco-German war, there was one day — one single day — when the French were presented with the opportunity of defeating — indeed, of destroying — the chief instrument of the German military machine, and of making good their escape. Whether that would have influenced the final course of the war is a matter for speculation. What is certain beyond argument is that the war — and with it the future of Europe — was decided at Mars-la-Tour on 16 August 1870.

****

APPENDIXES
A - D

APPENDIX A

ORDERS OF BATTLE OF THE FRENCH AND GERMAN FIELD ARMIES

The following Orders of Battle show the opposing sides as they were at first light on 16 August. Formations and units directly involved in the day of battle are shown in bold type (administrative units have been omitted). Those which took no part in the fighting on that day — viz. MacMahon's Army of Alsace, the German Third Army, and the larger part of the German First Army — are printed in roman. Notes are shown in italic. Some observations may assist the reader:

1.   The infantry strength of a German army corps may be taken as 25,000, with the exception of the Guard and XII (Royal Saxon) Corps which numbered 29,000. The average strength of a cavalry division was 3000, with either one or two 6-gun horse artillery batteries. Corps artillery consisted normally of 84 guns (viz. III Corps) or 90 guns (viz. X Corps).

2.   Because of the chaotic process of mobilization, it is a matter for speculation what the actual equivalent strength of French formations was on the Gravelotte plateau. For example, because of the piecemeal arrival of reservists in the forward area, Frossard's 2 Corps, despite its losses at Spicheren on 6 August, actually totalled 2000 more men on the morning of the 16th, quite apart from the unexpected bonus of Lapasset's brigade from Failly's 5 Corps ten days earlier. Secondly, the French passion for pecking-orders meant that army corps commanded by Marshals (viz. 1, 3 and 6) consisted of four divisions, while Generals (viz. 2, 4, 5, 7) had to be content with three. The Germans were wiser. Each of their thirteen army corps consisted of just two infantry divisions.

Thus a broad view of the French strength suggests the following: a 'large' army corps, 30,000; a 'small' army corps, 20,000 or less. A cavalry division, about 3000. The artillery of a corps, including mitrailleuse batteries, anywhere between 60 and 90 guns.

3.   Canrobert's 6 Corps is of special interest, not only because of its ineffective performance on the 16th, but because of its heroic failure on the 18th.

Originally designed as the army reserve at Châlons, it was sent forward to Nancy during the last week of July, but then swiftly returned whence it came, with predictable confusion on the only available railway line. After the defeat at Spicheren, it was again brought forward, this time to Metz, on 9 August. But it was too late, and as the note shows in the following table, it left behind its cavalry division; all but one regiment (the 9th) of its fourth infantry division; three-quarters of its corps artillery, including all its mitrailleuses; and its entire engineer park. It is just possible that these seemingly modest shortages tilted the balance, first at Rezonville, and then decisively on bloody Thursday.

I

FRENCH FIELD ARMIES

ARMY OF THE RHINE

Commander-in-Chief	**Marshal Bazaine**
Chief of Staff	**General Jarras**
Commanding Artillery	**General Soleille**

(Note: The Emperor handed over command to Bazaine on 12 August)

IMPERIAL GUARD
(Bourbaki)

DELIGNY'S DIVISION
1st Brigade
    Chasseurs of the Guard
    1st and 2nd Voltigeurs of the Guard
2nd Brigade
    3rd and 4th Voltigeurs of the Guard
2 x 4-pdr Batteries
1 x Mitrailleuse Battery

PICARD'S DIVISION
1st Brigade
    Zouaves of the Guard
    1st Grenadiers of the Guard
2nd Brigade
    2nd and 3rd Grenadiers of the Guard
2 x 4-pdr Batteries
1 x Mitrailleuse Battery

DESVAUX'S CAVALRY DIVISION
1st Brigade
    Guides
    Chasseurs of the Guard
2nd Brigade
    Lancers of the Guard
    Dragoons of the Guard
3rd Brigade
    Cuirassiers of the Guard
    Carabiniers of the Guard
4 x Horse Artillery Batteries

2 CORPS
(Frossard)

VERGÉ'S DIVISION
1st Brigade (Valazé)
    3rd Bn of Chasseurs
    32nd and 55th Regiments
2nd Brigade (Jolivet)
    76th and 77th Regiments
2 x 4-pdr Batteries
1 x Mitrailleuse Battery

BATAILLE'S DIVISION
1st Brigade (Pouget)
    12th Bn of Chasseurs
    8th and 23rd Regiments
2nd Brigade (Bastoul)
    66th and 67th Regiments
2 x 4-pdr Batteries
1 x Mitrailleuse Battery

LAPASSET'S BRIGADE Group   (*attached from Failly's 5 Corps*)
    14th Bn of Chasseurs
    49th and 84th Regiments
    3rd Lancers

LAVEAUCOUPET'S DIVISION (*detached as Metz garrison troops*)

VALABRÈGUE'S CAVALRY DIVISION
1st Brigade
    4th and 5th Regiments of Chasseurs
2nd Brigade
    7th and 12th Regiments of Dragoons

Reserve Artillery
    2 x 8-pdr Batteries
    2 x 12-pdr Batteries
    2 x Mitrailleuse Batteries

3 CORPS
(Leboeuf; *previously* Decaen)

MONTAUDON'S DIVISION
1st Brigade
> 18th Bn of Chasseurs
> 51st and 62nd Regiments

2nd Brigade
> 81st and 95th Regiments

2 x 4-pdr Batteries
1 x Mitrailleuse Battery

NAYRAL'S DIVISION
1st Brigade
> 15th Bn of Chasseurs
> 19th and 41st Regiments

2nd Brigade
> 69th and 90th Regiments

2 x 4-pdr Batteries
1 x Mitrailleuse Battery

METMAN'S DIVISION   (*not committed to action*)
1st Brigade
> 7th Bn of Chasseurs
> 7th and 29th Regiments

2nd Brigade
> 59th and 71st Regiments

2 x 4-pdr Batteries
1 x Mitrailleuse Battery

AYMARD'S DIVISION
1st Brigade
> 11th Bn of Chasseurs
> 44th and 60th Regiments

2nd Brigade
> 80th and 8th Regiments

2 x 4-pdr Batteries
1 x Mitrailleuse Battery

CLÉRAMBAULT'S CAVALRY DIVISION (*not committed to action*)
1st Brigade
  2nd, 3rd and 10th Chasseur Regiments
2nd Brigade
  2nd and 4th Dragoon Regiments
3rd Brigade
  5th and 8th Dragoon Regiments

Reserve Artillery
  2 x 8-pdr Batteries
  2 x 12-pdr Batteries
  4 x Horse Artillery Batteries

4 CORPS
(Ladmirault)

CISSEY'S DIVISION
1st Brigade
 20th Bn of Chasseurs
 1st and 6th Regiments
2nd Brigade
 57th and 73rd Regiments
2 x 4-pdr Batteries
1 x Mitrailleuse Battery

GRENIER'S DIVISION
1st Brigade
 5th Bn of Chasseurs
 13th and 43rd Regiments
2nd Brigade
 64th and 98th Regiments
2 x 4-pdr Batteries
1 x Mitrailleuse Battery

LORENCEZ'S DIVISION (*available but not engaged on 16 August*)

LEGRAND'S CAVALRY DIVISION
1st Brigade
 2nd and 7th Hussar Regiments (Montaigu)
2nd Brigade (Gondrecourt)
 3rd and 11th Dragoon Regiments

Reserve Artillery
 2 x 8-pdr Batteries
 2 x 12-pdr Batteries
 2 x Horse Artillery Batteries

6 CORPS
(Canrobert)

TIXIER'S DIVISION
1st Brigade
   9th Bn of Chasseurs
   4th and 10th Regiments
2nd Brigade
   12th and 100th Regiments

BISSON'S DIVISION (*only one regiment reached Metz*)
   9th Regiment

LAFONT'S DIVISION
1st Brigade
   75th and 91st Regiments
2nd Brigade
   93rd Regiment
   94th Regiment

LEVASSOR-SORVAL'S DIVISION
1st Brigade
   25th and 26th Regiments
2nd Brigade
   28th and 70th Regiments

(*Note: No Artillery is shown since only 36 guns out of an establishment of 114 reached Metz by 16 August. In addition, the entire Cavalry Division and three Infantry Regiments were left behind at Châlons*)

RESERVE CAVALRY

DU BARAIL'S DIVISION
    2nd Chasseurs d'Afrique
2 x Horse Artillery Batteries

(*Note: The two other regiments of Chasseurs d'Afrique of this Division provided the Emperor's escort to Verdun and took no part in the battle*)

FORTON'S DIVISION
1st Brigade
    1st and 9th Dragoon Regiments
2nd Brigade
    7th and 10th Cuirassier Regiments
2 x Horse Artillery Batteries

GENERAL ARTILLERY RESERVE

8 x 12-pdr Batteries
8 x Horse Artillery Batteries

(*Note: Largely deployed to fill the shortages in Canrobert's 6 Corps*)

ARMY OF ALSACE:
later ARMY OF CHÂLONS
(MacMahon)

1 CORPS
(MacMahon: *later* Ducrot)

Wolff's Division
Pellé's Division
L'Hériller's Division
Lartigue's Division
Michel's Cavalry Division
Reserve Artillery
    2 x 4-pdr Batteries
    2 x 12-pdr Batteries
    4 x Horse Artillery Batteries

5 CORPS
(Failly)

Goze's Division
L'Abadie's Division (*less* **Lapasset's Brigade Group** *detached to* **2 Corps**)
Guyot's Division
Brahaut's Cavalry Division
Reserve Artillery
    2 x 8-pdr Batteries
    2 x 12-pdr Batteries
    2 x Horse Artillery Batteries

7 CORPS
(Félix Douay)

Conseil-Dumesnil's Division
Liébert's Division
Dumont's Division
Amiel's Cavalry Division
Reserve Artillery
     2 x 8-pdr Batteries
     2 x 12-pdr Batteries
     2 x Horse Artillery Batteries

RESERVE CAVALRY

Margueritte's Division
Bonnemain's Division

II

GERMAN FIELD ARMIES

Commander-in-Chief	**King William I of Prussia**
Chief of Staff	**General von Moltke**
Inspector-General of Artillery	**General von Hindersin**

(Note: Also present at GHQ were the Chancellor, Bismarck, and the Minister of War, General von Roon)

FIRST ARMY
(Steinmetz)

VII CORPS — WESTPHALIA
(Zastrow)

13th Division
14th Division

VIII CORPS — RHINE PROVINCES
(Goeben)

15th Division
16th Division
31st Brigade
32nd Brigade (*late afternoon*)
    40th Regiment
    72nd Regiment
3rd Cavalry Division

I CORPS — EAST PRUSSIA
(Manteuffel)

1st Division
2nd Division
1st Cavalry Division

SECOND ARMY
(Prince Frederick Charles)

GUARD CORPS — GENERAL
(Prince Augustus of Württemberg)

1st Guard Infantry Division
2nd Guard Infantry Division
Guard Cavalry Division
1st Brigade
2nd Brigade
3rd Brigade (*early afternoon*)
    1st Guard Dragoon Regiment
    2nd Guard Dragoon Regiment

III CORPS — BRANDENBURG
(Alvensleben II)

5TH DIVISION (STUELPNAGEL)
9th Brigade (Doering)
    8th Leib-Grenadier Regiment
    48th Brandenburg Regiment
10th Brigade (Schwerin)
    12th Brandenburg Grenadier Regiment
    52nd Brandenburg Infantry Regiment
    3rd Brandenburg Jäger Battalion
12th Brandenburg Dragoon Regiment
2 x Heavy Artillery Batteries
2 x Light Artillery Batteries

6TH DIVISION (BUDDENBROCK)
11th Brigade (Rothmaler)
    20th Brandenburg Infantry Regiment
    35th Brandenburg Fusilier Regiment
12th Brigade (Bismarck)
    24th Brandenburg Infantry Regiment
    64th Brandenburg Infantry Regiment
1st Brandenburg Dragoon Regiment
2 x Heavy Artillery Batteries
2 x Light Artillery Batteries

Corps Artillery
2 x Horse Artillery Batteries
2 x Heavy Artillery Batteries
2 x Light Artillery Batteries

IV CORPS — LOWER SAXONY AND ANHALT
(Alvensleben I)

7th Division
8th Division

IX CORPS — SCHLESWIG-HOLSTEIN AND HESSE
(Manstein)

18th Division
35th Brigade
36th Brigade
  11th Grenadier Regiment (*late afternoon*)
  85th Infantry Regiment
  9th Jäger Battalion
6th Magdeburg Dragoon Regiment
4 x Field Artillery Batteries

25th (Hessian) Division
49th Brigade (*late afternoon*)
50th Brigade

X CORPS — HANOVER, OLDENBURG AND BRUNSWICK
(Voigts-Rhetz)

19TH DIVISION (SCHWARZKOPPEN)
37th Brigade (Lehmann)
  78th East Friesian Infantry Regiment
  91st Oldenburg Infantry Regiment
38th Brigade (Wedell)
  16th Westphalian Infantry Regiment
  57th Westphalian Infantry Regiment
9th Hanoverian Dragoon Regiment
2 x Heavy Artillery Batteries
2 x Light Artillery Batteries

20TH DIVISION (KRAATZ-KOSCHLAU)
39th Brigade (Woyna)
  56th Westphalian Infantry Regiment
  79th Hanoverian Infantry Regiment
40th Brigade (Diringshofen)
  17th Westphalian Infantry Regiment
  92nd Brunswick Infantry Regiment
  10th Hanoverian Jäger Battalion
16th Hanoverian Dragoon Regiment
2 x Heavy Artillery Batteries
2 x Light Artillery Batteries

Corps Artillery
2 x Horse Artillery Batteries
2 x Heavy Artillery Batteries
2 x Light Artillery Batteries

XII CORPS — KINGDOM OF SAXONY
(Crown Prince of Saxony)

23rd Division
24th Division
12th Cavalry Division

II CORPS — POMERANIA
(Fransecky)

3rd Division
4th Division

RESERVE CAVALRY

5TH DIVISION (RHEINBABEN)
11th Brigade (Barby)
    4th Westphalian Cuirassier Regiment
    13th Hanoverian Uhlan Regiment
    19th Oldenburg Dragoon Regiment
12th Brigade (Bredow)
    7th Magdeburg Cuirassier Regiment
    16th Altmark Uhlan Regiment
    13th Schleswig-Holstein Dragoon Regiment
13th Brigade (Redern)
    10th Magdeburg Hussar Regiment
    11th Westphalian Hussar Regiment
    17th Brunswick Hussar Regiment
2 x Horse Artillery Batteries

6TH DIVISION (DUKE OF MECKLENBURG-SCHWERIN)
14th Brigade (Diepenbroick-Grüter)
    6th Brandenburg Cuirassier Regiment
    3rd Brandenburg Uhlan Regiment
    15th Schleswig-Holstein Uhlan Regiment
15th Brigade (Rauch)
    3rd Brandenburg Hussar Regiment
    16th Schleswig-Holstein Hussar Regiment
1 x Horse Artillery Battery

THIRD ARMY
(Crown Prince of Prussia)

V CORPS — POSEN AND LIEGNITZ
(Kirchbach)

9th Division
10th Division

XI CORPS — HESSE-NASSAU AND SAXE-WEIMAR
(Bose)

21st Division
22nd Division

VI CORPS — SILESIA
(Tümpling)

11th Division
12th Division
2nd Cavalry Division

I BAVARIAN CORPS
(von der Tann)

1st Division
2nd Division

II BAVARIAN CORPS
(Hartmann)

3rd Division
4th Division

WÜRTTEMBERG DIVISION
(Obernitz)

BADEN DIVISION
(Beyer)

4TH CAVALRY DIVISION
(Prince Albert of Prussia)

APPENDIX B

'NI VIVRES NI MUNITIONS'?

Since Bazaine repeatedly stated that his reason for retiring towards Metz after the battle of Mars-la-Tour was for the purpose of replenishing stocks of food and ammunition,[1] it is revealing to describe the true state of affairs as presented in the evidence given at the Marshal's trial.

On the morning of the battle, there were available to the Army of the Rhine (even if the incompetent General Soleille, Bazaine's artillery commander, was unaware of the fact): 106,493 rounds of 4-pounder and 8-pounder ammunition, an immense quantity of mitrailleuse shot, and 17,580,000 chassepot cartridges. Expenditure during the fighting on the 16th was approximately 26,000 artillery rounds and 1,100,000 chassepot cartridges, and indeed a further 12,400 4-pounder shells were ready loaded on wagons during the evening of the 16th, waiting to be called forward to the artillery park at Gravelotte. It follows therefore that, despite Soleille's gloomy advice that the ammunition supply was insufficient to sustain another battle on the same scale as the 16th, the Army of the Rhine was fully capable, in terms of both men and material, of resuming a major offensive on the following morning.

If anyone had cause for concern, it was Frederick Charles, his Army strung out across a front of forty miles, his artillery reduced to some ten rounds per gun, his infantry battered and exhausted, his cavalry incapable of anything other than heroic *chevauchées*. Bazaine had only to look at a map of Lorraine to see the scale of victory which beckoned him. He did not look at the map of Lorraine. He looked at Metz. And Metz offered him naught for his comfort.

It is impossible to establish how or why Soleille arrived at so massive an underestimate of available ammunition, the more so since he was to write

---

1   *'Nous n'avons plus ni vivres ni munitions et il est nécessaire de procéder, avant toute chose, à un ravitaillement.'*

to Bazaine on 22 August, four days after the siege of Metz had started, with the curious intelligence that the magazines of the fortress were '*more fully stocked than at the start of the campaign*'. At no time on the 16th did he once communicate with any of the corps commanders. He ignored the substantial stocks of chassepot cartridges held by line regiments. He overlooked the vital fact that a large part of the Army of the Rhine had not been engaged at all during the day of battle and had therefore consumed no ammunition. And it does not appear to have been of any significance to him that as late as 6 p.m., Bourbaki had been able to throw back in disorder the late arrivals from VIII Corps and IX Corps by mounting a great battery of 54 guns of the Guard to the south of Rezonville. There are two probable answers: first, that Soleille had no means of knowing the true facts and was not disposed to find them out; and secondly, and more likely, that his pessimistic forecast provided Bazaine with a very convenient justification for his subsequent course of action.

The alleged shortage of provisions is an altogether different matter, and a bleak commentary on the administrative shambles which marked the French conduct of the whole August campaign. Here is General de Rivière's summing up at Bazaine's trial:

> On leaving Metz [15 August] the Army had with it 3,390 vehicles which carried 750,000 rations for the men and 200,000 of forage for the horses, that is to say four and a half days' supply. In addition, considerable stocks had been established on the fertile plateau which lies between Metz and Verdun.[2]

But contrary to the normal practice of sending the supply trains on ahead of a retreating army, this immense convoy had, for the most part, been left at Ban St Martin, a suburb of Metz, largely because of the extreme congestion on the Verdun road. Thus, by dawn on the 16th, only a small part of the train reached Gravelotte, not without causing much confusion among the marching columns. This convoy carried supplies for Frossard's 2 Corps and, with typical disregard for the fighting troops, for Army Headquarters. Yet even then it contained 173,000 rations for the men, 136,000 for horses, and three days' iron rations *for the entire army*. Thus, including the food which the men carried in their packs, the supplies were more than sufficient to see the Army of the Rhine safely to Verdun. But this was an unlucky, one might almost say a doomed, army from the start.

At this critical hour, the Quartermaster was a M. de Préval, whose ability to handle a problem which would have taxed an administrative genius was severely tested by the fact that he had held the appointment for

---

2   There is absolutely no other evidence that this was so. Rivière can only have been suggesting that the Army of the Rhine could have lived off the country during its westward march.

less than forty-eight hours. His first contact with his commander-in-chief was not until the evening of the 16th; and by then much had happened.

Towards 6 p.m., Bazaine, already gratified by Soleille's gloom, discovered the modest convoy assembled at Gravelotte, and unaware of what it contained, sent Préval to report on the position at Ban St Martin, but without instructions. '*Ni vivres ni munitions.*' Bazaine was already seeking the other half of his alibi.

Préval, unaware of the darker recesses of his Marshal's mind, repaired to Metz and there, with some presence of mind, loaded 500 wagons with food and medical supplies; and at dawn on the 17th set off for the plateau '*avec une surabondance des vivres*'. He was too late.

He was greeted on his arrival by Captain Fix of Bazaine's staff, who informed him that the army was retiring to the Amanvillers line. Préval was later to say: 'There was now no question of any shortage of rations, but only of a means of distributing them to the retiring troops *de manière à nous débarrasser de notre immense convoi.*'[3] The answer, as it was to prove the answer for General Robertson on the retreat from Mons, was to dump rations and equipment and leave the men to help themselves. But there was a difference. The BEF fell back slowly, fighting as it went. The Army of the Rhine fell back in confusion, its morale shaken, its discipline suspect. It helped itself, and added a good measure of looting as it went.

By early morning on the 17th the area around the Gravelotte crossroads was encumbered with a mass of material of every kind. And a mass of wounded. The wagons could not serve two purposes; and so — on whose direct order the evidence is silent — the material was off-loaded and, to the anger of an already despondent army, was consigned to the flames 'to ensure that it did not fall into the hands of the enemy'. The largest bonfire was lit in the Mance ravine; and the pillars of smoke were to mark the scene of a very different conflagration the following afternoon. Meanwhile, Préval, his convoy of wagons loaded with more than 2000 wounded men, made his melancholy way back to Metz.

And Bazaine? The other half of his equation had been solved. '*Ni vivres ni munitions.*' He had both in abundance. Both were an embarrassment; and he had, to his own satisfaction, proved that a commander could support the spectacle of success with the débris of defeat. Thus he wrote absurdly to his Emperor, promising an early sortie from a trap from which he had the means but not the will to escape.

****

3 *Procès Bazaine.*

APPENDIX C

BAZAINE'S DESPATCH OF 22 AUGUST

On 22 August Bazaine wrote his only despatch of the campaign. It is printed here verbatim apart from the correction of numerous misspellings which are themselves revealing of the Marshal's absolute lack of command of his subject. It is above all revealing of Bazaine's incomprehension of the true events of the day of battle; of his stubborn conviction of a threat — or series of threats — to his left flank which never existed; of a German superiority which was a fiction of his own imagination; and of an absurd assumption, at the end, of a victory which he knew he had not won. Significantly, despite the date and place of the document, he does not even mention bloody Thursday, and the defeat of the Army of the Rhine. It can only be assumed that this despatch, which reached neither Châlons nor Paris, was intended as a hostage to history. An attempt has been made to capture in translation Bazaine's infelicitous style.

'After the brilliant battle of Borny [*14 August*], the troops who took part in it received their orders to continue the march on the morning of the 15th, and which had been already indicated to them,[1] the 2nd and 6th corps-d'armée following the southern route by Rezonville, Mars-la-Tour, Manheulles, the 3rd and 4th by the more northern route by Conflans and Étain, the Guard, the general reserve, and the parks marching in rear of No. 6 corps. The first column was covered by the cavalry of reserve of Forton, the second by the division of chasseurs d'Afrique of Barail. The points to be occupied on the 15th were — Vionville by the 2nd corps, Rezonville by the 6th, Doncourt-les-Conflans by the 4th, St Marcel and Vernéville by the 3rd, the Imperial Guard in rear at Gravelotte, the division Forton at Tronville, with orders to scout well along the road to St

---

1 But without sufficient detail, for which Bazaine was responsible.

Mihiel, the division of General Barail at Jarny (along the northern of the two roads). The delays caused by the blocking of convoys, and those resulting from the participation of the 3rd and 4th corps in the combat at Borny, did not permit these two corps to commence early enough their movements, nor to carry them out in the limited time accorded to them. The 3rd corps, which should have been in rear of the 4th, had got ahead, and only had three of its divisions on the plateau of Gravelotte by 10 p.m. With regard to the 4th corps, it could only commence its movement early on the 16th.

The left column, composed of 2nd, 6th, and Guard, had pretty well got into positions on the 15th, but I was obliged to order it to maintain these on the 16th till midday, so that the 4th corps should take its place on the ridge; the news I had received of a strong concentration of the enemy to the south, and on my left, and prudence dictated that the two columns of retreat should act so as to support each other on whichever side the enemy might present himself.

On the 16th August, in the morning, the 2nd corps was in front of Rezonville, to the left of the direct and most southern road to Verdun; the 6th on higher ground to the right of this route; the 3rd, with three divisions, had its cavalry between Vernéville and St Marcel. The division Metman was 'en marche' to join the 4th,[2] which was proceeding to Doncourt; the Guard was at Gravelotte.

Such was the position when, shortly after 9 a.m., the advanced guard of Forton's cavalry signalled the approach of the enemy (they allow themselves that they were surprised by shell). Three batteries of horse-artillery, coming in sight from near Tronville, shelled them violently, obliging them to retire in all haste in rear of the camp of the two corps-d'armée, a little distance from Rezonville.

On hearing the guns, General Frossard at once occupied his positions above Flavigny, with one brigade (Lapasset) facing the left rear, to watch the great woods of St Arnould and Ognons, and to cover the head of the ravine leading to Gorze. Marshal Canrobert also took up his positions, and deployed his corps in front of Rezonville, between the route to Verdun and the village of St Marcel. The appearance of some of the enemy's cavalry and cannonade against the division Forton was only the prelude to a general action which was coming on. Two attacks could now be made out as about to occur: one coming from the woods of Vionville and St Arnould on the left, the other more on our front by Mars-la-Tour and Vionville. When I heard of the fighting, I left Gravelotte with my staff, giving orders to the Guard to hold itself in reserve on the right and left of the route, and warning Marshal Leboeuf that he must pivot on his left to support No. 6 corps and take the enemy in flank. I counted also on General Ladmirault

2 Bazaine's error. Metman's division was part of 3 Corps.

marching to sustain the turning movement of the 3rd corps, beyond which he ought to come into position, when he heard the guns.

On arriving, I found the 2nd corps heavily engaged along its entire front and under a tremendous artillery fire. Keeping his positions a little in rear of the crests, Marshal Canrobert, on his part, had arrested the offensive movement of the enemy, who was only keeping up an artillery fire against him. It was evident the enemy was going to make a great effort on our left from the woods which sheltered his men, and to cut us off from any line of retreat on Metz. Although I saw the meaning of this attack, I was anxious that our right should be solidly supported. Before the coming into line of the troops of Marshal Leboeuf, I ordered the Forton division of cavalry to go and take position in rear of the 6th corps (Canrobert), on the ancient Roman road which runs from Gravelotte to Doncourt, having at his back the woods of Villers-au-Bois, and with orders to charge the enemy at any opportune moment.

Having made these first dispositions, I called forward the batteries of twelve-pounders of the general reserve to reply to the enemy's, which were very trying to the 2nd corps. It was now between twelve and one o'clock. General Bataille was wounded, and his division got into confusion, and caused this also in the division Vergé. I therefore ordered the 3rd Lancers and the Cuirassiers of the Guard to charge the Prussian infantry. The former were repulsed, and the cuirassiers forming in three lines as if they had been at the manœuvres, threw themselves with heroic bravery on the enemy's squares, which they could not break. Some squadrons of Prussian hussars (Brunswickers) now pursued them on their retreat, advancing as far as some of the batteries, near one of which I found myself. I got separated from my staff, and was obliged to draw my sword, as also all of them, and to fight hand to hand not far from my officers.

The temporary hesitation produced among the Prussians enabled me to get up the division Picard, Grenadiers of the Guard, with General Bourbaki, relieving Bataille's and Vergé's divisions, on each side of Rezonville, while a division of No. 6 corps came up to the supports on the ridge of the ravine of Vionville. The Voltigeurs of Deligny's division faced the Bois des Ognons, which was occupied by a battalion of chasseurs, and to observe the approaches by which the Prussians might get their foot on the plateau of Gravelotte.

At the same moment that the enemy made his attack on Rezonville, he endeavoured to turn our right by a great attack of his cavalry.

Three of his regiments,[3] the cuirassiers of the King and two regiments of lancers, charged through the right of the 6th corps, our batteries, and even passed the crest that we occupied, and tried to take our infantry in reverse. The division Forton, the presence of whom he had not the slightest

3 There were only six squadrons in all, three of No. 7, and three of No. 16, of Bredow's brigade.

suspicion, took them in flank and rear, and this mass of cavalry was completely broken down under the sabres of our dragoons and cuirassiers. Our right was now quite disengaged, and the fire of Marshal Leboeuf commenced to be felt. It was now past two o'clock, and the enemy was thrown back everywhere on our right; in the centre the grenadiers of the Guard had stopped the attack, and on the left he [*the enemy*] had not taken the initiative that I had been expecting, but which he was still intending.

The fire of his guns had nearly ceased, and he was evidently making preparations for a new effort. Completely reassured as to my right by the entry into line of the first troops of my 3rd corps, I ordered Marshal Leboeuf to maintain firmly his position with the division Nayral, to unite with the 6th corps by means of the division Aymard, and to direct the division Montaudon on Gravelotte, which I destined to occupy stronger, and the points of debouch from Ars-sur-Moselle. I brought up also to the same point the divisions of the 2nd corps, which had been re-formed, and I placed batteries of twelve-pounders as also mitrailleuses at the opening of the ravine to destroy the enemy's masses if he attempted to come out. I knew that his reinforcements had passed Ars and Novéant, and I preoccupied myself above all with the attack which might be made on our left flank. My line of battle, which at the commencement of the action was nearly parallel to the line of the ravine of Rezonville, had taken now, shortly after 3 p.m., a direction nearly perpendicular to the woods of Les Ognons and stretching towards Mars-la-Tour, to the north of which was Ladmirault's 4th corps. In fact, at this moment the 4th corps was fast coming into line. The division Grenier, led by General Ladmirault in person, had pursued the enemy on his front, had thrown him back from St Marcel, Bruville, and on to Mars-la-Tour, and prepared itself for the attack on Tronville. The division Cissey supported the movement, and on the right marched the divisions Legrand and Clérambault, the 2nd chasseurs d'Afrique, and the brigade of the Guard, composed of lancers and dragoons, who had come up in support on hearing the fighting after having escorted the Emperor to Étain. General Ladmirault recognised that Tronville was too strongly occupied to be taken with two divisions, and he contented himself in occupying temporarily the enemy, and in establishing himself on the ground he had gained.

The enemy's artillery fire, which had for some time ceased, recommenced stronger than ever towards 3 p.m., to cover a new attack that the Prussians were going to attempt. After two hours of this, their attacking column showed itself in dense masses, and a charge of cuirassiers was attempted by them (1st and 2nd dragoon-guards) on the division of Lafont de Villiers to pierce our centre. The 93rd lost its eagle and one gun, but the Prussian cuirassiers found near them the division Valabrègue of the 2nd corps, which had established itself on the crest above Rezonville.[4] They

4   This is nonsense (*Author's note*).

were brought forward vigorously, and the eagle and gun retaken.

I then stopped the movement of the division Montaudon on Gravelotte, and called it back to the 3rd corps, to prepare for any eventuality on this side.[5] The division of cavalry Forton, that I had also ordered to retire, retook its position close to the wood of Villers-au-Bois. General Deligny rejoined with the four battalions of voltigeurs, which remained with them, and his 2nd brigade, which had been supporting and relieving a part of the grenadiers on the crest of the ravine of Rezonville. At the same time General Bourbaki, bringing up all his guns, established a great battery of fifty-four pieces, which thundered on the masses of the enemy, and disorganised him, while the fire of our infantry drove him back. On our left the enemy vainly endeavoured to debouch from the woods, which he found strongly guarded; he then tried to advance by the ravine which separates the Bois de St Arnould from the Bois des Ognons, but our mitrailleuses stopped his attempts (although there is a regular road), and made him submit to enormous losses.

About dark he attempted with a great mass of cavalry to turn our right flank (4th corps), but General de Ladmirault's cavalry under Legrand, which he had ready to hand, charged him, and after successive attempts, where both sides fought with great bravery, the enemy retreated.

General Cissey's division covered our rallying, and by his efforts put the left wing of the Prussians definitively in retreat.

The enemy, beaten, retreated on all points, leaving us masters of the battlefield. When a last attempt was made by him, as the night closed, at Rezonville, where I happened to be at the moment, I called in haste the Zouaves, whom I placed in a position perpendicular to the route, and, aided by General Bourbaki, who reassembled the troops whom he had at hand, I repulsed this last attack, after which the fire ceased completely.

It was then past 8 p.m. Our troops had been fighting ten hours under a terrible artillery fire, and remained mistresses of the field of battle, where they stopped in part till midnight without any interference with them. I gave them orders to retire to the positions around Gravelotte in order to reprovision in food and war material.'

Head-quarters, Ban-St-Martin, 22nd August 1870
The Marshal Commanding-in-Chief the Army of the Rhine.
Bazaine.

---

5 Not so. (*Author's note*)

APPENDIX D

BAZAINE'S MILITARY CAREER

Fusilier, 37th Regiment of the Line	21 March 1831
Corporal, 37th Regiment of the Line	July 1831
Quartermaster Sergeant, 1st Foreign Legion	Jan 1832
Sergeant Major, 1st Foreign Legion	Nov 1832
Sous-Lieutenant, 1st Foreign Legion	Nov 1833
(Spain. Carlist War, 1835)	
Captain, 1st Foreign Legion	Dec 1837
Chef de Bataillon, 1st Foreign Legion	Mar 1844
Lieut. Colonel, 1st Foreign Legion	Apr 1848
Colonel, 1st Foreign Legion	June 1850
(Crimean War 1854-56; Italian War 1859)	
Général de Brigade	Aug 1860
(Mexican expedition 1862)	
Général de Division	Sept 1862
Marshal of France	8 Sept 1864
(commanding 3 Corps, Imperial Guard, and again 3 Corps)	
Commander-in-Chief, Army of the Rhine	12 Aug 1870

Court-martialled at Versailles on 10 December 1873, stripped of his rank and decorations, and sentenced to death, subsequently commuted to twenty years imprisonment

SELECT
BIBLIOGRAPHY

I

The Historical Sections of the French and German General Staffs both produced elaborate and exhaustive accounts of the war, the former running to 22 volumes, the latter to 5 volumes (published in an indifferent translation in London between 1874 and 1884) accompanied by a small library of separate commentaries and individual tactical studies. For the general reader possessed of patience and stamina the following selected volumes and commentaries from these Histories will provide a more than adequate fund of source material.

La Guerre de 1870/71
(Paris, 1901-1913)

La Guerre de 1870. Juillet 1866 − 23 août 1870

Les opérations autour de Metz, 3 vols

Der deutsch-französische Krieg, 1870-71
(Berlin, 1872-1906)

Heft 18. III Armee Korps bei Spicheren und Vionville

Heft 19. Der Kriegzug in Frankreich 1870. Von Mainz bis Sedan

Heft 25. Die 38 Infanterie Brigade in der Schlacht bei Vionville−Mars-la-Tour, 16 August 1870

Studie V. Der 18 August 1870

II

Andlau, Baron d'
Metz: Campagnes et négoçiations
Paris, 1871

Assemblée Nationale
Enquête Parlementaire sur les actes du Gouvernement de la Défense Nationale, 18 vols
Versailles, 1873-75

Bazaine, François Achille (see also **Procès Bazaine**)
L'Armée du Rhin
Paris, 1872

Barail, François Charles du
Mes Souvenirs, 1820-1879
Paris, 1894-6

Episodes de la guerre de 1870 et le blocus de Metz
Madrid, 1883

Benedetti, Vincent
Ma mission en Prusse
Paris, 1871

Bismarck, Otto v.
Gedanken und Erinnerungen
Berlin, 1898

Bonnal, Guillaume Auguste
L'esprit de la guerre moderne: La Manœuvre de Saint Privat, 18 juillet − 18 août 1870, 3 vols
Paris, 1904-1912

Borbstädt, A, and Dwyer, F
The Franco-German War to the catastrophe of Sedan
London, 1873

Busch, Moritz
Bismarck: some secret pages of his history, 3 vols
London, 1898

Coffinières de Nordeck, Grégoire
Capitulation de Metz
Brussels, 1871

Ducrot, Auguste
La Journée de Sedan
Paris, 1871

Favre, Jules
Le Gouvernement de la Défense Nationale, 3 vols
Paris, 1871-75

Forbes, Archibald
My Experiences of the War between France and Germany, 2 vols
London, 1871

Förster, Wolfgang
Prinz Friedrich Karl von Preussen. Denkwürdigkeiten, 2 vols
Stuttgart, 1910

Frossard, Charles Auguste
Le deuxième corps de l'Armée du Rhin dans la campagne de 1870
Paris, 1871

Gramont, Alfred, Duc de
La France et la Prusse avant la Guerre
Paris, 1872

Guedalla, Philip
The Two Marshals. (Bazaine; Pétain.)
London, 1943

Hofffbauer, Carl Edouard v.
Die deutsche Artillerie, 1870-71, 3 vols
Berlin, 1873-78

Hohenlohe-Ingelfingen, Kraft Carl zu, Prinz
Letters on Artillery
London, 1888

Letters on Infantry
London, 1889

Letters on Cavalry
London, 1889

Hönig, Fritz
Gefechtsbilder aus dem Kriege 1870-1871, 3 vols
Berlin, 1891-94

24 Hours of Moltke's Strategy
Woolwich, 1895

Hooper, George
The Campaign of Sedan
London, 1906

Howard, Michael
The Franco-Prussian War. The German Invasion of France, 1870-1871
London, 1961

Jarras, L
Souvenirs
Paris, 1892

Krosigk, Hans v.
Generalfeldmarschall von Steinmetz
Berlin, 1900

Lebrun, Barthélemy
Guerre de 1870, Bazeilles-Sedan
Paris, 1884

Lecomte, Ferdinand
Relation historique et critique de la Guerre en 1870-71, 4 vols
Paris, 1872-74

Moltke, Helmuth v., Graf
The Franco-Prussian War
London, 1893

Napoleon III, Emperor
Les forces militaires de la France en 1870
Paris, 1872

Newdigate, Edward
The Army of the North German Confederation
London, 1872

Ollivier, Emile
L'Empire libéral, 16 vols
Paris, 1895-1912

Palat, Barthélemy
Bibliographie générale de la Guerre de 1870-71
Paris, 1896

La Stratégie de Moltke en 1870
Paris, 1907

Bazaine et nos désastres en 1870, 2 vols
Paris, 1913

Pflugk Hartung, Julius v.
The Franco-German War, 1870-71, trs. and ed. Major-General J.F. Maurice
London, 1900

Procès Bazaine (Capitulation de Metz)
Compte rendu sténographique in extenso
Paris, 1873

Rauch, Fedor v.
Briefe aus dem grossen Hauptquartier
Berlin, 1911

Roon, Albrecht v., Graf
Denkwürdigkeiten, 3 vols
Breslau, 1897

Rousset, Leonce
Histoire générale de la Guerre Franco-Allemande, 1870-71, 6 vols
Paris, 1895-99

Russell, William Howard
My Diary during the last great War
London, 1874

Trochu, Louis Jules
L'Armée Française en 1867
Paris, 1867

Verdy du Vernois, Julius v.
With the Royal Headquarters in 1870-71
London, 1897

Widdern, Cardinal Georg v.
Kritische Tage, 5 vols
Berlin, 1897-1900

Wimpffen, Emmanuel de
Sedan
Paris, 1871

INDEX

Italicized page references refer to illustrations. For military units, see Appendix A, Orders of Battle, and under the names of commanders.